W9-BVF-733

ADVANCED TOPICS
IN SCIENCE AND TECHNOLOGY IN CHINA

ADVANCED TOPICS IN SCIENCE AND TECHNOLOGY IN CHINA

Zhejiang University is one of the leading universities in China. In Advanced Topics in Science and Technology in China, Zhejiang University Press and Springer jointly publish monographs by Chinese scholars and professors, as well as invited authors and editors from abroad who are outstanding experts and scholars in their fields. This series will be of interest to researchers, lecturers, and graduate students alike.

Advanced Topics in Science and Technology in China aims to present the latest and most cutting-edge theories, techniques, and methodologies in various research areas in China. It covers all disciplines in the fields of natural science and technology, including but not limited to, computer science, materials science, life sciences, engineering, environmental sciences, mathematics, and physics.

Weidong Geng

The Algorithms and Principles of Non-photorealistic Graphics

Artistic Rendering and Cartoon Animation

With 314 figures, mostly in color

Author
Prof. Weidong Geng
State Key Lab of CAD&CG
Digital Media Technology Department
College of Computer Science
Zhejiang University, Hangzhou
310027, China
E-mail: gengwd@zju.edu.cn

ISSN 1995-6819 e-ISSN 1995-6827
Advanced Topics in Science and Technology in China

ISBN 978-7-308-06600-6
Zhejiang University Press, Hangzhou

ISBN 978-3-642-04890-6 e-ISBN 978-3-642-04891-3
Springer Heidelberg Dordrecht London New York

Library of Congress Control Number: 2009935705

Cover design: Frido Steinen-Broo, EStudio Calamar, Spain

Printed on acid-free paper

Springer is a part of Springer Science+Business Media (www.springer.com)

Preface

Non-photorealistic computer graphics is a multidisciplinary field in the research community, involving computer arts, computer graphics, computer vision, digital image/video processing and visual cognitive psychology. It aims at the computer generation of images and animations that are made in part "by hand" in appearance, and are characterized by their use of randomness, abstraction, ambiguity, or arbitrariness rather than completeness and adherence to the portrayed objects' properties. In essence, it mimics the eyes and minds of artists and designers to create, view and depict the graphics world, effectively carrying-out the visual communication between computers and human beings.

Coverage and Audience

This book mainly focuses on the following five core issues in non-photorealistic computer graphics.

(1) How to create the paintings, artworks or sculptures from a digitized blank canvas or a standard shape with the tools simulated by the computer.
(2) How to convert a series of reference images into the resultant depiction with the desired visual effect.
(3) How to automatically generate the artistic rendition or technical illustrations from the 3D models in terms of the stylized parameters.
(4) How to produce the comprehensive and expressive visualizations from a set of graphical and textual information on the basis of the semantic meanings to be conveyed.
(5) How to speed up the production of cartoon animation by computer-assisted refinement of traditional pipeline and the exploration of novel approaches.

The author not only take a survey of the state-of-the-art research as well as trends and open-ended questions regarding the aforementioned five core issues, but also discuss the theoretical underpinnings of the field. This includes detailing a host of useful algorithms and addressing two applications of particular interest: artistic rendering and cartoon animation.

The book will be useful to practitioners in the field. It contains a wealth of examples, particularly in the form of images, which the author hope will motivate the reader in the use of non-photorealistic computer graphics. The methods introduced are explained in enough detail so that programs can be written directly without a major conceptual effort.

Anothers use of the book is for reference by researchers in the field. The bibliographic references at the end of the chapters give the necessary pointers to the important publications. In the case of researchers in the field of non-photorealistic computer graphics, the methods that are built up are referenced appropriately, and a comprehensive index aids in selective readings.

Objective

Non-photorealistic computer graphics is a relatively young field, and new works are constantly being published. The intent of this book is to bring together a coherent conceptual framework for all of the research to date in the context of computer graphics, art history and theory, and cognitive psychology.

Although the field of non-photorealistic rendering has existed for more than two decades, it has for a long time not been taken seriously by large parts of the research community. The area has thus far been unstructured, making it increasingly difficult to identify and assess new open problems. Indeed, sometimes papers have even "reinvented the wheel," albeit in a different context and application concern. Recent years have seen many algorithms, papers, and software tools devoted to artistic rendering and computer-assisted cartoon animation. The time has become ripe for a systematic assessment of the literature. The following are our goals:

(1) To become the seminal reference for core issues surrounding artistic rendering and cartoon animation.
(2) To describe and review state-of-the-art advances in the field of non-photorealistic computer graphics, and to distill the breadth of cutting-edge non-photorealistic modeling, rendering and animation technologies into a coherent, accessible treatise.
(3) To provide the guidelines for researchers and software developers to assess and implement the best solution for their interactive arts application.

Acknowledgement

I would like to thank my family for their love, support, and patience, and a few of the great many people for their instrumental contributions in taking this book from an initial suggestion to a final product. I express my gratitude to Prof. Yunhe Pan, fellow of Chinese Academy of Engineering, for his time reviewing this book and contributing his many deep insights into the topic in the final chapter of the book.

A number of colleagues in the State Key Lab of CAD & CG at Zhejiang University gave the author support, offered constructive criticisms, or provided illustrations to include in the book. These include Profs. Hujun Bao, Yueting Zhuang, Dongming Lu, and Duanqing Xu. I am also indebted to the graduate students, faculty, and researchers in the research group of Computer Animation and Perception at Zhejiang University.

I wishes to thank those persons who provided the support to make this book appear, including the administrative, technical, and secretarial staff in our college who kept things up and running, even under adverse workloads (Ms Qi Shen, Ms Xuefang Zhang, etc.). I also thanks the graduate students at Zhejiang University who studied the topic with previous versions of the manuscript, and all of the colleagues and peers around the world who did great research and gave me the copyrights of their images.

The continuous research and development on non-photorealistic computer graphics in the past years were supported by the following grants: National Natural Science Foundation of China (Grant Nos.: 6960302, 69973044, 60373032, 60773183 and 60633070), National High Technology Research and Development Program of China (Grant Nos.: 2006AA01Z313 and 2006AA01Z335), New Century Excellent Talents in University (NCET-07-0743), and Program for Changjiang Scholars and Innovative Research Team in University (PCSIRT0652).

Finally, I also acknowledges the prodigious work of the people at Zhejiang University Press and Springer.

Weidong Geng
Hangzhou, China
August 16, 2009

Contents

1

Introduction

Non-photorealistic computer graphics are used to imitate the eyes and minds of artists and designers to create, view, and depict the graphical world. These computer-generated graphics are used instead of achieving the illusion of photorealism via an optical camera. With the advent of many algorithms, papers, and software tools dedicated to generating the artistic and meaningful images, the entire field was exploded into existence in the 1990s. Now the field appears to be approaching maturity. Many questions remain open, but many have been settled. This book presents a detailed treatment of this field in a coherent conceptual framework.

1.1 The Brief History: from Photorealism to Non-photorealism

Photorealism in the context of computer graphics is a "faithful" rendering of the material world based on a number of depiction principles, such as convincing details, anatomical correctness, correct color rendition, and the correct perceptions of space, volume, and texture, etc. Therefore this field of computer graphics is also called *photorealistic rendering,* denoting algorithmic techniques that resemble the output of a photographic camera even make use of the physical laws being involved in the process of photography. A truly photorealistic image needs to be generated accurately from an extremely detailed object description requiring a great modeling effort. For the time being, a vast number of different computational models have been explored that to approximate these physical processes. The creation of realistic pictures has made great progress in the computer graphics community. This can be judged by viewing feature films and TV commercials, where it is often impossible for the audience to decide which are the virtual objects generated by the computer and which are the real objects captured by the camera.

It is no doubt that highly realistic graphics are very useful, e.g., they can support designers to evaluate and refine new products and turn computer games into a more enjoyable experience. But in general photorealism considers only part of the imagery traditionally used in simulation, design, entertainment, advertising, research and education, etc. For instance, it may be useful for designers to be able to generate photorealistic images of the finished product. But, during the design process they prefer to work with sketches and conceptual drawings that are better suited for explaining the basic concept of a new product or showing its inner structure. In educational course books, most of the pictures are not photographs, but rather diagrams and illustrations that are better able to communicate the important aspects of a topic. Furthermore, there are many research areas that can benefit from automatically generated images based on purely abstract data. But, how can one create photorealistic images of data that have no counterpart in the visual world? As computer graphic is getting closer to its holy grail of achieving photorealism, people finally realizes that there is more to images than realism, and, computer-generated imagery should not be restricted to photorealistic renderings.

Thus a new type of quest has emerged—creating imagery that is more effective at conveying information, expressive or beautiful—rather than just being physically realistic. Researchers started to explore alternative rendering techniques other than mimicking the effect of a traditional photographic camera. They needed to differentiate themselves from the rest of the computer graphics community, and *non-photorealism* was thus proposed. From the point of view of rendering an image, non-photorealistic images can be anything from a drawing or a diagram to a painting, as long as it helps to communicate the intended idea.

1.2 What is Non-photorealistic Computer Graphics

As with many new and young areas of scientific endeavor, there is no uniform definition of what we have called non-photorealistic computer graphics. The border between photorealism and non-photorealism is also fuzzy. Examining the primary literature on the topic, a number of different points of view have been summarized as follows [Gooch & Gooch, 2001; Strothotte & Schlechtweg, 2002]:

(1) The process of image production that is being mimicked (or non-photorealistic to be more precise, processes that are definitely not being mimicked): *non-photorealistic rendering*.
(2) The freedom not to have to reproduce the appearance of objects precisely as they are: *non-realistic rendering*.
(3) The process of adapting presentation to a dialog context and the dynamic informational wishes of users: *abstraction*.
(4) A specific drawing style: the terms *sketch rendering*, *pen-and-ink illustration*, and *stipple rendering* are examples.

(5) The effect a rendition has (or will hopefully have) on its viewers: *comprehensible rendering.*
(6) The use of renditions for conveying information, perhaps in the context of other media of expression: *illustrative rendering*, or *expressive illustration.*
(7) The possible deformations of images: *elastic presentations.*

In order to better explain non-photorealistic computer graphics, we will first explore the fundamental concepts of image, picture, and visualization for visual representation. We will then further discuss the essential aspects of non-photorealistic computer graphics by comparing the photorealistic and non-photorealistic computer graphics in terms of their goals and algorithmic techniques.

1.2.1 Image, Picture, and Visualization

Image, picture, and visualization are the different levels of visual representations. They are often mixed when used to describe the resulting output of a rendering in the computer graphics community. In order to help readers to better understand the rest of this book, these vocabularies should be clarified from the point of view of computer depiction. Computer depiction deals with all aspects of picture production, encompassing both photorealistic and non-photorealistic styles. Based on the definitions from the Webster dictionary, the differences between image, picture, and visualization are given as follows [Durand, 2002]:

(1) *Image.* An image is a "reproduction or imitation", or "the optical counterpart of an object" [Webster, 1983]. It is an optically formed duplicate, characterized by optical accuracy to a visual scene or object.
(2) *Picture.* A picture is "a design or representation", or "a description so vivid or graphic as to suggest a mental image or give an accurate idea of something" [Webster, 1983]. A picture is more loosely defined than an image, and it corresponds to both to the graphical object and to a representation. Pictures always have a purpose, which can be a message, collaborative work, education, aesthetics, emotions, etc. The term "picture" can be used to describe a visual representation of a visual scene, but this representation is not necessarily optically accurate. Moreover, a picture is not necessarily the representation of an existing real scene or object. The extreme example of impossible figures shows that a picture can superficially look like the representation of a 3D reality, while no objective scene that can be projected to such a picture.
(3) *Visualization.* Visualization is "the act or process of interpreting in visual terms or of putting in visual form" [Webster, 1983]. A visualization can represent visually data or subjects that are not themselves visual. Visualization therefore mainly relies on metaphors to communicate the meaningful information to the audience.

1.2.2 Photorealistic versus Non-photorealistic Rendering

The major goal of photorealistic rendering is to generate images that mimic the effect of a traditional photographic camera. It depicts only "What I See"—the extrinsic properties of objects such as outgoing light varying with light conditions, and the resultant output is a photography-like image. Its rendering process is a unidirectional optical projection of a 3D model onto a 2D plane. A scene consisting of 3D objects is illuminated by a number of virtual light sources, and images are generated by a virtual camera that is placed in the scene. The idea is to generate 2D images of the scene by emitting light from the light sources into the scene, computing the interaction of the light with the surface of the 3D models, and capturing that portion of the light that reaches the camera on a virtual film plate.

Non-photorealistic rendering (NPR), not only depicts "What I See", but also depicts "What I Know"—the intrinsic parameters and constancy that are invariant and constant properties of the objects such as reflectance and relative sizes. This gives freedom to encode an impression of the scenes rather than being forced to follow physical constraints. Its resulting output is a hybrid picture balanced between extrinsic and intrinsic properties of objects. The NPR process is a bi-directional interaction between a 3D model and a 2D plane, involving feedback and influence from the picture space to the object space. Therefore the NPR is essentially becoming a very complex optimization problem, producing the best picture with back-and-forth exchanges, given constraints, and goals linking the scene and the picture.

The function to minimize image information, and the degrees of freedom to vary it, heavily depend on the rendering of context and goal. For example, the goals and constraints for picture creation of art and craft are often set by the medium, the social context, the artistic fashion, clarity, representation of intrinsic vs. extrinsic qualities, 2D layout, etc. There are three main strategies to solve this optimization problem. The user can solve it, the computer can solve it, or the solution might involve both user and computer decisions. All approaches are of course not contradictory and can be blended. The frequently used case is the mixed one. The computer has to make decisions automatically, but the user needs to keep some control and influence the decisions. For example, in game and movie making, it is the equivalent of the movie director wanting to keep control of the style of the pictures, and the computer has to respond automatically to the user's interaction.

As a summary, the differences between photorealistic and NPR are investigated as follows:

(1) *Content of rendition.* Photorealistic rendering is merely based on the 3D geometry and topological information of the scene, and the resulting image is an "objective" depiction of that scene, and nothing else. In contrast, NPR encodes the "subjective" artifacts into the picture that clearly do not exist in the world. These artifacts may stem from the way

in which the geometric model represents the original object, or result from the manner, or style in which the geometric model is rendered.

(2) *Manners for presentation.* In photorealistic rendering, the external world is presented in an "objective" way. The depiction corresponds exactly to the object being modeled, following physical constraints and leaving nothing for the imagination. However, the presentation manner in NPR is a graphical abstraction such that the resultant picture comes from, and is "higher" than the underlying models, with certain features of the model being enhanced. It gives freedom to encode an impression of scenes, and introduce a broader variety of styles. This not only enables better recognition of certain features of the object being modeled by changing the model, but also enables selected features of the geometric model to be exaggerated in the rendition, in order to emphasize them. Moreover, it can show more of the relevant parts of an object than what would otherwise be possible, while less relevant parts may no longer be visible.

(3) *The cognition process of the resulting depiction.* The output of photorealistic rendering comes from the intuitive observation of the real world, and its cognition process is consistent with the visual perception of human beings in their daily lives. However, a reasoning process is needed to interpret non-photorealistic images. It is assumed that the viewers are able to build up a mental model of the object being portrayed with creative thinking and imagination, and then to perform the cognitive process for the visual understanding of the NPR results. This reasoning process gives the greatest communicative power for NPR.

(4) *The algorithmic mechanism.* The photorealistic rendering technique is based on the working model of another kind of machine, a camera. It simulates the particle-by-particle lighting exposure principle with the pixel-by-pixel rendering mechanism. The correspondence between pixels and the drawn primitive object is direct. In contrast to the pixel-by-pixel mechanism, NPR employs a relative global mechanism beyond pixels, and paints. The resulting picture is in a region-by-region mode. Each region has a set of pixels with attributes of shape, an area as a whole. These regions may be formed by a stroke, or more generally, may come from the interactional areas between the pen/brush with the canvas.

(5) *The interplay between 3D and 2D aspects of depiction.* Photorealistic rendering is a unidirectional projection from a 3D objective scene onto a 2D image. The typical object space inputs are a 3D geometric description of the objects, their material properties, and light sources. Perspective matrices, hidden-surface removal, and lighting simulation are then used to project this model onto the 2D image. However, the NPR is a complex bidirectional process between the 2D picture and the 3D model. A typical feedback loop is that the user and the computer work together, cooperatively generating an initial picture, viewing it, assessing the qualities, and then re-generating the new interim pictures via necessary modifica-

tions and refinements. The process is iterated, and the final picture is retouched until it looks right.

1.3 The Framework for Non-photorealistic Computer Graphics

The default tendency of non-photorealistic computer graphics is to generate imagery that superficially looks like that made by artists [Lansdown & Schofield, 1995]. It involves a fundamental issue of simulating the intelligence of artists, i.e., to emulate human facilities for producing an artist's handwork. Artists and other picture makers have developed a rich set of techniques to produce effective pictures. Non-photorealistic computer graphics should learn from this large body of knowledge, as well as from the analysis performed in the perception community. However, fine arts are still believed to be of a purely "metaphysical" nature and that there is no underlying theoretical knowledge of them. Every creative act is partly guided by intangible "forces" and "feelings" that are not easily translatable to algorithms.

Non-photorealistic computer graphics not only has been concerned with simulating traditional drawing and painting techniques, but also aims at improving visualization based on the findings from cognitive psychology. Conveying meaning is beyond scientific curiosity for pursuing NPR. There is ample evidence that non-photorealistic renditions are in fact more effective for communicating specific information than photographs of photorealistic renditions in many situations. Many studies have been carried out by cognitive and educational psychologists that attest to the superiority of such handmade graphics over photo-like images. NPR therefore enables users to lead human-computer dialogs with information exchange in a graphical form. The style of the picture generated should be flexible so as to be most appropriate for the dialog at hand. To this end, a model of information transfer must be assumed or developed. Methods and tools need to be developed to enable designers and programmers of interactive systems to have appropriate pictures rendered for their end users.

The core scientific problems in non-photorealistic computer graphics can be categorized as the following ones in terms of its input/output information.

(1) *How to create art crafts from a blank canvas.* When an artist sets out to paint a picture, he or she must have three types of physical tools. The first is a medium, such as oil paint, acrylic or watercolor, to be used to construct the picture. The second is some type of applicator or brush/pen for the application of the medium. The third is a surface, such as paper or canvas, on which the medium is applied. Therefore the computer should first model and simulate these authoring tools and the physical interaction among them, and then the user can employ the

digitized authoring tools to interactively or semi-automatically create the art craft of pen-and-ink illustration, watercolor/oil painting, or engraving.

(2) *How to convert the source images into pictures with the desirable visual effects.* By the techniques from image processing, analogical reasoning, computer vision, etc., it attempts to semi-automatically translate the input images into the resulting pictures with the desired artistic styles, which may be specified by numerical parameters, textual keywords, or the reference images.

(3) *How to generate artistic renditions from 3D models.* Its input is a 3D model of the scene, character, the viewpoint, etc., and the algorithmic steps for rendering are very similar to those in photorealistic renderings. However, the affine transformations, viewing projections, texture-mappings or lighting models are usually with non-photorealistic properties, and can help generate the output picture, which gives the visual impression of the artistic rendition styles specified by the user.

(4) *How to synthesize expressive pictures from textual, graphical or pictorial data.* The "expressive" picture embodies various levels of meaning for the communication among artists and designers. Its input might be a combination of 3D models, 2D images, or semantic text. It attempts to render objects and scenes to resemble how artists and designers might want to see them. The resulting pictures are made meaningful and comprehensible. The viewer is encouraged to make the same imaginative, perceptual contributions as those in the interpretive art.

(5) *How to accelerate the production of cartoon animation sequences with temporal coherence.* 2D animation can only be automated to the extent that the computer acts as an interactive assistant to the animator. The key problem is that the modeling, rendering and motion which are implicitly and tightly coupled in the animated drawings of key frames are unavailable. The temporal coherence problem will arise if we want to speed up the cartoon animation production by decoupling the modeling, rendering, and motion as that in 3D animation production. For example, some features of the frames in a cartoon sequence are chosen randomly (e.g., stroke placement for hatching), and they will look different in each frame. Although this may be desirable in some cases, it will in general distract the beholders' attention, and can put a considerable strain on the eyes. Similar artifacts appear if the rendering algorithm is unstable with respect to small changes of the viewing angle or small body deformations. It is therefore important to ensure that small (or no) changes in the scene result only in small changes in the cartoon animation production.

This book is accordingly organized in terms of the aforementioned five scientific core issues, providing a systematic, in-depth insight into non-photorealistic computer graphics. The structure of the book is shown in Fig. 1.1.

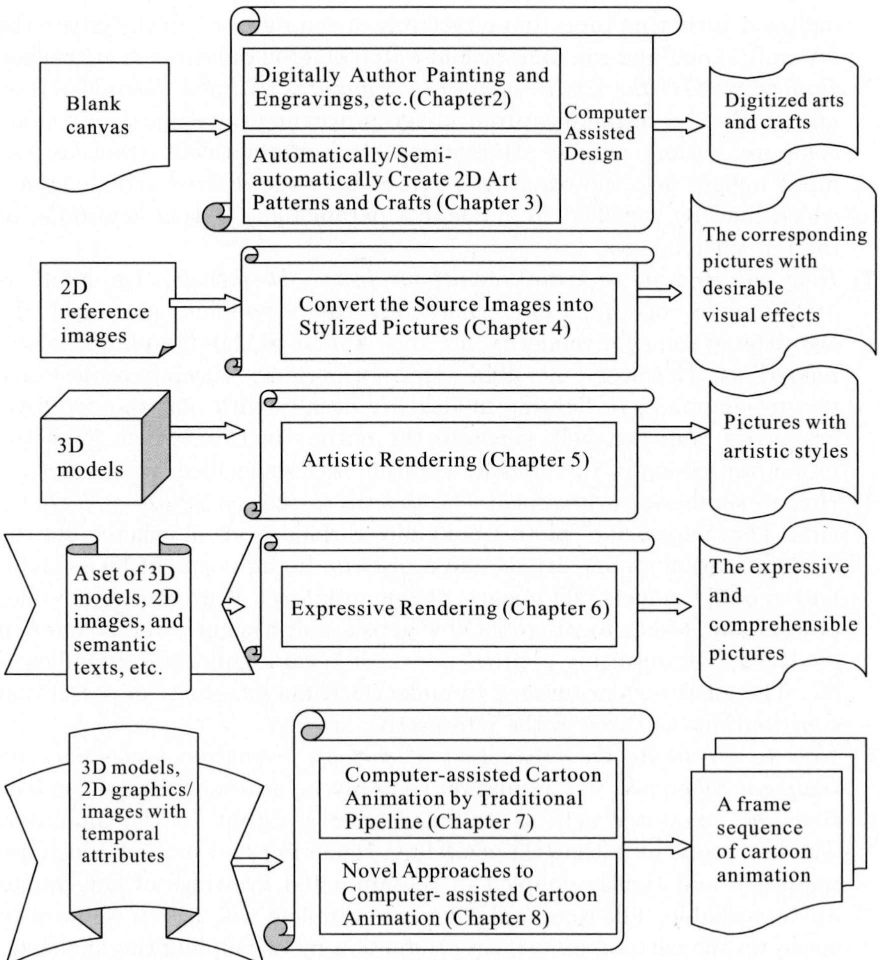

Fig. 1.1 The structure of the book based on a consistent framework of non-photorealistic computer graphics

An overview of the remaining chapters is given below:

Chapter 2 employs the *computer-aided design* (CAD) principles to enable the artist to explore the inner and outer world and our relation to them using the digitized media and tools. Its core technical issue is how to let the computer replace the paper/canvas, pigments, and pens/brushes by the natural media simulation.

Chapter 3 moves into how to automatically/semi-automatically synthesize the 2D art patterns in terms of the fractal computing, shape-grammars, spatial-layout, and the aesthetic knowledge/rules.

Chapter 4 deals with how to transform the source images into the resulting pictures with the desirable visual effects, which can be specified in three ways.

(1) The user explicitly specifies the resultant artistic style based on parameters or semantic keywords.
(2) The desirable visual effects are intuitively specified by a set of reference images/pictures.
(3) The user implicitly specifies the artistic transformation by the analogical mapping between pairs of images, instead of the final visual effect.

Chapter 5 discusses how to automatically/semi-automatically render the 3D objects or scenes into the artistic pictures. The rendition techniques include artistic simulation based on a traditional 3D rendering pipeline, conversion from the interim reference images, silhouette drawing, and the dedicated illustrational algorithms for 3D surfaces, 3D landscapes, and 3D volumes, respectively.

Chapter 6 structures and treats artistic communication methods that can visually convey meanings, purpose, intent, etc., including comprehensible rendering, expressing shape features, communications of design intent, and artistic presentation for transparent objects.

Chapter 7 describes a variety of computer-assisted cartoon animation techniques on the basis of traditional animation production pipeline, including computer-assisted auto-coloring, transforming black-and-white cartoon sequence into colorful ones, and computer- assisted "inbetweening" for cartoon characters.

Chapter 8 explores the novel approaches to assisting cartoon animation production beyond the traditional animation production pipeline, including video-driven cartoon animations, cartoon animation production guided by 2.5 D or approximate 3D geometry, cartoon animation production accelerated by artistic rendering with temporal coherence, and computer-assisted cartoon animation by reusing the graphical models, motions and rendition.

Chapter 9 concludes the book with a summary of research methodologies, scientific problems, current hot topics, and future directions in non-photorealistic computer graphics.

References

Durand F(2002) An invitation to discuss computer depiction. In: Proceedings of the 2nd International Symposium on Non-photorealistic Animation and Rendering 111–124

Lansdown J, Schofield S(1995) Expressive rendering: a review of non-photorealistic techniques. IEEE Computer Graphics and Applications 15(3): 29–37

Gooch B, Gooch A(2001) Non-photorealistic rendering. AK Peters, Ltd., Wellesly Massachusetts

Strothotte T, Schlechtweg S(2002) Non-photorealistic computer graphics: modeling, rendering, and animation. Morgan Kaufmann, San Francisco

Webster M(1983) Websters Ninth New Collegiate Dictionary. Merriam Webster, Springfield

2

Simulating Artistic Media for Digitized Creation of Artworks

One of the fundamental issues in non-photorealistic computer graphics is how to replace the natural media such as canvas, pigment, and pen/brush by the computer, in such a way that the artist can create the digital artworks by interactively manipulating these digitized artistic media. This chapter will provide in-depth coverage of algorithms for digitized drawing, painting and engraving. The relevant topics are broadly categorized into the following three parts:

(1) *Artistic tools modeling.* It describes the digitization of drawing tools (pen, pencil, crayon, charcoal, etc.), painting tools such as brushes, and engraving tools such as knives and chisels.
(2) *Modeling and simulation of natural medium and its interaction with tools.* It includes the modeling of natural media such as papers and canvases, and their interaction process with artistic tools such as pens and brushes.
(3) *Visual effect illustration for the final artwork.* It discusses the diffusion, sediment and drying process of pen-and-ink, water coloring and oil-painting, and the rendering of dried pigments.

2.1 Stroke-based Artistic Drawing

Strokes are the indivisible pictorial subunits or "building blocks" for constructing the new artistic images. It is of utmost importance to clarify how such pictorial subunits can be defined in terms of modeling their shape and attributes and how they can be rendered one by one. Here we will examine the different approaches for the creation of artistic lines, charcoal sketching, pen-and-ink, pencil-drawing and wax crayons.

2.1.1 Interactive Drawing Based on Brushstrokes

In the 1980s, the computer could generate the 2D graphical primitives in real-time. Then the graphics researchers began to extend the real-time drawing algorithms to mimic the brushstrokes by setting up the 2D lines, poly-lines, polygons and circles as the path of strokes and specifying the types of pixel distribution along the stroke path. The user can then interactively choose the various types of drawing strokes, and create the vivid pictures as shown in Fig. 2.1. The Paint on Windows platform is a typical application of it. The simplest brushstroke merely has a constant visual effect along the stroke path, ignoring the modeling of the paper and the temporal interplay of consecutive strokes.

Fig. 2.1 Interactive drawing based on 2D graphical primitives [Beach *et al.*, 1982]. Copyright of ACM, used with permission

In order to enhance the painting effect of a brushstroke, the researchers started to mimic the drawing with the stroke of stylized lines. For instance, the brushstrokes can be illustrated as shining tubes by employing the depth information, and it looks like it's being drawn by a brush with a shiny ball, as shown in Fig. 2.2.

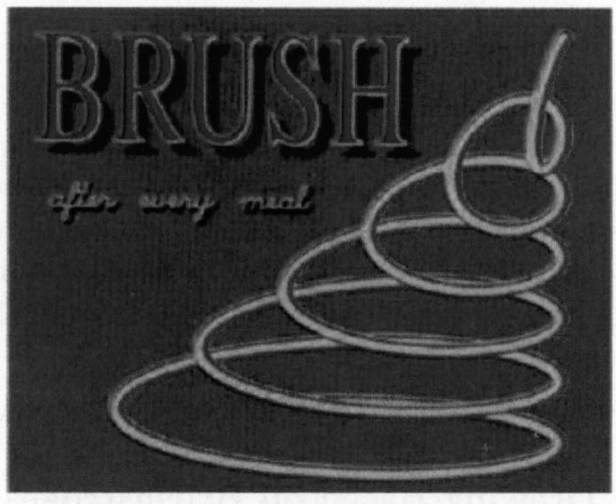

Fig. 2.2 Stylized line-drawing [Whitted, 1983]. Copyright of ACM, used with permission

From the point of view of interaction, the path of a brushstroke is usually controlled by a mouse or one of many tablet input devices that merely provide only (x, y) spatial information. The brushstroke itself is rendered with a single "brush shape" of a fixed size and orientation. However, a mouse-based interface does not support the fine control needed for detailed stroke work. A number of interruptions of the drawing act will make it difficult or impossible for the artist to maintain the kind of continuous control over his or her medium that is required for such tasks as changing "brush" shapes or the stroke styles. Thus digitized tablets with pressure-sensitive styluses become attractive devices for interactive drawing with brushstrokes. As the user draws on the tablet, the artist can change the shape of its contact point with the drawing surface. By changes in pressure exerted with the stylus against the surface, it is possible to control both the darkness (value) and width (weight) of the stroke. All of these factors are controlled by the artist in real time and with continuous feedback. Existing methods for modeling brushstrokes fall into two classes: "raster brushstroke", which models some brushstroke attributes at the pixel level and paints the result into a bitmap. The second class is the "vector brushstroke", which models a brushstroke outline and relies on scan-conversion for rendering.

The raster brushstroke approach is based on a digitization process called "brush extrusion". With the help of fast hardwired "BitBlt" operators, a bitmapped brush is dragged along a trajectory, leaving the image of the brushstroke. Fig. 2.3 shows a particular example of raster brushstroke sketching with a piece of a simulated charcoal drawing via a stylus. Raster brushstroke is well adapted to real-time sketching. Realistic models of paintings have been developed which make raster brushstrokes more expressive and simulate real paintings. Fig. 2.4 shows an example of a charcoal drawing. However, raster brushstrokes present two major drawbacks: they are resolution-dependent, and they cannot be edited. Resolution-dependence can be overcome by working at the maximum resolution of all possible output images. In any case, individual strokes cannot be easily, if at all, retouched nor edited.

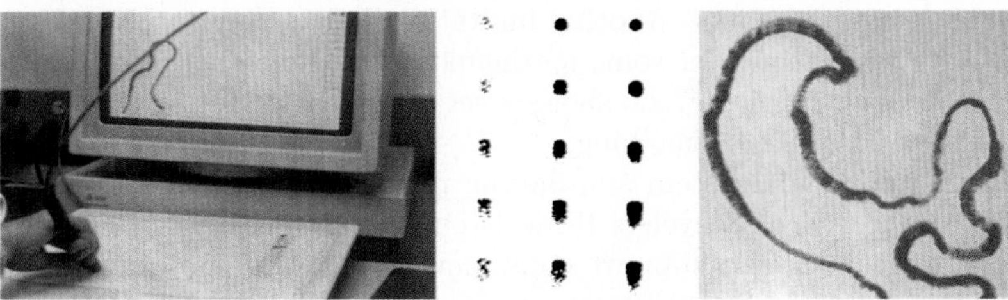

Fig. 2.3 Tilt stylus in use with dynamically brushed effects, varying with the magnitude and direction of tilt, the user pressure, etc. [Bleser *et al.*, 1988]. Copyright of ACM, used with permission

Fig. 2.4 An example of a charcoal drawing [Bleser *et al.,* 1988]. Copyright of ACM, used with permission

In the vector brushstroke approach, the stroke outline is computed from the brush outline and trajectory. Vector brushstrokes share two significant advantages of vector graphics: resolution-independence and editing capabilities. Strokes can be created, scaled, rotated or flipped very easily. Interactive retouching operations such as re-computing the stroke from the same trajectory using a different brush or different pressure data are straightforward. Moreover, the outline of the stroke is accessible to the user and can be edited like any other shape outline. However, vector brushstrokes have two major limitations. They often need heavier computations for curve fitting, as analytically solving the equations of the outline is too slow in the range of accessible shapes. Another limitation is that they sometimes require the user to explicitly enter some mathematical parameters, and thus are not suitable for sketching. Fig. 2.5 shows a set of typical vector brushstrokes and some instances of hand-sketching.

Furthermore, Finkelstein and Salesin proposed a multi-resolution vector brushstroke based on wavelets [Finkelstein & Salesin, 1994]. It requires no extra storage, and can support continuous levels of smoothing as well as direct manipulation of an arbitrary portion of the curve. Moreover, the control points and discrete nature of the underlying hierarchical representation are hidden from the user, which are preferred by hand-sketching. Fig. 2.6 shows some examples of multi-resolution brushstrokes.

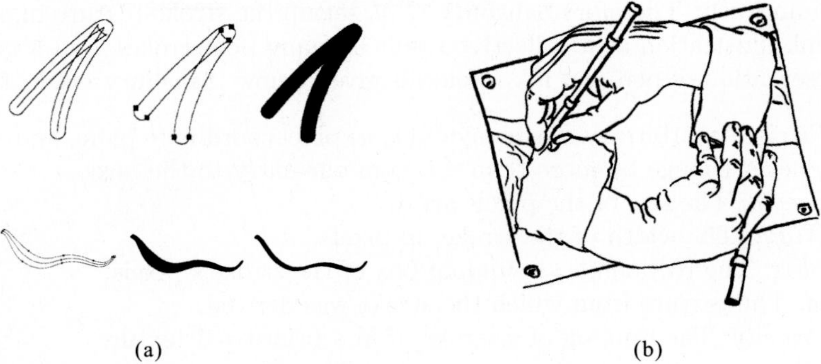

Fig. 2.5 Hand sketching with vector brushstrokes [Pudet, 1994]. (a) Vector brushstroke examples; (b) Hand drawing with vector brushstroke. Copyright of Blackwell Publishers, used with permission

Fig. 2.6 Line-drawings with multi-resolution brushstrokes [Finkelstein & Salesin, 1994]. Copyright of ACM, used with permission

2.1.2 Pen-and-ink Illustration by Stroke Textures

Brushstrokes are to emulate traditional artists' tools, and the resulting artwork is composed of the strokes which are individually drawn by the user. However, pen-and-ink illustration incorporates a wealth of textures, tones, and styles formed by thousands of individual monochromatic strokes of the pen. The creation of pen-and-ink illustration will require a great deal of technical skills and patience. In order to remove the burden of placing individual strokes from the user, Salisbury *et al.* proposed to emulate pen-and-ink illustration via stroke textures [Salisbury *et al.*, 1994].

Stroke textures refer to collections of strokes arranged in different patterns. In pen-and-ink illustration, its tone and texture are not independent parameters, as every stroke contributes both tone (darkness) and texture. Furthermore, pen and ink strokes work together to express tone and texture. The pen artist must take care to convey both of these qualities simultaneously. Therefore Salisbury *et al.* set up the stroke texture in a pen-and-ink illustration as a collective result of many pen strokes, and a typical representation of pen and ink strokes is given below [Salisbury *et al.*, 1994]:

(1) *Pixels:* An arbitrary-size array of (x, y) pixel coordinate pairs, and x and y never change by more than ± 1 from one entry to the next.
(2) *Length:* The size of the pixels array.
(3) *Width:* The width of the stroke, in pixels.
(4) *Bbox:* The rectangular bounding box of the stroke's pixels.
(5) *Id:* The texture from which the stroke was derived.
(6) *Priority*: The ranking of a stroke, if in a prioritized texture.

The Salisbury's interactive pen-and-ink illustration system supports a library of user-defined stored stroke textures and built-in procedural stroke textures (as shown in Fig. 2.7). A stored texture is simply a collection of strokes. Drawing a texture at a given darkness is a matter of choosing from the collection a subset that has enough strokes to reach the desired tone. Procedural stroke textures are computed procedurally to depict interesting texture effects such as stippling (randomly distributed points or short strokes), parallel hatching, and curved strokes. To draw procedural stroke textures, the system simply generates appropriate candidate strokes under the region of the brush and tests them.

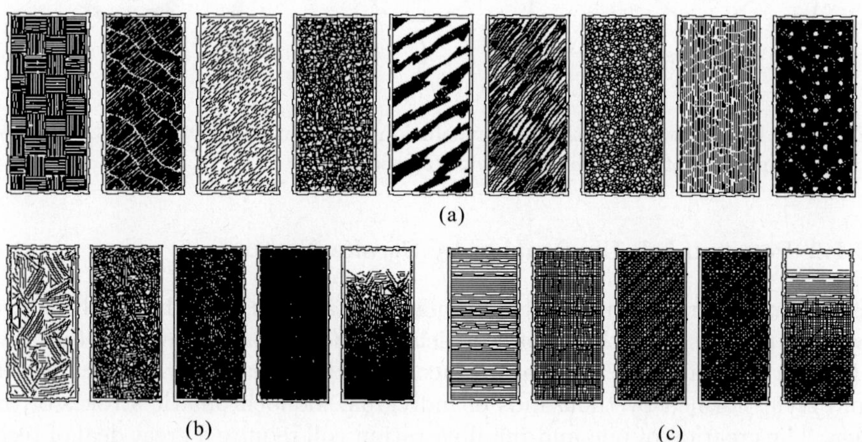

Fig. 2.7 Instances of stroke textures [Salisbury *et al.*, 1994]. (a) Assorted stored stroke textures; (b) A single texture drawn with several tone values; (c) The prioritized textures: the most significant strokes are drawn for light tone values, less important strokes are brought in to darken the texture. Copyright of ACM, used with permission

The overall paint pipeline in this system is given as follows:

```
Paint:
For Each brush position P
    While S←GenerateCandidateStroke(P)
        ClipStroke(S)
        If TestStrokeTone(S) then
            DrawStroke(S)
        End If
    End While
End For
```

GenerateCandidateStroke(P): At each brush position P, the system may in general try to draw many strokes. Each invocation of *GenerateCandidateStroke* returns the next stroke instance from a set of candidates. The next stroke returned may be generated dynamically based on the success of the previous strokes.

ClipStroke(S): The candidate stroke S is subjected to a series of clipping conditions such as to the bounds of the overall image, to the brush, to clipedges, etc. The clipping operations return a "first" and a "last" index into the stroke's pixels array, but before actually trimming the stroke, these indices are perturbed up or down by a small random amount to achieve ragged clipping.

TestStrokeTone(S): Two tests are performed to see how stroke S affects the image. First, the stroke's pixels in the image buffer are tested. If all the pixels are already drawn, the stroke has no effect on the image and is trivially rejected. Next, the effect of the stroke on the image tone is determined. The stroke is temporarily drawn into the image bitmap and the resulting tone is computed pixel-by-pixel along its length, by low-pass filtering each pixel's neighborhood. The stroke fails if it makes the image tone darker than the desired tone anywhere along its length.

DrawStroke(S): To draw stroke S, its pixels in the image bitmap are set, the display is updated, and an instance of S is added to the main stroke database. For stored stroke textures, the system checks to see if the new stroke S overlays an existing instance of the same stroke—such an occurrence could happen, for example, if the earlier stroke was clipped to the brush and the user has now moved the brush slightly. Rather than adding the new stroke, the previously-drawn stroke is extended to include the new stroke's pixels in order to avoid overwhelming the data structures.

Compared to the tedious individual stroke drawing, pen-and-ink simulation by stroke textures goes beyond emulating the traditional artists' tools. This enables the higher-level cumulative effect that the strokes can achieve: texture, tone, and shape. The user "paints" with a desired stroke texture to achieve a desired tone, and the computer draws all of the individual strokes. Fig. 2.8 shows some resulting pen-and-ink illustrations based on stroke textures.

Fig. 2.8 Interactive pen-and-ink illustrations [Salisbury *et al.*, 1994]. Copyright of ACM, used with permission

2.1.3 Interactive Pencil Drawing

Pencil drawing is a flexible medium, providing a variety of styles of line quality, hand gestures, and tone building. It is excellent for preparatory sketches, and is popularly used in the contexts of scientific and technical illustrations, architectural and design drawings. From the point of view of media simulation, pen-and-ink illustrations are relatively simple, as we merely take into consideration the attributes of a pen-and-ink stroke such as width and contact area. But pencil drawings are much more complicated, as we should additionally consider the modeling of the pencil, drawing papers and the interactions between them. There are two types of pencils: graphite and colored. Thus we will discuss them respectively in the following subsections.

2.1.3.1 Graphite Pencil Drawing

The representative work on graphite pencil drawing comes from Sousa and Buchanan[Sousa & Buchanan, 2000]. They took the observational approach to simulating pencil drawing, capturing the essential physical properties and behaviors observed to produce quality pencil marks at interactive rates. Its core is an observational model of the interaction among the real graphite pencil drawing materials (pencil, paper, eraser and blender).

(1) *Graphite Pencils.* Their pencil model is from the category of a wood-encased artist-grade graphite pencil. Every pencil contains a writing core (or lead) which is made of graphite, wax, and clay. The hardness of the lead depends on the percentage amounts of graphite and clay. The more graphite it contains the softer and thicker it is. Pencil hardness usually ranges from 9H to 8B. Table 2.1 presents the percentage values of the mass amounts of graphite, wax, and clay particles for the nineteen grades of pencil hardness.

Table 2.1 The percentage values of the mass amounts of graphite, wax, and clay particles for the nineteen grades of pencil hardness

Pencil Number	Graphite	Clay	Wax
9H	0.41	0.53	0.05
8H	0.44	0.50	0.05
7H	0.47	0.47	0.05
6H	0.50	0.45	0.05
5H	0.52	0.42	0.05
4H	0.55	0.39	0.05
3H	0.58	0.36	0.05
2H	0.60	0.34	0.05
H	0.63	0.31	0.05
F	0.66	0.28	0.05
HB	0.68	0.26	0.05
B	0.71	0.23	0.05
2B	0.74	0.20	0.05
3B	0.76	0.18	0.05
4B	0.79	0.15	0.05
5B	0.82	0.12	0.05
6B	0.84	0.10	0.05
7B	0.87	0.07	0.05
8B	0.90	0.04	0.05

(2) *Pencil Points.* Sharpening a pencil in different ways changes the shape of the contact surface between the pencil and the paper. The tip shape is defined as a polygonal outline based on the shape of three canonical types of sharpened pencil points (typical, broad, and chiseled) (see Fig. 2.9). A pencil tip shape is defined as T_s=$\{(x_i,\ y_i),\ s$: $3\leqslant i \leqslant n\}$, where $(x_i,\ y_i)$ is one of the n vertices of the polygon, and s is the scale factor of the polygon used to account for the thickness of the lead.

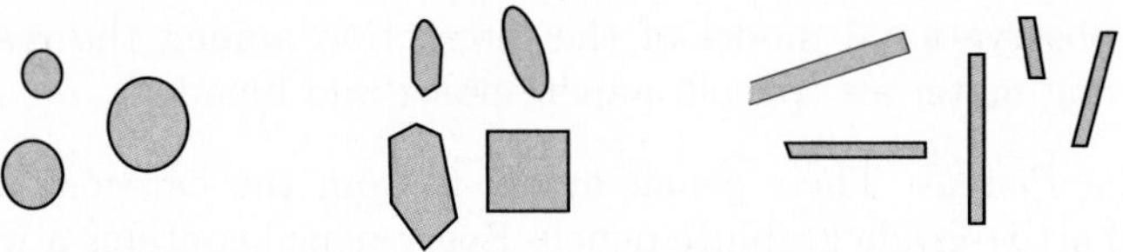

Fig. 2.9 Typical polygonal shapes of pencils

Pressure distribution coefficients are values between 0 and 1, representing the percentage of the pencil's point surface that, on average, makes contact with the paper. These pressure distribution coefficients are defined as

$$P_c = \{(c, x, y), (c_i, x_i, y_i) : 3 \leqslant i \leqslant n\}.$$

where c is the value of the main pressure distribution coefficient whose location (x, y) can be anywhere within the polygon defining the tip shape, and c_i is the pressure distribution coefficient at the vertex (x_i, y_i) from the polygonal tip shape. The value between c and c_i is calculated by linear interpolation, and thus defining the general shape of the pencil's tip (see Fig. 2.10).

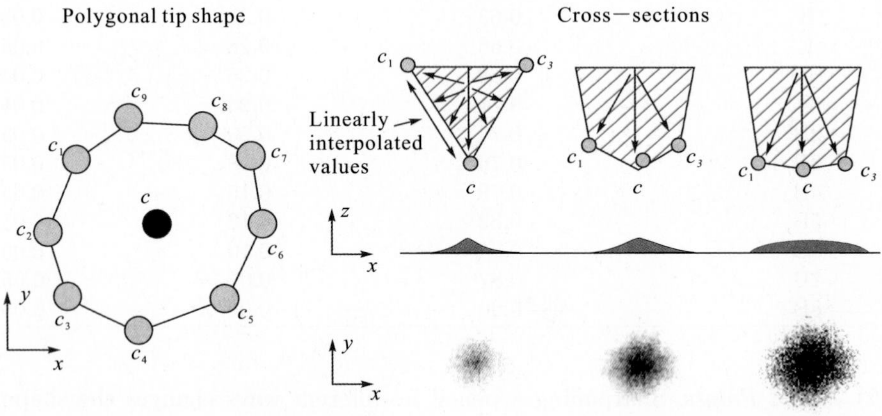

Fig. 2.10 Different values of pressure distribution coefficients (c, c_i) across the polygonal shape results in different distributions of the lead material onto the paper's surface [Sousa & Buchanan, 2000]. Copyright of Blackwell, used with permission

(3) *Drawing paper.* Papers are made in a variety of weights and textures. The smallest element of the paper's roughness is the grain. A grain is defined by 4 paper heights, where h_1 is at the paper location (x, y), and its three neighbors h_2 at $(x, y+\mathrm{d}y)$, h_3 at $(x+\mathrm{d}x, y+\mathrm{d}y)$, and h_4 at $(x+\mathrm{d}x, y)$ (see Fig. 2.11 (a)). The units $(\mathrm{d}x, \mathrm{d}y)$ are defined as in the normalized coordinate space, and the volume above the grain is to be filled with lead (see Fig. 2.11 (b)).

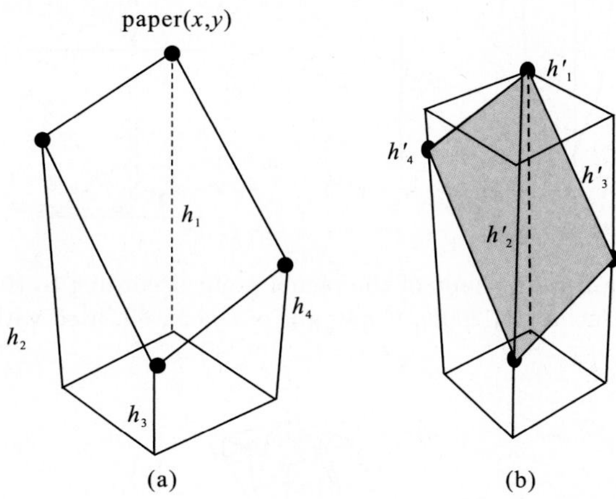

Fig. 2.11 The grain model of drawing paper

(4) *Pencil and paper interaction.* Pencil strokes are left on a paper through the friction between the lead and the paper. The paper grains react to the hardness of the pencil and to the pressure exerted upon it. In Sousa and Buchanan's system, the pencil and paper interaction is modeled as follows [Sousa & Buchanan, 2000].

For each new position of the pencil tip over the paper:

- Evaluate the polygonal tip shape of the pencil point in terms of the slant angle of the pencil (see Fig. 2.12).
- Initialize the local threshold volume of the paper.
- Distribute the pressure applied to the pencil across the tip shape.
  ① Compute the grain porous threshold volume.
  ② Process the grain biting the lead. It is composed of five steps (see Fig. 2.13):
    a. Compute the depth of the lead into the grain.
    b. Compute the volume bitten.
    c. Scale it according to the current lead degree of hardness.
    d. Distribute it among the paper grain heights.
    e. Compute the amount of lead deposited.
  ③ Compute the damage caused by the lead to the paper grain.

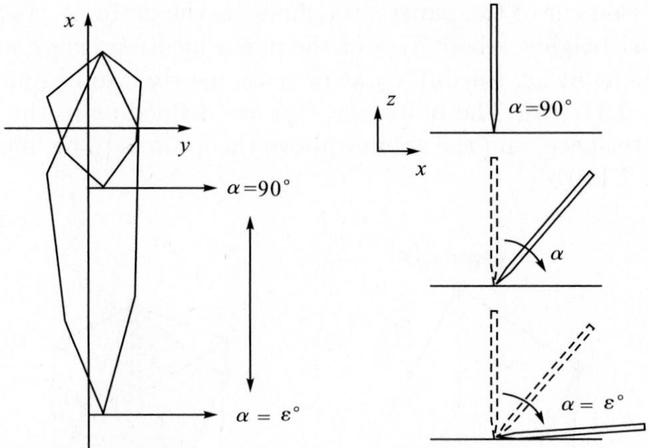

Fig. 2.12 Scaling the tip shape of the pencil point according to the slant angle of pencil [Sousa & Buchanan, 2000]. Copyright of Blackwell, used with permission

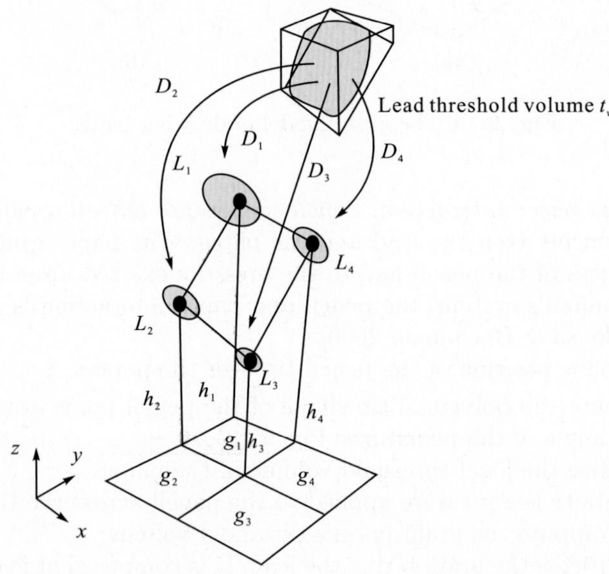

Fig. 2.13 Proportional distribution among the grain heights. In the example, $D_1 > D_4 > D_2 > D_3$ and $D_1 + D_2 + D_3 + D_4 = 0$. h_3 is shared by four grains g_1, g_2, g_3 and g_4. This means that h_3 accumulates the lead material by four grains [Sousa & Buchanan, 2000]. Copyright of Blackwell, used with permission

Finally, the reflected intensity of lead material is computed to form the resulting pencil drawing.

(5) *Eraser and blender interacting with lead and paper.* The eraser rubs the paper surface, and the lead material will be lifted away. When the blender is first being pushed, no lead material is deposited back onto the paper. As the blender continues to rub the paper surface, lead material is removed sticking to the blender's point, and a certain amount of lead will be deposited back on the paper. Fig. 2.14 shows some examples of the interaction effects between an eraser and a blender.

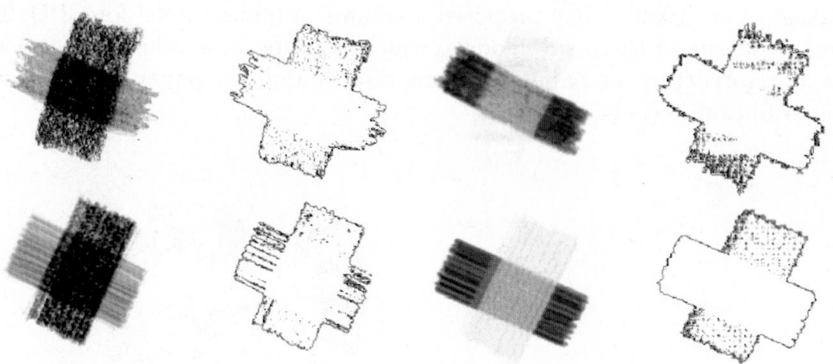

Fig. 2.14 Some examples of interaction effects between an eraser and a blender [Sousa & Buchanan, 2000]. Copyright of Blackwell, used with permission

Based on the aforementioned models of drawing materials and their interactions, the artist can create the pencil drawings interactively. Fig. 2.15 shows some instances of pencil drawings.

Fig. 2.15 Some instances of pencil drawings [Sousa & Buchanan, 2000]. Copyright of Blackwell, used with permission

2.1.3.2 Colored Pencil Drawing

Colored pencil drawing (CPD), is not only used as a means of study or for preliminary sketches to be developed further for painting and sculpture, but it also becomes an art form in its own right. In particular, a CPD is often being used for package illustrations and picture books. One of the salient features of a CPD is a gentle appearance for human eyes because of the soft, harsh, and almost misty representation. A colored pencil drawing can be emulated on a screen by combining several functions provided by existing digital paint systems, e.g., Painter (see Fig. 2.16) Takagi *et al.* developed the first system to directly support the CPD appearance and techniques [Takagi *et al.*, 1999]. They proposed a volume graphics model for CPD. The model consists of three sub-models, which describe in a volumetric fashion, the microstructure of paper, pigment distribution on paper, and pigment redistribution, respectively.

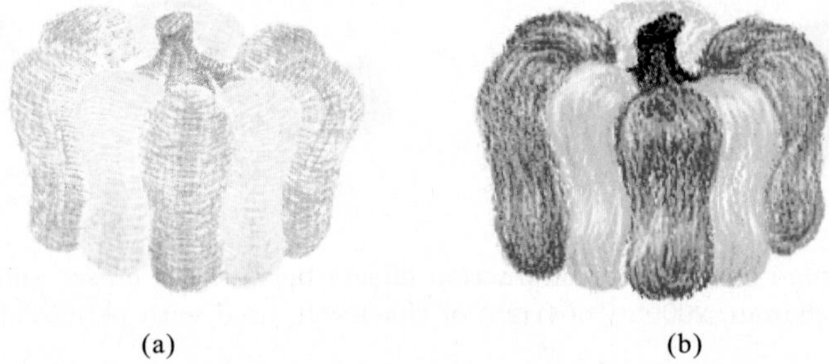

(a) (b)

Fig. 2.16 An actual colored pencil drawing and an image drawn with painter [Takagi *et al.*, 1999]. (a) Hand made colored pencil drawing; (b) Colored pencil drawing with painter.Copyright of IEEE, used with permission

The point of a pencil and the tip of a brush are assumed to be a sphere, and the *volumetric offset distance accessibility* is used for calculating the roughness of a paper. The system performs a binary classification on voxels of the CPD volume according to the density of composition materials with respect to prefixed thresholds. A colored pencil stroke is assumed to be a straight line segment with a constant width, and specified with the coordinates of the starting point, the direction vector on the (x, y) plane, and the width. There are two ways in which pigment is distributed onto the surface of paper (see Fig. 2.17):

(1) Pigments are shaved off from a pencil's lead by friction and deposited on the convex part of the paper.
(2) Pigments adhere to the surface of the paper, when a pencil's lead runs through areas covered with loading matter and pigments.

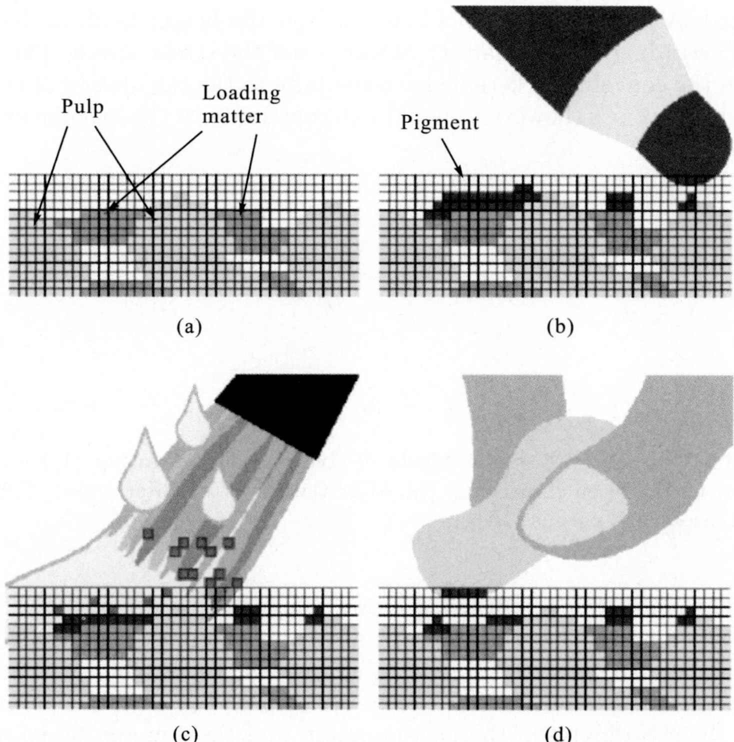

Fig. 2.17 Volumetric diagram of paper volume, pigment distribution, and redistribution concept in cross section [Takagi *et al.*, 1999]. (a) Paper; (b) Drawing; (c) Watering; (d) Eraser effects. Copyright of IEEE, used with permission

The *line integral convolution* (LIC) is extended to 3D by adding height information to the 2D data, and then adopted to approximate the movement of pigments in the pigment redistribution sub-mode. Pigment redistribution corresponding to the pencil pigment characteristics and the brush stroke speed can be simulated using the LIC by adjusting the length of the convolution kernel, estimating the location of the voxels which contribute to the LIC calculation, and finding the contribution of the convolution kernel.

For the colored pencil drawing *watering* effect (see Fig. 2.18), they assume that a pigment dissolves in water when a wet brush touches the pigment voxel. If a pigment voxel in the stroke region is accessible, the voxel has the possibility of dissolving. For these voxels, the degree of possibility is determined from the quantity of water contained in the brush, the quality of the bonding agent contained in the lead, and the stroke pressure. When the degree of dissolving exceeds a pre-specified threshold, the voxel is emptied, that is, it becomes a *source* voxel. After the source voxels are located, the brush stroke vector is used as a streamline for the LIC, and the pigment movements are calculated. A convolution kernel is defined on the height field. Its length is decided according to the quantity of water and the stroke speed. The source voxels in the convolution kernel also contribute to the calculation of the LIC. Non-pigment voxels, however, should not contribute to the calculation.

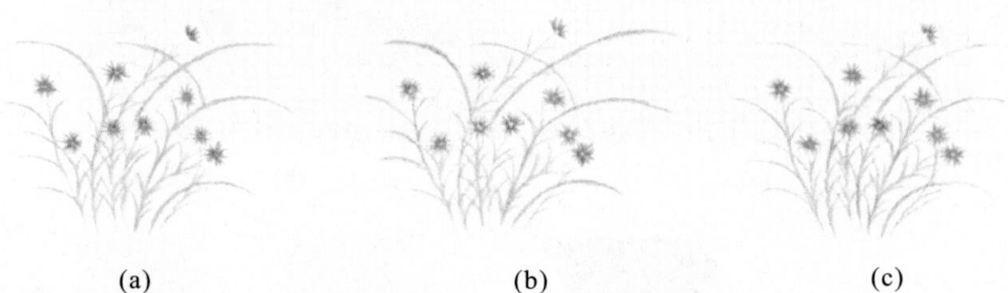

(a) (b) (c)

Fig. 2.18 Watering and eraser effects of colored pencil drawing [Takagi *et al.*, 1999]. (a) Colored pencil drawing; (b) After watering; (c) After eraser. Copyright of IEEE, used with permission

For the colored pencil drawing *eraser* techniques (see Fig. 2.18), Takagi *et al.* focused on the soft tint effect. A soft tint is obtained by applying light eraser strokes to colored pencil drawing surfaces. The shape of the patted area with an eraser stroke is assumed to be an ellipse. The involved parameters include the coordinates of the patting point, and the size and orientation of the ellipse. Additional key parameters are the softness of the eraser and the pressure of the eraser stroke.

This CPD model takes advantage of volumetric offset distance accessibility and LIC, and thus is highly controllable with a small number of parameters. The resultant CPD data sets are rendered using a volume visualization algorithm.

2.1.4 Simulating Wax Crayons

Wax crayons possess certain characteristics making them challenging to simulation. First, the crayon contact area is large enough that the paper is not flat over the entire region of contact. Secondly, wax is much more viscous than paints and inks, and so its interactions are different than these other media. The previously deposited wax will be obviously smeared by the action of later crayon strokes. Thirdly, the crayon footprint can change shape over a short period of time, changing substantially even within a single stroke. Rudolf *et al.* synthesized wax crayons drawings from collections of user-specified strokes based on a physically-inspired model [Rudolf *et al.*, 2003].

Paper is represented by a height-field texture. There are two types of paper textures in Rudolf's system. One is the lunar texture which has a suitable combination of roughness and coherence. It's generated by convolving a quarter-circle arc with a lattice populated by uniform noise. The other one is fundamentally different from the lunar texture. It is generated by using 2D stipple restriction masks to scale the amplitude of uniform noise. This mask is tiled across the noise lattice to impose a repetitive structure upon the generated texture. Examples of such textures are shown in Fig. 2.19.

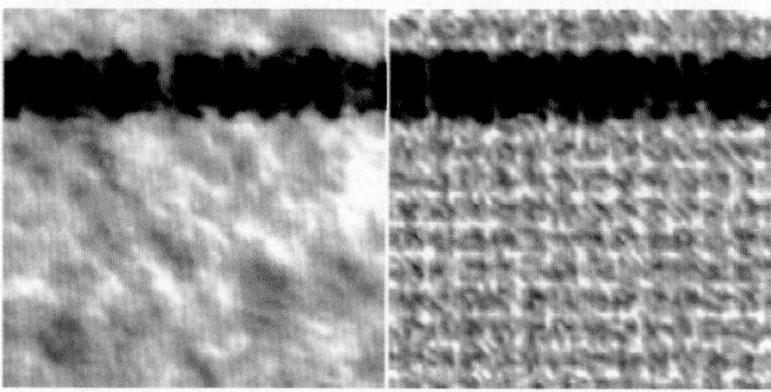

Fig. 2.19 Paper textures generated with lunar convolution and stipple restriction masks respectively [Rudolf *et al.*, 2003]. Copyright of IEEE, used with permission

There are two cases with real crayons interacting with the underlying paper. First, wax is deposited by the crayon. The volume of deposited wax depends on the size of the contact area between the crayon and paper, the slope of the paper over that area, and the pressure on the crayon. Second, wax that has been deposited onto the paper can be smeared around when another crayon passes over it. This smearing process pushes wax from the peaks of the paper texture, and down into adjacent lower regions. Smearing also has a directional component, in that the crayon can push wax over ridges in the paper. Fig. 2.20 illustrates the interactions of a crayon with the paper texture.

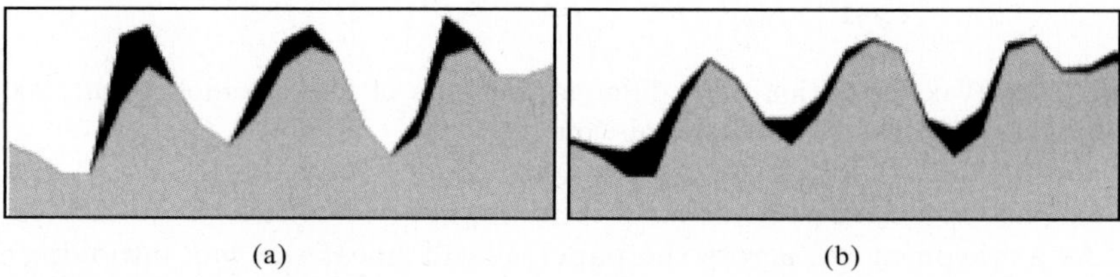

(a) (b)

Fig. 2.20 Hypothetical interaction between crayon and paper [Rudolf *et al.*, 2003]. (a) Wax deposition; (b) Smearing. Copyright of IEEE, used with permission

When creating wax renditions, they use line strokes as the drawing primitives. The parameters of its line-drawing include the endpoints P_1 and

P_2, the crayon's height mask M, the scalar force f applied by the crayon to the paper, and the set C for color properties of the wax. When drawing a line stroke with a crayon, the system must remove some volume of wax from the crayon and deposit it onto the paper underneath. The volume of deposited wax depends on the values of the crayon's height mask, relative to the local height of the paper. The difference between these heights determines how much wax is deposited, as well as how much wax is smeared from that region of the paper onto adjacent regions. Since the crayon's cells will potentially be worn away with each movement, the crayon's overall height must be adjusted at each step, so that, at the next step, the crayon is exerting the same amount of force upon the paper. In Rudolf's system, Hooke's Law of Compression is used to numerically determine the appropriate vertical displacement [Rudolf *et al.*, 2003]. Fig. 2.21 shows the crayon strokes varied with the pressure forces.

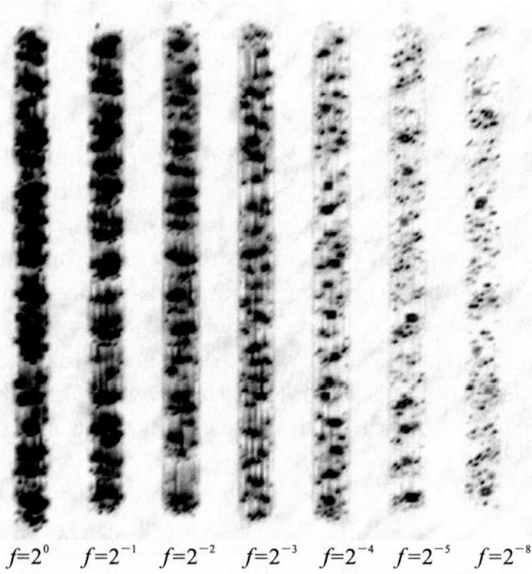

Fig. 2.21 Wax deposition with different amounts of force [Rudolf *et al.*, 2003]. Copyright of IEEE, used with permission

As a crayon moves across the paper, it will smear the wax into adjacent regions. It will force newly and previously deposited wax from that region to spread to adjacent regions. To simulate smearing, Rudolf *et al.* employed a smearing mask that encompasses the current paper cell and its eight neighbors. Each value in the mask determines the proportion of wax that is to be moved from the current cell to the cell underneath the given mask location. Fig. 2.22 shows the examples of wax deposition and its smearing effect.

Fig. 2.22 Modeled interaction between crayon and paper [Roudolf *et al.*, 2003]. (a) Wax deposition; (b) Smearing. Copyright of IEEE, used with permission

To render the wax model, a simplified Kubelka-Monk (KM) model is employed to generate the resulting images. The KM model approximates spectral transmittance, scattering, and interference. The value of these properties can be inferred by two specified colors. Each of these colors is the observed result of a layer of pigment overtop of a uniform background. One is the result with a black background, and the other with a white background. From these two results (see Fig. 2.23), KM theory provides a means of interpolating the resulting color, given arbitrary backgrounds. The KM model does so by inferring how much light is scattered by the pigment medium, and how much is transmitted through the medium. Fig. 2.24 shows examples of final wax crayon images generated from user defined strokes.

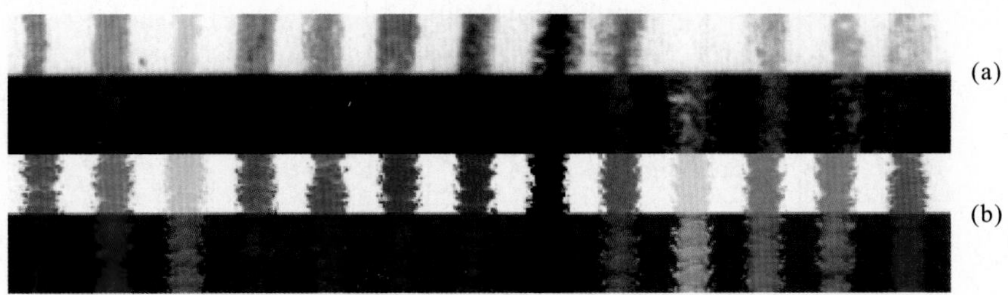

Fig. 2.23 Appearance of (a) real wax crayons and (b) simulated crayons [Rudolf *et al.*, 2003]. Copyright of IEEE, used with permission

Fig. 2.24 Sample simulated images (a) generated from real user-defined strokes (b) [Rudolf *et al.*, 2003]. Copyright of IEEE, used with permission

2.2 Oriental Calligraphy and Black Ink Painting

A typical pipeline to simulate oriental calligraphy and black ink painting is shown in Fig. 2.25. The input from the user usually consists of the position, pressure, tilt and trajectory of the brush. The dynamic and physical attributes of the tip mainly includes the global deformation and the shape of the tip, and the deformation of each bristle within the tip, etc. The dipping

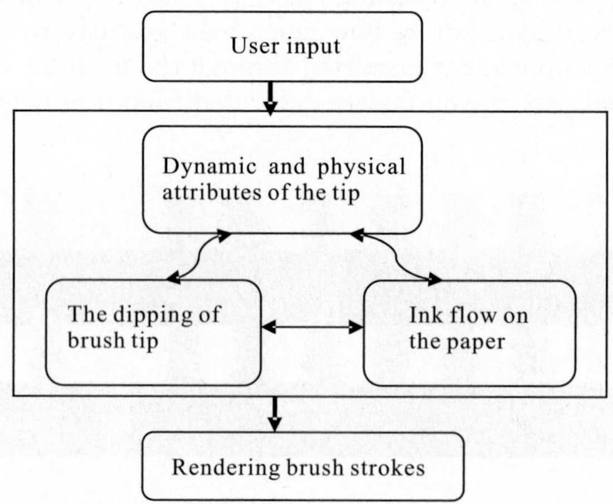

Fig. 2.25 A pipeline to simulate oriental calligraphy and black ink painting

of the brush tip is to calculate the ink flow distribution with the brush tip. The ink flow behaviors on the paper are mimicked in terms of the interaction model between paper and brush, including the ink absorption by the paper and the ink infusion on the paper. The rendering of brush strokes is to generate and display the resulting art work for the user.

2.2.1 Modeling of Soft Brushes

The brushes are usually modeled in terms of their shapes, the dipping and dyeing, and the interaction between brush and paper. The existing brush models can be classified as brush modeling with 2D strokes, parametric 3D brush, virtual brush with 3D geometry, and brush models driven by an expressive input device.

2.2.1.1 Brush Modeling with 2D Strokes

The "brushes" used in conventional computer painting systems are similar to automated rubber stamps They build up the resulting images by placing repeated copies of some static or simply derived patterns. Sometimes they simulate a spray of ink by painting pixels in a circular region around the brush. Strassmann described a typical brush modeling with 2D strokes [Strassmann, 1986]. He represents the brush as an array of bristles. Each bristle has a relative position to the center of the brush and an independent ink supply with a specified color whose intensity is from 0 to 1. When the bristle with dipped ink contacts the paper with sufficient pressure, it will leave a 2D stroke on the paper, and the 2D stroke is represented by position and pressure. The ink supply on each bristle is assumed to be a reservoir to a finite quantity of fluid, which gets replenished each time the brush is dipped. The quantity is decreased as the brush moves through the stroke, and eventually the bristle runs out. When the quantity drops to zero, that bristle no longer contributes to the image on the paper. If the stroke is known at the time of the act of dipping, its length is used to help determine the quantity of ink deposited on the bristles. If a scratchy breakup at the tail of each stroke is desired, the dip should put just the right amount of ink on the brush, including selecting a few bristles to be short-changed so they ran out early. There are parameters which control how many bristles get short-changed, and by how much, either as a fraction of the total stroke length or in units of absolute distance.

Chan *et al.* modeled the brushes in terms of the interaction effect between paper and bristles [Chan *et al.*, 2002]. The brush model consists of many bristles and they are arranged somewhat randomly within a circular area. The circular area is divided into small squares and each bristle is positioned randomly within that square. In order for a bristle to paint, it has to have ink on it and also the pressure applied to the brush needs to be sufficient for the bristle to touch the paper. In this brush model, each bristle draws a line on the paper. Combining all of the lines that each bristle draws makes a stroke. The thickness of the lines can be varied to get different effects. Also, the bristle does not stay at a fixed position all the time. It keeps moving to draw a more irregular line. These two are important procedures that affect how a stroke will look on paper. When ink is added to a brush, some bristles are randomly selected and their ink content is increased by a random amount. Also, it implements the "ink stealing" effect. As the artist paints a stroke, a bristle can steal ink from neighboring bristles. This allows the possibility of the *Feibai* effect because some bristles can dry up completely and then regain ink by stealing from others. Fig. 2.26 shows the model of a brush and several typical painting effects.

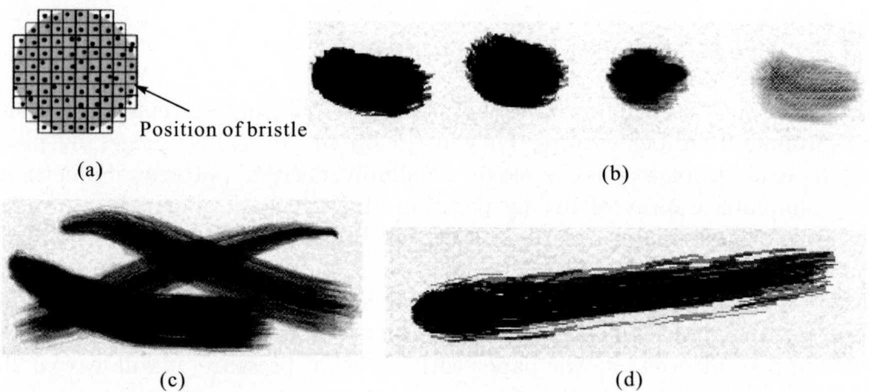

Fig. 2.26 Brush modeling in terms of interaction effects between bristles and paper [Chan *et al.*, 2002]. (a) Cross-section of a brush; (b) Brush strokes painted using increasing amount of water added to the ink from left to right; (c) Each stroke's transparency depends on how much water is in the ink; (d) *Feibai* effect is created by adding ink to randomly selected bristles and ink stealing. Copyright of ACM, used with permission

2.2.1.2 Parametric 3D Brush Modeling

The brush model with 2D strokes is simple and easily implemented. However, it lacks 3D and other physical properties of the brush, and is difficult to mimic the complex stroke effects for art works. Therefore Wong and Ip proposed a parameterized brush model to simulate the physical process of brush stroke creation [Wong & Ip, 2000]. It takes the following brush aspects into consideration: (a) 3D geometric parameters for the brush; (b) The brush hair properties; (c) The variations of ink deposition along a stroke trajectory.

Its brush geometry model (BGM) specifies the necessary information relating to the geometry of the brush bundle, i.e., the radius of the brush stem R, the length of the brush bundle L and the number of hairs M that form the bundle. These parameters are fixed for a given brush and do not change during the stroke creation process. In the normal state, the brush bundle, while suitably inked, can be approximated by an inverted cone as shown in Fig. 2.27. O_i is the location of the hair root relative to the center of the base of bundle O; h_i (i=1, 2,..., M) is the piece of hair within the brush bundle. A typical example of a real brush has the following values: (a) brush stem radius R=0.9 cm; (b) length of brush bundle L=3 cm; (c) number of hairs M=10,000 approx.

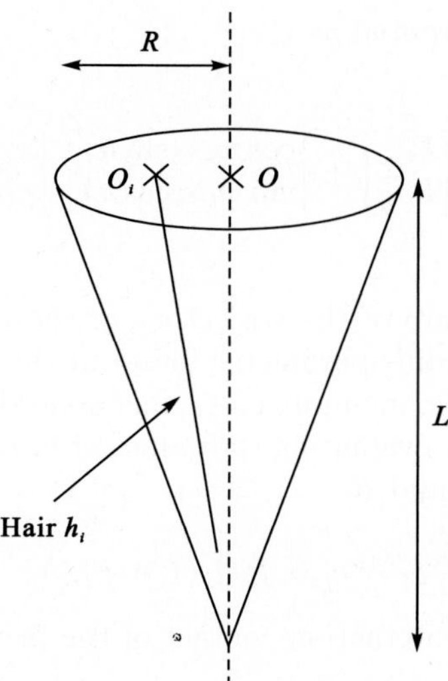

Fig. 2.27 Brush bundle in a normal state [Wong & Ip, 2000]. Copyright of Elsevier, used with permission

The brush motion dynamic model consists of two components: the instantaneous position of the brush tip P_t, and the 'footprint' of the brush on the paper U_t. The instantaneous position of the brush tip is the three-dimensional coordinate of the brush tip at any instance of time during the stroke creation process:

$$P_t = (P_{t \cdot x}, P_{t \cdot y}, P_{t \cdot z}),$$

where t=0, 1, 2,... is the discretized instances of strokes, $P_{t \cdot x}$, $P_{t \cdot y}$ are the planar coordinates on the paper, and $P_{t \cdot z}$ is the vertical distance from the root of hair bundle, O, to the paper, such that,

$$|P_{t \cdot x} - P_{(t-1) \cdot x}| \leqslant 1, \quad |P_{t \cdot y} - P_{(t-1) \cdot y}| \leqslant 1.$$

For the computation of U_t, paper is assumed to be non-blocking and the brush bundle can pass through its surface. The intersection of the brush bundle and the paper is a rotating ellipse (as shown in Fig. 2.28).

The "footprint" U_t, of the brush at any instance of time is modeled as 3-tuple:

$$U_t = (u_t, v_t, w_t),$$

where u_t is the major radius of the intersecting ellipse, v_t is the minor radius of the intersecting ellipse, and w_t is the degree of rotation of the intersecting ellipse. Then, together with the root of each piece of hair o_i, where $o_i = (x_i, y_i)$ is the 2D coordinate with respect to the center of the base of brush bundle O, the location of the pixels to be painted by each piece of hair can be computed as

$$\begin{bmatrix} x \\ y \end{bmatrix} = \begin{bmatrix} P_{t \cdot x} \\ P_{t \cdot y} \end{bmatrix} + \begin{bmatrix} \cos w_t - \sin w_t \\ \sin w_t \times \cos w_t \end{bmatrix} \begin{bmatrix} x_i v_t / R \\ y_i u_t / R \end{bmatrix},$$

where P_t is the coordinate of the trajectory of the brush stroke at instance t, and R is the brush radius parameter found in the brush geometry model. Suppose the brush bundle maintains a perfect cone shape and is vertical, our computational model for evaluating the values of u_t and v_t can be formulated as a function of $P_{t \cdot z}$, L and R,

$$u_t = v_t = R/L \left(L - P_{t \cdot z}\right).$$

Fig. 2.28 shows the interaction contact of the brush with the paper.

Fig. 2.28 The interaction contact of the brush with the paper [Wong & Ip, 2000]. Copyright of Elsevier, used with permission

Lee proposed a parametric brush model focusing on the elastic property of each single bristle of the brush [Lee, 1999]. He modeled the brush bristles using Hooke's law, simulating bristles as long, thin, elastic rods. The theory of elasticity is applied to model their deformation (as shown in Fig. 2.29). The brush path is defined interactively by the user or as a list of control points comprised of parameter conditions (time, position, pressure). For the stroke rendering, it provides two methods. The first one is straightforward in that the strokes are straightforward so that the paper pixels in contact with each bristle are simply painted according to the ink quantity remaining in the bristles. The second one is called *boundary-shading rendering*. The boundary of the stroke segment and the amount of ink within are both calculated iteratively. The *brush mark* at any instant in time is defined as the area of the paper to be painted by the bristles, represented by the convex hull of the paper points in contact with bristles. The outline of a brush mark is the *stroke segment*, later used to compute the *stroke*. The *stroke* or *boundary of the stroke* is the trail left by the brush as it moves along a path, with the resultant image computed as the connection or union of all stroke segments at every node along the brush path. Simultaneously with computing the boundary of a stroke, shading within the stroke is applied in a left-to-right linear shading pattern, across each shading segment. Fig. 2.30 shows some examples of stroke rendering.

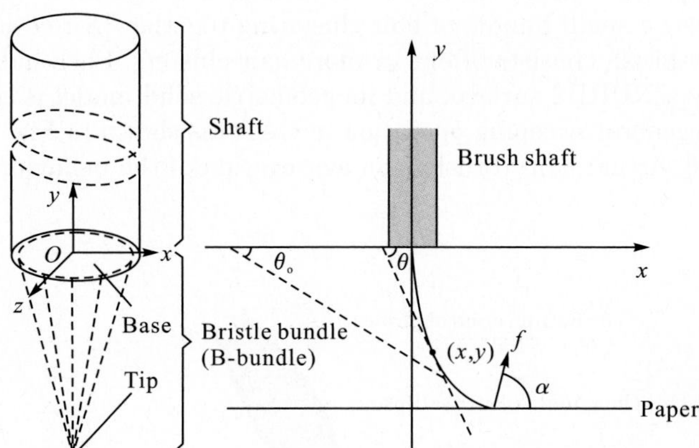

Fig. 2.29 The brush model and its bristle deformation [Lee, 1999]. Copyright of IEEE, used with permission

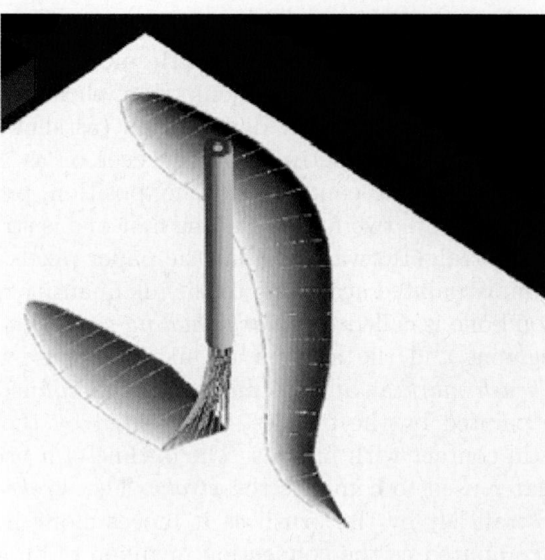

Fig. 2.30 Example of stroke rendering [Lee, 1999]. Copyright of IEEE, used with permission

2.2.1.3 Virtual brush with 3D solid geometry

Xu *et al.* proposed a virtual brush model with 3D solid geometry on the basis of hair cluster, a small bundle of hair clustering together [Xu *et al.*, 2002]. A virtual hairy brush consists of one or more hair clusters. Each hair cluster is described by a NURBS surface, and its geometric solid model is constructed through the general sweeping operation in CAD (as shown in Fig. 2.31). The behavior of a virtual hairy brush is an aggregation of the behavior of all hair clusters.

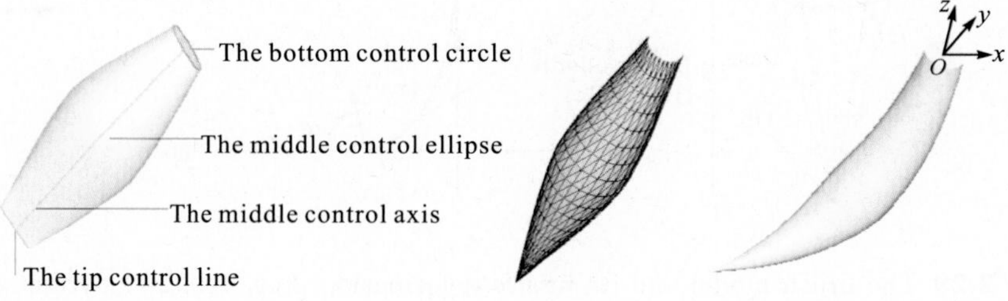

Fig. 2.31 The virtual brush model with 3D geometry [Xu *et al.*, 2002]. Copyright of Blackwell, used with permission

A virtual hairy brush is assumed to have three possible states in its lifecycle: the initial state, the dipping state, and the working state. In the initial state of a virtual hairy brush, the tip control line, the middle control axis, and the middle control ellipse are reduced to a point, a straight line, and a circle, respectively. In the dipping state, the hair cluster acquires ink-related information, which includes color and degree of wetness according to how the brush is dipped. The working state of a virtual brush is the *deformation* state of the brush. The brush deforms due to touching or pressing against the paper. By varying the eccentricity of the middle control ellipse, the tip control line and middle control axis, a series of solid modeling effects can be achieved (see Fig. 2.32).

Fig. 2.32 The modeling effects of the virtual brush with 3D geometry [Xu *et al.*, 2002]. Courtesy of Songhua Xu

However, hairy-cluster-based modeling for a virtual brush is not sufficient to deal with the highly chaotic geometry of the brush. Therefore they further proposed an improved virtual brush with a two-level hierarchical geometry [Xu *et al.*, 2003]. At the lower level of the hierarchy, hair threads whose position and geometry in 3D space are close to each other are gathered together and modeled as one hair macro. At the upper level, disjointed hair macros whose geometries are similar are classified into the same cluster of hair macros. A hair macro represents the smallest granularity in the modeling, and its geometric model is created by sweeping an ellipse along a skeleton. The shape of the moving ellipse can be varied during sweeping, and the ellipse always lies on the normal plane with respect to its skeleton. Based on this two-level hierarchical representation, it can efficiently represent the complex geometry as well as simulate the dynamic behavior of real paintbrushes having thousands of disjointed hair clusters (see Fig. 2.33).

Fig. 2.33 Complex brush geometries of the virtual brush [Xu *et al.*, 2003]. Copyright of IEEE, used with permission

2.2.1.4 Brush Modeling Driven by an Expressive Input Device

The aforementioned brush models are mainly based on the mathematic or physical properties of the real brush. They are transparent to the users. The user can not feel or touch these virtual brushes. However, without an input device as expressive as a real brush, the current virtual brushes will not be very user-friendly. There are two typical approaches to designing expressive input devices. One is to employ the real brush with additional sensors to expressively capture the control and intension of the user. The other one is to use the haptical devices with sufficient degrees of freedom as a substitute of the real brush.

Chu & Tai proposed an expressive device based on a real brush with ultrasound sensors [Chu & Tai, 2002]. The elastic brush built in the computer is driven by the movements sensed from a real brush. As shown in Fig. 2.34

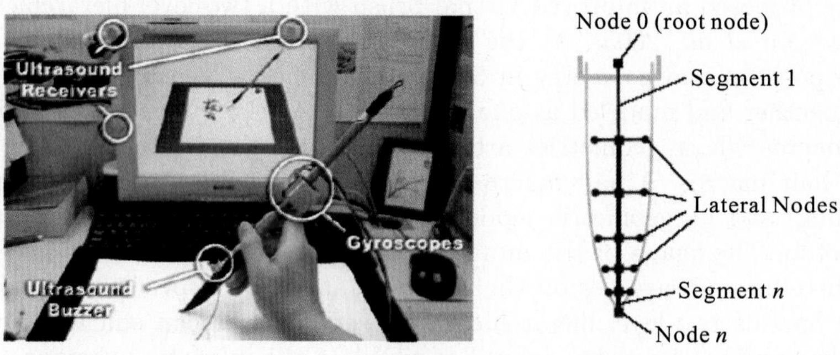

Fig. 2.34 The expressive input device and the internal structure of the elastic brush [Chu & Tai, 2002]. Copyright of IEEE, used with permission

the brush models are constructed in a two-layer approach: brush skeleton and brush surface. The brush skeleton determines the dynamics of the brush. It is composed of a spine and lateral nodes. The spine is a set of connected line segments for general bending of the brush. Lateral nodes are slides along the sides of a spine node for lateral deformation. Brush surface determines the footprint of the brush. It is created by sweeping the cross-section (two half-ellipses) along the spine. In the skeleton spring system of the brush, the angular springs are generated from the consecutive spine nodes or lateral nodes. The displacement springs are generated from the spine nodes and its lateral nodes. The brush flattening and splitting are simulated by the lateral nodes. The brush splitting at the bristle level is carried out by an alpha map. The brush plasticity is simulated by zero-shifting the spring energy function.

Yeh *et al.* proposed a brush model driven by a force feedback device with six degrees of freedom (DOF) (see Fig. 2.35). With force feedback, a user experiences the interaction between the pen and paper and one can feel it more realistically. The brush model is constructed by using physical-based springs as the skeleton of the brush. The springs used in this system adapt to the bending angle as the control variable. By using the information retrieved from the six DOF device, the brush model changes its position and orientation and simulates the shape it represents. Then, the detection of collision between the brush and paper is performed. Furthermore, the shape, orientation, position of brush, as well as volume of ink and water contained in brush determine the stroke drawing on the paper. In the meantime, force information is sent back to the force feedback device to simulate the feeling that the user touched a paper. Lastly, the ink-water transfer model is responsible for the transfer of ink and water in brush and paper.

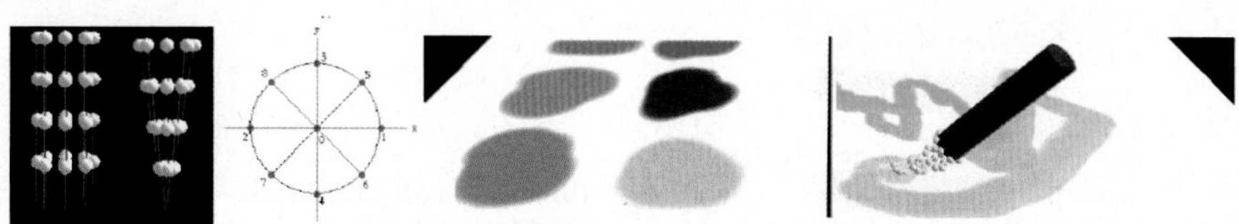

Fig. 2.35 The six DOF force feedback device, the brush model and some simulated brush strokes [Yeh *et al.*, 2002]. Copyright of IEEE, used with permission

2.2.2 Calligraphy with Soft Brushes

The objective of calligraphy simulation is to allow users to "practice" calligraphy electronically by generating the aesthetic character images using the digitized brush. From the point of view of technology, its core issues are how to capture and create the aesthetic features found in brush-written images, e.g., the natural running of stroke shapes produced by calligraphers, the impression of physical rubbing between the brush and the underlying paper, and the varying shades and trails of grey created by fast movement of a drying brush, etc.

A representative work on calligraphy simulation comes from Wong and Ip [Wong & Ip, 2000]. The user can specify the set of physical parameters or apply a predefined set of standard parameter values appropriate for that style of writing. The contact between the brush hair bundle and the writing paper is modeled using an elliptic footprint whose principal axes can be dynamically adjusted according to different brush bending and turning control. The result is a good approximation to real brush-written characters. By varying the different parameters which control the profile of ink absorption and deposition variants, etc., along a stroke, realistic calligraphic effects can be produced. They analyzed the four commonly used Chinese brush writing styles *Li* (clerical script), *Zhuan* (seal character), *Kai* (regular script), and *Xing* (running style), and decomposed the stroke creation process into I–IV stages.

I is the stage when only x, y coordinates of the stroke trajectory are specified. II is the result of varying the brush stem distance from the paper to create a stroke with a sharp end. III is used to affect the rotation of the brush at the turning point. This resembles the effect when the artist turns the brush head in a direction in preparation for the ensuing downward tick. During IV, the completed stroke is created. Note that in the resultant stroke, the turning portion changes to a sharper box shape, which simulates the artist's action of pressing down on the brush head. Fig. 2.36 shows the four stages with the horizontal strokes and the parameters to create the final resultant stroke.

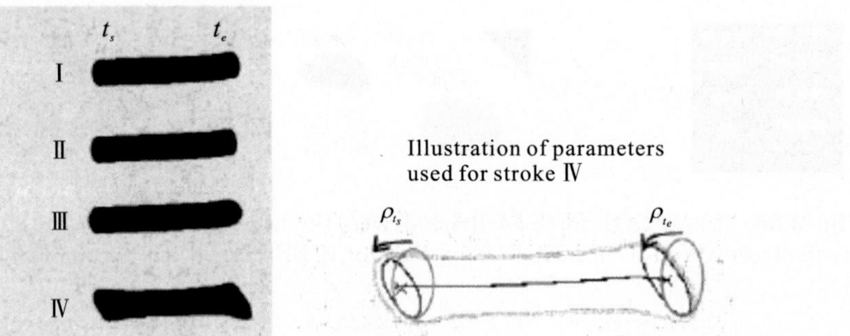

Fig. 2.36 The four stages of creating the horizontal strokes [Wong & Ip, 2000]. Copyright of Elsevier, used with permission

The amount of ink deposited by each piece of hair is modeled by two parameters: (a) A parameter g_t (0.0-1.0), which is a global reference of the ink depositing level which can vary over time instances t; (b) A range ($-s$-s), where s (0.0-1.0), within an individual piece of hair is allowed to deviate from the global reference g_t. Then, for each hair h_i, the degree at which it deviates from g_t is s_{q_i}, where q_i is a uniform random number in the range (−1.0-1.0). The amount of ink deposited by a single piece of brush hair h_i at the instance t is

$$g_{i,t} = g_0 + \sum_{j=1,\ldots,t} (g_j - g_{j-1})(1 - s_{q_i}).$$

With this we are able to model the amount of ink deposited by each piece of the brush hair. However, there exists interaction between the brush hair and the surface of the writing paper. Therefore a parameter for the absorption variant e_t (0.0-1.0) is used. Consider a brush moving on the paper surface, the tips of the hair move against the paper at a certain speed. If the speed is relatively high and the brush is rather dry, then at certain instances some hairs are probably not depositing any ink at their contact points on the paper. The role of e_t is to control the probability of this "non-inking effect" at any instance t of the stroke painting. Moreover, the on and off of inking is also related to the degree of brush hair spreading b_t, which is the consequence of a drying brush bundle, and the perpendicular distance of the pixel to the stroke trajectory, i.e., the r_i value of the location of the root of each piece of hair h_i. As a result, this on and off function is formulated as $E(e_t, r_i)$ such that

$$E(e_t, r_i) = \begin{cases} \text{on}, & \text{if } d_{i,t} < e_t(R - r_i)/R - b_t/R, \\ \text{off}, & \text{otherwise}, \end{cases}$$

Where $d_{i,t}$(0.0-1.0) is a uniform number generated for hair h_i at instance t.

An analysis of some well-known Chinese brush writing styles is given, with a view to establishing the relationship of these writing styles and the modeling process of simulating these different writing styles. The visual appearance of brush-written characters is the combined effects of the speed and direction of stroke writing, the orientation of the brush, the force asserted on the paper, and the ink content of the brush. The simulated calligraphy characters with different styles are shown in Fig. 2.37.

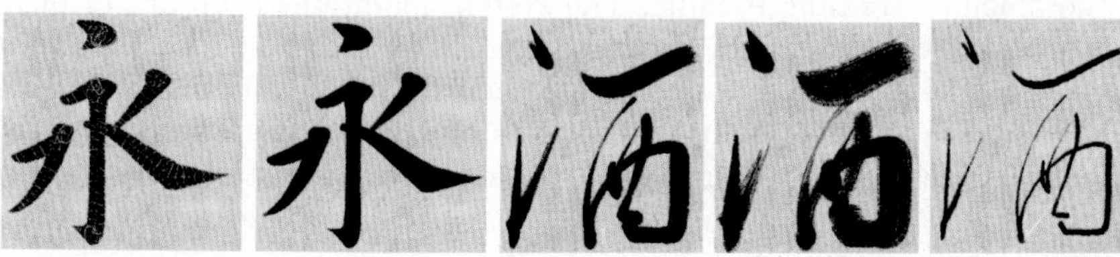

Fig. 2.37 Calligraphic characters with different styles [Wong & Ip, 2000]. Copyright of Elsevier, used with permission

Chu & Tai employed a real brush with the ultrasound sensors as an expressive device to simulate the Chinese calligraphy[Chu & Tai, 2002]. The character simulation is controlled by an energy function as $E = E_{\text{deform}} + E_{\text{frict}}$, where E is the total energy, E_{deform} is the tuft deformation energy and E_{frict} is the frictional work done by dragging the brush against the paper surface. The resultant character images are generated by texture mapping. Fig. 2.38 shows some examples of the resultant calligraphic characters.

Fig. 2.38 Some examples of the resultant calligraphic characters [Chu & Tai, 2002]. Copyright of Elsevier, used with permission

Xu *et al.* built a 3D geometric model for the typical brush typically in Chinese calligraphy [Xu *et al.*, 2002]. From the point of view of calligraphy simulation, their main contribution lies in the setting-up of the quality parameters of the virtual hairy brush in terms of the real brush. In real life, brushes having soft hair tend to branch out easily during writing. Some brushes have a great deal of hair and tend to take in more ink and cause serious paper saturation during the writing process. Other brushes have rather long hair and their tips tend to get deformed and easily rotated to a greater extent. In order to ease the configuration of a virtual brush to achieve the desired quality, they carried out a special procedure to train the computer by employing the principle of the *MiaoHong* process in Chinese calligraphy. The number of the training samples can be set by the users. The trained results of a virtual brush are brush strokes whose boundaries are specified by the machine-training module. The system maintains a library of quality configurations contributed by the users themselves or by the machine training procedure. The end users can configure their favorite virtual hairy brush by assigning values to the quality parameters by themselves. The implemented system provides a window in which the users can adjust these parameters visually. Fig. 2.39 shows an example of real calligraphic artwork and an electronicallic simulated one.

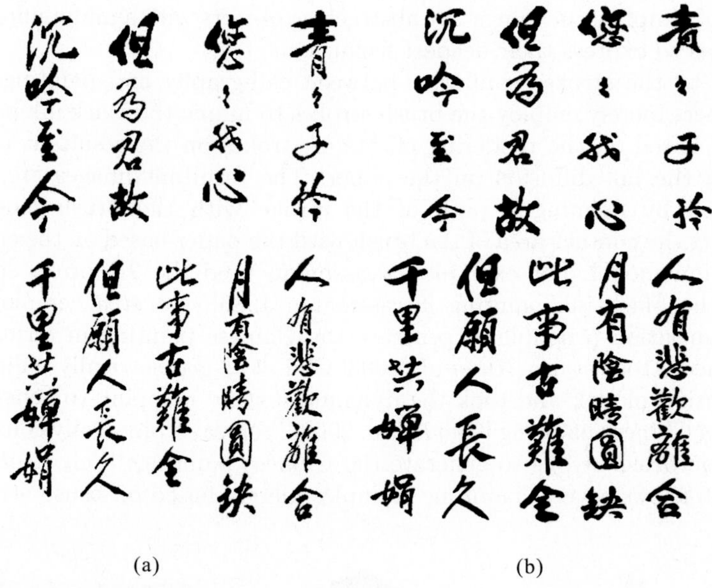

Fig. 2.39 (a) Real calligraphic artwork vs. (b) artwork created by the virtual hairy brush [Xu *et al.*, 2002]. Copyright of IEEE, used with permission

2.2.3 Oriental Black Ink Painting

Oriental black ink painting originated from Chinese painting, which is a spontaneous and expressive form of art, and has spanned more than three thousand years. These black ink paintings were drawn by brushes made from very fine animal hair which were dipped in ink and water. The interaction between ink particles, water particles and paper produces different aesthetically appealing effects unique to the ink-and-brush medium. The secret of Chinese painting is in putting the correct tones in the proper parts of the brush and in being able to call them forth by the proper handling of the brush. Every brush stroke in a Chinese painting conveys meaning to the viewer. Oriental black ink paintings have several unique features when compared with oilcolor and water-color paintings. Firstly, a black ink painting usually consists of a few well-placed strokes. Overlapping of strokes is not often done and white spaces are necessary and meaningful. Secondly, in black ink paintings the emphasis is in the quality of each stroke as well as in that of the entirety. Artists usually draw each stroke in one sweep without re-touching. Thirdly, from the point of view of rendering effects, black ink paintings not only separate light and color, but also avoid depth and other three-dimensional effects such as shadows to preserve the desired features of an object. Finally, the black ink painting heavily stresses the notion of "implicit meanings" by abstracting objects with a minimum amount of strokes to express their deepest feelings.

Due to the strokes similarity between calligraphy and paintings, some researchers merely employ the brush strokes to mimic the black ink paintings directly based on the rendering effects of strokes on the resultant pictures, ignoring the ink diffusion on the paper. The resultant images are usually generated by defining a path of the stroke with the brush model and rendering the contact area of the brush with the paper based on the empirical interaction model. For example, Strassmann used the 2D brush stroke to create the black ink painting [Strassmann, 1986]; Xu *et al.* employed the stroke imitation principle to generate the Chinese painting in terms of the predefined stroke styles [Xu *et al.*, 2003] Chu *et al.* geometrically built the 3D deformation model, and took the dynamic texture mapping to generate the resulting Chinese painting [Chu & Tai, 2002]. Yeh *et al.* physically constructed an elastic brush stroke to generate the Chinese paintings [Yeh *et al.*, 2002]. Fig. 2.40 shows several painting examples merely based on brush strokes.

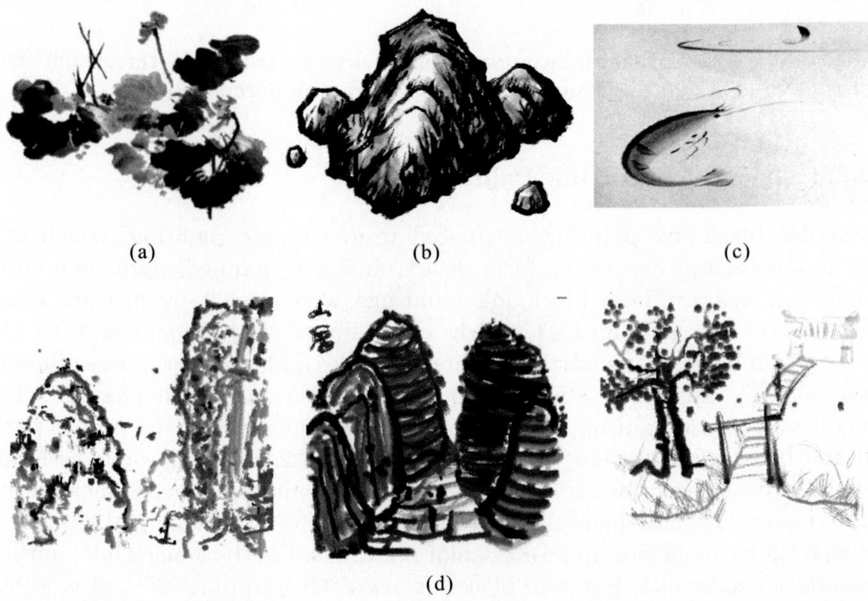

Fig. 2.40 Example of simple simulation of oriental painting merely by the brush strokes. (a) Selected from [Xu *et al.*, 2002; 2003]; (b) Selected from [Chu & Tai, 2002]; (c) Selected from [Strassmann, 1986]; (d) Selected from [Yeh *et al.*, 2002]. Copyright of ACM, used with permission

However, ink diffusion on the paper is perhaps the most admired unique feature of oriental black ink. A type of halo appearing around the original stroke adds a mysterious touch, being caused by letting ink spread beyond the stroke's original border, while ink seeping into special paper with high absorbency creates a feathery, blurred edge. These diffusion features represent complex physical phenomena which cannot be completely simulated by simple degradation functions, fractals, or texture mapping techniques, since purely mathematical methods generally result in flatly blurred images which are different compared to realistic diffusion images. In order to get the more natural and sophisticated visual effect of oriental painting, the ink diffusion mechanism should be incorporated into its simulation algorithm. Therefore we will further discuss the ink diffusion mechanism and the interaction model with the paper respectively.

2.2.3.1 The Ink Diffusion Principles and Mechanism on the Paper

Development of the appropriate model for simulating ink diffusion requires attention to be focused on the occurring physical mechanism. Kunii *et al.* presented the first multi-dimensional ink fusion model which proved to provide exactly the same intensity distribution as in real images of the oriental black ink painting [Kunii *et al.*, 1995]. When a drop of diffusing ink falls on the surface of highly absorbent paper, it begins to spread throughout the paper. As a result of this process, the final image appears to be sufficiently bigger than the initial zone to which the ink was directly applied. As shown in Fig. 2.41, the remarkable feature of the diffused ink image is a kind of black border which appears along the edge of the initial zone, i.e., the zone where ink was directly applied to paper. Outside the initial zone there finally appears a sufficiently large grey zone with not very high ink concentration, but has more or less a homogeneous intensity of color. This grey zone is one where ink was not directly applied to the paper. Carbon particles collect there as a result of diffusion.

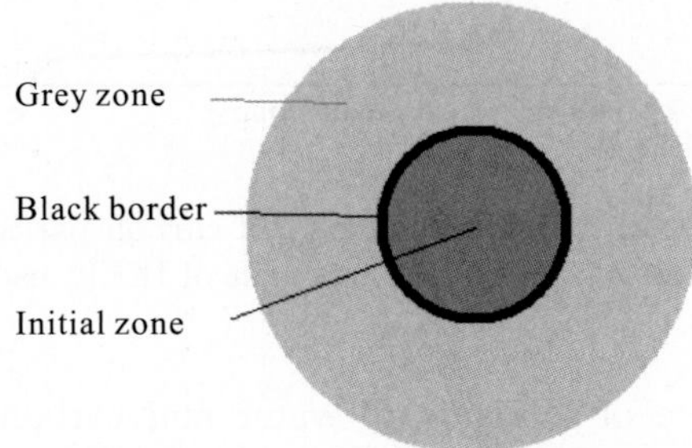

Fig. 2.41 Three zones of different intensity appear in the image: initial zone where ink was directly applied to paper; black border, a dark line along the border of the initial zone; grey zone, the area where solid particles of the ink collect as a result of diffusion [Kunii *et al.*, 1995]. Copyright of IEEE, used with permission

Due to the spread of water outside of the initial zone, the density of carbon in water will decrease inside this zone. Consequently, the concentration of carbon particles in water (i.e., ratio of carbon to water) rises sharply along the boundary of initial zone. Thus, the points with high concentration occur when the diffusion of carbon particles slow down. It results in the appearance of a barrier for carbon particles near the border of the initial zone. Many carbon particles which diffuse to the boundary of the initial zone from the inner parts of this zone, begin to slow down there and can not leave the vicinity of the border. After the water dries up, they remain near the boundary. That is how the above-mentioned black boundary effect may occur. Some carbon particles which are able to overcome this barrier, appear outside the initial zone. Those particles immediately fall into a zone, where there is much more water than carbon. Although there might be little water outside the initial zone, the decrease in the number of carbon particles can be even greater than the decrease of water density. In this case, concentration of carbon particles in water appears to be sufficiently low outside of initial zone which results in a diffusion with a maximal rate for carbon outside the initial zone. Carbon particles there diffuse freely in water and draw a grey zone around the initial zone. In this grey zone, the intensity of grey color will be approximately constant. Due to the effects described above, the grey zone will be separated from the initial zone by a dark line—black boundary. Therefore the density distribution function will look as shown in Fig. 2.42.

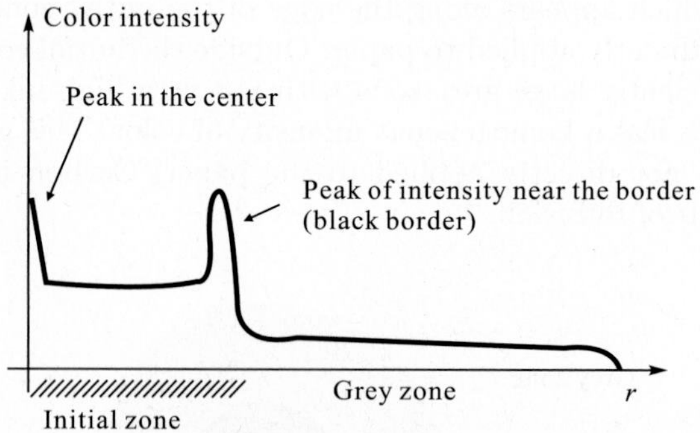

Fig. 2.42 Typical diagram of surface density of carbon particles within a certain point of the image [Kunii *et al.*, 1995]. Copyright of IEEE, used with permission

Indeed, the nature of diffusion of water and carbon particles is quite different. Water spreads in the paper mainly due to microscopic capillary effects. The summary macroscopic effect can be satisfactorily described in terms of diffusion. The diffusion coefficient in this case is determined mainly by the structure of the paper and so is approximately constant. And it might be different in different directions—depending on the manufacturing method of the paper. As to carbon particles, they are much bigger than the molecules of water. Their motion is not based on the capillary effect of paper. Motion of carbon particles in water is the well-known Brownian motion. Its nature is due to microscopic collisions between molecules of water and carbon particles. The faster such collisions occur and the higher the average speed of water molecules is, the bigger the diffusion coefficient for Brownian motion of carbon particles will be. Thus, the diffusion coefficient of the motion of carbon particles depends on the temperature and the local concentration (in the zone where this concentration is low) of these particles in water. Diffusion of carbon particles does not depend directly on paper structure. Assuming that the temperature is constant, the diffusion coefficient for carbon particles will depend only on the concentration of carbon particles in water. The higher this concentration is, the slower the diffusion might be. But the concentration of carbon in water changes with time at each point of the image. Thus, the diffusion coefficient for the motion of carbon particles can strongly depend on time and the point of the image. As aforementioned, the density of carbon in water will decrease inside this zone. The sharpest decrease of this density will occur near the border of the initial zone because the gradient of density function is maximal there. Consequently, it seems that distribution of water density would soon become like the distribution shown in Fig. 2.43.

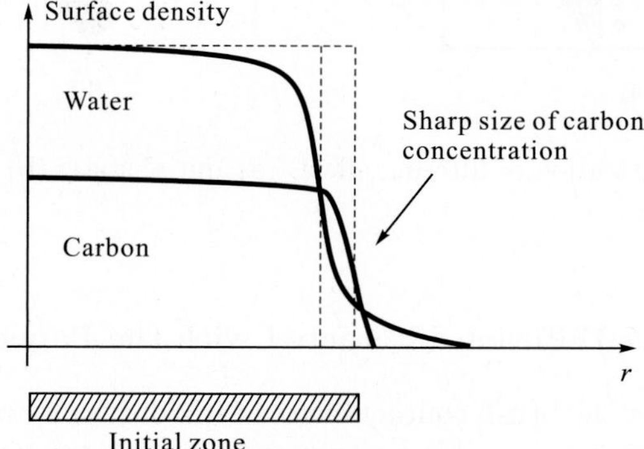

Fig. 2.43 Distribution of water and carbon in the stain made by diffused ink on the surface of the paper after the diffusion process starts [Kunii *et al.*, 1995]. Copyright of IEEE, used with permission

Huang *et al.* proposed the diameter-filtering mechanism to simulate the ink diffusion observation and analysis [Huang *et al.*, 2003]. Water is a liquid which can move to anywhere in the paper under the forces associated with capillary action. All water particles are defined as objects with the same volume, mass, color and response to external forces. They only differ in position recorded as coordinates in the paper cells. The quantity of water accordingly governs the span of the diffusion image or the number of diffusion steps. The carbon particles can be most simply simulated like water particles. They have mass, position, diameter and color. These attributes all vary among particles. The diameter and mass of a carbon particle are determined by the fineness to which the ink is initially ground. If the ink is initially ground coarsely, it contains small and large particles that produce observably different color intensities at the border of the initially brushed area. However, most homogeneous, small and uniform carbon particles move in water unhindered by the fibers, as such the intensity changes smoothly across the diffusion area. Only carbon particles that are smaller than the space between the fibers can seep into the mesh in the water. Particles larger than this space remain in their initial positions. As shown in Fig. 2.44, two adjacent cubes represent two neighboring paper cells [Huang *et al.*, 2003]. Black grains in the paper cells are carbon particles of different sizes. It is chaotic between the two paper cells represented fibers. The arrow represents the direction in which the water flows. The carbon particles move in this direction. Larger carbon particles cannot pass through the holes in the paper.

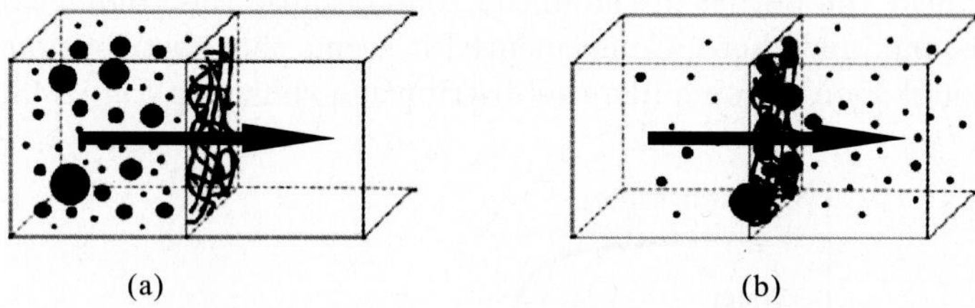

Fig. 2.44 An illustration of filtering effect. (a) Initial state; (b) Equilibrium state

2.2.3.2 The Ink Diffusion Interacted with the Paper

In order to render the brush contact effect of ink diffusion, we should take the interaction model between ink and paper into consideration. The capillary attributes of paper should also be modeled to display the ink diffusion effect. A typical approach to modeling the paper in painting is to represent the paper as a cellar model based on fiber meshes, in which the entire paper is divided into an array of cells. Each cell will act as a container of the ink. The fiber mesh structure of the paper provides information about each point on the paper [Lee, 2001]. As shown in Fig. 2.45, simulating diffusion rendering is to determine the schema simulating the point-to-point flow of ink through the fiber mesh. Lee developed a “wave” schema for representing how ink flows through a fiber mesh. Diffusion is considered to originate from the “boundary points of strokes”, being analogous to the outward-moving circular waves produced when an object is thrown into a lake. In other words, water oscillates up and down during wave movement and the paper cells diffuse color when the diffusion wave arrives.

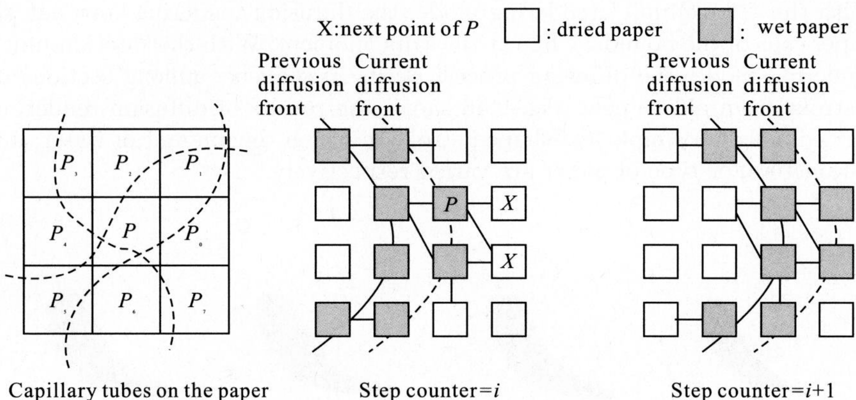

Fig. 2.45 Wave schema of ink diffusion in the paper [Lee, 2001]. Copyright of Elsevier, used with permission

At any particular moment, the points at the edge of a profile of the diffusion area are collectively termed as the "diffusion front" such that the "boundary points" are the "initial diffusion front". The diffusion process accordingly involves using the current diffusion front to successively determine the next diffusion front as a time sequence represented by a step counter as it changes from zero to n. Fig. 2.45 depicts the main principles of ink flow, and the important aspects are as follows:

(1) From a point P at the current diffusion front, ink can only flow to point P' if it is connected to P and is dried.
(2) Point P' absorbs some amount of liquid ink before it transports ink to other points.
(3) The ink absorbed at P' evaporates after a unit of time Δt, where it is assumed that $\Delta t = 2$.

In this wave schema, (a) The ink density at the diffusion front is determined before the diffusion wave continues on; (b) The points covered by the diffusion front will not be included in the next diffusion front for a short period of time, hence the number of points involved in the diffusion process can only linearly increase over time; (c) The ink cannot flow backward because the diffusion wave travels only outward.

The ink diffusion algorithms are constructed based on the aforementioned principles of ink flow and paper cells intensity. When a short stroke is produced quickly, the diffusion process starts at the points along the boundary of the brush stroke almost at the same moment. For a long and slowly drawn brush stroke, diffusion in the older sections may start earlier than in the newer sections, and the ink within the oldest sections may even dry up. Therefore the system provides two rendering modes: "stroke-unit" and "section-unit". With the "stroke-unit" rendering mode, the diffusion rendering starts at all paper cells of the boundary line at the same moment. With the "section-unit" rendering mode, the diffusion process starts in sequence among sections of a stroke from old to new. Fig. 2.46 shows the results of diffusion rendering carried out on a simple leaf-shaped stroke in which the amount of water, ink parameters, or type of paper are varied respectively.

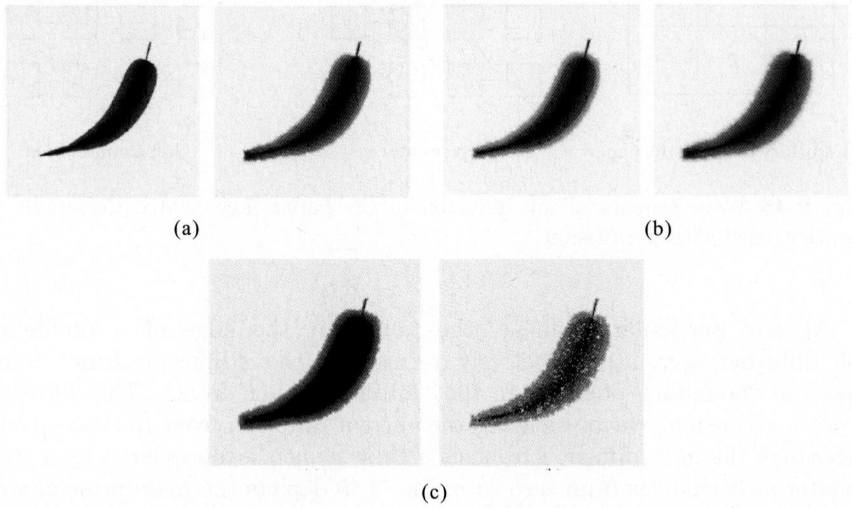

Fig. 2.46 Diffusion rendering on a leaf stroke with the variables water, ink parameters and types of paper [Lee, 2001]. (a) The amounts of water are different; (b) The sizes of the carbon particles are different; (c) The densities of the paper cells are different. Copyright of Elsevier, used with permission

Guo and Kunii proposed a similar structure model of paper with small circular regions, in which the fibers are distributed with homogeneously randomness in terms of the given density [Guo & Kunii, 2003]. This means that the fiber density and the average fiber orientation are globally uniform, but the local fiber density varies irregularly from place to place.

Their algorithmic schemas to simulate and render the ink diffusion effects are as follows:

(1) The tree transportation schema determines how liquid ink flows in a fiber mesh by three rules:
   - Liquid ink can flow from point P to point P', if there is a capillary tube connecting them, and P' has not gotten any ink yet.

- Liquid ink can flow from point P to zero, at one or more than one point.
- Point P absorbs a maximum amount of liquid ink $Q(p)$ before it transports liquid ink to other points.

(2) The source of ink quantity variation schema determines how long a diffusion process will persist by two rules:
- If point P absorbed the amount of liquid ink $Q(p)$, the amount of liquid ink remaining at its source point decreases by $Q(p)$.
- When all the source points have no liquid ink remaining, the diffusion process gets stopped.
- The grey zone calculation schema determines the intensity for every pixel on the paper by the following steps:
- The grey zone (or intensity) at each pixel is determined by the amount and density of liquid ink absorbed there, i.e., $I = Q(p) \times V(p)$.
- The amount of liquid ink $Q(p)$ is evaluated as a statistical function of the number of fibers passing through the point;
- The density of liquid ink $D(p)$ is evaluated as a function of the time counter value and the density of ink on its corresponding source point. Fig. 2.47 gives the circle strokes based on different fiber meshes.

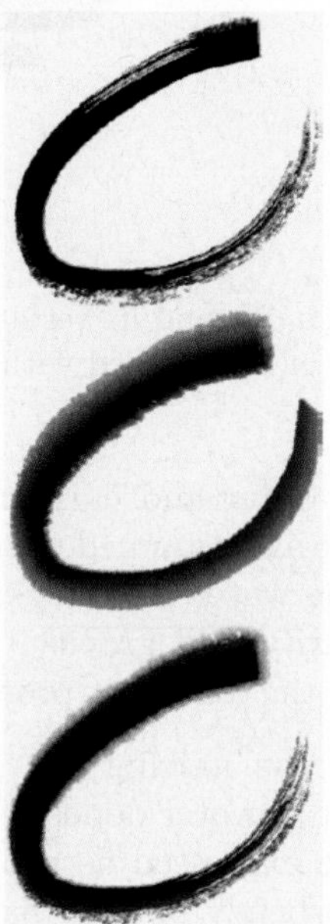

Fig. 2.47 One stroke in various rendering effects [Guo & Kunii, 2003]. Copyright of IEEE, used with permission

During the digital painting process, the user picks up the control points to define a boundary for a stroke. Each stroke is defined by two boundary wire-lines with the picked control points placed on them. The next step is to specify the rendering mode and to set the parameters for each stroke. Rendering parameters include paper absorbency, paper type, ink density, ink quantity, drawing speed, and brush size. Fig. 2.48 shows the interim painting process of a dog and its resultant black ink painting artwork.

Fig. 2.48 A painting process of a dog and its resultant black ink painting artwork [Guo & Kunii, 2003]. Copyright of IEEE, used with permission

Way *et al.* assumed that water and carbon particles are the two main constituents of Chinese ink. He also assumed that the forces that move the ink include the interactions among water molecules, water and carbon particles, and the forces due to capillarity and gravity, etc. [Way *et al.*, 2003]. The motion of ink is simulated by the following processes:

(1) *Paper absorbency.* When the moving ink passes through paper cell p with N fibers, the amount of water deposited in p is Q. The relationship between N and Q can be expressed as proportional to Absorbency(p). An equation for the absorbency of each paper cell is (Absorbency(p)= Base+Var×rand).
(2) *Movement of water particles.* Water is a liquid which can move anywhere in the paper under the forces associated with capillary action. When the water in a certain paper cell flows out, its quantity and direction must be

determined. The approximate equation for $K(p)$, the ratio of the quantity of out-flowing water to the quantity of water left in the paper cell, is represented as $K(p) = F_{\text{base}} + F_{\text{diff}} \times (1 - (1 - \text{Absorbency}(p)^2))$, where F_{base} is a real number between zero and one, that represents the basic flow rate p, and F_{diff} is a real number between zero and one, that represents the difference between the highest flow rate and the lowest. The quantity of water that flows in all directions into the neighboring paper cells is determined by associated probabilities. Fig. 2.49 illustrates how the water propagation is influenced by the capillary force and the gradient of the quantity of water relatively to each other in two neighboring cells [Way *et al.*, 2003].

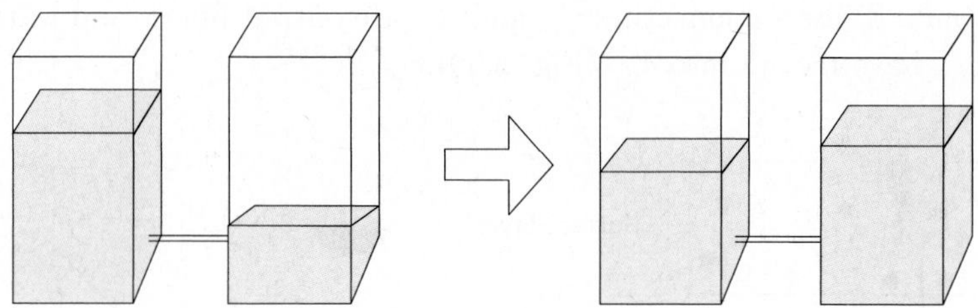

Fig. 2.49 Illustration of water propagation during ink diffusion

(3) *Movement of carbon particles.* The carbon particles can be most simply simulated like water particles. They have mass, position, diameter and color. The diameter and mass of a carbon particle are determined by the fineness to which the ink was initially ground. Only carbon particles that are smaller than the space between the fibers can seep into the mesh in the water. Particles larger than the space between the fibers remain in their initial positions. This filtering effect can be represented as follows, where p is the paper cell in which the carbon particle is located.

If carbon_diameter>hole_diameter(p) **Then** carbon_position← p
Else carbon_position←water_outflow_direction (p)

Fig. 2.50 shows the simulated result using the proposed ink diffusion method. The strokes of the resulting image are similar to those of an artist's painting on real Hsuan paper.

Yu *et al.*, proposed a local equilibrium model to calculate the movement of water and ink effectively [Yu *et al.*, 2003]. Their paper model is composed of cells which are minimal components. A cell has eight neighboring cells, and these neighboring cells are connected by fibers. When two or more strokes are intersected, the shapes of the strokes in the intersected parts are different from those in the other parts due to the moisture included in each cell. To simulate this phenomenon, each cell on the paper is divided into three layers:

surface layer, absorption layer, and deposition layer (Fig. 2.50). Water and ink in the surface layer are moved to neighboring cells or are absorbed in the absorption layer. In the absorption layer, the water and ink are desorbed to the surface layer or deposited in the deposition layer. Water in the deposit layer evaporates over time. A local equilibrium model is employed to determine the state of water and ink movement of each cell at each time step interactively. Let a cell $c_{i,j}$ denote a front cell if $c_{i,j}$ has water and ink moving into neighboring cells. Let $c_{i,j}^k$ denote the kth neighboring cell of $c_{i,j}$, and $W_{i,j}$ and $I_{i,j}$ denote the quantity of water and ink of the cell $c_{i,j}$ respectively. A fiber connecting neighboring cells is defined as input or output according to the quantity of water in each cell. If $W_{i,j} > W_{i,j}^k$, then the fibers connecting $c_{i,j}$ and $c_{i,j}^k$ are regarded as output fibers. Otherwise, they are regarded as input fibers. If fibers connecting $c_{i,j}$ and $c_{i,j}^k$ are output fibers, and water and ink in $c_{i,j}$ have moved into $c_{i,j}^k$ (Fig. 2.50).

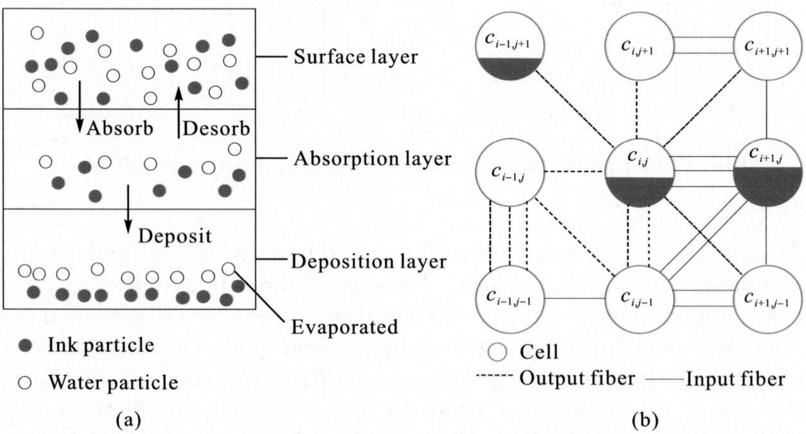

Fig. 2.50 The layer structure of paper and the relationship between a front cell $c_{i,j}$ and neighboring cells. (a) The layer structure of paper; (b) The relationship between cells

2.3 Simulation of a Colored Painting

The pipeline to simulate a colored painting is similar to that of the black ink painting. However, the colored painting involves the blending and rendering of colorful pigments on the canvas, and this makes the simulation process of a colored painting much more complex than that of the black ink painting. Fig. 2.51 gives an iterative diagram of the interactive colored painting. In this section, we will first present the computational rendering model for color pigments, and then describe the simulation process for watercolor and oil painting respectively.

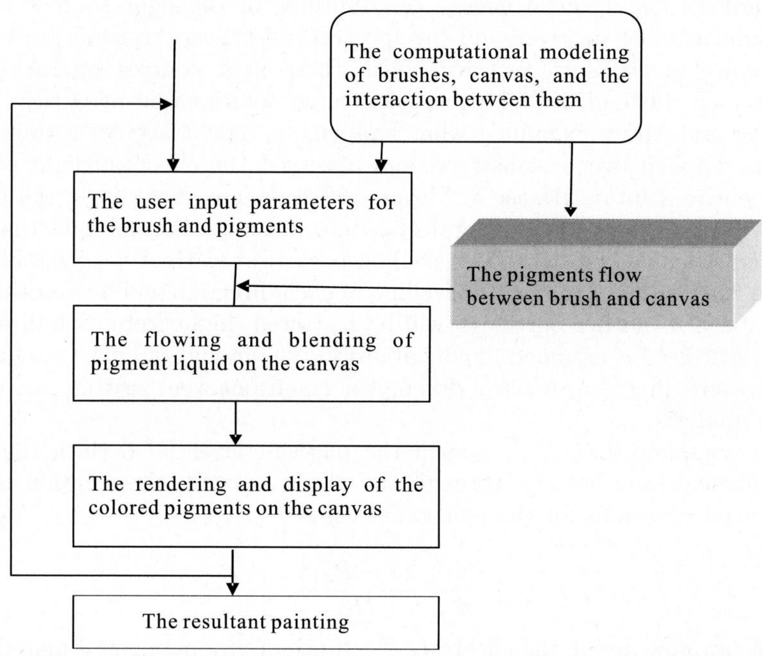

Fig. 2.51 A typical pipeline to simulate the interactive colored painting

2.3.1 The Computational Model of Rendering Colored Pigments

The colored pigments are the manufactured objects in the real world. The illumination of them should take into consideration the physical makeup of their pigmented surfaces. To render the color of any pigmented object, the physical interactions on the pigmented surface must be included. The straightforward way of specifying color in a graphic scene is via the common red, green, and blue (RGB) triplet. However this method is far removed from reality—the RGB method is only appropriate for additive colorants, such as colored light (e.g., the phosphors in the monitors screen). A second approach for specifying color is in the cyan, magenta, and yellow (CMY) space. This specification is in the domain of subtractive color synthesis and accurately models the effect of light transmission through a colored surface. However, this method is insufficient for representing pigmented surfaces, since CMY color synthesis works best for purely transmitting materials and a pigmented surface can have both transmitting and reflecting characteristics.

The most accurate way of dealing with light in a synthetic imaging application is on a wavelength-by-wavelength basis. It is only in this way that more subtle illumination modeling and color calculation problems can be handled. The spectral energy distributions of the light sources in the environment must be given and the spectral reflectance, transmittance, and absorbance of the surfaces with which these light sources interact must be specified. Instead of looking at pigmented solutions on a particle level, Kubelka and Munk examined what happens as light traverses a thin layer of paint applied over a substrate, and observed the effects of light energy in the entire solution [Haase & Meyer, 1992]. At any location in the paint, light from the surface is moving deeper into the material and light that has reflected from the substrate is travelling back toward the top of the film. A certain fraction K of the light travelling in each direction will be absorbed by the material. Another portion S will be scattered. Light from each direction that is scattered is assumed to contribute to the amount of light travelling in the opposite direction. A set of differential equations were written as a result of this analysis.

For complete hiding, i.e., when the pigment layer is so thick that the substrate can not be seen through the pigment layer, the solution of the differential equations for the reflectance R_x is:

$$\frac{K}{S} = \frac{(1 - R_x)^2}{2R_x}.$$

We can now derive the spectral reflectance of any pigmented material at complete opacity if we know its respective K and S values (and the spectral properties of the solution in which the pigments are immersed). Fig. 2.52

(a) (b)

Fig. 2.52 Comparison of the resulting illumination of real pigments and the simulated ones by the KM model [Haase & Meyer, 1992]. (a) Canvas painted with real pigments showing mixtures of cadmium red and napthol red with titanium white; (b) Resultant rendition of using the KM model to simulate the mixture of cadmium red and napthol red pigment with titanium white. Copyright of IEEE, used with permission

shows the comparison of the resulting rendition of real pigments and the simulated one by the Kubelka and Munk thoery. This is often rewritten as:

$$R_x = 1 + \frac{K}{S} - \sqrt{\left(\frac{K}{S}\right)^2 + 2\frac{K}{S}}.$$

This approach incorporats the ideas behind the pigment particle scattering and absorption interactions, but allows a much easier and more comprehensive calculation of entire pigmented system. Due to the fact that the combination of absorption and scattering are linear, we can compute the properties of mixtures of pigmented solutions by the following equations:

$$K_M = \sum_{i=1}^{n} K_i c_i, \quad S_M = \sum_{i=1}^{n} S_i c_i, \quad \left(\frac{K}{S}\right)_M = \frac{\sum_{i=1}^{n} K_i c_i}{\sum_{i=1}^{n} S_i c_i},$$

where
K_M=absorption of pigment mixture, S_M=scattering of pigment mixture, n=number of pigments in mixture, c_i=concentration of ith pigment in mixture by weight of dry pigment, K_i=absorption of ith pigment, S_i=scattering of ith pigment.

There is lots of further work to be done on the KM model and their shortcomings. An important example is the work of Saunderson [Saunderson, 1942], which can work well for the illumination of an oil painting layer. Saunderson's formula attempts to account for both external and internal surface reflection. This formula is used to adjust the measured reflectance from which K and S are determined. Given the Fresnel reflectance equation:

$$k_1 = \left(\frac{n_2 - n_1}{n_2 + n_1}\right)^2,$$

where
n_1=refraction index of the external medium (i.e., the air), n_2=refraction index of the internal medium (i.e., the oil).

Saunderson's formula is as follows:

$$R_t = k_1 + \frac{R_m - k_1}{1 - k_1 - k_2 + k_2 R_m},$$

where
R_t=theoretical reflectance, spectral reflectance adjusted for use in determining K and S; R_m=measured reflectance, spectral reflectance measured by a spectrophotometer, k_1=front surface reflectance of the film, k_2=internal reflectance of the film.

For the time being in the computer graphics community, the KM model theory is the most popular model being used to predict the reflectance that will result when two or more pigments are mixed.

2.3.2 Simulation of Watercolor Painting

Watercolor images are created by the application of watercolor paint to paper. Watercolor paint is a suspension of pigment particles in a solution of water, binder, and surfactant. It exhibits beautiful textures and patterns that reveal the motion of water across paper, much as the shape of a valley suggests the flow of streams. Its vibrant colors and spontaneous shapes give it a distinctive charm. And it can be applied in delicate layers to achieve subtle variations in color, giving even the most mundane subject a transparent, luminous quality.

The simulation of watercolor paint can be broken down into three parts [Small, 1990]. First, pigment and water are applied to the paper in a variety of ways. The paper characteristics are specified, as well as the environmental variables such as humidity and gravity. Second, the movement of pigment and water in response to various forces at discrete time steps is computed. Finally, given the state of the simulation at some discrete time, the image can be rendered in a variety of ways.

To simulate the watercolor effectively, it is important to study not only the physical properties of the medium, but also the characteristic phenomena that makes watercolor so popular with artists. A simulation is successful only if it can achieve many of the same effects. In the following sections, the modeling of water paper, the fluid simulation of pigment and water, and the illumination of the color pigment will be described in detail.

2.3.2.1 Watercolor Canvas Modeling

Watercolor canvas/paper is typically made from linen or cotton rags pounded into small fibers. The canvas itself is mostly air, laced with a microscopic web of these tangled fibers. Such a substance is obviously extremely absorbent to liquids, and so the paper is impregnated with sizing so that liquid paints may be used on it without immediately soaking in and diffusing. Sizing is usually made of cellulose. It forms a barrier that slows the rate of water absorption and diffusion.

The fundamental model to simulate the watercolor canvas is the *cellular automata*. The basic unit of the simulation is a paper cell, which can be thought of as a group of paper fibers and the spaces between the fibers. The water and pigments are assumed to be evenly distributed across the area of a paper cell, which has constant absorbency and an initial color. The cell can communicate only with its immediate neighbors. Fig. 2.53 is a typical water canvas/paper model based on a complex cellular automata [Cockshott *et al.*, 1992].

(x, y) is the coordinate of the cell, and h_i is the reservoir height of the corresponding cell. In each paper cell, it has the properties of initial color, absorbency, water content, and pigment content, etc. In addition to the specific information stored with each cell, there is also certain global information

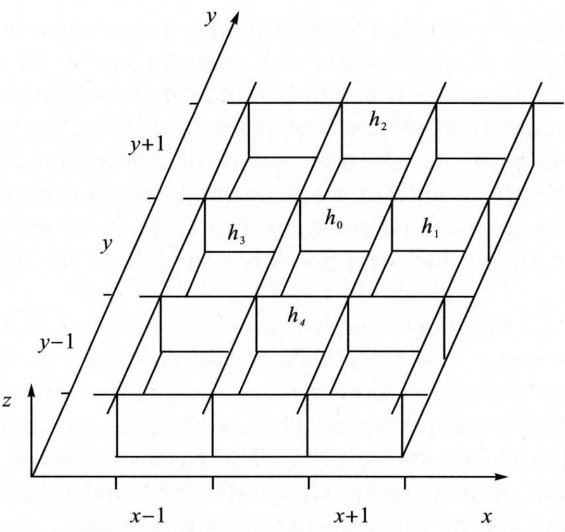

Fig. 2.53 A typical water paper model of cellular automata

such as humidity, gravity, the surface tension of the pigment-carrying medium (i.e., water), and the weight of the pigments used.

In order to achieve more realistic watercolor effects, a more sophisticated watercolor canvas model was proposed by Curtis *et al.* [1997]. As shown in Fig. 2.54, the watercolor paper is modeled by three layers from top to bottom in terms of the fluid movement of water and pigment. The shallow-water layer—where water and pigment flow above the surface of the paper. The position-deposition layer—where pigment is deposited onto ("absorbed by") and lifted ("desorbed") from the paper. And lastly the capillary layer—where water that is absorbed into the paper is diffused by capillary action.

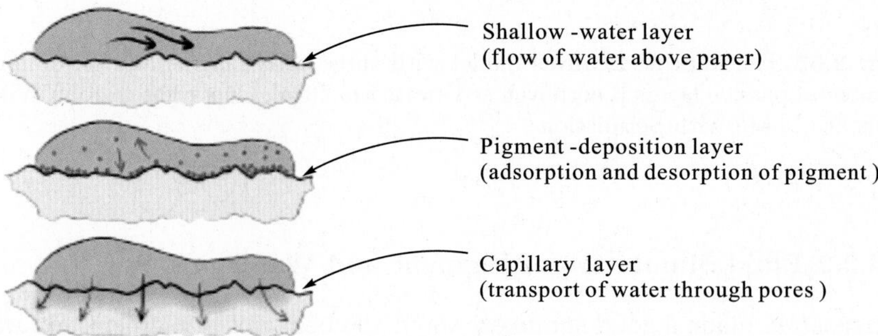

Fig. 2.54 The three-layer canvas model for watercolor paint [Curtis *et al.*, 1997]. Copyright of ACM, used with permission

This three-layer watercolor canvas model makes sense when examining the different states in which water and pigment can exist during painting activity. First, some sort of brush puts a mixture of water and pigment onto a paper canvas. At this instant, the paint fluid acts like a flow of water, carrying pigment particles. At some point, depending on the paper fabric, the water will be absorbed into the paper and spread throughout the paper structure. As the pigment particles are too large to be absorbed, they will be deposited on the surface and possibly picked back up by the paint fluid later on.

Laerhoven and Van Reeth further improved the three-layer canvas model for their real time water color simulation [Laerhoven & Van Reeth, 2005]. As shown in Fig. 2.55, their layered canvas consists of three active layers and an unlimited number of passive layers. The active layers are very similar to that in Curtis' model [Curtis *et al.*, 1997]. The passive layers are considered to contain previously drawn strokes that have dried and no longer participate in the simulation, except when the canvas is rendered.

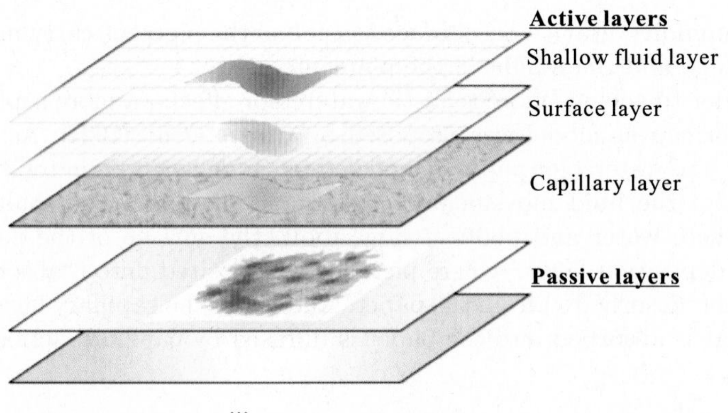

Fig. 2.55 The improved canvas model with three active layers and an unlimited number of passive layers [Laerhoven & Van Reeth, 2005]. Copyright of John Wiley& Sons,Ltd., used with permission

2.3.2.2 Fluid Simulation of Pigment and Water

Curtis *et al.* made a good summary about the behavior of pigment and water when they are applied to watercolor paper [Curtis *et al.*, 1997]. A pigment is a solid material in the form of small, separate particles. Watercolor pigments are typically ground in a milling process into a powder of grains ranging from about 0.05 to 0.5 microns. Pigments can penetrate into the paper, but once in the paper they tend not to migrate far. Pigments vary in density, with lighter pigments tending to stay suspended in the water longer than the heavier ones and thus spreading further across the paper. Staining power, an estimate of the pigment's tendency to adhere to or coat paper fibers, also varies between pigments. Certain pigments exhibit granulation, in which particles settle into the hollows of rough paper. Others exhibit flocculation, in which particles are drawn together into clumps usually by electrical effects. The behaviors of water are also summarized from the point of view of simulation. For example, the water flow must remain within the wet area mask. A surplus of water in one area should cause flow outward from that area into nearby regions. The water flow will be dampened to minimize oscillating waves. The water flow must be perturbed by the texture of the paper to cause streaks parallel to the flow direction. Local changes should have global effects. e.g., adding water in a local area should affect the entire simulation. There should be an outward flow of the fluid toward the edges to produce the edge-darkening effect.

In the watercolor paper model based on *cellular automata* [Small, 1990], each cell is required to know only about itself and its immediate environment. The simulation takes into account diffusion, surface tension, gravity, humidity, paper absorbency and the molecular weight of each pigment. A small number of rules defining simple local behavior between a cell and its immediate neighbors results in a complex global behavior of the fluid simulation. The simulation of the fluid can then be broken down into three steps. First the movement of water and pigment is calculated for the surface. Then it is calculated for the infused material. And finally any movement of material between these two states is computed.

The movement of water and pigment is considered to be driven by a composite (gravity, surface tension, spreading force, etc.) displacement force D, which is divided into horizontal and vertical components. Assuming that D_x and D_y are the horizontal and vertical components respectively, and g, s and sp are the coefficients that define the relative strengths of gravity, surface tension, and diffusion coefficient. water_x is the surface component at some location x. This equation of computing D_x and D_y are as follows:

$$\begin{aligned} D_x =& g \times \text{water}_x + s \times \left(\sum_{n=1}^{n=10} \frac{1}{n} \text{water}_{x+n} - \sum_{n=1}^{n=10} \frac{1}{n} \text{water}_{x-n} \right) \\ &+ sp \times \left(\text{water}_{(x-1)} - \text{water}_{(x+1)} \right), \end{aligned}$$

$$\begin{aligned} D_y =& g \times \text{water}_y + s \times \left(\sum_{n=1}^{n=10} \frac{1}{n} \text{water}_{y+n} - \sum_{n=1}^{n=10} \frac{1}{n} \text{water}_{y-n} \right) \\ &+ sp \times \left(\text{water}_{y-1} - \text{water}_{y+1} \right). \end{aligned}$$

Let Δwater be the amount of water that will move from each cell, and a positive displacement indicates that the material has moved to the right (or higher numbered cell). The following equations show the displacement in the horizontal direction only:

$$\begin{aligned}
&\Delta\text{water}_x = D_x \times \text{water}_x,\\
&\textbf{If}\,(\Delta\text{water}_{x-1} > 0)\,\text{from_left} = \Delta\text{water}_{x-1}, \textbf{Else}\ \text{from_left} = 0,\\
&\textbf{If}\ (\Delta\text{water}_{x+1} < 0)\,\text{from_right} = \Delta\text{water}_{x+1}, \textbf{Else}\ \text{from_right} = 0,\\
&\text{water}_x = \text{water}_x - |\Delta\text{water}_x| + \text{from_left} + \text{from_right}.
\end{aligned}$$

Note that the displacement force is determined by the water content, regardless of the pigments. The pigment content (cyan, magenta, and yellow) are assumed to be in solution and will flow in equal proportion with the water.

Now we can compute displacement of the water and pigment which have become infused in the paper. The gradient, denoted by ∇, is the difference between a cell and its neighbor. Again the horizontal and vertical components are calculated for the water and pigment separately.

$$\nabla\text{water} = \text{water}_x - \text{water}_{x-1}, \quad \nabla\text{cyan} = \text{cyan}_x - \text{cyan}_{x-1}, \text{etc.}$$

The displacement field, Δ, is then computed for each component by the following formulas:

$$\Delta\text{water} = g \times a\nabla\text{water}, \Delta\text{cyan} = g \times W_{\text{cyan}}a\nabla\text{cyan}, \text{etc.},$$

where g is the gravity constant and a is the field which describes the absorbency of each cell; W_{cyan} is the weight of cyan pigment, which controls the pigment component to diffuse faster or slower.

In addition to the surface and infused components of water and pigments, how much of the surface material is absorbed by the paper should also be simulated. This is affected by the absorbency of the cell a, the fluid capacity of the cell c, and a constant k which is used to set the overall speed of the absorption. For each cell the amount of fluid absorbed is described by the following formulas:

$$\begin{aligned}
&A = k \times a \times \text{water}_{\text{surface}},\\
&\textbf{If}\ A\,(c - \text{water}_{\text{infused}})\ \textbf{Then}\ A{=}c - \text{water}_{\text{infused}},\\
&\text{water}_{\text{infused}} = \text{water}_{\text{infused}} + A,\\
&\text{water}_{\text{surface}} = \text{water}_{\text{surface}} - A.
\end{aligned}$$

Curtis *et al.* further improved the cellar automaton to simulate the fluid flow and pigment dispersion of watercolor by adopting a more sophisticated paper model and a more complex shallow layer model [Curtis *et al.*, 1997]. The painting consists of an ordered set of translucent glazes or washes, the results of several independent fluid simulations, each with a shallow-water layer, a pigment-deposition layer and a capillary layer.

In the shallow-water layer, water flows across the surface in a way that is bounded by the wet-area mask. As the water flows, it lifts pigment from the paper, carries it along, and re-deposits it on the paper. The quantities involved in this simulation are:

(1) The wet area mask M, which is one if the paper is wet, and zero otherwise.
(2) The velocity v of the water u in the x and y directions.
(3) The pressure p of the water.
(4) The concentration g^k of each pigment k in the water.
(5) The slope ∇h of the rough paper surface, defined as the gradient of the paper's height h.
(6) The physical properties of the watercolor medium, including its viscosity μ and viscous drag ρ(set μ=0.1 and ρ =0.01).

Based on the aforementioned parameters, the shallow water equations to update the velocities of water are as follows:

$$\frac{\partial u}{\partial t} = -\left(\frac{\partial^2 u}{\partial x^2} + \frac{\partial u \partial v}{\partial y^2}\right) + \mu \nabla^2 u - \frac{\partial p}{\partial x},$$

$$\frac{\partial v}{\partial t} = -\left(\frac{\partial^2 v}{\partial y^2} + \frac{\partial u \partial v}{\partial x^2}\right) + \mu \nabla^2 v - \frac{\partial p}{\partial y}.$$

In the pigment-deposition layer, each pigment k is transferred between the shallow-water layer and the pigment-deposition layer by adsorption and desorption. While the pigment in the shallow-water is denoted by g^k, the deposited pigment is denoted by d^k. The physical properties of the individual pigments, including their density ρ, staining power ω, and granularity γ—all affect the rates of adsorption and desorption by the paper.

The function of the capillary layer is to allow for expansion of the wet area mask due to capillary flow of water through the pores of paper. The relevant quantities in this layer are:

(1) The water saturation s of the paper, defined as the fraction of a given volume of space occupied by water.
(2) The fluid-holding capacity c of the paper, which is the fraction of volume not occupied by paper fibers.

The main loop of our simulation takes as input the initial wet-area mask M, the initial velocity v of the water u, the initial water pressure p, the initial pigment concentration g^k, and the initial water saturation of the paper s. The main loop iterates over a specified number of time steps, moving water and pigment in the shallow-water layer, transferring pigment between the shallow water and pigment-deposition layers, and simulating capillary flow.

```
Proc MainLoop(M, u, v, p, g^1,..., g^n, d^1,..., d^n, s):
    For each time step Do:
    MoveWater(M,u, v, p)
        MovePigment(M, u, v, g^1, ..., g^n)
        TransferPigment(g^1, ..., g^n, d^1, ..., d^n)
        SimulateCapillaryFlow(M, s)
    End For
End Proc
```

Their model is capable of producing a wide range of effects from both wet-in-wet and wet-on-dry painting (see Fig. 2.56). Due to its complexity, the painting process is not real-time. Therefore Laerhoven and Van Reeth made a trade-off between "real-timeness" and the simulation complexity. They proposed a new model for the real-time simulation of watery paint [Laerhoven & Van Reeth, 2005]. They employ a variant of the two dimensional Navier-Stokes equation to simulate the fluid movement:

$$\frac{\partial \boldsymbol{v}}{\partial t} = -(\boldsymbol{v} \cdot \nabla)\boldsymbol{v} + \upsilon \nabla^2 \boldsymbol{v},$$

where, υ represents the two-dimensional vector field of velocities and $\upsilon = \eta/\rho$ is a constant indicating the rate at which the fluid diffuses. ρ and η are the mass density and viscosity of the fluid respectively.

Fig. 2.56 The simulated watercolor effects [Curtis *et al.*, 1997]. Copyright of ACM, used with permission

A time step in this simulation starts from adding water, pigments and velocities values. And then the state of the velocities of a fluid body at any given time and space is updated by the Navier-Stokes equation based on the fast and stable algorithm from Stam [Stam, 2003]. Finally, the water quantities w and pigment quantities P_{idx} for each pigment can be similarly updated with the following two equations:

$$\frac{\partial w}{\partial t} = -(\boldsymbol{v} \cdot \nabla)w + v_w \nabla^2 w,$$
$$\frac{\partial p_{\text{idx}}}{\partial t} = -(\boldsymbol{v} \cdot \nabla)P_{\text{idx}} + v_P \nabla^2 P_{\text{idx}}.$$

Fig. 2.57 shows the simulated examples of strokes with various watercolor effects.

Fig. 2.57 The simulated examples of strokes with different watercolor effects [Laerhoven & Van Reeth, 2005]. Copyright of John Wiley & Sons, Ltd., used with permission

Besides the traditional Navier-Stokes approach to fluid simulation, Chu and Tai proposed a novel fluid flow model based on the lattice Boltzmann equation. It combines the simulations of spontaneous shape evolution and porous media flow under a unified framework [Chu & Tai, 2005]. The main idea of the lattice Boltzmann equation approach is to model fluid dynamics using a simplified particle kinetic model. This approach divides the simulation domain into a regular lattice. At each lattice site x and time t, the fluid particles moving at arbitrary velocities are modeled by a small set of particle distribution functions $f_i(x, t)$.

2.3.2.3 Illumination of Watercolor Pigment

The final appearance of watercolor is derived from the interaction between the movements of various pigments in a flowing medium, the adsorption of these pigments by the paper, the absorption of water into the paper, and the eventual evaporation of the water medium. While these interactions are quite complex in nature, they can be used by a skilled artist to achieve a wide variety of effects.

In the simulated watercolor painting, there are two approaches to rendering the resulting watercolor artwork. The first one is to employ the CMY color system to calculate the resulting color [Small, 1990]. The final color at each pixel is calculated by the following equations:

$$\text{pixel}_\text{r}=\text{initial\_color}_\text{r}-(\text{cyan}_\text{surface}+\text{cyan}_\text{infused})$$
$$\text{pixel}_\text{g}=\text{initial\_color}_\text{g}-(\text{magenta}_\text{surface}+\text{magenta}_\text{infused})$$
$$\text{pixel}_\text{b}=\text{initial\_color}_\text{b}-(\text{yellow}_\text{surface}+\text{yellow}_\text{infused})$$

However, as aforementioned in Section 2.3.1, CMY color synthesis works best for purely transmitting materials, and pigmented surfaces have both transmitting and reflecting characteristics. Therefore the second approach using the KM model is proposed to calculate the illumination of colorful pigments. It is becoming the most popular model to perform the optical composition of pigment layers.

In typical applications of the KM model theory, the K and S coefficients for a given colorant layer are determined experimentally, using spectral measurements from layers of known thicknesses. However, in watercolor painting, it is much more convenient to allow a user to specify the K and S coefficients interactively, by choosing the desired appearance of a "unit thickness" of the pigment over both a white and a black backgrounds. Given these two user-selected RGB colors R_w and R_b, respectively, the K and S values can be computed by a simple inversion of the following equations:

$$S = \frac{1}{b} \times \coth^{-1}\left(\frac{b^2-(a-R_w)(a-1)}{b(1-R_w)}\right), \quad K = S(a-1),$$

where

$$a=\frac{1}{2}\left(R_w + \frac{R_b - R_w + 1}{R_b}\right), \quad b = \sqrt{a^2-1}.$$

The above computations are applied to each color channel of S, K, R_w, and R_b independently. In order to avoid any divisions by zero, we require that $0 < R_b < R_w < 1$ for each color channel. This restriction is reasonable even for opaque pigments, since the user is specifying reflected colors through just a thin layer, which should still be at least partially transparent.

After we get the scattering and absorption coefficients S, and K for a pigmented layer of given thickness x, the KM model allows us to compute reflectance R, and transmittance T through the layer:

$$R = \sinh \times (b \times S \times x/c), \; T = b/c,$$

where

$$c = a \; \sinh \times (b \times S \times x) + b \times \cosh \times (b \times S \times x).$$

We can then use the Kubelka's optical compositing equations to determine the overall reflectance R and transmittance T of two abutting layers with reflectance R_1, R_2 and T_1, T_2, respectively:

$$R = R_1 + \frac{T_1^2 R_2}{1 - R_1 R_2}, \qquad T = \frac{T_1 T_2}{1 - R_1 R_2}.$$

This computation is repeated for each additional glaze. The overall reflectance R is then used to render the pixel. Fig. 2.58 shows examples of watercolor renderings using the KM model. For individual layers containing more than one pigments of thicknesses $x^1, \ldots, x^n$, the S and Kcoefficients of each pigment k are weighted in proportion to that pigment's relative thickness x^k. The overall thickness of the layer x is taken to be the sum of the thicknesses of the individual pigments. Fig. 2.59 shows several objects in a resultant watercolor artwork rendered by the KM model.

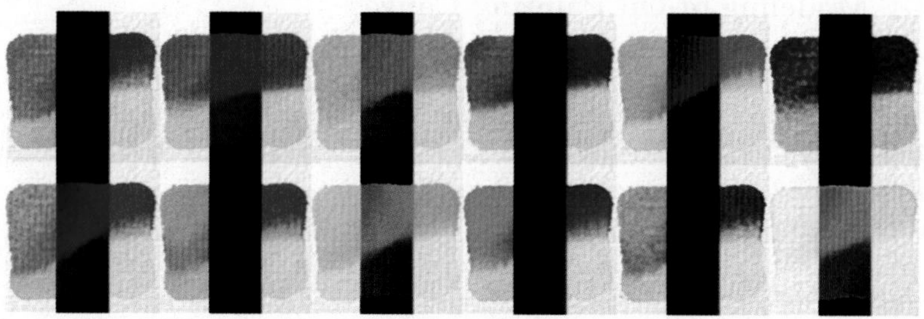

Fig. 2.58 Watercolor effects rendering by the KM model [Curtis *et al.*, 1997]. Copyright of ACM, used with permission

Fig. 2.59 Simulated watercolor artwork rendered by the KM model [Laerhoven & Van Reeth, 2005]. Copyright of ACM, used with permission

2.3.3 Simulation of Oil Painting

Each paint medium has its own characteristics. Watercolor is a very low-viscosity painting, and it is relatively easy to model the fluid-like behavior and generate physically-based realistic effects. Oil painting is a kind of highly viscous paint media which is popular among artists for its versatility and ability to capture a wide range of expressive styles. It is a challenge to design an interactive model that correctly captures the physical behavior of viscous paint, because of the complex underlying set of partial differential equations that govern that motion. In this section, modeling of the oil painting canvas, brushes, and the coloring will be discussed respectively.

2.3.3.1 Modeling of Oil Painting Canvas

Oil-based painting supported by a textile canvas constitutes the major part of museum art collections in Europe and is still the favorite expressive medium of modern painters. Even digital artists often try to reproduce the quality and feel of the traditional masterpieces.

A typical model of oil painting artwork is shown in Fig. 2.60. The first level of oil paint, the foundation for an oil painting, is called the "ground". It is composed of binding agents and pigments, traditionally chalk or gypsum, white lead, and linseed oil. The ground preparation is applied directly on the support to flatten the surface and provide a better adherence of the upper layers to the structure. The other four layers in the oil painting artwork are:

(1) A dark initial layer composed of one or a few transparent colors related closely to each other. These colors can be used as a block in the painting.

(2) A middle layer of opaque colors, including the lightest values in the painting.

(3) A glaze painted with transparent colors that modify the underlying tone and bring richness to the surface.

(4) A varnish that protects the paint from the effects of light, pollution, and dirt and enhances the optical properties of the painting.

The representative work on simulation of oil-painting canvas modeling comes from Drago and Chiba (2004). They present a synthesis of woven canvas in three dimensions. There are two algorithmic steps to reproduce the oil painting canvas. First, it generates a basic geometrical model which can be offset by two successive displacing functions to form the macroscopic structure of the thread. Secondly, procedural displacements are employed to refine the model and simulate the microgeometry of the fabrics, surface reflectance characteristics, etc. There are four basic types of weaving patterns: simple tabby weave, ribbed tabby weave, rep weave consisting of doubled wrap and weft threads, and twill weave (see Fig. 2.61).

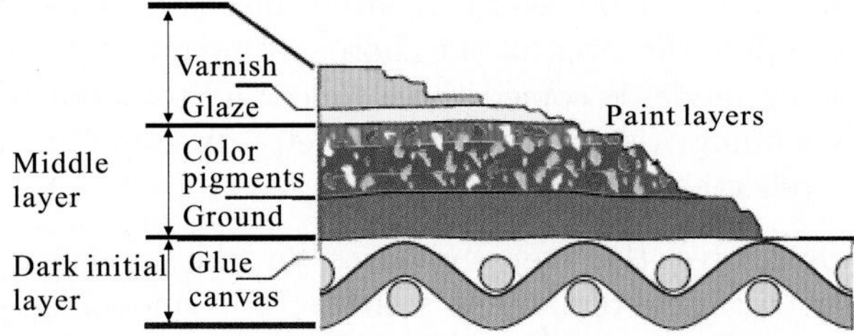

Fig. 2.60 Anatomy of an oil painting canvas with traditional oil-based medium [Drago & Chiba, 2004]. Copyright of Springer Science and Business Media, used with permission

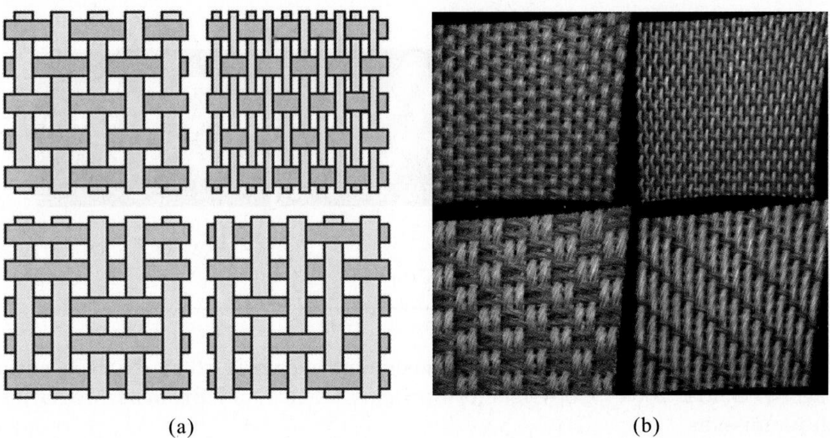

Fig. 2.61 Typical weaving patterns and the corresponding oil painting canvas generated by computer. From top left in clockwise order: simple tabby weave, ribbed tabby weave, rep weave consisting of doubled wrap and weft threads, and twill weave [Drago & Chiba 2004]. (a) Weaving patterns; (b) The corresponding canvas simulated by computer. Copyright of Springer Science and Business Media, used with permission

The algorithmic pipeline to create a generic woven fabric geometry is as follows:

(1) With a step function, the surface shading divides the underlying geometry in a pattern of straight lines and transparent areas. Each line segment represents the top or bottom half of a thread.
(2) The weaving of the pattern is formed by displacing the geometry with an explicit function.
(3) Each segment is displaced in a semicircular curve along new surface normals to form the three dimensional characteristic of the thread.

(4) The microgeometry is modeled by a third displacement and bump shading is used to simulate the twist of the chords forming the thread.
(5) The underlying model is copied three times and textured with different parameters defining orientation (wrap or weft), direction (upper or lower), and surface reflectance characteristics.

Fig. 2.62 illustrates the steps involved in the modeling process of the macrogeometry. The remaining steps involve modeling each yarn's microstructure and shading of the surface. The following sinusoidal function is used to displace the geometry in forming the variations of weave:

$$\text{Weave}(x) = \sin(2\pi x \times T_{\text{freq}} + \text{Phase}) \times \text{Height}.$$

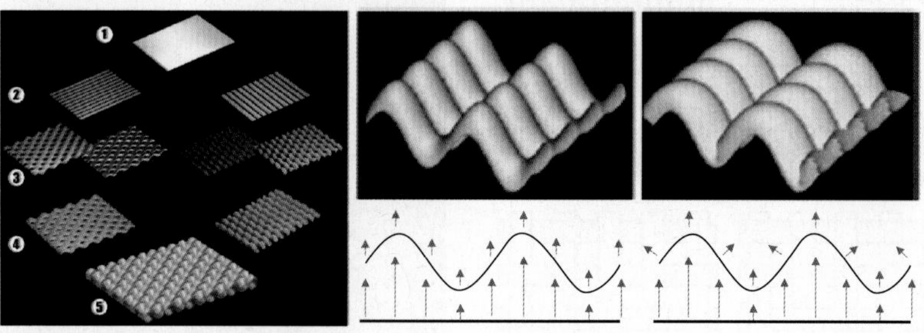

Fig. 2.62 Five steps to build the macrogeometry of canvas from a NURBS surface [Drago & Chiba, 2004]. Copyright of Springer Science and Business Media, used with permission

Where the periodic curve is a function of x, which is ideally chosen in one of the surface parametric coordinate directions u or v. T_{freq} is the number of threads requested. It determines the coarseness or delicacy of the structure and will dictate the choice of the other parameters characterizing weaving attributes. Height is the total amplitude of the curve and should ideally be twice the radius of each thread. In the case of the tabby weave, the phase constant is either zero if the geometry represents even rows of threads or π for odd rows.

The simulated canvas examples based on the four weaving patterns are shown in Fig. 2.61 (b). This method is potentially applicable to the representation of many types of woven fabrics.

2.3.3.2 Modeling of Oil Painting Brushes

Paint brushes are often regarded as the most important tools at an artist's disposal. In oil painting, there are four common and widely used brush styles (see Fig. 2.63), including:

(1) Rounds. Have a simple tubular shape with a semi-blunt point, allowing for a great variety of strokes.
(2) Flats. Thinner and wider than rounds with bristles squared off at the point. Flats are typically longer than they are wide.
(3) Brights. The same shape and construction as flats but typically shorter, with width nearly equal to length.
(4) Filberts. Have a thicker collection of bristles that increase their ability to hold paint. Filberts usually have oval-shaped heads.

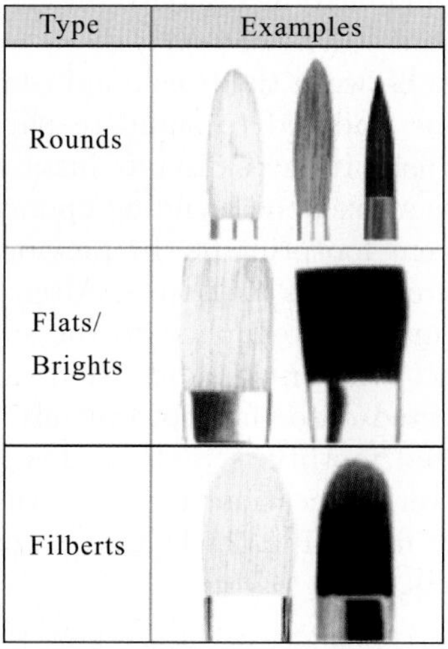

Type	Examples
Rounds	
Flats/ Brights	
Filberts	

Fig. 2.63 Typical brush styles commonly used in oil painting [Baxter *et al.*, 2001]. Copyright of ACM, used with permission

The major difficulty in simulating the oil paint brushes used in acrylic and oil-like painting is that the brushes are numerically stiff dynamical systems, and suffer from numerical instability. Bristles have very little mass. As they bend, energy stored in them can induce large accelerations and velocities when they are abruptly released. The representative work on the oil brush modeling comes from Baxter *et al.* They present a physically-based, deformable 3D brush model, which gives the user control of complex brush strokes intuitively. The haptic feedback enhances the sense of realism and provides tactile cues that enable the user to better manipulate the paint brush [Baxter *et al.*, 2001].

Compared with the brush modeling in watercolor, the most significant feature of oil painting brushes is the bi-directional pigments transfer, i.e., paint is transferred both from the brush to canvas, and back from the canvas to the brush. This is because the oil pigments are more viscous than those used in water color. During the contact between brush and canvas, the oil pigments on the brushes will be deposited on the canvas and simultaneously the oil pigments on the canvas will be obviously taken away by the brush. Baxter *et al.* developed a bi-directional, two-layer paint model to simulate the bi-directional color transfer [Baxter *et al.*, 2001]. Paint information is stored on both the canvas and brush in multiple textures. When the brush surface intersects the canvas geometry, the brush is considered to be in contact with the canvas. The bi-directional pigment transfer must correctly modify the paint textures to simulate paint volume being interchanged between two surfaces. The paint transfer problem is first reduced to two dimensions to simplify computation while introducing only slight inaccuracies. In the general case, a projection plane will be chosen that maximizes the area projected by the intersecting curve between the brush and canvas surfaces.

The textures must be updated to simulate paint transfer and mixing. The simulation of the brush produces discrete instances of the brush surface. To produce a continuous stroke, the blending operation is performed over a line connecting the current footprint to the previous one. The centroids of the footprint ploygons are used as endpoints. After the 2D blending is complete, the updated textures are reapplied to the surfaces. This is achieved by rendering a variation of the brush subdivision surface mesh. The surface vertices that were projected onto the footprint are used as texture coordinated into a new updated footprints texture. The original surface texture coordinates are used as vertex locations to render the updated textures back into the surface's texture maps. Fig. 2.64 shows an example of the simulated bi-directional paint effects.

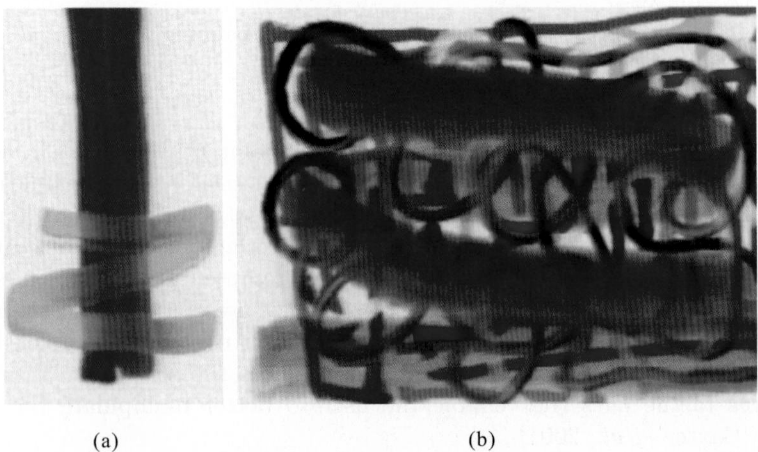

(a) (b)

Fig. 2.64 (a) Bi-directional paint transfer is demonstrated by dragging a yellow paint stroke through wet purple; (b) A purple glaze of paint has been thinly applied over dry paint [Baxter et al., 2001]. Copyright of ACM, used with permission

Later on, they further improved the bi-directional paint transfer model in their IMPaSTO system by the following realistic brush-canvas paint transfer heuristics principles [Baxter *et al.*, 2004a]:

(1) Paint moves in the push direction.
(2) Paint is conserved (neither created nor destroyed).
(3) Brush-canvas paint transfer requires physical contact and is greater when the brush is moving.
(4) The more paint is loaded on a brush, the more it will be deposited on the canvas.
(5) The more paint is on the canvas, the more it will be picked up by the brush.

Their paint transfer algorithm is responsible for determining how much paint moves from the brush to the canvas and vice versa. They made the assumption that at any given cell where brush-canvas contact is occurring, the transfer flow is unidirectional. That is to say, if the pigments are being deposited onto the canvas at a particular cell, it cannot also be loading into the brush simultaneously. The direction of the flow is determined by whether there is more paint on the canvas, or on the brush. When paint is transferred in either direction, or is moved by the advection algorithm, the new pigment concentrations on the affected brush or canvas cells are determined by simple volume-weighted averaging.

2.3.3.3 Coloring of Oil Painting

There are two typical approaches to rendering the resultant oil painting artwork. The first one is relatively simple, and it merely takes into account the pigments on the contact area between brush and canvas. The resulting color is calculated by empirical equations, ignoring the motion of oil painting pigments. The second approach is complex. It takes into consideration the fluid motion of oil pigment based on the physical behaviors of the oil fluid and the resulting oil painting artwork is usually rendered by the KM model.

The DAB system [Baxter *et al.*, 2001], employs the first approach to simulate the coloring of oil paintings based on additive RGB blending for thick paint. Each paint surface contains two color layers: the surface layer and a deeper layer. The surface layer is the boundary at which paint transfer between objects occurs, and it is completely wet. The deeper layer represents the reservoir of paint contained within the bristles, and it is completely dry. The paint transfer between surface layers occurs upon a collision between the brush and canvas. Transfer from the brush's reservoir layer to the surface is performed whenever the surface is no longer saturated (and paint remains in the reservoir layer). Drying paint from the canvas's surface layer to the deeper layer occurs on a timed interval or as requested by the user.

The surface and deeper layers are stored in color textures. The amount of volume of paint transfers between surface layers is dependent on the volume of paint within each layer. The volume leaving, V_l, is computed from the initial volume V_i and transfer rate R over the elapsed time T by the equation:

$$V_l = V_i \times T \times R.$$

The resulting paint color C_{new} is computed by the weighted portions of remaining paint volume and color, $V_r = V_i - V_l$ and C_i. The incoming volume and color from the other surface, V_l' and C_i' are calculated by the equation:

$$C_{\text{new}} = V_r \times C_i + V_l' \times C_i'.$$

To generate realistic paint effects, the wet and dry layers of the painting are composited together with an embossing of the paint volume. The volume of the wet layer V_w is multiplied by the optical thickness O_t of the paint, and then used for alpha blending of the wet and dry layer colors C_w and C_d as follows:

$$C_{\text{displayed}} = \alpha \times C_w + (1-\alpha) \times C_d, \ \alpha = \min(V_w \times O_t, 1).$$

The composited color of the paint must not change during drying. The optical blending function is used with this constraint to compensate for the new dry layer C_d', when some volume δ_α is removed from the wet layer.

$$C_d' = \frac{\alpha \times C_w + (1-\delta) \times C_d - a'C_w}{1-\alpha'}, \ \alpha' = \alpha - \delta_\alpha.$$

The dry layer of the canvas uses a relative height field to allow for unlimited volume of paint to be added, with a constraint only on the relative change in height between texels. An embossing of the height field is also computed. The additive blending is employed to combine this embossing and color buffer to create the final rendered image of the paint. As shown in Fig. 2.65, this paint model also supports variable wetness, which is accomplished by gradually moving paint from the completely wet surface layer of the canvas to the completely dry deeper layer. Fig. 2.66 shows some simulated oil painting rendered by this additive blending model.

Regarding the fluid motion of oil pigments in the second approach, the paint motion is often driven and dominated by boundary conditions. On the one side is the paint's boundary with the moving canvas, and on the other, the boundary with the stationary canvas. In the IMPaSTO system [Baxter *et al.*, 2004a], a conservative advection scheme is proposed to simulate the basic dynamics of paint, which preserves both overall paint volume and pigment mass even when the paint is spread thinly. Moreover, it is augmented with heuristics that models the remaining key properties needed for painting. Assuming that the concentration of a pigment q is a scalar quantity, how this

Fig. 2.65 Variable wetness is displayed as yellow paint has been painted over the purple color stripes of 100%, 50%, 0%, 75%, 25% dryness (from left to right) [Baxter *et al.*, 2001]. Copyright of ACM, used with permission

Fig. 2.66 Oil painting examples generated by the DAB system [Baxter *et al.*, 2001]. Copyright of ACM, used with permission

quantity evolves over time under a specified velocity v can be determined by the following partial differential equation:

$$\frac{\partial q}{\partial t} = -(v \times \nabla)q.$$

This advection calculation is predicated on the priori knowledge of which velocity field to use. In real painting this velocity field comes from a number of sources. The main source is the frictional forces imposed by the brush on the one side of a layer of paint, and by the stationary canvas on the other. Any viscid fluid will have zero slip (tangential) velocity at the interface between the fluid and a solid boundary. So during a paint stroke, within the thin layer of paint trapped underneath the brush, the paint in contact with the brush has the canvas's velocity, while paint in contact with the canvas has the brush's velocity. All possible velocities between zero and the brush speed must exist within the layer of paint. Thus as a first approximation, a reasonable 2D velocity relative to the canvas surface is used. This kinematic brush velocity, v_b, is the first component of the total velocity used. However, the paint will flow outward in any unconstrained direction. They use a simple heuristic rule to model this "squishing" behavior. First, for every cell in the 2D paint grid where the brush penetrates the height field surface, the amount of penetration p, and the 2D gradient of the penetration amount ∇p are computed. The heuristic pressure-driven velocity v_p is defined to be a constant c times that value,

$$v_p = -c \times \nabla p.$$

This pressure-driven velocity v_p is then simply added onto the brush velocity v_b to get the total velocity at each cell of brush-canvas contact. The color pigment mixing and compositing is rendered in real time based on the diffuse reflectance model described by Kubelka and Munk (see Section 2.3.1). Fig. 2.67 shows some simulated oil paintings by this coloring model.

Fig. 2.67 Simulated oil paintings from IMPaSTo [Baxter *et al.*, 2004a]. Copyright of ACM, used with permission

However, the fluid simulation in the IMPaSTO system is just an empirical approximation of the dynamics of oil pigments, and is not sufficiently accurate for the highly viscous oil paintings. Therefore Baxter *et al.* further presented a viscous paint model based on the well-known stokes' equations for viscous flow [Baxter *et al.*, 2004b]. It is the first unconditionally stable numerical method that treats viscous fluid with a free surface boundary. The viscous fluid behavior uses the 3D incompressible Stokes equations:

$$\frac{\partial v}{\partial t} = v\nabla^2 u - \nabla p + F, \ \nabla \times u = 0,$$

where u was the velocity of the fluid, v is the kinematic viscosity, and p is the pressure. F represents externally applied forces. The density is assumed to be constant, since most familiar viscous materials are homogenous. The second part of the equation is the equation for continuity, which enforces incompressibility and the conservation of mass. The Stokes' equation is a simplification of Navier-Stokes', which is applicable for highly viscous flows. The simplification arises from the observation that the contribution of the advection term which appears in Navier-Stokes' equation,

$$(u \cdot \nabla) \times v,$$

is negligible for viscous fluids with low Reynolds number flows. This can be understood as the velocity field is diffusing so rapidly throughout the fluid that the fluid's inertia does not have time to exert influence on the flow.

The numerical method used to solve the fluid flow equations is as follows: a provisional velocity field u is first computed, and captures the effect of the viscous term $v \times \nabla^2 \times u$ and any externally applied body forces F. The new pressure p is used to compute the final divergence-free velocity field u. A three-step temporal discretization scheme of the solver can be written succinctly as follows:

$$\begin{aligned} u^* &= u^n + \Delta t \left[v \times \nabla^2 \times u^* + F \right], \\ \nabla^2 p &= \nabla \times u^* / \Delta t, \\ u^{n+1} &= u^* - \Delta t \times \nabla \times p. \end{aligned}$$

where n refers to the time step for which the variables are to be evaluated. The resulting oil painting artwork is rendered by the KM model.

2.4 Digitized Sculpting

The history of sculpture art can be traced back to the birth of human beings. It originates from the tools made by human beings for hunting, farming and the other daily living activities, which in essence differentiates the human beings from animals. As it gradually evolves from the making of tools towards the intentional creation of artificial models, solid logos or characters based on the material of wood, stone and metal, etc., sculpting has become an art form. In this section, we will describe the two most common forms of sculpture: wood sculpting and mental embossing.

2.4.1 Digitized Wood Sculpting

The representative work on the virtual sculpting of wood comes from Mizuno *et al.* [1998, 1999]. They employed an interactive modeling technique to form a solid object with curved surfaces by carving a virtual piece of work, as we do it in the real world. Original solid objects to be carved are polyhedral with plane or carved surfaces, defined with a CSG (Constructive Solid Geometry) expression by planes or quadric surfaces as the primitives. Any shaped solid object can be used as an original object. A carved solid object is also defined by a CSG expression. The user can form a 3D sculpting solid object interactively by carving a workpiece with virtual chisels. An ellipsoidal chisel is defined with one quadric surface, and a cubic surface of a flat chisel is defined with three quadric surfaces which are actually pairs of parallel infinite planes. The tip of a virtual chisel is defined with an ellipsoid or a cube, and can remove or attach their own shape, from or to the virtual piece of work, which is rendered with shadowing. By performing this carving operation repeatedly, the user can form arbitrarily shaped solid objects. Since this virtual sculpting uses an ellipsoid as one of the virtual chisels, the surfaces of the carved solid objects look like surfaces carved by a round chisel (gouge) in the real world (see Fig. 2.68).

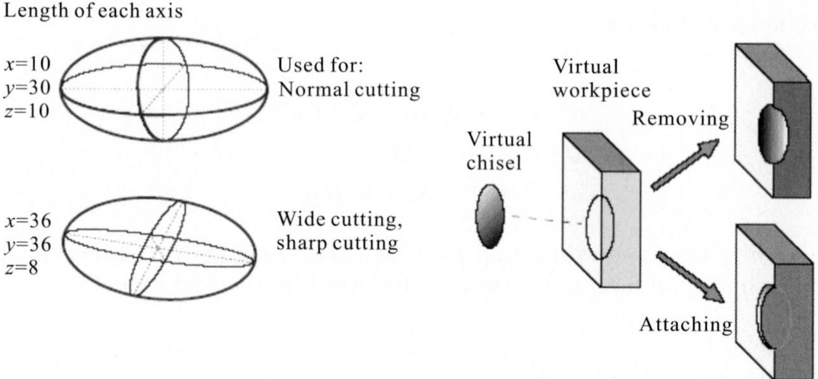

Fig. 2.68 Examples of virtual chisels and their sculpting operation of removing and attaching [Mizuno *et al.*, 1999]. Copyright of Blackwell, used with permission

During the sculpting operation, the user can specify the following parameters:

(1) *Chisel type*: to be selected from different ellipsoids.
(2) *Chisel depth*: moves along the normal axis of the object surface.
(3) *Chisel direction*: rotates around three axes.
(4) *Sort of operation*:to be selected from removing or attaching.

The surface of the solid object needs to be changed after each carving operation in terms of the CSG modeling. Fig. 2.69 shows some examples of virtual carving operations on the workpiece.

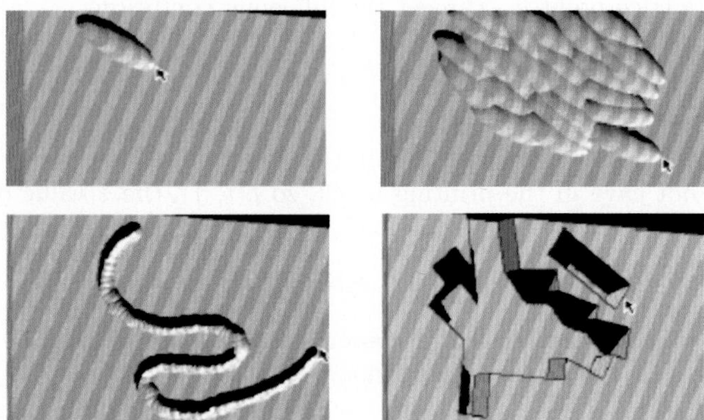

Fig. 2.69 Examples of the virtual carving process [Mizuno *et al.*, 1999]. Copyright of Blackwell, used with permission

The entire carving process will be recorded with a logical formula, which will be used to generate a high quality image of the carved object by the ray tracing method. Fig. 2.70 shows some resulting wood sculpture of the virtual sculpting.

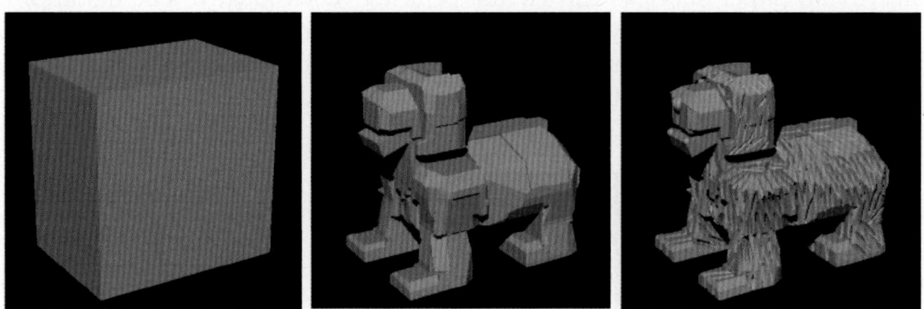

Fig. 2.70 Resulting wood sculpture examples [Mizuno *et al.*, 1999]. Copyright of Blackwell, used with permission

Mizuno *et al.* also described how to synthesize a woodcut printing image in terms of the wood sculpture. A virtual woodcut printing is generated with virtual items consisting of "a printing block", "a paper sheet", and "a printing brush" in a virtual 3D space. The grey value of each point on the virtual paper sheet is decided by the distance from the sheet to the virtual printing block at each point, and the grey value increases inversely to the distance. A virtual paper sheet is expressed as a 2D lattice $(i,\ j)$ and is at first placed in parallel with the x-y plane in the virtual space. The x and y values of a lattice point $(i,\ j)$ meet the following conditions:

$$x = s_i,\ y = s_j\ ,$$

where s is sampling interval.

The lattice points can move only in the direction of the z axis. The paper sheet does not cave in the printing block, so $p(i,\ j)$, the z value of a lattice point, satisfies the following condition:

$$p(i, j) \geqslant b(x, y).$$

The distance $d(i,\ j)$ from the paper sheet to the printing block at the lattice point $(i,\ j)$ is expressed as follows:

$$d(i, j) = p(i, j) - b(x, y).$$

A grey value $f(i, j)$ at each lattice point of the virtual paper sheet is computed with the following expressions:

$$f(i, j) = \begin{cases} 0, & \text{if } d(i, j) > t_d, \\ a(t_d - d(i, j)), & \text{otherwise,} \end{cases}$$

where a, t_d are constant > 0.

Thus, removed areas of the printing block print the sheet white and other areas black. A virtual printing brush is used to change the distance from the virtual paper sheet to the virtual printing block locally. The distance is decreased little by little by operating the virtual printing brush, and a virtual print is synthesized interactively. Fig. 2.71 shows some examples of a virtual sculpture and its woodcut printing.

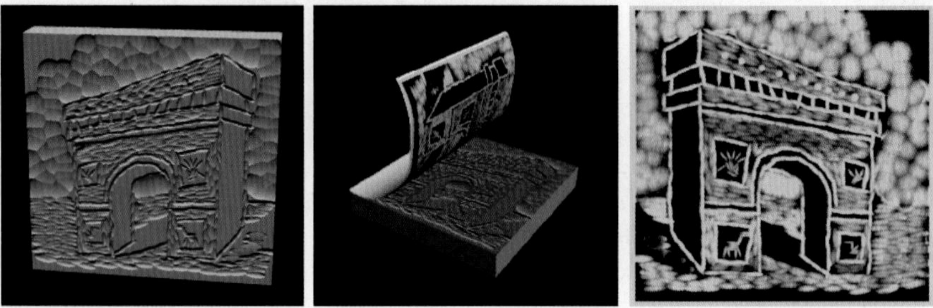

Fig. 2.71 Virtual sculpture and its synthesized woodcut printing [Mizuno *et al.*, 1999]. Copyright of Blackwell, used with permission

2.4.2 Digitized Metal Embossing

Embossing is the art of decorating metals. It is usually performed on a sheet of metal about 0.3-1.0 mm thick. It can be copper, brass, aluminum, silver or any other soft and flexible metal. The ornamental design is raised from the back of the metal by means of hammers and punches followed by hammering from the front, which is called chasing. The tools used for embossing are hammers with specially shaped handles and faces, and different punches are used for raising metal from the back as well as for chasing it from the front. The punches are so shaped that they are capable of producing any effect that may be required. There are also "tracers" that are used for making contours of the drawings onto the metal. A sheet of raw rubber or an asphalt block is also needed as a foundation.

In order to simulate the virtual embossing, Sourin proposed a functionally based approach to modeling the embossing [Sourin, 2001]. Each tool, a sheet of metal, and a final embossed picture are defined with the Function Representation or just F-Rep. Each individual function in the F-Rep is an inequality $f(x, y, z) \geqslant 0$, that is greater than zero for the points inside the respective shape, equal to zero on the surface of the shape, and less than zero for the points outside the shape. The resulting function is an inequality as well. It is a superposition of other functions representing shapes and operations over them.

First, let's represent a sheet of metal of size $2w \times 2h \times 2d$ as a thin solid plate by intersecting six plane half-spaces as follows:

$$\begin{aligned} f_{\text{embossed}} &= f(x, y, z) \\ &= \min(x + w, \min(w - x, \min(y + h, \min(h - y, \min(z + d, d - z))))) \\ &\geqslant 0. \end{aligned}$$

The intersection operation is implemented with the min function.

Next, the contours of the drawing are outlined by dragging lines. Mathematically, each curve drawn on the surface of the plate is interpolated by segments of straight lines, where for each segment the negative offset operation is applied along the normal to the surface.

About the raising up operation of the relief regions, it can also be modeled with the offset operations and/or the set-theoretic operations over the plate and the shapes representing the tools. In our case, for bossing up the portions of the plate by hammering or pressing it from behind with the punches, the offset is the most appropriate method. For each application of the punch to point $P_1(x_1, y_1, z_1)$, the following is to be done for any point $P(x, y, z)$:

$$P' = P - P_1,$$
$$f_{\text{offset}} = \frac{pa^3}{q|P'|^2 + a^2},$$
$$f_{\text{embossed\_new}} = f_{\text{embossed}} + f_{\text{offset}},$$
$$f_{\text{tool}} = f_{\text{sphere}}(x, y, z) = r^2 - (x - x_1)^2 - (y - y_1)^2 - (z - z_1)^2 \geqslant 0,$$

where a, p, and q are parameters defining the size of the affected region and the height of embossing.

In order to visualize the simulated embossing, Sourin employed the ray tracing algorithm to render the resulting embossing artwork [Sourin, 2001]. To make ray tracing interactive, only the region that has been affected by the most recent application of the tool is to be redrawn (see Fig. 2.72). This method ensures the required fast rendering time of the affected regions.

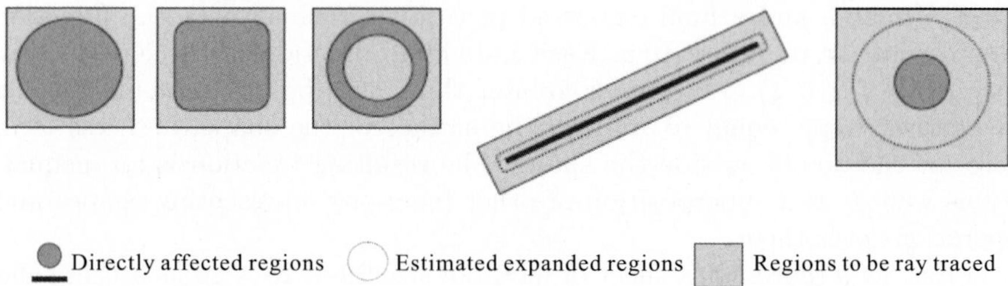

Fig. 2.72 The affected regions by different tool shapes [Sourin, 2001]. Copyright of Springer Science and Business Media, used with permission

At last, the background is to be made by beating down the metal with differently shaped hammers and punches. To simulate the stroke of the punch with a semi-spherical tip, the offset and/or the theoretic operations similar to those can be used as follows:

Offsetting: $f_{\text{embossed}} = f_{\text{embossed}} - f_{\text{offset}} \geqslant 0$.

Subtraction: $f_{\text{embossed}} = \min(f_{\text{embossed}}, -f_{\text{tool}}) \geqslant 0$.

Subtraction with blending:

$$f_{\text{embossed\_new}} = f_{\text{embossed}} - f_{\text{tool}} - \sqrt{f_{\text{embossed}}{}^2 + (-f_{\text{tool}})^2} - \frac{a_1}{1 + \left(\frac{f_{\text{embossed}}}{a_2}\right)^2 \left(\frac{-f_{\text{tool}}}{a_3}\right)^2},$$
$$f_{\text{embossed}} = f_{\text{embossed\_new}}, \ f_{\text{embossed}} \geqslant 0.$$

The process of embossing continues if other contours, raised regions, and background patterns are to be made. Fig. 2.73 shows an offset function and its resulting embossing effects.

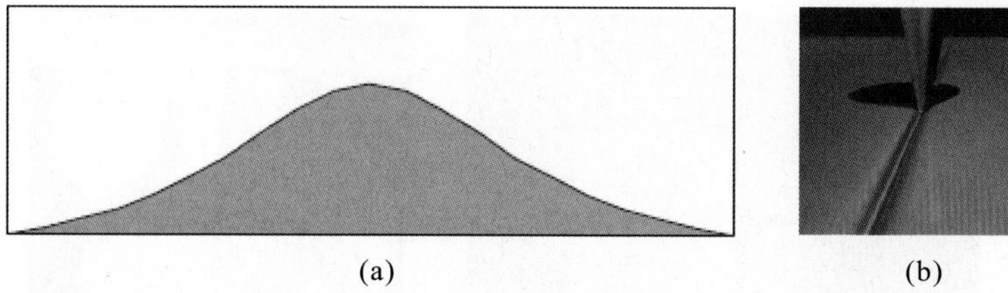

(a) (b)

Fig. 2.73 Example of offset function and its resulting embossing effects [Sourin, 2001]. (a) Offset function; (b) The resulting embossing effects. Copyright of Springer Science and Business Media, used with permission

2.5 Creation of Artwork in a Virtual Environment

The creation of artwork in a virtual environment presents many challenges. Besides taking advantage of the many possibilities that a virtual environment can offer, it must support design without restricting the artist's creative process, and provide sufficient immersion for the user as if they were creating the artwork in the real environment. Lalioti *et al.* explored a research interface for a Ndebele wall painting in a virtual environment [Lalioti *et al.*, 2001]. The system consists of three parts: a set of patterns; virtual tools that let users select, manipulate, and paint a pattern; and the algorithms that facilitate positioning and applying colors to the patterns. The users can select colored and uncolored patterns from a pre-scanned set and then manipulate and position them on a virtual surface. The users can also employ different colors typical of the Ndebele wall painting to paint areas of the selected pattern. The virtual tools in their system have two categories: one that allows manipulation of the patterns and the other that lets the user choose colors and paint the interior of patterns. In order to keep the interaction metaphors as close as possible to the real wall painting process, they experimented with a nonintrusive and seamless interaction method that uses image-analysis techniques and stereo vision to track a real paintbrush or the user's hand, mimicking the real painting paradigm. Fig. 2.74 shows the pictures of a real and virtual Ndebele painting.

Keefe *et al.* went further by extending the 2D brush strokes into a 3D analog to create 3D works of art (CavePainting) in a fully immersive virtual environment [Keefe *et al.*, 2001]. The system is designed to take advantage of the 8 ft.×8 ft.×8 ft. space in which the artist works. Physical props and gestures are used to provide an intuitive interface for artists who may not be familiar with virtual reality. It enables the artist to create a new type of art medium and provides a novel approach to viewing this artwork after it has been created. Fig. 2.75 shows its setup and examples of how to create CavePainting.

The artist start the CavePainting by defining a ground plane and a wall rising out of it. The strokes are animated as they leave the artist's brush.

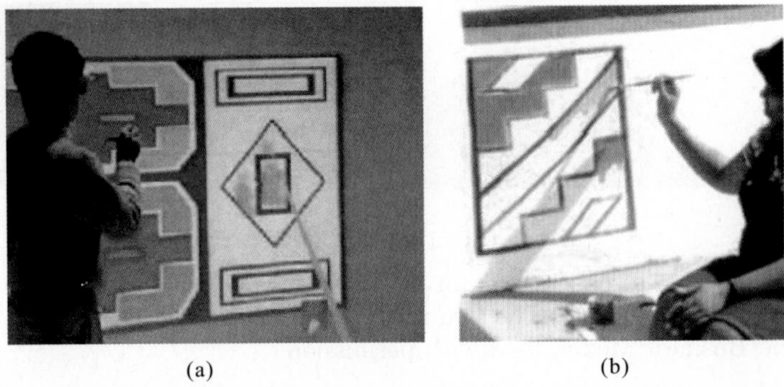

(a) (b)

Fig. 2.74 Virtual (a) and real (b) Ndebele painting [Lalioti *et al.*, 2001]. Copyright of IEEE, used with permission

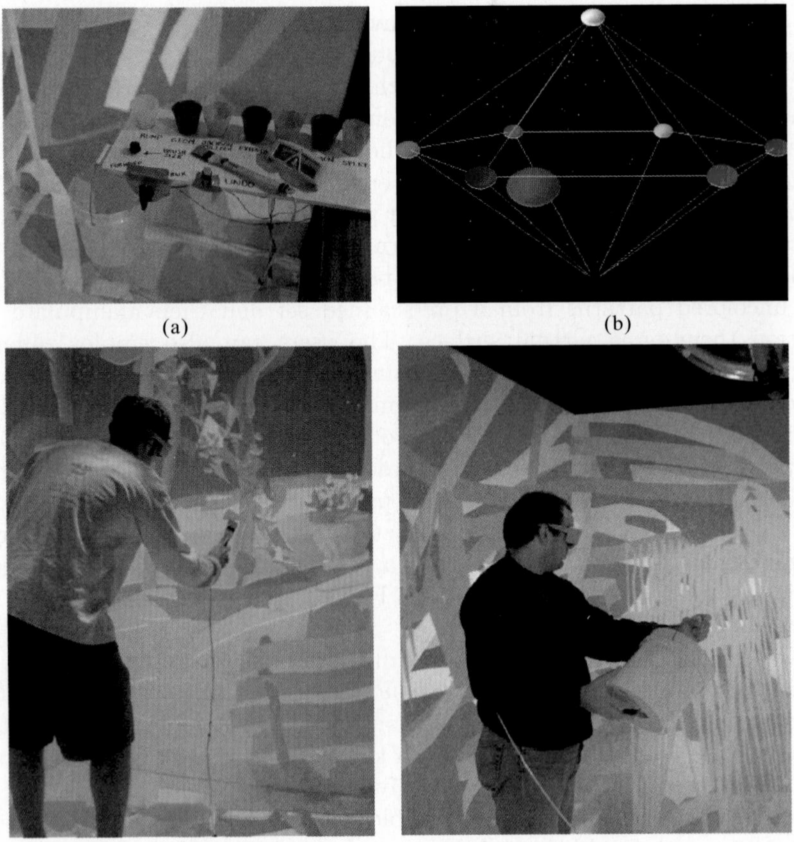

(a) (b)

(c) (d)

Fig. 2.75 The system setup of CavePainting [Keefe *et al.*, 2001]. (a) The painting table interface; (b) A 3D color picker; (c) Virtual painting with a brush; (d) Virtual paint dripped out of a real bucket. Copyright of ACM, used with permission

They fall in the direction that the brush points until they reach one of the walls of the Cave, where they splatter in the virtual world, as if they had actually hit the physical wall of the Cave. Both strokes provide an interesting link between the physical space the user occupies and the virtual world in which he finds himself immersed. The artist is free to create long expressive brush strokes and then step back to observe the work from different angles. Interaction with the computer is accomplished through the use of simple gestures and props that are commonly used in painting and positioned on a table inside the Cave. Scenes are created by layering and arranging virtual 3D brush strokes in space.

The resulting CavePainting is composed of many 3D paint strokes. These individual strokes are layered and arranged in space to produce a scene. The artist can choose between several stroke types. The current stroke types in the system are line, ribbon, tube, bumpy tube, trail of any type of geometry, Jackson Pollock++, splat, extrusion, and bucket. The artist picks a stroke type to indicate the general characteristics of the stroke. This is analogous to choosing application of oil paint with a large flat brush, a small round brush, a sponge, or a palette knife, since the artist can obtain considerable variation in a stroke, even after a stroke type has been chosen. The artist actually applies the virtual paint by moving a tracked paint brush prop around in the Cave. The virtual strokes respond to fine variations in the position and orientation of the paint brush prop. The immediacy of the response of the virtual paint to the artist's movements is very important. The direct control over the 3D paint is what allows them to create expressive variations in strokes. Fig. 2.76 show an example of CavePainting artwork.

Fig. 2.76 A CavePainting artwork [Keefe *et al.*, 2001]. Copyright of ACM, used with permission

They also discussed the dispute about CavePainting. What are the main differences between CavePainting and free form modeling? The first can be attributed to the fact that their system runs in a fully immersive Cave environment. The Cave provides the artist with enough space to stand up and walk around in while working. This directly affects the type of work that the artist creates, as well as the way in which the artist works. Additionally, since the user wears shutter glasses in the Cave, he or she is able to see both the real world and the virtual world at the same time.

Second, CavePainting provides the artist with fine control over color and a large, varied set of brush strokes with which to work. CavePainting3 does not attempt to be a modeling system in a traditional sense, where the user is often concerned with exact coordinate representations for the size or shape of objects. Rather, CavePainting aspires to be an extension of painting in three dimensions. Just as an oil painter builds up a painting with layers of varied brush strokes, the Cave-painter creates many different 3D strokes to convey the impression of a 3D scene.

Finally, CavePainting promotes the idea that art created by this dynamic 3D tool is meant to be viewed in an interactive 3D display environment, since a static 2D print, no matter how large, cannot truly convey the 3D nature of this type of work. CavePainting presents a viewing mode of its own which takes this notion a step further by providing the observer with additional insight into the artistic process that produced each work.

2.6 Summary

In this chapter, we mainly discussed the fundamental principles and algorithms about how to create artwork from a blank canvas, including the simulation of pencil-drawing, pen-and-ink illustration, black ink, watercolor, oil painting, etc. In recent years, there are more works published about how to speed up the digitized painting by real-time implementation. The readers who are interested in this topic can refer to [Coconu *et al.*, 2006; Lee *et al.*, 2006; Luft & Deussen, 2006].

From the point of view of fine arts, the digitized creation of artwork rapidly changes the mind and thinking mode of an artist. Its birth has not only enabled the artist to employ an ever-increasing variety of medium and tools to conveniently control, manipulate and generate the traditional artwork, but it also has made the entire working space surrounding the artist fully digitized. It provides a technical platform for the artists to explore a new art medium. In moving from physical canvas to the computer screen, the artist gains an incredible amount of flexibility. However, this is often in exchange for the kind of subtlety and presence that are found only in fine art tools and papers. The modeling of brushes, canvas, and pigment in the digitized painting are simplified from that found in the real painting.

With the advancement of computer graphics, the technical research work on digitized painting will make for a more natural interface for the digital painting. The techniques of digital painting will become strong enough to make the content of the resulting artwork be only limited to the imagination capability of the user. On the other hand, the novel interactive graphics techniques will motivate the artists to explore and experiment with the new art medium, greatly enriching the current art forms.

References

Baxter B, Scheib V, Lin MC, Manocha D(2001) DAB: interactive haptic painting with 3D virtual brushes. In: Proceedings of the 28th Annual Conference on Computer Graphics and Interactive Techniques 461–468

Baxter W, Wendt J, Lin MC(2004a) IMPaSTO: a realistic, interactive model for paint. In: Proceedings of the 3rd International Symposium on Non-photorealistic Animation and Rendering 45–148

Baxter W, Liu Y, Lin MC(2004b) A viscous paint model for interactive applications. Computer Animation and Virtual Worlds 15(3-4):433–441

Beach RJ, Beatty JC, Booth KS, Plebon DA, Fiume EL(1982) The message is the medium: multiprocess structuring of an interactive paint. In: Proceedings of the 9th Annual Conference on Computer Graphics and Interactive Techniques 277–287

Bleser TW, SIbert JL, McGee JP(1988) Charcoal sketching: returning control to the artist. ACM Transactions on Graphics 7(1):76–81

Chan C, Akleman E, Chen J(2002) Two methods for creating Chinese painting. In: Proceedings of Pacific Graphics 2002 403–412

Chu NS, Tai CL(2002) An efficient brush model for physically-based 3D painting. In: Proceedings of Pacific Graphics 2002 413–421

Chu NS, Tai CL(2005) MoXi: Real-time ink dispersion in absorbent paper. In: International Conference on Computer Graphics and Interactive Techniques 504–511

Cockshott T, Patterson J, England D(1992) Modelling the texture of paint. Computer Graphics Forum 11(3): 217–226

Coconu L, Deussen O, Hege HC(2006) Real-time pen-and-ink illustration of landscapes. In: Proceedings of the 4th International Symposium on Non-photorealistic Animation and Rendering 27–35

Curtis CJ, Anderson SE, Seims JE, Fleischery KW, Salesin DH(1997) Computer-generated watercolor. In: Proceedings of the 24th Annual Conference on Computer Graphics and Interactive Techniques 421–430

Drago F, Chiba N(2004) Painting canvas synthesis. The Visual Computer 20(5): 314–328

Finkelstein A, Salesin DH(1994) Multiresolution curves. In: Proceedings of the 21st Annual Conference on Computer Graphics and Interactive Techniques 261–268

Guo Q, Kunii TL(2003) "Nijim" rendering algorithm for creating quality black ink paintings. Computer Graphics International 2003 136–143

Haase CS, Meyer GW(1992) Modeling pigmented materials for realistic image synthesis. ACM Transactions on Graphics 11(4):305–335

Huang SW, Way DL, Shih ZC(2003) Physical-based model of ink diffusion in chinese ink paintings. Journal of WSCG 2003

Keefe DF, Feliz DA, Moscovich T, Laidlaw DH, Jr JJL(2001) CavePainting: a fully immersive 3D artistic medium and interactive experience. In: Proceedings of the 2001 Symposium on Interactive 3D Graphics 85–93

Kunii TL, Nosovskij GV, Hayashi T(1995) A diffusion model for computer animation of diffuse ink painting. Computer Animation 1995 98–102

Laerhoven TV, Van Reeth F(2005) Real-time simulation of watery paint. Computer Animation and Virtual Worlds 16(3∼4):429–439

Lalioti V, Malan A, Pun J, Wind J(2001) Ndebele painting in VR. Computer Graphics and Applications 21(2):10–13

Lee H, Kwon S, Lee S(2006) Real-Time Pencil Rendering. In: Proceedings of the 4th International Symposium on Non-photo realistic Animation and rendering Animation and Rendering 37–45

Lee J(1999) Simulating oriented black-ink painting. Computer Graphics and Applications 19(3):74–81

Lee J(2001) Diffusion rendering of black ink paintings using new paper and ink models. Computers and Graphics 25 (2):295–308

Luft T, Deussen O(2006) Real-time watercolor illustrations of plants using a blurred depth test. In: Proceedings of the 4th International Symposium on Non-photorealistic Animation and Rendering 11–20

Mizuno S, Okada M, Toriwaki J(1998) Virtual sculpting and virtual woodcut printing. The Visual Computer 14(2):39–51

Mizuno S, Okada M, Toriwaki J(1999) An interactive designing system with virtual sculpting and virtual woodcut printing. Computer Graphics Forum 18(3):183–194

Pudet T(1994) Real-time fitting of hand-sketched pressure brushstrokes. Computer Graphics Forum 13(3):205–220

Rudolf D, Mould D, Neufeld E(2003) Simulating wax crayons. In: 11th Pacific Conference on Computer Graphics and Application Pacific Graphics 2003 163–172

Salisbury MP, Anderson SE, Barzel R, Salesin DH(1994) Interactive pen-and-ink illustration. In: Proceedings of the 21st Annual Conference on Computer Graphics and Interactive Techniques 101–108

Small D(1990) Simulating watercolor by modeling diffusion, pigment, and paper fibers. Image Handling and Reproduction Systems Integration 1460: 140–146

Sourin A(2001) Functionally based virtual embossing. The Visual Computer 17(4): 258–271

Sousa MC, Buchanan JW(2000) Observational model of graphite pencil materials. Computer Graphics Forum 19(1):27–49

Stam J(2003) Real-time fluid dynamics for games. In: Proceedings of the Game Developer Conference

Saunderson JL(1942) Calculation of the color pigmented plastics. Journal of the Optical Society of America 32(12):727–736

Strassmann S(1986) Hairy brushes. In: Proceedings of the 13th Annual Conference on Computer Graphics and Interactive Techniques 225–232

Takagi S, Fujishiro I, Nakajima M(1999) Volumetric modeling of colored pencil drawing. In: Seventh Pacific Conference on Computer Graphics and Applications 1999 250–258

Way DL, Huang SW, Shih ZC(2003) Physical-based model of ink diffusion in chinese paintings. Journal of WSCG 2003

Whitted T(1983) Anti-aliased line drawing using brush extrusion. In: Proceedings of the 10th Annual Conference on Computer Graphics and Interactive Techniques 151–156

Wong HTF, Ip HHS(2000) Virtual brush: a model-based synthesis of Chinese calligraphy. Computer and Graphics 24(1):99–113

Xu S, Tang M, Lau F, Pan Y(2002) A solid model based virtual hairy brush. In: Proceedings of Eurographics 2002 299–308

Xu S, Lau FCM, Tang F, Pan Y(2003)Advanced design for a realistic virtual brush. Computer Graphics Forum 22(3):533–542

Yeh J, Lien T, Ouhyoung M(2002) On the effects of haptic display in brush and ink simulation for Chinese painting and calligraphy (short paper). In: 10th Pacific Conference on Computer Graphics and Applications 439–441

Yu YY, Lee DH, Lee YB, Cho HG(2003) Interactive rendering technique for realistic oriental painting. Journal of WSCG 2003

[illegible]

3

Computer-aided Design of Art Patterns

Human artists often do the design of art patterns manually. The designer first imagines the art patterns in his mind, and then draws them on paper or canvas. This process is repeated until the desirable art patterns are created. It is time consuming and the novelty of the resulting art patterns is limited to the human's imagination, which is difficult to meet the requirements for a huge amount of art patterns in a manufacturing industry such as textile. This chapter will mainly discuss how to let the computer assist in the generation of the art patterns, including:

(1) *Art pattern creation by fractals.* It is based on the principles of fractal geometry, and performs the numerical calculation by the iterative function system. The output of the numerical data are colored to generate the resultant art patterns.
(2) *Art pattern creation by shape grammars.* Shape grammars specify a mechanism for selecting and performing recursive rules for shape computations. The computer handles the representation and computation of shapes, rules, and the presentation of correct design alternatives. This frees the designer to specify, explore, develop design languages in terms of the shape grammar, and select alternatives for the desirable art patterns.
(3) *Layout-based creation of art patterns.* Three basic layout-based art pattern design methods are presented: (a) How to convert the graphical layout into the resulting art patterns in terms of the specified structure of craftwork. (b) How to create an aesthetic layout of an art pattern by the regular layout. (c) How to automatically/semi-automatically place the user specified graphical entities by a specific artistic style.
(4) *Knowledge-based creation of art patterns.* The artificial intelligence techniques are employed to represent the design knowledge and aesthetic conventions of art patterns, and then generate the resultant art patterns by reasoning on them.

3.1 The Overview of Art Pattern Design

From the point of view of artwork, the art pattern design is a creative modeling activity that aims at the generation of planar decoration and ornamentation. There are four major components in the art patterns: graphical entities, layouts, colors, and textures [Lu *et al.*, 1997].

The graphical entity is composed of a set of geometric primitives such as points, lines, and faces. The graphical entity is defined relatively to the entire art pattern, and itself could be considered a kind of sub-art-pattern that is generated by the transformations, translation, scale, rotation, skew, etc., applied on the geometric primitives (see Fig. 3.1).

Fig. 3.1 A graphical entity generated from a rhombus primitive by composite transformations [Lu *et al.*, 1997]. Courtesy of Weilin Lu *et al.*

When multiple graphical entities are integrated into a novel art pattern, the spatial relationships among the graphical entities are called the "layout" of the art pattern. The typical layouts involved in the art pattern can be summarized as follows:

(1) *Planar layout.* All of the graphical entities are placed on the same plane, ignoring their depths to the view point, and there is no overlapping among the graphical entities.
(2) *Perspective layout.* All of the graphical entities are presented to the viewer in terms of the perspective projection principles.
(3) *Scattered layout.* The silhouettes of the graphical entities are generated first. The desirable art pattern is generated by randomly scattering the relevant graphical entities onto the canvas in terms of the predefined density model.
(4) *Radial layout.* There is a central graphical entity in the art pattern. The other graphical entities can be centripetally orientated towards the central graphical entity, or centrifugally, or spirally placed from the central graphical entity.

(5) *Evenly distributed layout.* The graphical entities in the art pattern are evenly distributed in terms of a central or a pre-specified axis. A typical method to generate this kind of layout is to let several graphical entities be evenly distributed within a small region, and then "copy and paste" it to the remaining regions in the canvas, until the entire canvas is filled.

(6) *Complex layout.* There are several types of graphical entities in the art pattern. The graphical entities of the same types are placed together with connectivity in a region, and each region with the same type of graphical entities will be surrounded by another type of graphical entities.

(7) *Continuous layout.* Several graphical entities are aesthetically formed into a sub-art-pattern, and this sub-art-pattern will be repeated with a spatial rhythm along a line, or within a specific region.

(8) *Overlapping layout.* The graphical entities are flattened out within a specific view volume. The foreground graphical entities closely interweave with the background graphical entities, but will not occlude the background ones. All the graphical entities have a suitable contrast with the neighboring ones, addressing the presentation principle of domination vs. subordination, strong vs. light emphasis, and virtual vs. real impression.

(9) *Layout with bi-directional continuities.* If one art pattern is stitched to the same art pattern horizontally or vertically, the resulting art pattern is seamless regarding their graphical entities placed on the horizontal or vertical boundaries. The layout inside this kind of art pattern is called bi-directional continuities.

(10) *Layout with four-directional continuities.* If one art pattern is stitched to the same art pattern with four directions: left, right, up and down, the graphical entities placed on the four directional boundaries in the resulting art pattern are all seamless. The layout inside this kind of art pattern is called four-directional continuities.

Color is one of the basic building blocks of creating art patterns. A color field's size and shape, the frequency of a foreground object with which a color appears in an art pattern, and the background color all affect our perception of a color. Therefore, the computer-aided creation of art patterns often involves a color palette, which enables the user to mix and organize colors, explore color combinations, and solicit historical, theoretical, or expert sources [Meier *et al.*, 2005]. The harmony of color is one of the fundamental factors in the visual style of the art pattern. The beauty of the art pattern is largely dependent on whether the colors used in the art pattern are harmonious. The designer can often choose, specify, and coordinate all the colors in the art pattern mainly by his individual perception of color, orders of colors and the other subjective preferences.

Texture is a high-level graphical primitive in the art pattern, in which there is a highly coupled structure inside it. The texture of an art pattern could be the background, or the special effects of graphical entities, which are often generated by a non-linear transformation applied on the graphical entities.

In the computer graphics community, lots of research work has been done to assist the generation of the aforementioned four major components of the art pattern, or even for the entire art pattern itself. In the following sections, we will mainly discuss how to create art patterns by fractals, from user-specified layouts, shape grammars, and by the aesthetic knowledge respectively.

3.2 Art Pattern Creation by Fractals

A fractal is generally "a rough or fragmented geometric shape that can be split into parts, each of which is (at least approximately) a reduced-size copy of the whole" [Mandelbrot, 1982]. A fractal often has the following features [Falconer, 2003].

(1) It has a fine structure at arbitrarily small scales.
(2) It is too irregular to be easily described in traditional Euclidean geometric language.
(3) It is self-similar (at least approximately or stochastically).
(4) It has a Hausdorff dimension which is greater than its topological dimension (although this requirement is not met by space-filling curves such as the Hilbert curve).
(5) It has a simple and recursive definition.

Because they appear similar at all levels of magnification, fractals are often considered to be infinitely complex (in informal terms). Fractals can be classified according to their self-similarity. There are three types of self-similarity found in fractals:

(1) *Exact self-similarity.* This is the strongest type of self-similarity; the fractal appears identical at different scales. Fractals defined by iterated function systems often display exact self-similarity.
(2) *Quasi-self-similarity.* This is a loose form of self-similarity; the fractal appears approximately (but not exactly) identical at different scales. Quasi-self-similar fractals contain small copies of the entire fractal in distorted and degenerated forms. Fractals defined by a recurrence of relations are usually quasi-self-similar but not exactly self-similar.
(3) *Statistical self-similarity.* This is the weakest type of self-similarity; the fractal has numerical or statistical measures which are preserved across scales. Most reasonable definitions of "fractal" trivially imply some form of statistical self-similarity. (A fractal dimension itself is a numerical measure which is preserved across scales.) Random fractals are examples of fractals which are statistically self-similar, but neither exactly nor quasi-self-similar.

Fractal art is a cross-disciplinary field of mathematics and art. Graphically, fractals are images created out of the process of a mathematical exploration of the space in which they are plotted. Most people recognize fractals only as pretty pictures useful as backgrounds on the computer screen or original postcard patterns. A fractal image is a graphical representation of fractals whose points diverge, or go out of control and converge, or stay inside the set. To make fractal images more elaborate and interesting, color is added to them in terms of empirical rules and conventions. Images of fractals can be created using by the following common fractal generation techniques:

(1) *Escape-time fractals* (also known as *"orbits" fractals*).These are defined by a formula or recurrence relation at each point in a space. Examples of this type are the Mandelbrot set (see Fig. 3.2), Julia set (see Fig. 3.3), the Burning Ship fractal, the Nova fractal(see Fig. 3.4), and the Lyapunov fractal. The 2D vector fields that are generated by one or two iterations of escape-time formulae also give rise to a fractal form when points (or pixel data) are passed through this field repeatedly.
(2) *Iterated function systems.* These have a fixed geometric replacement rule. Cantor set, Sierpinski carpet, Sierpinski gasket, Peano curve, Koch snowflake, Harter-Highway dragon curve, T-Square, and Menger sponge are some examples of such fractals.
(3) *Random fractals.* Generated by stochastic rather than deterministic processes, for example, trajectories of the Brownian motion, Lévy flight, fractal landscapes and the Brownian tree.
(4) *Strange attractors.* Generated by iteration of a map or the solution of a system of initial-value differential equations that exhibit chaos.

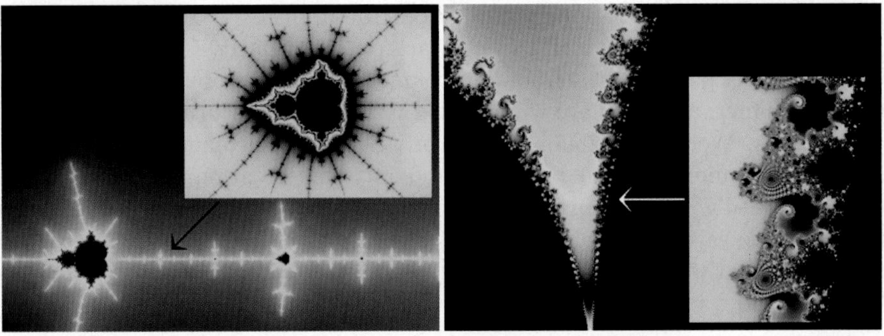

Fig. 3.2 Example image of Mandelbrot fractals [www.fractal.net.cn, 2007]. Copyright of www.fractal.net.cn, used with permission

Fig. 3.3 Example images of Julia fractals [www.fractal.net.cn, 2007]. Copyright of www.fractal.net.cn, used with permission

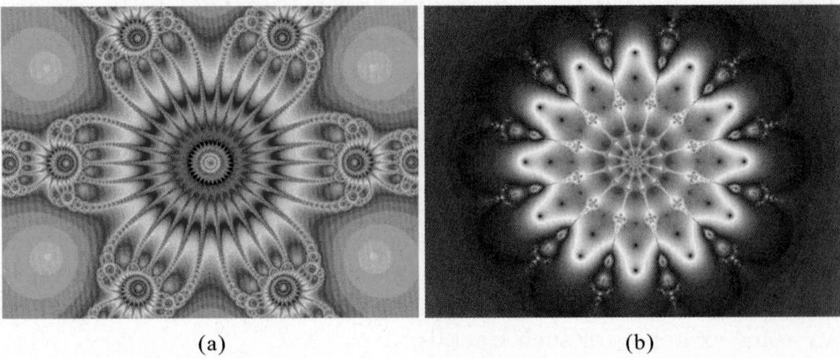

(a) (b)

Fig. 3.4 Example images of Newton and Nova fractals [www.fractal.net.cn, 2007]. (a) Newton Fractals; (b) Nova Fractals. Copyright of www.fractal.net.cn, used with permission

The fractal art brings the artists a new method to design art patterns. One of the well-known websites of fractal arts in China is

www.fractal.net.cn/aboutfractal/aboutfractal.htm.

There are lots of beautiful fractal art patterns on it. Compared to the traditional art patterns, the fractal art patterns present a novel aesthetic style to the designer, and they are widely used in the manufacturing industry [Luo *et al.*, 2004; Wei *et al.*, 2006]. Moreover, the digital geometrical processing and shading methods can be integrated into the creation of art patterns, thus generating more colorful art patterns. For example, Suffern employed the recursive ray-tracing algorithm to calculate the global lighting, and used the bump-texture mapping technique to process highlights and reflections based on the fractal geometry by Brownian motion [Suffern, 2002].

3.3 Art Pattern Creation by Shape Grammars

Shape grammars were formally proposed by Stiny [Stiny, 1980]. A shape is defined as a limited arrangement of straight lines in a Cartesian coordinate system with real axes and an associated Euclidean metric. A finite set of shapes may be used as the vocabulary for the formation of other shapes. It is said that a shape is made up of elements in a given set of shapes, whenever it is the shape union of transformations of shapes within this set. The set of all shapes made up of shapes in a given set of shapes S is denoted by S^+. For a given set of shapes S, the set of shapes S^* contains in addition to all of the shapes in the set S^+ the empty shape S_Φ.

Labeled shapes can be formed from given vocabularies of shapes and symbols. It will be said that a labeled shape σ is made up of shapes in a set S and symbols in a set L whenever it has one of the following three forms:

(1) $\sigma = \langle s, \Phi \rangle$, where s is a shape in the set S^+.
(2) $\sigma = \langle s, p \rangle$, where P is a finite, nonempty set of labeled points in which any symbol associated with a point is an element of the set L.
(3) $\sigma = \langle s, P \rangle$, where s is a shape and P is a set of labeled points satisfying conditions (1) and (2) respectively.

The set of all labeled shapes made up of shapes in the set S and symbols in the set L is denoted by $(S, L)^+$. The set of labeled shapes $(S, L)^*$ contains in addition to all the labeled shapes in the set $(S, L)^+$, the empty labeled shape (S_Φ, Φ).

A shape grammar has four components:

(1) S is a finite set of shapes.
(2) L is a finite set of symbols.
(3) R is a finite set of shape rules of the form $\alpha \rightarrow \beta$, where α is a labeled shape $(S, L)^+$, and β is a labeled shape in $(S, L)^*$.
(4) I is a labeled shape in $(S, L)^+$ called the initial shape.

The shapes in the set S and the symbols in the set L provide the building blocks for the definition of the shape rules, in the set R, and the initial shape I. Labeled shapes generated using the shape grammar are also built up in terms of these primitive elements. Labeled shapes are generated by a shape grammar by applying the shape rules one at a time to the initial shape, or to labeled shapes produced by previous applications of the shape rules. A given labeled shape γ is generated by the shape grammar if there is a finite series of labeled shapes, beginning with the initial shape and ending with γ, such that each term in the series, except for the first, is produced by applying a shape rule to its immediate predecessor. From the point of view of art pattern creation, a shape grammar defines a set of shapes called a language. This language contains all of the shapes s generated by the shape grammar, which have no symbols associated with them. That is, each of these labeled shapes is derived from the initial shape by applying the shape rules. Each is made up of shapes or sub-shapes of shapes in the set S. The resulting art pattern can be considered as a specific language sequence defined by shape grammar.

From the point of view of the user, the process to create an art pattern by shape grammar consists of three major phases [Tapia, 1999]:

(1) *Creating and modifying the shape grammar.* The designer creates the rules and initial shape, and verifies or changes the spatial and logical constraints.
(2) *Compiling the grammar.* While converting the grammar into an internal form, the computer checks that each rule always applies in only a finite number of ways.
(3) *Exploring the resulting art patterns defined by the grammar.* The designer explores the language of designs, generating designs, imposing additional constraints, halting the generation process, backtracking to a previous design, or saving the current state. The designer may interpret the resulting designs in a curvilinear world and use them as the basis for a design.

Wong *et al.* applied the principle of shape grammars to create the traditional floral ornamental design by "adaptive clip art", which encapsulates the rules for creating a specific ornamental pattern [Wong *et al.*, 1998]. They defined adaptive clip art as two parts: *elements* and *growth rules.*

Elements correspond to the 2D geometric primitives that appear in the ornament, e.g., flowers, leaves, and stems. They are the objects upon which the growth rules operate. To provide simplicity without sacrificing the ability to draw details, each element is defined as a collection of one or more proxies. A proxy is a relatively simple geometric shape that represents the element, or a part of the element, for the purposes of locating empty spaces and testing for intersections. When producing the final output, a more complicated rendering procedure can be invoked. The use of proxies, therefore, keeps the details of rendering an element separate from the mechanics of positioning it in the design.

Growth is a particularly good source for continuous patterns that fill space and that can logically transport a design into new regions. The *growth rules* are specified as procedures. When a rule is invoked on a parent element, the code associated with that rule (the rule body) is executed. This code can perform environmental queries and create child elements, among other things. A support library is provided for common environmental queries and for conveniently manipulating geometrical primitives such as proxy shapes. Finally, the framework for elaborating adaptive clip art uses a limited form of planning in selecting the element for growth on each new iteration. It attempts first to grow the ornament into a large open space, then shifts to filling in the corners of the desired region (see Fig. 3.5 (a)). If the region is resized or reshaped, the ornament can be automatically regenerated to fill this new area in an appropriate way.

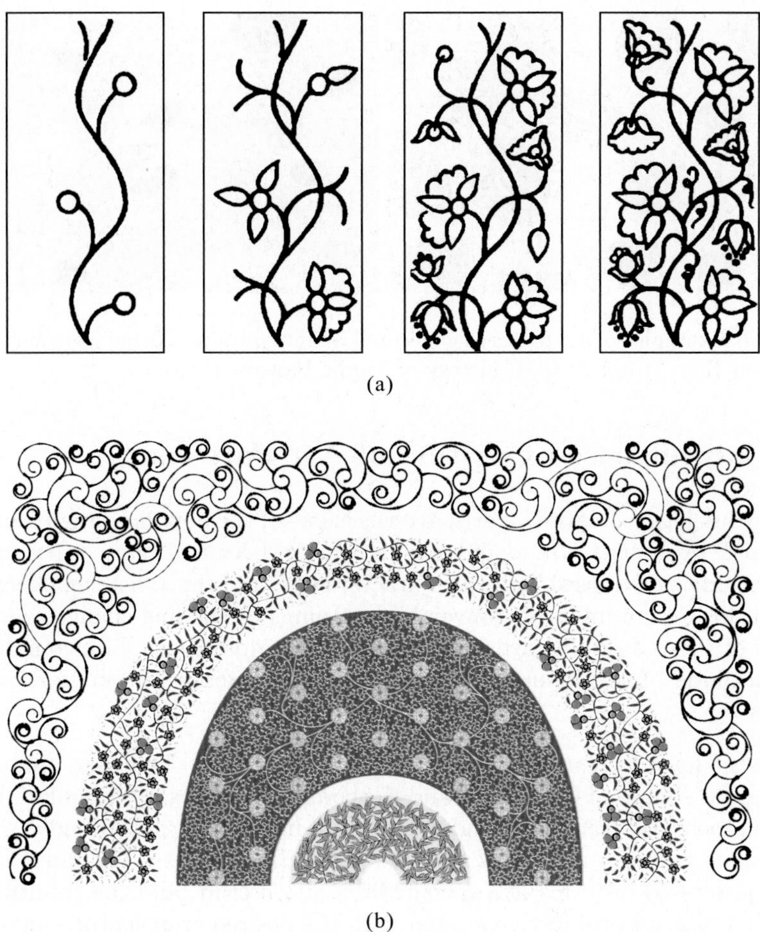

(a)

(b)

Fig. 3.5 Examples of (a) *growth rules* and (b) ornaments [Wong *et al.*, 1998]. Copyright of ACM, used with permission

Lu *et al.* embedded the fuzzy logic into the shape grammar to automatically generate the art patterns, and the major improvements on the shape grammar are as follows [Lu *et al.*, 1996]: A shape rule schema $\alpha \rightarrow \beta$ is replaced by a fuzzy logic rule, and labeled shapes are defined as a fuzzy set of shapes. Whenever specific values are given to all of the variables in α and β by a fuzzy logic assignment g to determine specific labeled shapes, a new shape rule $g(\alpha) \rightarrow g(\beta)$ is defined in fuzzy logic principles. This new shape rule can then be used to change a given shape into a new one by the fuzzy logic reasoning. The resultant art patterns are generated by the integrated process of fuzzy logic reasoning and rule rewriting, and Fig. 3.6 gives some examples of the resulting art pattern for textile.

Fig. 3.6 Examples of art patterns generated by integration of fuzzy logic and shape grammar [Pan *et al.*, 2002]. Courtesy of Yunhe Pan *et al.*

3.4 Layout-based Creation of Art Patterns

The layout-based creation of art patterns is one of the popular design methods preferred by artists. Its popularity is partly because many types of art patterns have obvious structural characteristics, and the artist can effectively present his design intent or convey his meanings by making changes onto the layout of these desirable art patterns. In the computer graphics community, the methods of layout-based creation of art patterns are summarized as follows:

(1) *Novel layout creation based on regular structures.* The user inputs the regular shapes of the layout, and the computer makes it "irregular" based on stochastic principles, and generates a new layout accordingly.
(2) *Layout creation integrated with the fabrication process.* The input layout is processed in terms of a specific fabrication craft, and the resulting art pattern is accordingly generated with the desired craft features or styles.
(3) *Art pattern creation by stylized layout.* The global layout of the art pattern is often determined by the specified style. The resulting art pattern is semi-automatically/automatically generated with placing graphical entities by their shapes in terms of the aesthetic conventions or spatial constraints.

3.4.1 Novel Layout Creation Based on Regular Structures

The layout with regular structures is convenient to be input. However, the resulting art pattern with regular layout looks "artificial" and "rigid". In order to generate the layout with natural forms by the computer, the researchers proposed to let the user input the regular shape first, and then transform it into a desirable "natural" appearance by applying random disturbance on it. Yessios was one of the pioneers to employ this approach to generating the stone and wood patterns [Yessios, 1979]. A regularly laid out pattern is derived first and next disturbed by randomly moving its points left or right and up or down. A decisive part of this algorithm is the random number generator, which determines a variety of structural details, as well as the degree of disturbances. The one used is based on the linear congruential formula

$$X_{n+1} = (aX_n + C) \bmod m,$$

where, the "magic numbers" X, a, C and m are assigned values in accordance with principles of numerical computing.

Such a sequence of disturbances, when applied to what may initially look like a regularly laid out brick-wall, changes it to a stone wall. Or, by applying the proper disturbances to a set of concentric circles/ ellipses, the points of the basic ellipse are disturbed in the X and/or Y directions and the wood patterns can be derived. By regulating the degree and extent of the disturbances, variable types of walls and woods can be derived (see Fig. 3.7).

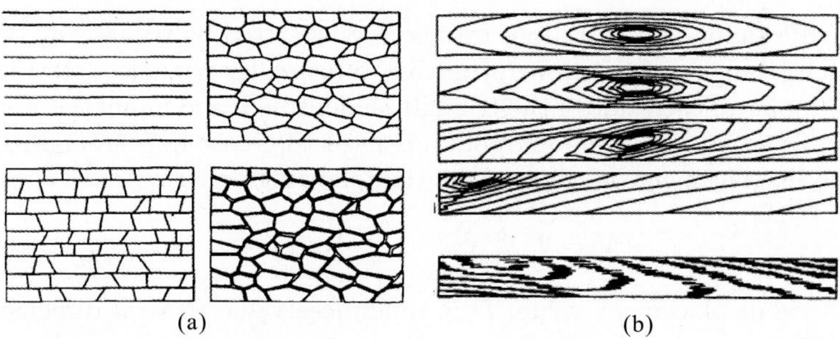

Fig. 3.7 Examples of generating stone and wood patterns by introducing disturbance on regular shapes [Yessios, 1979]. (a) Stone pattern; (b) Wood pattern. Copyright of ACM, used with permission

Miyata represented the stone wall as a combination of the joint pattern and stone textures, and explored how to generate a variety of stone wall patterns by specifying a few simple parameters regarding its layout and visual appearance [Miyata, 1990]. The joint pattern is in essence the layout of stones, represented by a "node and link model". Each node has position and link data. Each enclosed space of the joint pattern is equivalent to the space occupied by a stone in the wall. The texture of the stone is generated by using a fractal technique, and each line segment of an inter-node is subdivided recursively to generate a natural joint pattern. The average size of stone, the roughness of its surface, the variance of its size and so on, are used as input parameters. Two output data files are generated: a bump data file, which represents the stone's height data, and an attribute data file, which represents the stone's attributes. The overall process to generate the stone pattern is as follows:

(1) The basic joint pattern is generated by using the average size of a stone in the wall and the variance of its size.
(2) The basic joint pattern is deformed by relocating its nodes. After node relocation, each line segment is subdivided recursively, using the fractal method.
(3) The space occupied by each stone is found by using the link information of the basic joint pattern. The stone space is a polygon formed by nodes and line segments.
(4) The texture of individual stones is generated by subdividing the stone primitive recursively. For this, the fractal method and the roughness value of the stone are used.
(5) The stone texture is clipped by cut polygons, which are contracted polygons of the stone spaces.
(6) The height data and the attributes of the clipped stones are placed in the bump plane and the attribute plane, respectively, by the scan-line method.

The 3D shape of a stone in a wall is reconstructed by recursively dividing the patch triangles of the stone primitive into smaller triangles (see Fig. 3.8). The midpoint of each side of the triangle is identified, and a point at a vertical distance V from one of the midpoints is used to create new triangles, where V is the displacement value given by the following equation:

$$V = 2^{-(n+1)(D-1)} \times \text{Rnd} \times L,$$

where V is displacement value, D is roughness value (fractal dimension), n is subdivision level, L is edge length, Rnd is regular random number.

Fig. 3.8 The examples of resulting stone patterns with 3D effect [Miyata, 1990]. Copyright of ACM, used with permission

3.4.2 Layout Creation Integrated with Fabrication Craft

In many hand-made artworks, their art pattern is often closely related to the craft that fabricates them. While generating this kind of art pattern with the computer, it usually first lets the user specify the global layout or structure with simple graphical primitives such as points, lines/edges or faces. Then the computer will convert the input layout into the desired art pattern output in terms of the styles or features of fabrication crafts specified by the user.

One of the popular fabrication art works is the "knotwork", and many researchers explored how to generate its art pattern by the computer. For example, Kaplan and Cohen presented a technique for automating the construction of Celtic knotwork and decorations [Kaplan & Cohen, 2003]. This knotwork is analogous to closed loops of rope that cross over and under one another, becoming entangled. The loops of rope are called threads that, when entangled, form the knot. In computer-aided Celtic design, the layout of the knotwork is often represented by a planar graph, which can produce all possible knots. The underlying graph structure provides an easy, intuitive method for altering thread order via breakpoints.

In Kaplan and Cohen's system, graph edges are represented by strokes that are drawn by the user and vertices are represented by junctions. Users are allowed to draw strokes with the mouse using either the free-form or straight line styles. The system separates strokes where they intersect and culls tiny overlaps that occur due to the hand drawn nature of the strokes. Next, a set of junctions is automatically created at the endpoints of every stroke. A junction records a location consisting of the strokes that have endpoints near that location and a counterclockwise ordering, in which the strokes connect to that junction. Junctions that are close to one another are combined. After defining the layout of a knotwork by graph, the following algorithmic steps are employed to generate the resulting knotwork (see Fig. 3.9):

(1) Find the midpoint of each edge. Put crossings at each midpoint.
(2) Compute the threads that compose the knot by connecting the crossings.
(3) Inflate the threads.
(4) Calculate the overlapping order of the threads and offset their height values based on the overlapping order.

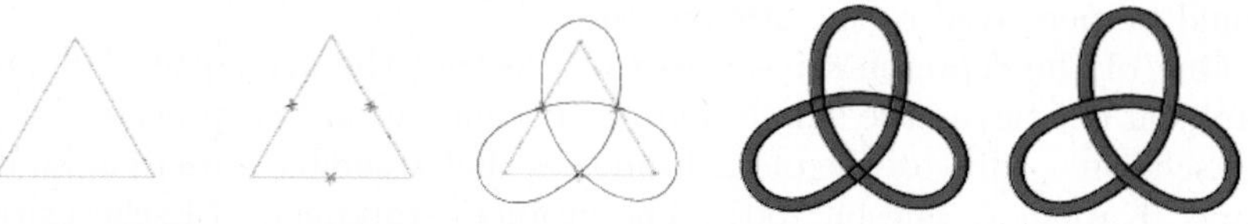

Fig. 3.9 Overview of the algorithmic steps to generate knotwork by graph [Kaplan & Cohen, 2003]. Copyright of ACM, used with permission

In addition, they also presented techniques for interweaving and attaching images to the knotwork, and techniques to encapsulate knot patterns to simplify the design process. It can help design the knotwork intuitively, quickly, and easily. Fig. 3.10 shows examples of knotwork created by the computer.

Fig. 3.10 Examples of knotwork created by the computer [Kaplan & Cohen, 2003]. Copyright of ACM, used with permission

3.4.3 Art Pattern Creation by Stylized Layout

While creating the new art patterns, the designers are often asked to employ the specified graphical entities (such as characters/text, and icons/images), which will be placed on specific objects/trajectories, or filled into a specific region, in terms of aesthetic conventions, spatial constraints, or styles. In most cases, the outline shapes of these graphical entities implicitly determine the overall layout of the resulting art patterns. Sometimes small deformational changes on the graphical entities are necessary while satisfying the requirements of the desired layout.

Inside this kind of art patterns, one of the frequently used graphical entities is "text." The text entity will be artistically deformed to place it along a specific trajectory or on a specific surface (see Fig. 3.11). The text entity can also be placed and rendered in terms of the lighting distribution and tone. If we utilize the 2D image or graphical entities to create this kind of art patterns, the deformation tolerance of the basic entities should be taken into consideration, as it is preferred that the deformed entities in the art pattern should be perceived as the original one.

One of the representative works of creating the art pattern by specific graphical entities is the simulation of "Escherization"—a process that finds an Escher-like tiling of the plane from tiles that resemble a user-supplied goal shape. [Kaplan & Salesin, 2000]. The problem statement of Escherization is: given a closed plane figure S (the "goal shape"), find a new closed figure T such that: (a) T is as close as possible to S; (b) Copies of T fit together to form a tiling of the plane.

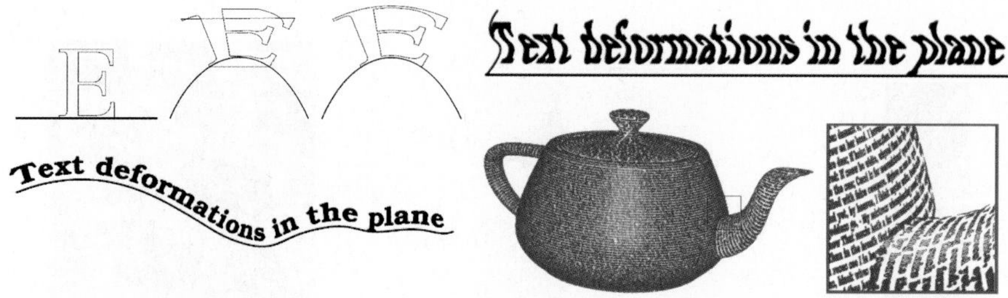

Fig. 3.11 The geometric layout of texts [Surazhsky & Elber, 2002]. Copyright of Blackwell, used with permission

Kaplan & Salesin presented a solution to the Escherization problem that is able to find reasonable-looking tiles for many real-world shapes [Kaplan & Salesin, 2000]. It works by using a simulated annealer to optimize over a parameterization of the "isohedral" tiling, a class of tiling that is flexible enough to encompass nearly all of Escher's own tiling, and yet simple enough to be encoded and explored by a computer. Fig. 3.12 gives an example of illustrating the processing pipeline of generating Escherization.

Fig. 3.12 The processing pipeline of generating Escherization [Kaplan & Salesin, 2000]. Copyright of ACM, used with permission

Later on, they extended it to solve the following dihedral Escherization problem [Kaplan & Salesin, 2004]: given closed plane figures S_1 and S_2 (the "goal shapes"), find new closed figures T_1 and T_2 such that: (a) T_1 and T_2 are as close as possible to S_1 and S_2 respectively; (b) T_1 and T_2 admit a dihedral tiling of the plane.

They augmented the representation of a tile shape with a curve that splits it into two pieces, and optimized over this new configuration space using an objective function that compares the two pieces with two goal shapes. Fig. 3.13 shows the examples of dihedral Escherization art patterns.

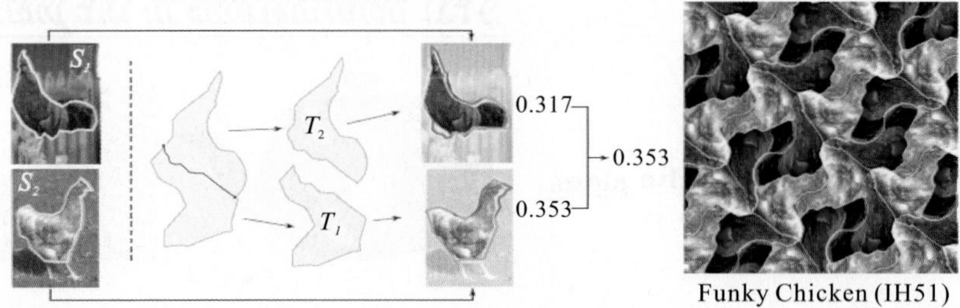

Fig. 3.13 Examples of dihedral Escherization [Kaplan & Salesin, 2004]. Copyright of ACM, used with permission

3.5 Knowledge-based Creation of Art Patterns

The researchers from computer graphic and artificial intelligence communities explored a number of knowledge-based approaches to automating the creation of art patterns by artificial intelligence techniques, including rule-based reasoning, expert systems, case-based reasoning, etc. One of the representative works comes from the research group led by Prof. Yunhe Pan at the Artificial Intelligence Institute of Zhejiang University. They successfully developed a computer-aided design system for automatic creation of art patterns, which has been widely applied in the textile industry. The major components of their systems are shown in Fig. 3.14. It collects the layout,

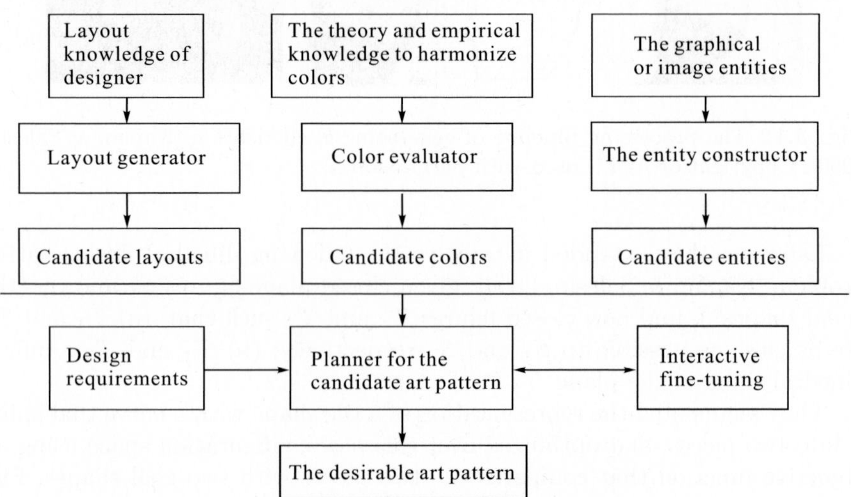

Fig. 3.14 The typical components in CAD system for automatic art pattern creation

color conventions, and knowledge from a designer. Then it employs the artificial intelligence techniques to apply them for the automatic creation of the desirable art patterns. In this section, we mainly discuss the knowledge representation and generative reasoning for automatic art pattern creation.

3.5.1 Aesthetical Knowledge Representation for Art Pattern Generation

A typical design pipeline of creating an art pattern is as follows: at first, the designer looks for the candidate graphical entities, and then makes changes on them to fit the current design requirements. Secondly, the revised entities are composed together on the canvas by the aesthetical harmony principles and layout conventions regarding spatial and visual properties for art patterns. At last, the colors and illustration techniques are applied on the composed entities to generate the resulting art patterns.

In order to create the art patterns automatically or semi-automatically, two kinds of aesthetical knowledge, layout generation and entity manipulation knowledge, should be represented and computed [Zhuge *et al.*,1997]. The layout generation knowledge is the core of art pattern creation, and consists of semantic, spatial, and visual description of layouts in art patterns. The entity manipulation knowledge depicts the allowable transformations or operations that can generate novel entities from the source ones. Aiming at the automatic creation of art patterns, we presented an integrated model for representing the knowledge of both layout generation and entity manipulation [Geng & Pan, 1999]. It is based on a symbolic matrix, and composed of three major parts:

(1) *The spatial description of entities.* The symbols in the matrix depict the spatial position of entities and geometric transformations.
(2) *The sub-layouts and their hierarchical structure in the overall layout.* It is described by the sub-matrices at different levels.
(3) *The overall description of art pattern.* It is represented by a symbolic semantic model, which includes the styles, types, templates of layout, etc.

A formalized BNF-like description of the knowledge representation scheme based on symbolic matrix is given below:

<Art-Pattern>::={<Sub-Art-Pattern>}|<Spatial-Placement-of-Entities>
        <Composition-of-Entities>
        <Aesthetic-Deformation-of-Entities>
<Sub-Art-Pattern>::=< Art-Pattern >
<Spatial-Placement-of-Entities>::={<Sub-Spatial-Placement-of-Entities>}|
        <Basic-Entities><Spatial-Position>
<Basic-Entities>::=<Sub-Art-Pattern> | <Primitive-Element>
<Primitive-Element>::=<Symbol><Identification-Number><Color>

<Spatial-Position>::=<Space-of-Layout><Location-in-layout-Space>
<Space-of-Layout>::=<Identification-Number-of-Layout-Space>
<Level-of-Layout-Space><Dimension-of-Layout-Space>
<Identification-Number-of-Layout-Space>::=<Identification-Number-of-Underlying-Matrix>
<Level-of-Layout-Space>::=<Hierarchical-Level-of-Underlying-Matrix>
<Identification-Number-of –Underlying-Matrix>::=
<Identification-Number-of–the-Parent-Matrix >
<Hierarchical-Level-of–the-Underlying-Matrix >
<Location-in-the-Parent-Matrix> | <0-for-Root-Matrix>
<Dimension-of-Layout-Space>::=<Length-of Matrix><Width-of-Matrix> |
<Length-of Matrix><Width-of-Matrix><Height-of-Matrix>
<Location-in-layout-Space>::=<x, y> | <x, y, z>
<x>::=0..Length-of-Matrix
<y>::=0-Width-of-Matrix
<z>::=0-Height-of-Matrix
<Composition-of-Entities>::=<Element-to-be-Composed><Composition-Relationship>
<Element-to-be-Composed>
<Element-to-be-Composed>::=<Composed Elements> | <Primitive element>
<Composed Elements>::=<Elements-Applied-with-Composition-Relation-ship>
<Composition-Relationship>::=<Up, Down, Left, Right> |
<Transparent, Semi-transparent, Overlapping> |
<Harmony composition such as appearing simultaneously> |
<Other conventional compositions>
<Aesthetic-Deformation-of-Entities>::=<Elements-to-be-Deformed><Deformation-Parameters>
<Elements-to-be-Deformed>::=<Primitive-Element> | <DeformedElement>
<Deformed-Element>::=<Elements-Applied-with-Deformation-Parameters>
<Deformation-Parameters>::=<Scaling-Parameters> | <Rotation-Parameters> |
<Skewing-Parameters> |...

3.5.2 Generation of Art Patterns by Synthesis Reasoning

In the automatic generation of an art pattern, the generative reasoning techniques are preferred. Therefore, Pan borrowed the reasoning concept from artificial intelligence and presented a generative inference method, called "synthesis reasoning", for the automatic creation of art patterns [Pan, 1996]. Let S be the source to be used for synthesis; SS denotes the synthesis space of potential art patterns constructed from S; C represents the constraints to be involved in synthesis reasoning; R is the resulting art pattern. The synthesis reasoning process is defined as finding R from SS in terms of the constraints C (see Fig. 3.15).

The source of synthesis, S, is composed of three parts: primitive elements, structure, and the field of influence, and can be described as follows:

$$S = \{P, M, F\}.$$

Where P is a set of primitive elements, and $P = \{p_1, p_2, \ldots, p_n\}$ means that the synthesis source consists of n primitive elements. M describes both the constructional relationship among the primitive elements and how to build up the synthesis source by them. F defines its influence intensity distribution, while S is involved in the synthesis reasoning process. Based on the primitive elements and structure, F can be accordingly decomposed into two parts, FP and FM.

$$FP = \{FP_1, FP_2, \ldots, FP_n\}, FP_i,$$

where is the influence intensity of p_i during the synthesis reasoning ($i = 1, \ldots, n$). FM describes the influence intensity of structure M for synthesis reasoning.

The synthesis space is constructed from all the synthesis sources to be involved in the synthesis process. Assuming that there are m synthesis sources with n primitive elements, the synthesis space can be represented as

$$SS = \sum_{i=1}^{m} \sum_{j=1}^{n} (FP_{ij}P_j, FM_iM_i).$$

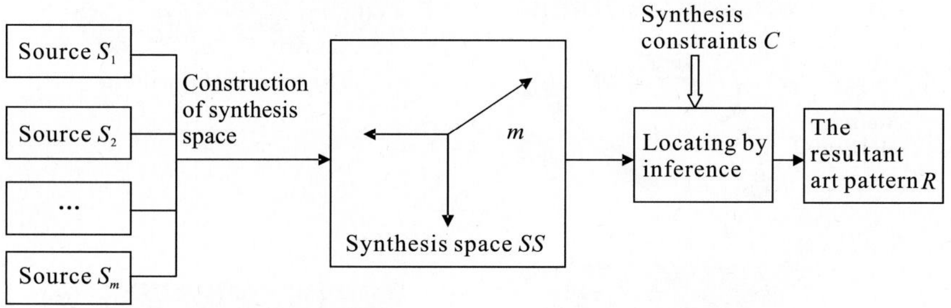

Fig. 3.15 The diagram of the synthesis reasoning process

In essence, the synthesis space can be considered as the span of two subspaces: the synthesis one for primitive elements and the others for structure. Each position in the synthesis space represents a potential synthesis result. An algorithmic diagram to create art patterns by synthesis reasoning is shown in Fig. 3.16.

Zhang *et al.* [2000, 2001] explored how to create art patterns by the synthesis reasoning scheme, and Fig. 3.17 gives an example of creating art patterns by synthesizing layout structures, graphical entities, and colors.

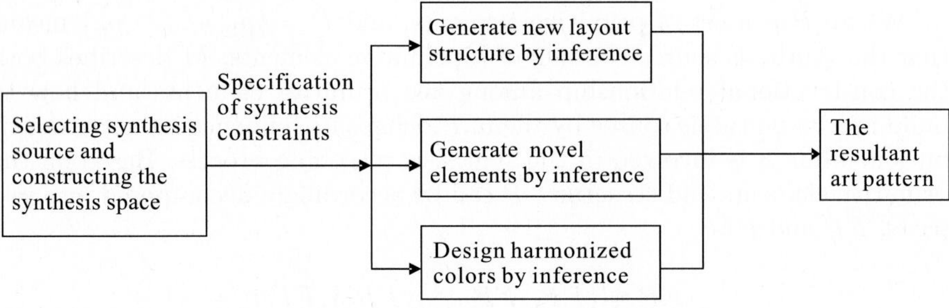

Fig. 3.16 The algorithmic scheme of creating art patterns by synthesis reasoning

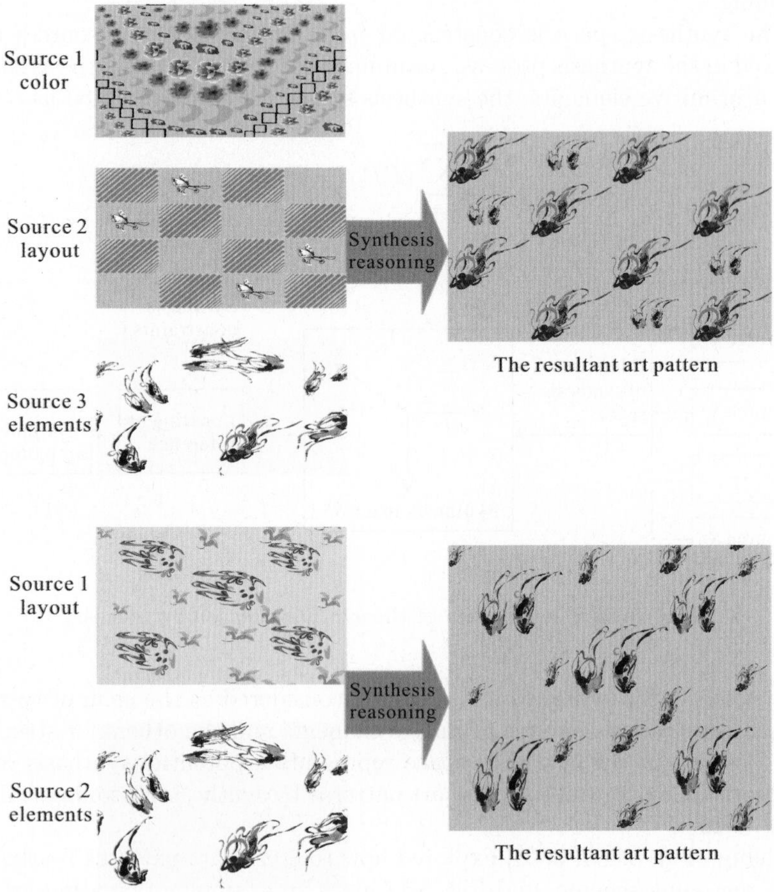

Fig. 3.17 The example of art pattern creation by synthesis reasoning [Pan *et al.*, 2002]. Courtesy of Yunhe Pan *et al.*

3.6 Summary

The application of computers in the design of art patterns provides a novel visual language and toolkit for the designer, expanding their imagination space as well as the media space for artistic presentation. From the point of view of computer aided design techniques, the computer can preform lots of the time-consuming and tedious work, and accordingly let the designer focus more on creative activities regarding art pattern generation. Besides the layout, entities, and colors, the designers also take into consideration the artistic painting effects such as water-coloring, oil-painting, etc. In the future, it may provide novel approaches to generating more sophisticated art patterns by embedding the digital painting techniques into the automatic creation of art patterns.

References

Falconer K(2003) Fractal geometry mathematical foundations and applications. John Wiley & Sons, Ltd, Chichester.

Geng WD, Pan YH(1999) Representation of generation-oriented aesthetic layout. Journal Of Computer-aided Design and Computer Graphics 11(3):193–195 (in Chinese)

Gooch B, Coombe G, Shirley P(2002) Artistic vision: painterly rendering using simple vision algorithms. In: Proceedings of the 2nd International Symposium on Non-photorealistic Animation and Rendering 83–91

Kaplan M, Cohen E(2003) Computer generated Celtic design. In: Proceedings of the 14th Eurographics Workshop on Rendering 9–19

Kaplan CS, Salesin DH(2000) Escherization. In: Proceedings of the 27th Annual Conference on Computer Graphics and Interactive Techniques 499–510

Kaplan CS, Salesin DH(2004) Dihedral Escherization. In: Proceedings of the 2004 Conference on Graphics Interface 255–262

Lu WL, Pan WH, Jiang JD(1996) Pattern-generating mechanism based on fuzzy grammar. Chinese Journal of Computers 19(8):636–640 (in Chinese)

Lu WL, Pan WH, Jiang JD(1997) A methed for 2D-shape design. Journal of Computer-aided Design and Computer Graphics 9(5) (in Chinese)

Luo XH, Wen G, Jia Y(2004) Study on the method of decorative pattern of ceramic product based on fractal theory. China Ceramic Industry 11(3):25–28 (in Chinese)

Mandelbrot BB(1982) The fractal geometry of nature. W.H. Freeman and Company, San Francisco

Meier BJ, Spalter AM, Karelitz DB(2005) Interactive color palette tools. IEEE Computer Graphics and Applications 24(3): 64–72

Miyata K(1990) A method of generating stone wall patterns. ACM SIGGRAPH Computer Graphics 24(4):387–394

Pan YH(1996) The theory of synthesis reasoning. Pattern Recognition and Artificial Intelligence 9(3):201–208 (in Chinese)

Pan YH *et al.*(2002) Intelligent CAD system for art pattern creation.Technical Report, Institute of Artificial Intelligence, Zhejiang University (in Chinese)

Stiny G(1980) Introduction to shape and shape grammars. Environment and Planning B 7(3):343–351

Suffern KG(2002) Painting with light. In: Proceedings of the 20th Annual Conference on Computer Graphics and Interactive Techniques 143–146

Surazhsky T, Elber G(2002) Artistic surface rendering using layout of text. Computer Graphics Forum 21(2):99–110

Tapia M(1999) A visual implementation of a shape grammar system. Environment and Planning B:Planning and Design 26(1):59–73

Wei BG, Pang XB, Zhu WH, Pan YH(2006) Using texture render in fractal pattern design. Journal Of Image And Graphics 11(5):689–694 (in Chinese)

Wong MT, Zongker DE, Salesin DH(1998) Computer-generated floral ornament. In: Proceedings of the 25th Annual Conference on Computer Graphics and Interactive Techniques 423–434

Yessios CI(1979) Computer drafting of stones, wood, plant and ground materials. ACM SIGGRAPH Computer Graphics 13(2):190–198

Zhang LL, Lu DM, Pan YH, Jan ZS(2000) The generation model of pattern design knowledge based on synthesis reasoning. Journal of Computer-aided Design and Computer Graphics 12(5):384–389 (in Chinese)

Zhang LL, Lu DM, Pan YH(2001) The synthetically generation of pattern element based on eigenvector. Journal of Image and Graphics, 6(6):547–551 (in Chinese)

Zhuge Y, Pan YH(1997) Knowledge representation of layout for art patterns based on computational mental image. Journal of Software 8(10):738–744 (in Chinese)

www.fractal.net.cn (2007)

4

Artistic Painting by Reference Images

The artistic painting by reference images is to convert the source input images into the corresponding paintings with the desired artistic effects. From the point of view of research methodology, the existing work can be summarized into three categories:

(1) The reference images are taken as source images, and then the artistic processing techniques (e.g., half-tone, heuristic image processing rules, empirical stroke-generation techniques, etc.) are employed to transform the reference images into the resulting painting in terms of the user specified rendering styles, and other parameters, to control the visual effect.
(2) The reference images are used to directly specify the desired visual effects or artistic features, which are extracted from reference images and then matched to that in the input source images. A computational model of feature association between input and reference images is then built, which will accordingly synthesize the resulting painting via optimization techniques.
(3) A set of reference images is used to implicitly specify the association relationship of visual effect between source and target images. Then the analogy-based learning techniques are employed to automatically convert the newly input images into the resulting painting with the desired visual effect consistent with the relationship among the reference images.

4.1 Artistic Effect Generation by Pixel-level Image Processing

The traditional image processing technique is the fundamental approach of converting the source image into the artistic painting. It can directly make the image, with the specified visual effect, by the image processing operators on its pixels. At the level of aesthetic meanings, the visual perception of the resultant image is equal to that in the source image in terms of color/tone, texture, shape, etc.

4.1.1 Artistic Processing via Digital Half-toning

Digital half-toning, also known as spatial dithering, is a classical image processing technique. The half-toning process is based on phychophysical characteristics of the human vision system. The eye integrates luminous stimuli over a solid angle of about 2 degrees. This means that human beings actually perceive the average intensities corresponding to small solid angles in our visual field. Half-toning algorithms exploit this phenomenon, effectively redistributing the state of the pixels in such a way that the average intensity in small areas of the dithered image is approximately the same as that of the original image. Therefore, in a sense of visual perception, the images with continuous tone can be simulated and approximated by the careful arrangement of individual displayed cells with properly selected colors or elements. At the beginning, half-toning research was mainly focused on the grey image, and the resultant image processed by half-toning was approximated by displayed cells filled with black and white colors only. Fig. 4.1 is an example of artistic half-tone on a grey image.

(a)

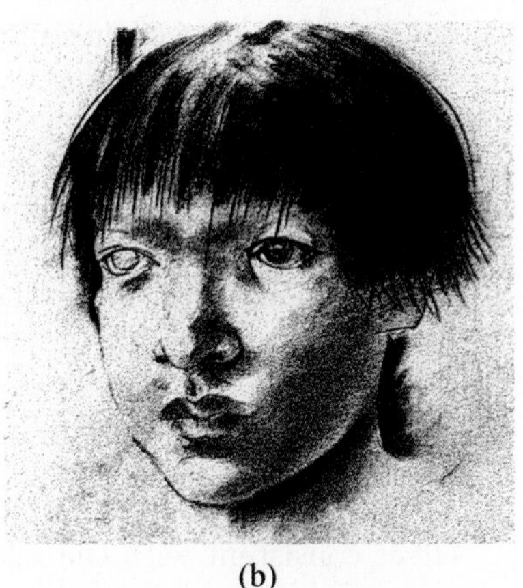

(b)

Fig. 4.1 Artistic half-tone on grey image [Luiz & Jonas, 1991]. (a) Source image; (b) The resultant image. Copyright of ACM, used with permission

The standard bi-level half-toning was soon generalized and extended to the multi-colored half-toning [Ostromoukhov & Hersch, 1999], in which the color image is converted into a barycentric combination of color intensities into a multi-color non overlapping surface coverage. The elements to be filled into the individual displayed cells are also extended to include non-standard colors, symbols, texture patterns, etc.

Some researchers further investigated how to mimic the special effects using half-toning, for example, Buchanan [1996] showed that half-toning methods can be altered to control the look and stylization of the images by parameters such as the region size and shape, and the approximation function. Freudenberg *et al.* [2002] applied the half-tone screen in texture space. This enables many effects to be generated, including indication mapping and individual stroke lighting. Its simulated rendering styles ranging from engraving, with lighting-dependent line width, to pen-and-ink style drawings using prioritized stroke textures.

4.1.2 Artistic Processing with Heuristic Rules

Image processing algorithms works well from the point of view of mathematics, however, there is no explicit relationship between its parameters and the artistic visual effects. This makes it difficult to precisely predict the resulting effects of the mathematical image processing operator under different parameters. In order to achieve the desired artistic effects, it usually needs lots of experiments to iteratively refine the relevant parameters. Therefore, the researchers started analyzing and summarizing the conventions and empirical rules of artwork design techniques, the rules of using color, artistic styles, how to convey the specified means, etc., and built a set of empirical rules for artistic processing. These rules are evaluated by a series of experiments, and then are embedded into a variety of image processing algorithms, which can explicitly and directly generate the desired visual effects without any experiments in advance. An artistic processing pipeline with heuristic rules is shown in Fig. 4.2.

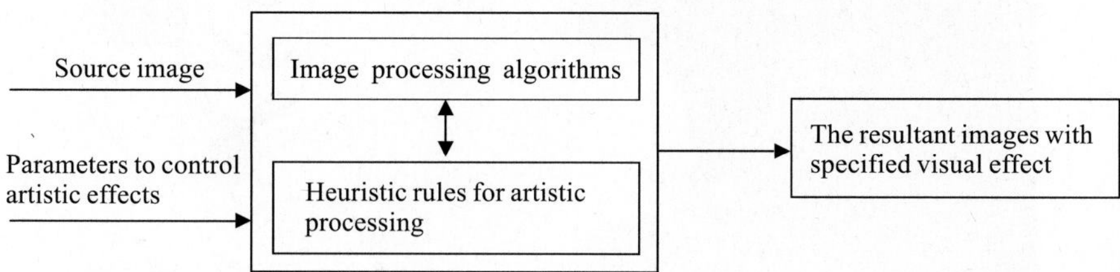

Fig. 4.2 The artistic processing pipeline embedded with heuristic rules

The heuristic rules are heavily dependent on the artistic styles, and here we mainly discuss the rules for sketching, engraving and cubist styles.

4.1.2.1 Shape and texture preserving for sketching

The sketching style is to generate an effect similar to a sketch with a pen or pencil, such as pen-and-ink. The major goal of sketching from images is to represent the intrinsic object's detail. Wang *et al.* [2004b] implemented the concept of self-quotient images (SQI), which is able to minimize the influence of shadow in an image and allows shape information to be used effectively. They also developed an edge-preserved low-pass filter to preserve the important features of an image. They employed the binary form of a SQI which can remove most of the object's irrelevant information, including the color, and keep only the shape and texture elements. The threshold controls how much texture and shape information should be displayed. The threshold is calculated by:

$$H = \text{average}(Q) \times h,$$

where Q is the SQI image and h is a controllable parameter. Different values of h give different threshold. h is usually chosen between 0.5 and 1.5. Fig. 4.3 is an example of sketching from images.

(a) (b)

Fig. 4.3 Example of sketching from images [Wang *et al.*, 2004b]. (a) Source image; (b) The sketching style. Copyright of John Wiley & Sons, Ltd., used with permission

4.1.2.2 Facial engraving

Engraving is among the most important traditional graphical techniques. It first appeared in the fifteenth century as an illustrative support for budding book-printing, but very quickly became an art in its own right. Ostromoukhov [1999] proposed a facial engraving system that can make a digital engraving from a photographic image with reasonable quality in a relatively short time. It is based on the analogy between the "universal" copperplate which imitated the true copperplate engraving technique and conventional dithering. The art of digital copperplate engraving may be presumed to be the art of building appropriate threshold structures. He developed the basic technique for building separate engraving layers (threshold structures) which roughly follow the features of the original image, as well as the rules for merging them together. These layers are superimposed to form various cross-etching and smooth transitions between different parts of the artwork rendered by different engraving layers. The resulting threshold structure is equilibrated in such a way that it generates a visually uniform output from a uniform input signal of any intensity. When applied on an input digital photo using a standard dithering algorithm, such a threshold structure generates a reasonably faithful reproduction, which imitates traditional engraving. Fig. 4.4 is an example of digital facial engraving.

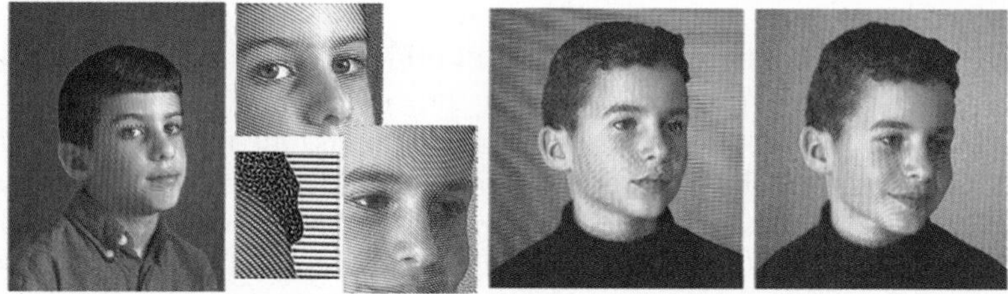

Fig. 4.4 Example of digital facial engraving [Ostromoukhov, 1999]. Copyright of ACM, used with permission

4.1.2.3 Cubist style simulation

Cubist art is an artwork by composing elements of a scene taken from multiple points of view. Paradoxically, the cubist style conveys a sense of motion without assuming temporal dependence between views. Collomosse and Hall proposed an approach to produce a cubist style painting using a set of two-dimensional images [Collomosse & Hall, 2003]. Salient features are first identified within the image set, such as eyes, noses, and mouths as compositional elements, and then geometrically distort them to produce the more angular forms common in cubist art. Finally, the composition is rendered to give a painterly effect using an automatic algorithm. The composition of each output image is stochastically decided, and so a potentially original rendering is possible with each new pass over the same input set. Fig. 4.5 shows an example of this cubist style.

Fig. 4.5 Cubist style generation from images [Collomosse & Hall, 2003]. Copyright of IEEE, used with permission

4.2 Converting Images into Artistic Painting by Strokes

From the point of view of content and meanings, an artwork consists of two components: one is the objective content abiding by the physical laws; the other one is the subjective meanings motivated from the perception of a human audience. The aforementioned pixel-level image processing operators are performed on the original pixel-represented objects in the source image, and it is difficult to embed the subjective meanings into the resultant paintings. However, human artists can easily insert their subjective imaginations into their artwork by their strokes. Therefore, the stroke-based artistic painting is proposed to transform the input images into the target paintings. A stroke-layer is built between the source images and the target painting (Fig. 4.6). It is composed of strokes, and each stroke has its individual parameters and attributes. These strokes are distributed in an aesthetic order. From the aesthetic point of view, this stroke layer is equal to the source image in terms of its abstraction or aesthetic principles, including semantics, logics, style, visual effects, etc. Human artists can interact with this stroke layer, and add their subjective understanding of the world into it by editing and revising the relevant strokes, such that the desired subjective meanings can be embodied in the resultant painting. Fig. 4.7 is a diagram of stroke-based artistic painting from the point of view of logical processing.

Fig. 4.6 An example of stroke-based artistic painting from images [Hertzmann, 2002]. (a) Source image; (b) The Stroke layer; (c) The resultant painting. Copyright of ACM, used with permission

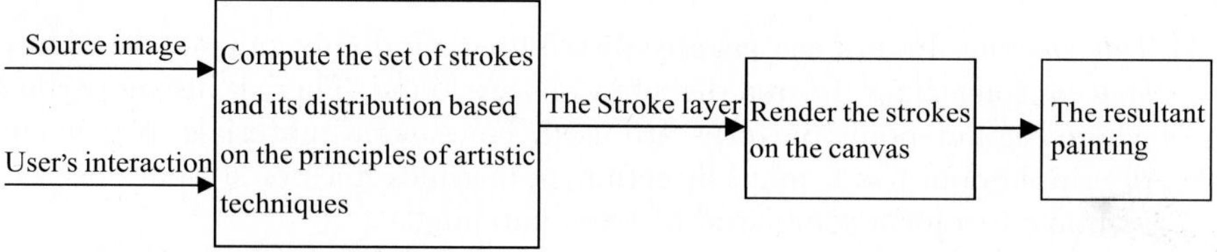

Fig. 4.7 A diagram of artistic painting from images

It is obvious that the key point in stroke-based artistic painting is how to build the stroke layer, which is properly matched to the source image in terms of the aesthetical principles and content. For the time being, a classical solution to compute the stroke layer is to transform it into an optimization problem, in which an energy function is defined to describe the differences between the stroke layer and the source image. Accordingly the stroke layer is built by minimizing the energy function. A typical definition of this energy function, *E(I)*, is described below [Hertzmann *et al.*, 2001; Hertzmann, 2003]:

$$E(I) = E_{\text{match}}(I) + w_{\text{abs}} E_{\text{abs}}(I),$$
$$E_{\text{match}}(I) = \sum_{(x,y)\in I} \| I(x,y) - S(x,y) \|^2,$$

where I is the input source images, $I(x,y)$ is the pixel value at (x,y) in the source image I, $S(x,y)$ is the stroke that passes through the (x,y) position on the canvas. $E_{\text{abs}}(I)$ is the number of strokes in the source image I. W_{abs} is a scalar weighted parameter to control the level of abstraction in a painting style.

In the following subsections, the stroke-based artistic painting for classical art forms will be discussed respectively.

4.2.1 Image-based Stippling Drawing

Stippling is an illustration technique that can create drawings by using mostly dots. Typically, several tens of thousands of dots are manually arranged to generate a single drawing. Many small dots of ink are carefully placed on paper to approximate different tones. Stipples are placed closer together to form dark regions and further apart to form lighter regions. The stipples must be placed evenly, yet randomly, so that the human eye does not see spurious patterns that are not a part of the intended impression. The stipples may vary in size and occasionally shape to convey subtle details. In general, the following degrees of freedom are used in stipple drawings [Deussen *et al.*, 2000].

(1) *Dot spacing.* Points are usually distributed randomly but nearly evenly spaced; sometimes jittered distributions are found. There is also a method where regular point patterns are used. For several materials, placement of stipple dots has a main direction, sometimes lines of stipple dots are combined to form some kind of cross hatching.
(2) *Dot size.* Point sizes may vary for lighter and darker regions. The largest dots are up to about twice as large as the smallest dots.
(3) *Dot shape.* The shape of the individual dots can vary, while in others very regular shapes are found. Sometimes special paper is used for additional variations.
(4) *Inverse drawing.* If very dark regions have to be generated, an inverse process is performed. The background is drawn in black, and white stipples are used.

Stippling is a powerful and widely used illustration method. It has significant artistic merit independent of its utility. The stipples can represent fine detail and texture with little cost in complexity. Stippling is particularly good at clearly representing smooth, rounded objects without sharp edges and so is often used in medical and archaeological texts. The only reason which prevents stipple drawings from being used much more widely is their expensive creation. To generate a good and large stipple drawing is a very time-consuming process. An artist creates a stipple drawing by locally placing dots. He/she has to take care that no macroscopic patterns arise, which is done by using a reduction lens during drawing. The lens allows the artist to directly observe the tonal value of a region by optical reduction. A dot which is set in the wrong position must be removed by a cutting knife, often large areas are destroyed by some misplaced dots. It is a highly time-consuming process until the result is reached.

One of the fundamental features of a good stipple drawing is that the stipples are *well-spaced*, that is, the stipples do not clump together, leave uneven voids, or form unwanted patterns. Therefore, the key point in computer-generated stippling is how to produce a good distribution of stipples in terms of the input reference image. A typical approach to generate the distribution of stipples is based on the centroidal Voronoi diagrams [Deussen *et al.*, 2000; Hertzmann, 2003].

An ordinary Voronoi diagram is formed by a set of points in the plane called the *generators* or *generating points*. Every point in the plane is identified with the generator which is closest to it by some metric. The common choice is to use the Euclidean L_2 distance metric:

$$|X_1 - X_2| = \sqrt{(x_1 - x_2)^2 - (y_1 - y_2)^2},$$

where $X_1 = (x_1, y_1)$ and $X_2 = (x_2, y_2)$ are any two points in the plane. The set of points in the plane identified with a particular generator form that generator's Voronoi region, and the set of Voronoi regions covers the entire plane.

A *centroidal* Voronoi diagram has the interesting property that each generating point lies exactly on the centroid of its Voronoi region. The centroid of a region is defined as:

$$C_i = \frac{\int_A x\rho(x)\mathrm{d}A}{\int_A \rho(x)\mathrm{d}A},$$

where A is the region, x is the position and $\rho(x)$ is the density function. For a region of constant density ρ, the centroid can be considered as the center of mass.

Fig. 4.8 gives the examples of a general Voronoi and a centroidal Voronoi diagram.

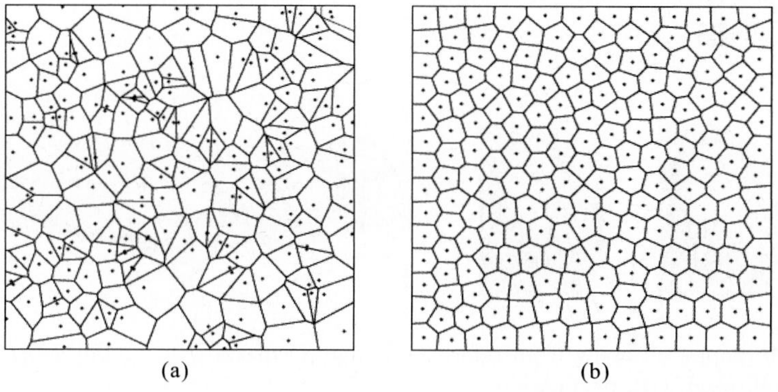

Fig. 4.8 General and centroidal Voronoi diagrams [Secord, 2002]. (a) General Voronoi diagram; (b) Centroidal Voronoi diagram. Copyright of Blackwell, used with permission

A centroidal Voronoi diagram is a minimum-energy configuration in the sense that it minimizes

$$\int_A \rho(x)|C_i - x|^2.$$

Practically speaking, a centroidal distribution is useful because the points are well spaced in a definite sense. The Lloyd's [1982] method is usually employed as a solver to generate a centroidal Voronoi diagram from any set of generating points. It is an iterative algorithm, and can be stated as [Secord, 2002]:

Algorithm: Lloyd's method
While generating points x_i not converged to centroids **do**
  Compute the Voronoi diagram of x_i
  Compute the centroids C_i
  Move each generating point x_i to its centroid C_i
End While

The iteration is repeated until it converges. In practice, the movement of the points is stopped if the differences are below a given threshold.

Deussen *et al.* [2000] presented the first system to create stipple drawings by generating an initial dot set, which is then processed by a relaxation method based on Voronoi diagrams. They introduced an interactive stipple editor similar to painting systems that were used to generate such drawings. The approach computes an initial dot distribution by a specialized half-toning technique by the given reference image. This dot set is modified automatically or semi-automatically to generate a final distribution similar to a stipple drawing. Fig. 4.9 shows an example of the simulated stipple drawing by reference image.

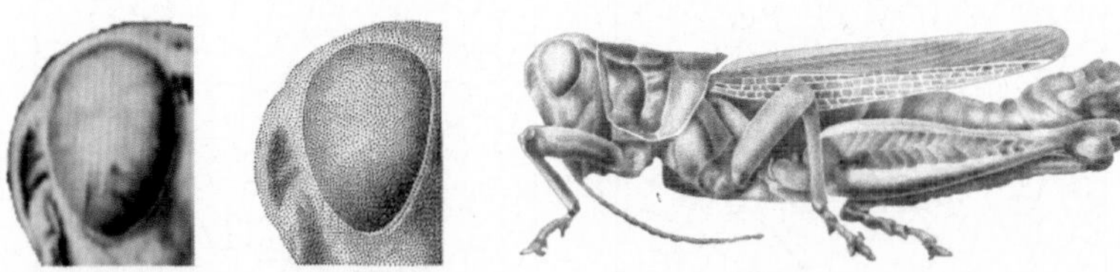

Fig. 4.9 Stipple drawing from reference image [Deussen *et al.*, 2000]. Copyright of Blackwell, used with permission

Secord [2002] presented an alternate stippling style and algorithm, by varying the dot spacing instead of the dot size. The idea is to define a spatially varying density function $\kappa(p)$ that determines how dense the stippling should be in different parts of the image. This density function is directly derived from the tones of the reference image $T(p)$, that is,

$$\kappa(p) = 1 - T(p)/m,$$

where m is the max grey level in T. The new energy function is:

$$E(I) = \sum_{p \in I} L_p^i \kappa(p) \left\| p - C_i \right\|^2 = \sum_{p \in I} L_p^i \kappa(p) \left((p_x - C_{ix})^2 + (p_x - C_{iy})^2 \right),$$

where $L_p^i \in \{0,1\}$ is a binary labeling of pixels: if $L_p^i = 1$, then the pixel p has been assigned to centroid i. Every pixel is assigned to exactly one centroid.

$$\sum_p L_p^i = 1.$$

The labeling step is the same, but the centroids are now re-estimated as:

$$C_i = \frac{\sum_p L_p^i \kappa(p) p}{\sum_p L_p^i \kappa(p)}.$$

This summation can be accelerated by precomputing sums of $\kappa(p)$.

Later on, Hiller *et al.* [2003] further extended the stipple drawing method by replacing the dots with arbitrary shapes. Lloyd's Method is also extended to enable small objects to be positioned on a place in a visually pleasing form. This allows us to generate new illustration styles. Fig. 4.10 gives an example of extended stipple drawing.

Fig. 4.10 A stipple drawing of fish by distributing various types of objects [Hiller *et al.*, 2003]. Copyright of Blackwell, used with permission

4.2.2 Image-based Mosaic and Stained Glass Simulation

The ancient art of mosaic is among the oldest, most durable, and most functional art forms, which have a history of more than 5,000 years. Mosaics are designs and pictures formed from the juxtaposition of small tiles of stones, terracotta, or glass. Mosaics derive much of their splendor from scale. Upon close scrutiny, the skillful placement of tiles and the intricate tessellations that define the work are prominently visible. On a larger scale, the tiles fit together like jigsaw pieces into an abstract puzzle, forming a unique and striking blend of colors, designs, and images. The interplay between these different levels of abstraction and our ability to resolve the "big picture" from the individual tiles is what makes mosaics visually compelling. The aesthetic pleasure of a mosaic results from the reduction of the visual data and the manual arrangement of important features. Some of the fundamental features are contour lines, colors, shapes, and positions of the basic primitives. Fritzsche *et al.* [2005] summarized the characteristic features of mosaics as follows:

(1) Constant splices between the tiles.
(2) Fundamental colors with stochastic variation in tone and luminance values.
(3) Slight variation of the tile's size and shape.
(4) Tiles are arranged along feature lines of the underlying master image.
(5) Smooth changes in tile orientation.

Hausner [2001] presented a formal problem statement of generating mosaic artwork by reference image: given a rectangular region I^2 in the plane R^2, and a vector field $\Phi(x, y)$ defined on that region, find N sites $P_i(x_i, y_i)$ in I_2 and place N squares of side s, one at each P_i, oriented with sides approximately parallel to $\Phi(x_i, y_i)$, such that all squares are disjointed and the area they cover is maximized.

Hausner employed a modification of the known Lloyd's method [1982] to approximate centroidal Voronoi tessellation and distribute quadratic tiles in a mosaic like arrangement. The rectangular region covers a colored image, and each square will be uniformly colored, representing the part of the image it covers. The direction field Φ usually tends to align tiles with edge features in the reference image. A good tile size is calculated as follows: for an $h \times w$ pixel image with n tiles, this yields tiles with sides of $d = \delta\sqrt{h \times w/n}$ pixels. The factor $\delta < 1$ accounts for packing inefficiencies due to variations in Φ.

However, Hausner's method reflects oversimplification and approximation, which prevents the user's input and restricts high quality output (Fig. 4.11). Elber and Wolberg [2003] improved this by establishing a tessellation in terms of the principal features and strokes in a digital image. The feature curves are first extracted from the image, and the offset curves are computed to delimit rows of rectangular mosaic tiles. In order to solve the self-intersection problem, the offset curves are trimmed by Voronoi diagrams that are computed using a Z-buffer. Finally, composition rules are applied to merge these tiles into an intricate jigsaw that conforms to classical mosaic styles. Fig. 4.12 shows the offset curves and the tiles along them. Fig. 4.13 gives the simulated mosaic art work from a reference image.

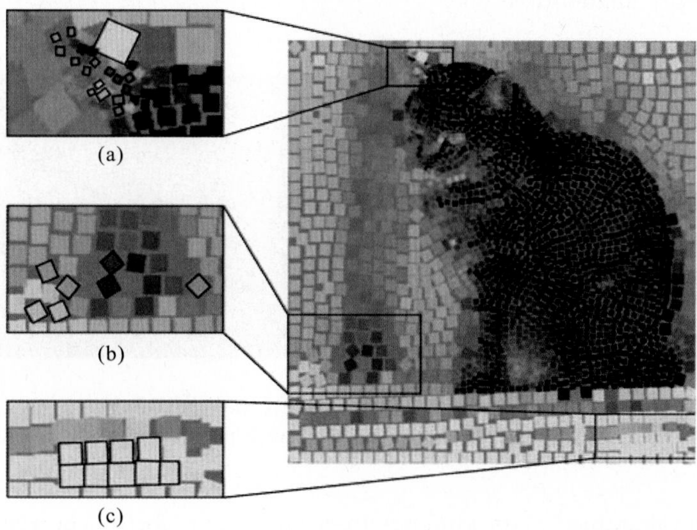

Fig. 4.11 Artifacts in the synthetic mosaic generated by Hausner [Hausner, 2001]. (a) Wrong tiles sizes too close together; (b) Random misalignment of tiles; (c) Unwanted tile overlapping. Copyright of ACM, used with permission

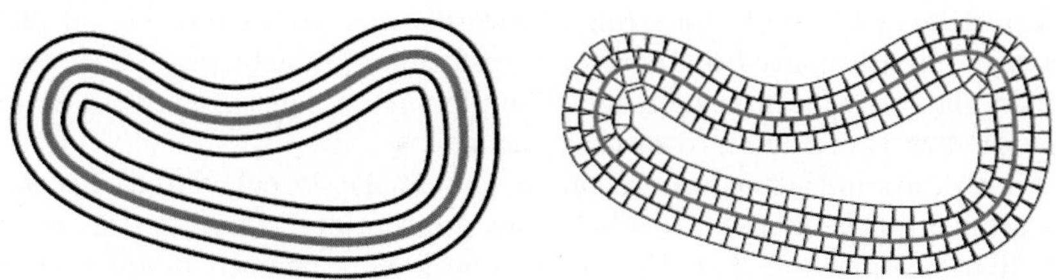

Fig. 4.12 Offset curves and the tiles arrangement [Elber & Wolberg, 2003]. Copyright of Blackwell, used with permission

A disadvantage of this method is that the resulting regular tile arrangement appears quite artificial, especially since the influence of the features and offset curves are not restricted (see Fig. 4.13). Therefore, Fritzsche *et al.* [2005] presented an interactive tool to efficiently create pleasing synthetic mosaics. It enables the user to arrange tiles of various shapes and sizes, especially for the small mosaic tiles. The user controls the distribution process by adding contour lines and directional information. Tiles can be sized or shaped in order to better approximate the master image features. It also allows for variations, and the resulting mosaics often have the appearance of a traditionally handcrafted one.

Fig. 4.13 Reference image and its mosaic effect [Elber & Wolberg, 2003]. Copyright of Springer Science and Business Media, used with permission

Medieval stained glass windows are a stylized art form. The visual effect of stained glass looks similar to that of mosaics. However, their concerns are different, and the key issues in designing a stained glass window are the tile boundaries and colors. The process for building a stained glass window involves designing a composition first, or *cartoon*, indicating the arrangement of tiles. The cartooned shapes are cut out of colored glass, assembled, and fixed in place with lead solder, or *leading*. The key points in simulating stained glass from a reference image are how to align tile edges with image edges, and to form tiles, which may be straightforwardly cut from glass. Mould [2003] presented an automated method for transforming an arbitrary image into a stained glass version of that image. The pipeline in constructing the stained glass window is divided into several stages.

Firstly, an initial segmentation of the image is calculated. Secondly, this segmentation is used to obtain an appropriate tiling by the erosion and dilation operators (see Fig. 4.14): one having smooth boundaries and approximately convex pieces, and lacking excessively large or excessively small pieces. Thirdly, for each tile, a color is properly chosen for it. Finally, a displacement map is applied to a plane, representing the leading and irregularities in the glass, and the resulting stained glass is rendered. Fig. 4.15 shows the examples of stained glass from reference images.

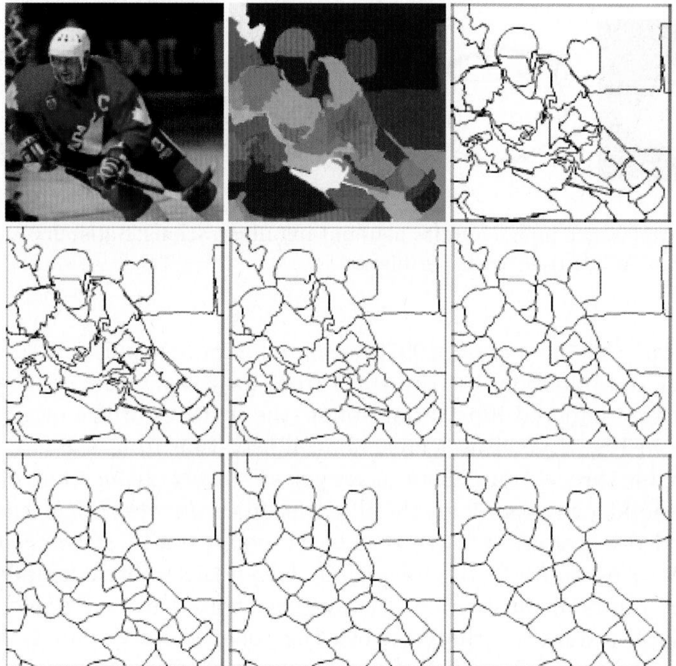

Fig. 4.14 The original image, segmentations, manipulated with erosion operators with different radiuses [Mould, 2003]. Copyright of ACM, used with permission

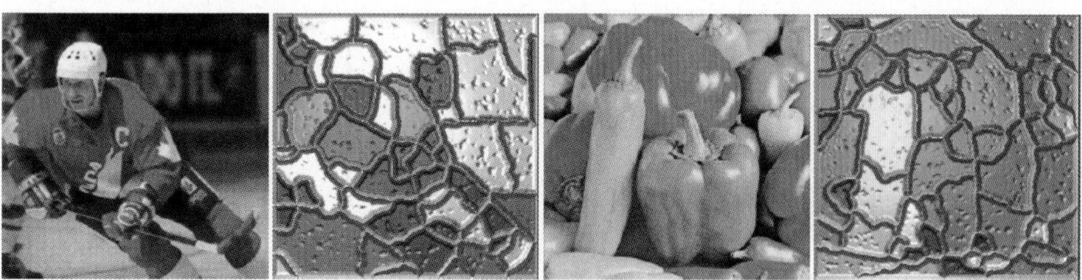

Fig. 4.15 Stained glass image pairs [Mould, 2003]. Copyright of ACM, used with permission

4.2.3 Image-based Pen-and-ink Illustration

Salisbury *et al.* [1994] proposed the first system to interactively create pen-and-ink illustration. They also used the reference image to assist the user to set up the parameters (such as tone, silhouette, orientation of stroke texture, etc.) to better generate the resulting pen-and-ink illustration. Fig. 4.16 shows the examples of generating pen-and-ink illustration from reference image.

Fig. 4.16 Reference image and its pen-and-ink illustrations [Salisbury *et al.*, 1994]. Copyright of ACM, used with permission

Later on, Salisbury *et al.* [1997] presented a more sophisticated system to create pen-and-ink-style line drawings from grey-scale images in which the strokes of the rendered illustration follow the features of the original image. As shown in Fig. 4.17, a user creates an illustration from a reference image by specifying three components: a grey-scale *target image* that defines the desired tone at every point in the illustration, a *direction field* that defines the desired orientation of texture at every point, and a *stroke example set*, or set of strokes, to fill in the tone areas. Given these three components and a scale for the final illustration, the system creates an *orientable texture*—generated procedurally—that conveys the tone, texture, and forms of the surfaces in the scene. An illustration is composed of one or more such layers of orientable textures, allowing an illustration to be rendered with several, potentially overlapping, types of strokes.

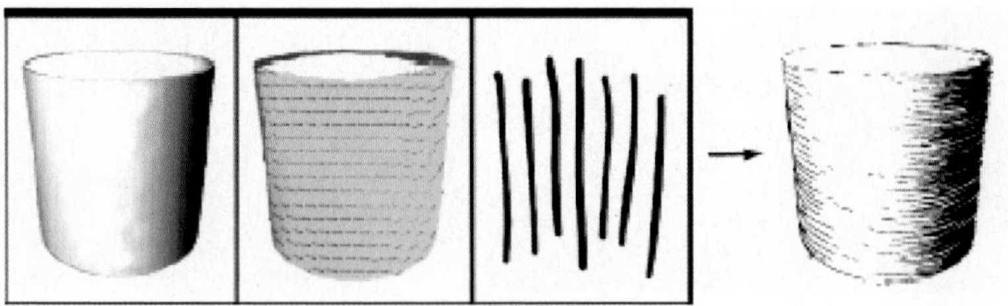

Fig. 4.17 From left to right: tone, direction, a stroke example set, and a resulting illustration [Salisbury *et al.*, 1997]. Copyright of ACM, used with permission

In implementation of Salisbury's system, a *stroke* is a mark to be placed on the page. Each stroke is *oriented*, in the sense that it can be rotated to any angle to follow the direction field where it is placed. The *stroke example set* is a collection of strokes, all drawn with respect to the vertical orientation, that serve as prototypes for the strokes in the final image. By aligning the direction field with surface orientations of the objects in the image, the user can create textures that appear attached to those objects instead of merely conveying their darkness. The result is a more compelling pen-and-ink illustration than that was previously possible from 2D reference imagery (see Fig. 4.18). One of the remaining key issues is how to place strokes in the illustration so that the tone of the illustration "matches" that of the original tone image. Matching is necessarily approximate, because the illustration is purely black and white, whereas the tone image is grey-scale. To facilitate this approximate matching, each stroke is thought of as adding darkness to a *region* of the illustration. One way of spreading the darkness of a stroke over a region is to blur the image of the stroke when considering the effect of its darkness. To measure the progress of a current illustration towards the reference image, a blurred version of the illustration is compared with the tone image. The blurring consists of applying averaging filters, of variable sizes, across the illustration, with the size increasing with the target lightness in a region. The diameter of the blurring filter is the same as the average inter-stroke distance required to achieve the target lightness.

Fig. 4.18 Pen-and-ink illustration with orientable textures [Salisbury *et al.*, 1997]. Copyright of ACM, used with permission

However, practical illustrations are somewhat different from illustrations generated using other previous systems. For clarity, dictionary illustrations express only the important characteristics of objects. As a result, many features of an object are simplified or omitted and fewer strokes are used. Kim *et al.* [2001] presented an approach to making more natural-looking pen-and-ink illustrations with fewer user strokes. Its concise pen-and-ink illustration generating procedure consists of three steps (see Fig. 4.19): (a) Boundary extraction; (b) Input of user strokes; (c) Generation of artificial strokes. In the first step, the boundaries of objects are extracted and smoothed by using the Bezier curve. User strokes are then drawn by the user to generate artificial strokes. In the final step, we use stroke morphing techniques to generate artificial strokes.

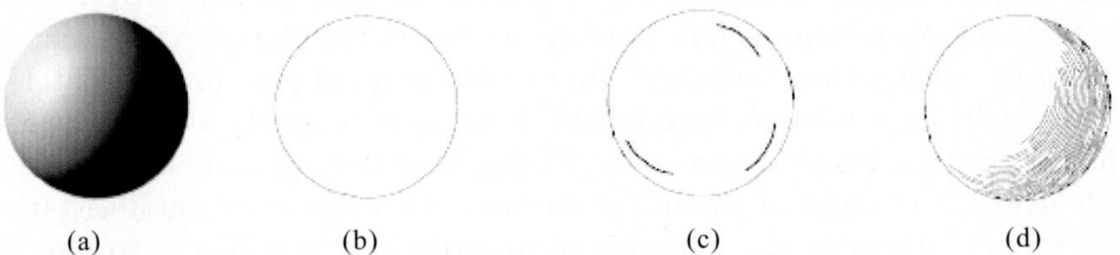

Fig. 4.19 Illustration generating procedure [Kim *et al.*, 2001]. (a) An original image; (b) Boundary extraction; (c) User stroke; (d) Illustration result. Copyright of IEEE, used with permission

From the technical point of view, stroke morphing is a technique used to automatically generate artificial strokes based on given user strokes. Two kinds of methods: flow-oriented stroke and shape-oriented stroke morphing are implemented in Kim's system (see Fig. 4.20). Flow-oriented stroke morphing is suitable when strokes are intended to show flow or direction, like smoke or water. Shape-oriented stroke morphing, on the other hand, is suitable when strokes are influenced more by shape than flow, so this can be applied to drawing leaves or feathers. Fig. 4.21 shows some examples of pen-and-ink illustration based on stroke morphing.

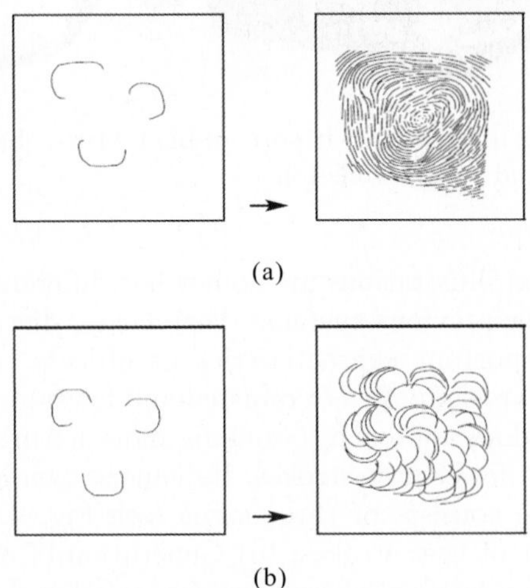

Fig. 4.20 Two types of stroke morphing methods [Kim *et al.*, 2001]. (a) Flow-oriented stroke morphing; (b) Shape-oriented stroke morphing. Copyright of IEEE, used with permission

Fig. 4.21 Pen-and-ink illustration based on stroke morphing [Kim *et al.*, 2001]. (a) Reference image; (b) Strokes given by the user; (c) The resultant illustration. Copyright of IEEE, used with permission

4.2.4 Image-based Pencil Drawing

There are two typical approaches to create pencil drawings from reference images. One is to implicitly recover or specify the pencil drawing strokes in terms of the tone values of the reference image, and then render the final pencil drawing based on the simulation model of interactive drawing (see Chapter 2). The other one is to employ the image processing and visualization techniques to directly simulate the visual effect of pencil drawing in terms of the empirical conventions.

In the stroke-based approaches, Sousa and Buchanan [1999] employed the blender and eraser model to render the tone values using one pencil hardness (degree). Certain portions of the drawing are smudged using blenders, a kneaded eraser is then used to lighten the areas where there are highlights. Its implementation is based on a two-stage rendering pipeline. The first stage is to evaluate pencil and paper model for each paper location (x, y) (correspondent to the reference image pixel location) on the polygonal shape for the pencil point (the smallest pencil point is equal to one pixel). The intensity $i_{(x,y)}$ is used to adjust the pressure p applied to a single pencil resulting in the correct amount of lead material deposited at paper (x, y). The pressure p applied to the pencil is the only parameter that changes at this stage and it is given by $p = 1.0 - i_{(x,y)}$. It is based on traditional pencil rendering methods to create tone values. If the user provides additional pressure p_a, then the final pressure calculation p is scaled as $p = p \times p_a$. In Fig. 4.22, pencil strokes are interactively defined over the photograph after the automatic evaluation of the pencil and paper model. The second stage is to adapt the blender and eraser model to an interactive illustration system. The user interactively controls the blender and the eraser model. For each paper location (x, y) (correspondent to the reference image pixel location (x, y)), the blender and eraser model is evaluated with *mpdc* from the blender's and eraser's point located at (x, y). The pressure distribution coefficients (*mpdc* and $vpdc_i$) have values equal to 1.0. The pressure applied to blenders/erasers is also adjusted according to $i_{(x,y)}$. In this case, $p_{i_{(x,y)}} = i_{(x,y)}$, this means that in order to achieve a lighter intensity more pressure is required.

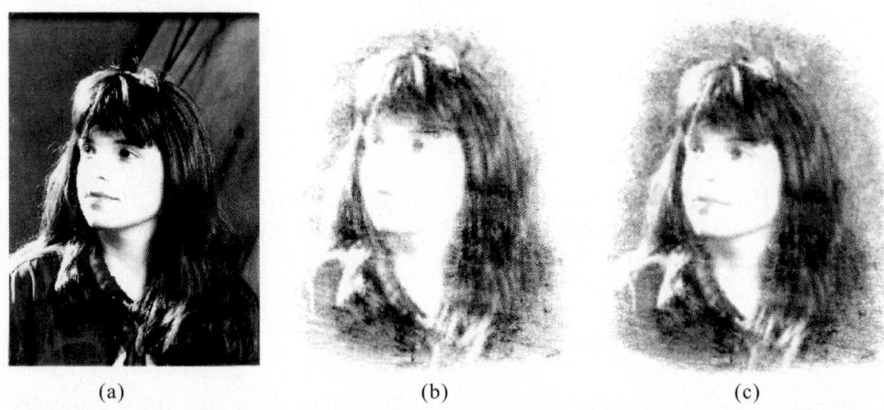

Fig. 4.22 (a) High contrast photograph of Patricia; (b) Automatic rendering using 6H pencil followed by interactive rendering with strokes interactively applied using medium-soft pencils applied with light pressure; (c) Smudging the darker tones, the background plane of the photograph, and lightly smudging the shadows and some of the face lines. Kneaded eraser lightly applied to emphasize the highlights [Sousa & Buchanan, 1999]. Copyright of IEEE, used with permission

The advantages of this approach are obviously. The rendering pipeline is very close to the real pencil drawing process. However, its strokes are limited to the simple "point" shape, and it is difficult to generate the sophisticated pencil drawings. Therefore, Durand *et al.* [2001] proposed a more general stoke model for the image-based stroke drawings. The strokes are modeled using a local threshold structure (threshold texture), which has a flat histogram and is represented as a grey-level texture map. Threshold textures can be either acquired by scanning real stokes or modeled directly. Individual strokes are described by a skeleton, a reference to a stroke threshold texture, and a target tone for strokes excluded from automatic modeling. A stroke skeleton is represented by a poly-bezier curve, along which the threshold texture is warped. The equilibration of threshold structures is performed by the merged probability of the histogram of overlapping strokes using the *max* mode. The histogram of a stroke as a probability density function $p(x) = 1$, for $x \in\{0,1\}$. The cumulative density function (corresponding to the cumulative histogram) is:

$$p(x) = 1,\ x \in \{0, 1\},\quad p[X \leqslant x] = \int_0^x p(\varepsilon)\mathrm{d}\varepsilon = x.$$

The main assumption is that there is no correlation between strokes. This is reasonable given the texture of our strokes and their irregular placement.

The probability and cumulative density of two overlapping strokes p_1 and p_2 are:

$$p_{\max(12)}(x) = p_1(x) \times P_2[X \leqslant x] + p_2(x) \times P_1[X \leqslant x] = 2x,$$
$$p_{\max(12)}[X \leqslant x] = x^2.$$

This formula can be generalized to the histogram of n overlapping strokes:

$$p_{\max(i=1,\ldots,n)}(x) = nx^{n-1},\quad P_{\max(i=1,\ldots,n)}[X \leqslant x] = x^n.$$

A flat is then obtained by multiplying each value x by the corresponding cumulative density

$$P_{\max(i=1,\ldots,n)}(x) = nx^{n-1}.$$

Equilibration can thus be performed by applying a power function depending on the number of overlapping strokes. Fig. 4.23 shows the examples of a flat histogram of overlapping strokes under the *max* mode.

It provides a controllable simulation of the variation of pencil pressure or stroke thickness traditionally used in tonal modeling. It provides the user with freedom on the creative and aesthetic side. The user can specify smudging and control the amount of detail over each part of the drawing. As shown in Fig. 4.24, the user provides a reference photograph Fig. 4.24(a), edits the tones, draws strokes and specifies a precision map Fig. 4.24(b) while interactively viewing the drawing Fig. 4.24(c).

In the approach of image processing and visualization, LIC (line integral convolution), a texture based vector field visualization technique, is usually employed to generate the desired pencil drawing [Mao *et al.*, 2001; Huang & Li, 2003]. Given a 2D vector field represented as a regular Cartesian grid, the LIC algorithm takes as input a white noise image of the same size as the vector field and generates an output image wherein the texture has been locally blurred in the direction of the vector field. There is a one-to-one correspondence between the grid cells of the vector field and the pixels of input and output image. To decide the value for each pixel in the output image, a local streamline passing through the corresponding grid cell in the vector field is generated. Then a low-pass filter kernel is defined on the local

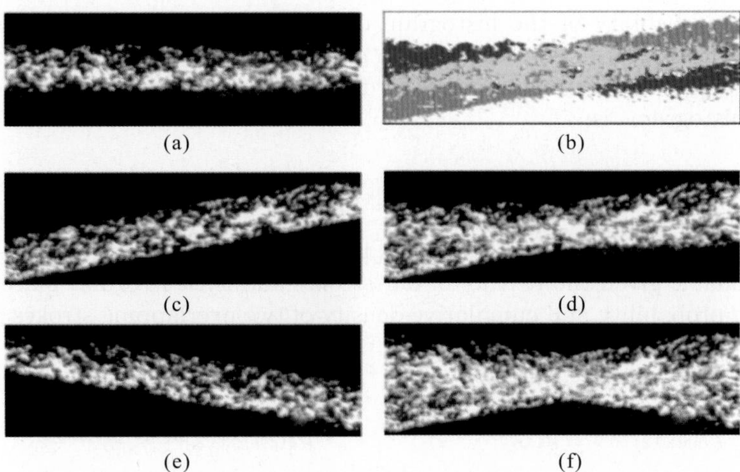

Fig. 4.23 A flat histogram of overlapping strokes under the *max* mode [Durand *et al.*, 2001]. (a) Stroke 1; (b) Overlapping of stroke 1 and stroke 2 (yellow); (c) Stroke 2; (d) Max(stroke1, stroke 2); (e) Stroke 3; (f) Max(stroke1, stroke 2, stroke 3). Copyright of Springer Science and Business Media, used with permission

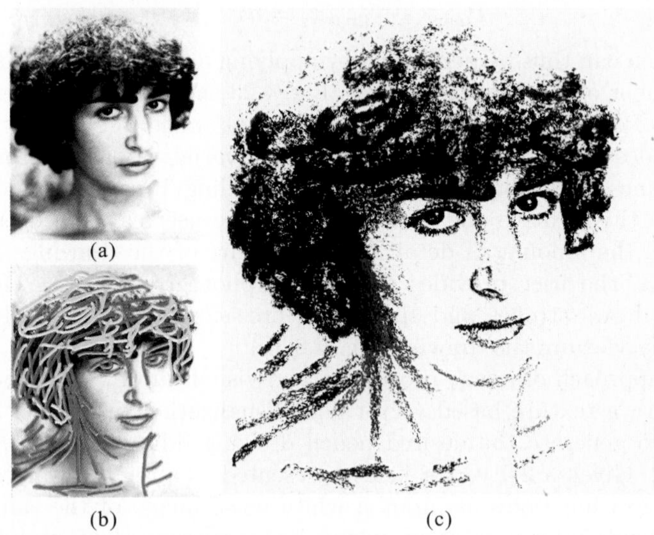

Fig. 4.24 Basic features of Durand's interactive drawing system [Durand *et al.*, 2001]. Copyright of Springer Science and Business Media, used with permission

streamline and the pixels lying on the streamline in the input image are convoluted with it. Since an LIC image is obtained by low-pass filtering the input image along the streamlines of a vector field, we can see traces along streamlines. On the other hand, the intensities of pixels within any local area vary randomly as the input image to the LIC is a white noise. Such similarity, between the LIC textures and the real pencil drawings, suggests to us that the tone of pencil drawings can be imitated with LIC textures to avoid performing complex and time consuming physical simulations. That is, a pencil drawing style image can be simply generated by taking a white noise matching the target tone of the subject and a vector field specifying the directions of strokes as the input to the LIC algorithm. The typical steps of a LIC algorithm, to convert the source image into the pencil drawing effects, are as follows [Huang & Li, 2003]:

(1) Use color-based image segmentation to subdivide the source image into different regions.
(2) Each region is considered as a feature region, whose boundary is extracted.
(3) Apply image moment functions and texture analysis to obtain the feature's geometric attributes.
(4) White noise image is generated from the original image.
(5) Apply the feature's geometric attributes to generate the vector field.
(6) Use LIC to generate the final rendering.

Yamamoto *et al.* [2004] further extended the LIC technique to generate the colored pencil drawing. It reproduces color images with custom inks to automatically select the best color set for individual regions in a source image. Then layers of stroke image for each color are generated and superimposed with the KM optical compositing model. The major algorithmic steps are below:

(1) Segment the source image into different regions and decide two best colors for each region.
(2) For each of the two colors chosen in Step 1, calculate its density required for building the target color. The density is calculated in a pixel-by-pixel manner. The result consists of two density values (one for each color) for each pixel. Two layers of grey scale images are subsequently generated with the density of each color.
(3) Generate noise images for the two layers respectively. Each region of the resulting noise images is a white noise with its pixels being either white or the color of the region with a probability proportional to the density value.
(4) For each layer, define a vector field representing the stroke directions.
(5) Apply LIC to the vector fields and noise images to generate two layers of stroke images.

(6) Modify the stroke images with the given paper model to obtain two improved stroke images.
(7) Blend the two layers with the KM model to finally produce the finished colored pencil drawing.

The users are also allowed to specify regions and to customize the color set for a specified region interactively. Fig. 4.25 shows the examples of employing different color sets to generate the colored pencil drawings from the same reference image. Fig. 4.26 shows an example of a image-based colored pencil drawing with custom colors.

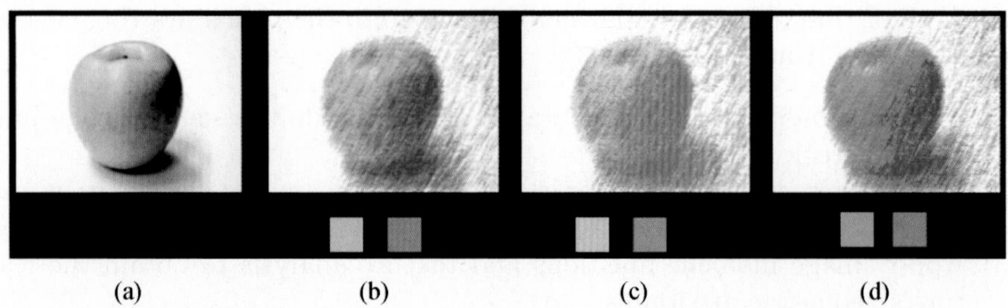

Fig. 4.25 Colored pencil drawing resulting from the same reference image with different color sets [Yamamoto *et al.*, 2004]. (a) Reference image; (b) Result 1; (c) Result 2; (d) Result 3. Copyright of IEEE, used with permission

Fig. 4.26 Image-based colored pencil drawing from reference images [Yamamoto *et al.*, 2004]. Copyright of IEEE, used with permission

4.2.5 Image-based Oriental Painting

Chinese painting stresses the notion of "implicit meaning" in which painters use a minimum amount of strokes to express their deepest feelings. Chinese landscape and figure paintings are the two major themes of Chinese painting. Chinese landscape painting is often based on the hemp-fiber and axe-cut texture strokes. The long hemp-fiber strokes express relatively smooth surfaces, while short hemp-fiber strokes indicate a more wrinkled surface. The axe-cut texture strokes best depict earthen forms and hills. It can also effectively describe angularly shaped rocks of crystalline quality and sedimentary rocks displaying layered structures. The simulation of different rock textures are controlled by changing stroke distribution, ink density, stroke length, etc. A typical pipeline to paint Chinese landscape with texture strokes is as follows [Way & Shih, 2001]:

(1) An artist begins to visualize a land formation with external contours, which define the overall shape. Internal contours are added to imply folds on the slopes, to reveal the position and direction of the ridge, and determines its volume.
(2) After the internal contours are defined, texture strokes are applied in the area.
(3) The texture stroke is used to symbolize the rock information.
(4) Finally, the brush moves along the path of the stroke and deposits ink on the canvas.

Regarding the oriental painting from reference images, the user merely specifies the contour and relevant painting parameters in terms of the reference image, the system will accomplish the remaining painting process. Fig. 4.27 shows an example of a reference image and its corresponding oriental painting.

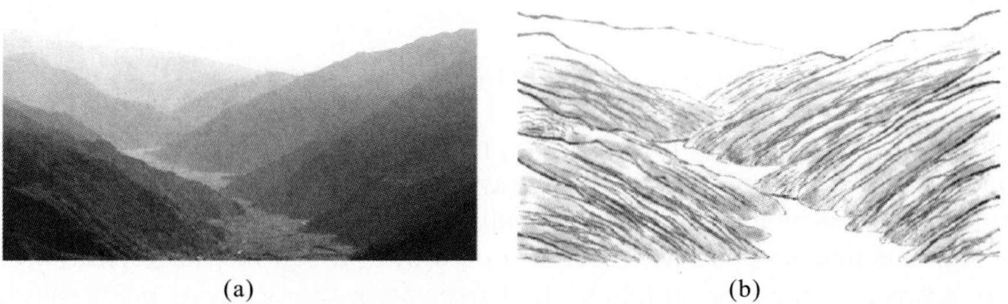

Fig. 4.27 Interactive oriental painting from reference images [Way & Shih, 2001]. (a) Reference image; (b) The oriental painting based on hemp-fiber texture strokes. Copyright of Blackwell, used with permission

The corresponding oriental painting is based on the axe-cut texture strokes.

The figure painting heavily depends on the painter and viewer. Users are responsible for component figuration and stroke specification. Therefore, Way *et al.* [2001] proposed a data-driven approach to generate the portrait painting from reference images. A database of different components together with their styles is established, and each component contains both figuration and intelligence of stroke skills. Brush movement and the ink depositing strategy are defined and saved in our components database. The component definition methodology consists of four steps:

(1) Define the component figuration by imitating existing paintings, actual photographs, or by user's origination.
(2) Specify each stroke with the necessary stroke mechanisms.
(3) Define geometric feature points for this component. It is defined to control component deformation, which occurs on primary elements or strokes.
(4) Define expression feature points for this component if necessary. Despite controlling the deformation, an expression feature point is for optional and expressional purposes.

The reference image is used to facilitate the structural design. The composition process comprises of the following steps:

(1) Draws assistant cross lines to determine the facing direction.
(2) Computes the component proportions.
(3) Determines the lip length.
(4) Refines the facial shape according to the lips length. Expand or contract the cheek width.
(5) Refines the component geometry according to scenography.

After the automatic drawing process, the user is allowed to conduct three refinements: geometrical refinement, expression refinement, and universal refinement.

4.2.6 Image-based Colored Painting

The work on an image-based color painting can be dated back to 1990. Haeberli [1990] proposed a painting system that can interactively convert the source image into the colored painting. A simple interactive program is implemented to allow the user to operate on a source image. The basic interactive technique is to follow the cursor across the canvas, point sample color of a stored image at the location of the cursor, and then paint a brush stroke of that color. Each stroke is described by a collection of attributes, including:

(1) *Location.* Position of the brush stroke.
(2) *Color.* The RGB and Alpha color of the stroke.

(3) *Size.* How big the stroke is.
(4) *Shape.* The look of the brush stroke.

By changing the size, direction and shape of brush strokes, many different representations of a single photographic image may easily be created.

The major advantage of Haeberli's colored painting method is that the user can have better control of the resultant painting. Its limitation is also obviously: it needs lots of manual input. Therefore, the researchers started looking for the automatic/semi-automatic approach to convert the reference images into the colored painting. The typical one is to generate the color painting directly over the entire image in terms of the visual features. For example, Curtis *et al.* [1997] presented a semi-automatic method to convert the source image into watercolor effect. The user interactively chooses the colored pigments that matches the source image. The system then computes the distribution of colored pigments and adds new strokes of specified pigments to approximate the desired color by the trial-and-error method. Fig. 4.28 is an example of converting a source image into a watercolor effect.

(a)

(b)

Fig. 4.28 Converting source image into a watercolor effect [Curtis *et al.*, 1997]. (a) Source image; (b) The resultant watercolor painting. Copyright of ACM, used with permission

Hertzmann [2003] proposed a system that can simulate the embossing painting effect. A "raw" color image is produced by compositing the brush strokes. A height map is assigned to each stroke, and a height field for the painting is produced by rendering the brush strokes textured with the height maps. The final painting is rendered by bump-mapping the painting's colors with the height map (see Fig. 4.29).

Shiraishi and Yamaguchi [2000] presented an automatic painterly rendering method that can synthesize an impressive image with a handcrafted look from a source image. The color difference image is first obtained by taking the differences between the local source images and stroke colors. The image momentum of the color images are then computed to generate

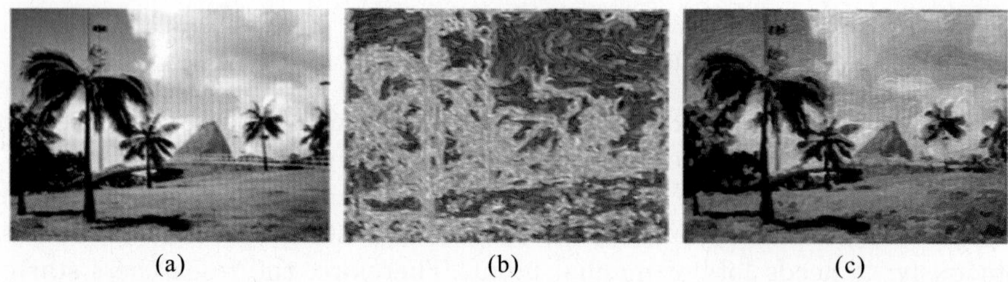

(a) (b) (c)

Fig. 4.29 Embossing painting effect from source image. (a) Source image; (b) Height map; (c) Painting with lightingc [Hertzmann, 2002]. Copyright of ACM, used with permission

rectangular brush strokes approximating the local regions of the source image with suitable locations, orientation, and sizes. The resultant image is composited with smaller strokes at the details while its flat regions are painted with larger ones. The density is controlled by a dithering method with space-filling curves. The painting process starts from the larger strokes and finishes with the finer ones. Fig. 4.30 shows the example of converting a reference image into a colored painting in terms of image momentum.

(a) (b)

Fig. 4.30 Colored painting based on image momentum [Shiraishi & Yamaguchi, 2000]. (a) Source image; (b) The resultant painting. Copyright of ACM, used with permission

However, these computer painterly rendering algorithms use very simple brush strokes over the entire image, and the resultant images tend to appear mechanical in comparison to hand-made work. In order to improve the artistic quality of the resultant painting effect, two typical divide-and-conquer strategies are employed to separate the source image into different layers, or extract the regions of interest by the "vertical" separation and the "horizontal" segmentation respectively. In the vertical separation approach, the reference image is separated into many layers in terms of simplification or abstraction principles. The automatic/semi-automatic painting methods are individually applied on each layer. The final painting is "vertically" composited from the interim painting of all layers. In the horizontal segmentation approach, the reference image is analyzed and segmented by the visual features such as depth and colors in terms of the conventions and principles of colored painting. In each segmented region, the computer automatically computes the basic parameters of strokes such as position, color, size, orientation, etc., and render the resultant painting according to the stroke parameters. The final painting is a "horizontal" composition of interim painting of all segmented regions.

A typical algorithmic pipeline on the "vertical" separation is shown in Fig. 4.31. The most representative work of this approach comes from Hertzmann [1998]. He observed that an artist would often begin a painting as a rough sketch, and go back over the painting with a smaller brush to add details. Therefore, he presented a technique of painting an image with multiple brush sizes in terms of the principle that each brush can only capture the details which are at least as large as the brush size. The resultant painting is built up in a series of layers, starting with a rough sketch drawn with a large brush. The sketch is painted over with progressively smaller brushes, but only in areas where the sketch differs from the blurred source image. The brush sizes are expressed in radii $R_1, \ldots, R_m$, and each interim layer of image, L_p, is generated by blurring the source image. Blurring is performed by convolution with a Gaussian kernel of standard deviation $f_\sigma L_p$, where f_σ is a constant factor. The initial canvas is a constant color image, and the algorithm then proceeds by painting a series of layers, one for each radius, from largest to smallest. Fig. 4.32 shows examples of painting with different sizes of brushes.

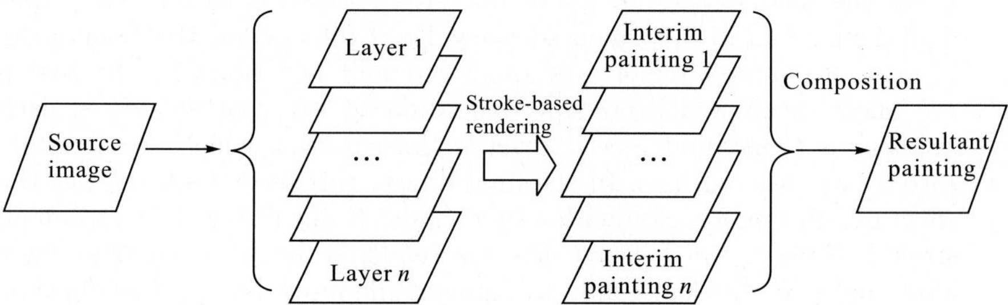

Fig. 4.31 The algorithmic pipeline for the "vertical" separation approach to colored painting

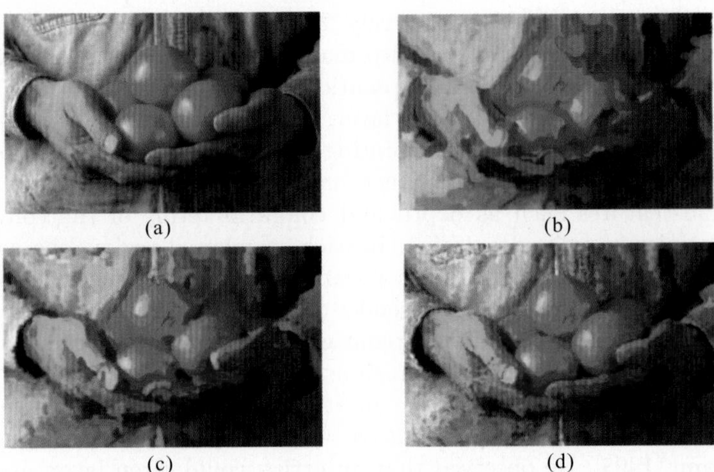

Fig. 4.32 Painting with three brushes. (a) A source image; (b) The first layer of a painting after painting with a circular brush of radius 8; (c) The image after painting with a brush of radius 4; (d) The final image, after painting with a brush size of 2. [Hertzmann, 1998] Copyright of ACM, used with permission

In the "horizontal" segmentation approach, the key points are how to extract the regions of interest from the source images and how to calculate the position, orientation, color, and the size of strokes in each segmented region. From the point of view of the visual features used for segmentation, the existing relevant work can be classified into the following methods:

(1) *Color painting by intensity and depth.* Gooch *et al.* [2002] presented a method that takes a raster image as input and produces a painting-like image composed of strokes. It works by segmenting the image into features, finding the approximate medial axes of these features, and using the medial axes to guide the brush stroke creation. The input digital image is first segmented using flood filling, and the boundaries of each segmented region are smoothed and any holes in the region are filled. Then a discrete approximation to the central axis of each segment is found and pieced together into tokens, which are spatially sorted into ordered lists. In the final image, this second sorting has the effect of painting a region with a single large stroke instead of many small strokes. Finally, the brush paths are rendered as brush strokes. They also employed the depth map to segment the input image. The depth is used as another information channel to the segmentation process. Objects are first differentiated using the depth, and these objects are further decomposed using intensity variation. This technique is chosen because depth tends to be quite good at resolving object-object interactions, but

poor at choosing how to lay strokes across a surface. Fig. 4.33 shows an example of a colored painting based on a depth map.

(a) (b) (c)

Fig. 4.33 A colored painting based on depth segmentation [Gooch *et al.*, 2002]. (a)Source image; (b) Depth image; (c) The resultant painting. Copyright of ACM, used with permission

(2) *Color painting by object detection.* Johan *et al.* [2004] presented a color painting technique that first detects the objects-to-be-rendered from the input image, and then generates strokes for each object according to the painting rules. Its major algorithmic steps are as follows:

- *Edge detection.* Edge detection is to find the boundary of objects. The edges in the input image are detected by Canny's algorithm [1986]. After the edges are detected, a distant image, whose pixels contain the distance to the nearest edge, is created, and the Voronoi diagrams are accordingly created by drawing cones with their apexes at the edge pixels on the screen. The vector field of stroke directions that follow the orientation of the nearby edges is generated by the direction perpendicular to the gradient of the distance image.
- *Object detection by image segmentation.* Image segmentation is to partition an image into meaningful regions. In many cases, each region is closely related to the object in the image, so it is employed to detect the objects in the input image. The input image is segmented using a simple approach, which generates regions by connecting neighboring pixels of similar colors. That is, a seed pixel is selected randomly from the input image, and the region is grown by successively connecting the neighboring pixels whose color differences to the seed pixel are below the user-specified threshold. The input image is segmented by repeating this process until all pixels are classified into specific regions. Two neighboring regions with similar average colors are merged into a single larger region. Small regions resulting from the segmentation process are then regarded as showing the details of the objects that are to be used in the detailed painting.

- *Simulation of the painting styles.* A painting style is defined as a set of parameters for controlling the properties of the generated strokes. The properties of strokes are defined as direction, width, length, average interval between strokes, and the maximum fluctuation of stroke direction. The direction of strokes can be determined by a constant direction specified by the user, or the direction of the vector field that follows the edge direction. The other parameters are interactively specified by the user. The color of the stroke is set to the color at the starting point in the input image. However, in order to avoid unnatural color, the average color of the pixels in the region is set as the color of the stroke if the difference between the color at the starting point and the average color exceeds a user given threshold value.
- *Color diffusion.* In order to render the generated strokes, considering the pigment-based features, the proposed method first approximates the strokes with sampling points, and then diffues their colors to nearby pixels considering the diffusion direction and features (edges) of the input image. The final color of a pixel is computed by weighted averaging of the colors that reached that pixel and the color of the paper. The basic idea of the color diffusion process is to diffuse two types of weights: weight of color and weight of shape. The weight of color is used to calculate the color of each pixel in the output image, which is affected by the roughness of the paper. The weight of shape determines the diffusion area, which is affected by the distance from the sampling point and the roughness of the paper.
- *Stroke rendering.* A stroke is rendered by performing the color diffusion process for all sampling points that approximate the stroke. The shape of a stroke is defined to be the union of the diffused areas of all the sampling points. The weight of the color of a stroke at a pixel is defined as the maximum weight of color values that reached the pixel. The output image is created by weighted averaging the colors of all strokes and the paper.

(3) *Segmentation by visual attention.* DeCarlo and Santella [2002] employed the eye-tracking device to capture the visual attention and identified the meaningful elements of this structure using a model of human perception and a record of a user's eye movements in looking at the source image. The resultant painting is a line-drawing style using bold edges and large regions of constant color. A summary of the process used to transform an image is as follows: (a) Instruct a user to look at the image for a short period of time, obtaining a record of his eye movements. (b) Disassemble the image into its constituents of visual form using visual analysis (image segmentation and edge detection). (c) Render the image, preserving the form predicted to be meaningful by applying a model of human visual perception to the eye-movement data. The fundamental principles behind the attention based image segmentation are that: each time we direct our

gaze and attention to an image, our visual intelligence interprets what we see by performing sophisticated inference to organize the visual field into coherent regions; to group the regions together as manifestations of meaningful objects; and to explain the objects' identities and causal histories. Once the identified object is in place, the remaining issue is to direct these resources of style to preserve meaningful visual form, while reducing extraneous detail. Visual form describes the relationship between pictures of objects and the physical objects themselves. Painterly abstraction can cue visual form heuristically by emphasizing parts and boundaries in an image through techniques such as aligning brush strokes perpendicular to the image gradient (see Fig. 4.34). Santella and DeCarlo [2004] also validated that such an abstraction will direct your attention to its most meaningful places and allow you to understand the structure there without conscious effort.

Fig. 4.34 A source image (1024×688), fixations gathered by the eye-tracker, and the resulting line drawing [DeCarlo & Santella, 2002]. Copyright of ACM, used with permission

4.3 Artistic Transfer of Color and Texture from Reference Images

Color distribution and texture structure are the two important components of the visual effect of an image. Given an artistic image or painting as a reference example, the input source image can be converted into the desired visual effects by imposing the reference images's color or texture characteristics on it. It is a popular approach to inheriting the given visual effects or artistic features from the specified image.

4.3.1 Artistic Transfer of Color

The problem statement of color transfer can be described as: given a reference image T and a source image S, the target color distribution is specified by T. The processing of color transfer is to create a new image S' from S, such that the cognition content of S' is the same as that of the source image S, and the color distribution of S' is coherent with that in the reference image T.

For the time being, a typical solution of color transfer is that: a color space is selected to make a statistical analysis of the color distribution of S and T, and then a mapping relationship model M_c between the color distribution of S and T is built. At last, the source image S is converted into the resultant image S' in terms of the mapping relationship model M_c. The key points in this approach include how to choose a best fit color space and how to build the mapping relationship model M_c. Reinhard *et al.* [2001] chose the $l\alpha\beta$ color space, which minimizes correlation between channels for many natural scenes. It assumes that the human visual system is ideally suited for processing natural scenes. Their main algorithmic steps of color transfer, based on $l\alpha\beta$ color space, are as follows:

(1) The source and reference images are converted into $l\alpha\beta$ color space from the RGB color space by the following equations:

$$\begin{bmatrix} L \\ M \\ S \end{bmatrix} = \begin{bmatrix} 0.3811 & 0.5783 & 0.0402 \\ 0.1967 & 0.7244 & 0.0782 \\ 0.0241 & 0.1288 & 0.8444 \end{bmatrix} \begin{bmatrix} R \\ G \\ B \end{bmatrix}, \quad \begin{bmatrix} L_{\log} \\ M_{\log} \\ S_{\log} \end{bmatrix} = \begin{bmatrix} \log L \\ \log M \\ \log S \end{bmatrix},$$

$$\begin{bmatrix} l \\ \alpha \\ \beta \end{bmatrix} = \begin{bmatrix} \frac{1}{\sqrt{3}} & 0 & 0 \\ 0 & \frac{1}{\sqrt{6}} & 0 \\ 0 & 0 & \frac{1}{\sqrt{2}} \end{bmatrix} \begin{bmatrix} 1 & 1 & 1 \\ 1 & 1 & -2 \\ 1 & -1 & 0 \end{bmatrix} \begin{bmatrix} L_{\log} \\ M_{\log} \\ S_{\log} \end{bmatrix}.$$

(2) In $l\alpha\beta$ space, the means and standard deviations for each axis are computed separately. The mapping relationship model M_c is built by substracting the means of data points in the source image S first, and then the data points comprising the synthetic image are scaled by factors determined by their respective standard deviations. This transformation makes the resulting data points have standard deviations that conform to the reference image, and the transformation equations are as follows:

$$l^* = l - l^S, \qquad l' = \frac{\sigma_l^t}{\sigma_l^s} l^*;$$

$$\alpha^* = \alpha - \alpha^S, \quad \alpha' = \frac{\sigma_\alpha^t}{\sigma_\alpha^s} \alpha^*;$$

$$\beta^* = \beta - \beta^S, \quad \beta' = \frac{\sigma_\beta^t}{\sigma_\beta^s} \beta^*.$$

(3) The averages computed from the reference image T are added back to $l'\alpha'\beta'$ previously computed, and then the resultant values in $l\alpha\beta$ color space are converted back into RGB color space by the following equations:

$$\begin{bmatrix} L_{\log} \\ M_{\log} \\ S_{\log} \end{bmatrix} = \begin{bmatrix} 1 & 1 & 1 \\ 1 & 1 & -1 \\ 1 & -2 & 0 \end{bmatrix} \begin{bmatrix} \frac{\sqrt{3}}{3} & 0 & 0 \\ 0 & \frac{\sqrt{6}}{6} & 0 \\ 0 & 0 & \frac{\sqrt{2}}{2} \end{bmatrix} \begin{bmatrix} l \\ \alpha \\ \beta \end{bmatrix},$$

$$\begin{bmatrix} R \\ G \\ B \end{bmatrix} = \begin{bmatrix} 4.4679 & -3.5873 & 0.1193 \\ -1.2186 & 2.3809 & -0.1624 \\ 0.0497 & -0.2439 & 1.2045 \end{bmatrix} \begin{bmatrix} L \\ M \\ S \end{bmatrix}, \quad \begin{bmatrix} L \\ M \\ S \end{bmatrix} = \begin{bmatrix} 10^{L_{\log}} \\ 10^{M_{\log}} \\ 10^{S_{\log}} \end{bmatrix}.$$

Fig. 4.35 shows an example of color transfer based on $l\alpha\beta$ color space.

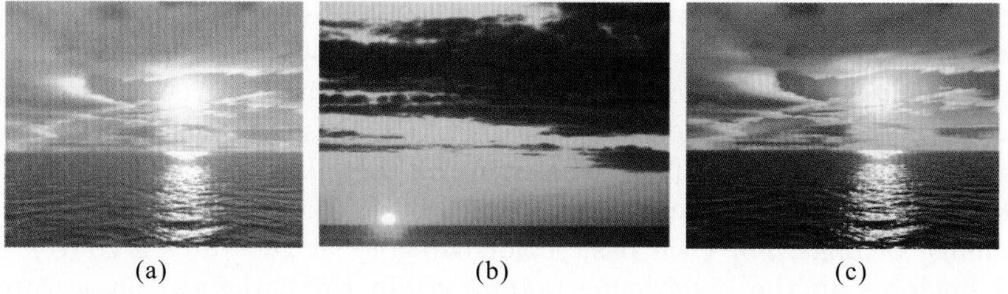

(a) (b) (c)

Fig. 4.35 Color transfer based on $l\alpha\beta$ color space. (a) Source image; (b) Reference image; (c) The resultant image [Reinhard *et al.*, 2001]. Copyright of IEEE, used with permission

However, the resulting quality of this general color transfer form depends on the two images' similarity in color composition. If source and target images that do not work well together are selected, then separate swatches of each color region must be manually set, and a match must be made between them.

In order to overcome this limitation, Chang *et al.*[2003] proposed an improved color transformation method in accordance with characteristics of human color perception. Human beings have an outstanding ability to discriminate between colors, and human color perception can also group similar colors into the same category. It is found that there are regularities in the number of basic colors and in their spreads on the color space in the developed languages. There are eleven basic color terms: black, white, red, green, yellow, blue, brown, pink, orange, purple, and grey. Based on the eleven perception-based color categories, Chang *et al.* made the following two assumptions [Chang *et al.*, 2003]:

(1) Color transformation within the same basic color category does not produce an unnatural result. This is clear because we perceive colors in the same basic color category as similar colors, so transferred color will not be very perceptually different from the original color. Therefore, such a transformation will not cause odd feelings in viewers.
(2) Color transformation within the same basic color category could create a different impression. This is reasonable because human color vision is sensitive. We are able to detect even small color differences, and the differences can cause different feelings compared with those inspired by the original color.

The first step in this approach is to divide the color space into the eleven basic color categories, and then, segments the input photograph and reference painting by using those categories. Chang *et al.* [2003] employed Uchikawa's 802 test colors taken from the regular grid of an x, y diagram in six different luminance, and each test color has been rated by subjects, which basic color category is the most appropriate for it. All of these test colors are converted into a CIE Lab color space and obtains the spreads for each color category. The color space is divided into eleven basic color categories just like Voronoi tessellation, regarding each data point as a site, and merges regions that belong to the same basic color category. By these categories, the image segmentation is performed by transferring all the pixel values to the CIE Lab color space, evaluating them that to which basic color category each pixel of an image belongs. For each basic color category, it generates a convex hull that encloses all the pixel value points within the category. These convex hulls are called basic convex hulls.

Now eleven basic convex hulls, ch_i^{pic}, for the input source image, and eleven basic convex hulls, ch_j^{pnt}, for the reference painting are obtained. For a pixel color value p^{pic} in the basic convex hull, ch^{pic} of the source image, its corresponding color value in the reference painting P^{pnt} is given by the following equation:

$$P^{\mathrm{pnt}} = \frac{||c^{\mathrm{pic}}, p^{\mathrm{pic}}||}{||c^{\mathrm{pic}}, b^{\mathrm{pic}}||}(b^{\mathrm{pnt}} - c^{\mathrm{pnt}}) + c^{\mathrm{pnt}},$$

where c^{pic} and c^{pnt} are the center of gravity of ch^{pic} and ch^{pnt} respectively. Assuming that l is a line that starts at c^{pic} and goes through p^{pic}. b^{pic} is the intersection point between ch^{pic} and l. l' is a line that starts at c^{pnt} and has the same direction as l, and b^{pnt} is the intersection point between ch^{pnt} and l'. The final color transfer process is carried out by substituting each pixel color value in the source image with its corresponding color in the reference painting. The color feature of the resultant image will be similar to those of the reference painting. Fig. 4.36 shows an example of a perception-based color transfer.

Fig. 4.36 Perception-based color transfer [Chang *et al.*, 2003]. (a) Source image; (b) Reference painting; (c) The resultant image after color transfer. Copyright of IEEE, used with permission

4.3.2 Artistic Transfer of Texture

The problem statement of texture transfer can be described as follows.

A reference image, R, specifies a texture effect to be transferred. Given a source image S, it is modified by replacing some high-frequency information with the texture in R, such that the resultant image is similar to the reference image in some degree in terms of the texture effect.

From the point of view of painting, the artistic style simulation based on texture transfer are global in the sense that the user need not deal with details such as defining and painting individual brush strokes. Texture transfer methods are also more general since they don't need to emulate any particular artistic style (line drawing, hatching, realistic oil painting, and so on). Fig. 4.37 is an illustration of texture transfer for artistic style simulation.

The representative work of texture transfer comes from Ashikhmin [2003]. He proposed a texture transfer method based on his coherent texture synthesis technique [Ashikhmin, 2001], which works by growing texture patches of irregular size, one pixel at a time. It proceeds in scan line order, choosing the best pixel from a short candidate list. This list is based on locations from which synthesized pixels were already taken. Each already synthesized pixel in a small (typically, L-shaped 5×2.5) neighborhood contributes to its appropriately forward shifted neighbor in the texture image

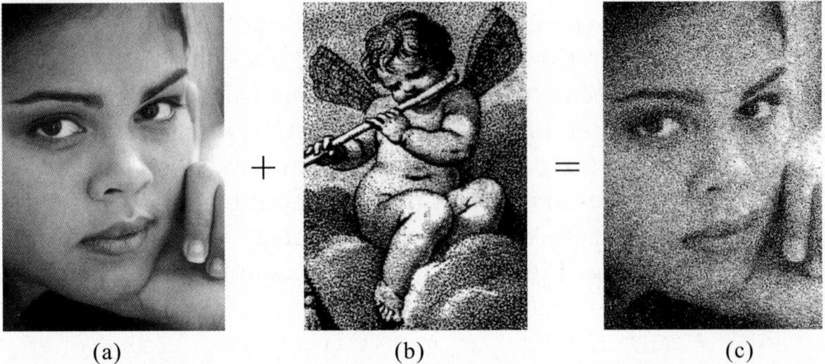

Fig. 4.37 An illustration of texture transfer for artistic style simulation [Ashikhmin, 2003]. (a) Source image; (b) Reference image; (c) The resultant image. Copyright from IEEE, used with permission

to the list. Certain texture transfer examples are created by extending the notion of the neighborhood to a full square that includes corresponding parts of the target image. He made two improvements on the coherent texture synthesis technique. First, he increased the algorithm's search space, as a slight increase in search space dramatically improves the convergence rate of coherent synthesis without compromising visual results. Second, problem-specific image similarity metrics were modified as the measure of neighborhood difference, which is the sum of two parts. First, the difference of neighborhood averages between the source and the target, and secondly the L_2 pixel-wise difference of only high-frequency components in the L-shaped neighborhoods of the result and the source texture images. Fig. 4.38 shows an example of texture transfer for this artistic style simulation.

Fig. 4.38 Texture transfer for artistic style simulation [Ashikhmin, 2003]. (a) Source image; (b) Reference image; (c) The resultant image. Copyright of IEEE, used with permission

Wang *et al.* [2004a] further presented a hierarchical patch-based approach to the synthesis of directional textures for painting style simulation. The major improvements of this method are: (a) Painting styles are represented as one or more blocks of sample textures selected by the user from the example painting, instead of using the entire reference image; (b) Image segmentation and brush stroke directions defined by the medial axis are used to better represent and communicate shapes and objects presented in the synthesized painting. The synthesized stroke textures can follow a direction field determined by the shapes of the regions to be painted. The major algorithmic steps of this method are that: the user specifies in the example painting one or more small blocks of sample textures that best represent the distinct styles to be simulated. Then, the image-to-be-synthesized is segmented according to the contents of the source image, and a direction field in each segmented region is defined. Finally, a hierarchy of texture patches, assisted with image masks, is employed to synthesize directional textures in each segmented region to form the final synthesized painting. Fig. 4.39 shows some examples of painting simulation by texture transfer.

Fig. 4.39 Examples of directional texture transfer for artistic style simulation [Wang *et al.*, 2004a]. (a) Source image; (b) Reference images with rectangles; (c) The resultant painting. Copyright of IEEE, used with permission

Guo *et al.* [2006] presented a texture transfer method in terms of painting technique. It is implicitly assumed that the textures in the example painting are embodied by the brush strokes. Therefore, the transfer of these artistic textures can be carried out by extracting the representative brush strokes from the example painting, and then reapplying them on the source image in terms of the painting conventions. The major algorithmic steps can be described as:

(1) *Brush library construction.* Representative brushes are extracted from example paintings of the given style to construct a brush library.

(2) *Region segmentation.* The photographic image is segmented by the mean shift method.
(3) *Grounding layer synthesis.* Suitable patches in the example painting are selected to synthesize the grounding layer.
(4) *Directional field construction.* Directional field is constructed by either interpolating user specified key directions, or synthesizing with extracted direction field from example painting.
(5) *Brush painting.* Seeds are generated using the direction field and brushes are placed over the seeds with perturbations added to the brush shape and color.
(6) *Fusion with image.* The painted result is composed into an original photographic image.

Fig. 4.40 shows an example of texture transfer for a painting.

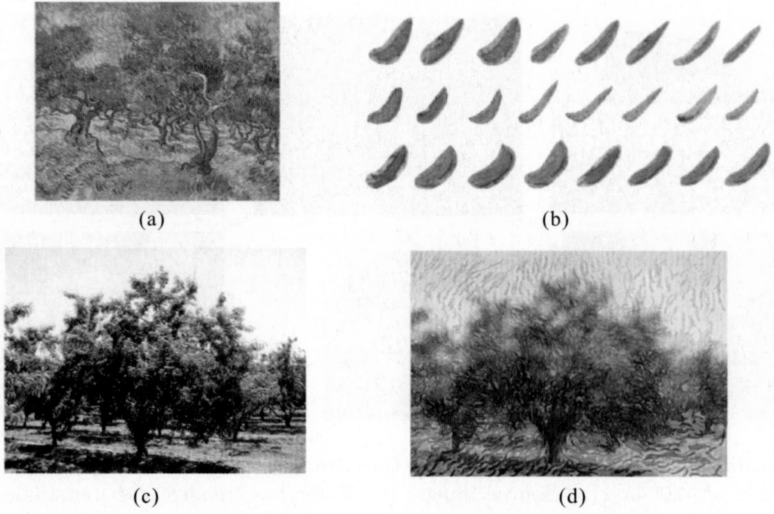

Fig. 4.40 Texture transfer by brush strokes [Guo *et al.*, 2006]. (a) The example painting; (b) Extracted brush strokes; (c) Source image; (d) The resultant image. Copyright of Journal Zhejiang University, used with permission

4.4 Image-based Painting Driven by Examples

From the point of view of image-based artistic rendering, a painting example is composed of two parts: a source image S and its corresponding painting image P. S and P depict the same content, but their visual effects are different. The relationship of S and P can be interpreted as: an image-based transformation, T, is implicitly specified, such that $T(S) = P$. From the point of view of artistic painting, T can be considered as a painting technique that can convert the source image into the desired artistic style. The example-based painting is to apply this transformation T to a source image S, and with the desire that the resultant image has the similar painting to style of P. This will make the example-based painting to be a challenging problem, as the transformation T is implicitly defined in the example.

There are two typical approaches for example-based painting. One is to employ the analogical reasoning and texture synthesis techniques to directly generate the resultant painting by the analogy in image space. The other one is to explicitly generate the empirical stroke templates by analyzing the painting examples. And the new painting is synthesized by applying the template on the source images based on pattern matching techniques.

4.4.1 Painting Style Simulation by Image Analogy

Analogy is a basic reasoning process. It is based on a systematic comparison between structures that uses properties of, and relations between, objects of a source structure to infer properties and relations between objects of a target structure. Image analogy is explored by Hertzmann *et al.* [2001] as a means for creating complex image filters, that can convert a photograph into various types of artistic renderings having the appearance of oil, watercolor, or pen-and-ink, by analogy with actual (real-life) renderings in these styles. The problem of image analogy can be given as follows:

Given a pair of images A and A' (the unfiltered and filtered source images, respectively), along with some additional unfiltered target image B, synthesize a new filtered target image B' such that $A : A' :: B : B'$.

In other words, "image analogy" is to find an "analogous" image B' that relates to B in "the same way" as A' relates to A.

A crucial aspect of the image analogy is the definition of similarity used to measure not only the relationship between each unfiltered image and its respective filtered version, but also the relationship between the source pair and the target pair when taken as a whole. This issue is tricky, in that we want to use some metric that is able to preserve recognizable features of the original image filter from A to A', while at the same time is broad enough to be applied to some completely different target image B. Moreover, it is not obvious what features of a training pair constitute the "style" of the filter: in principle, an infinite number of different transformations could be inferred from a pair of images. Hertzmann *et al.* [2001] employed a similarity metric that is based on an approximation to a Markov random field model, using raw pixel values and, optionally, steerable filter responses. Their image analogy algorithm is easy to describe. First, in an initialization phase, multiscale (Gaussian pyramid) representations of A, A' and B are constructed, along with their feature vectors and some additional indices used for speeding the matching process (e.g., an approximate-nearest-neighbor (ANN) search, as described below). The synthesis then proceeds from the coarsest resolution to the finest, computing a multiscale representation of B', one level at a time. At each level l, statistics pertaining to each pixel q in the target pair are compared against statistics for every pixel p in the source pair, and the "best" match is found. The feature vector $B'_l(q)$ is then set to the feature vector $\mathrm{A}'_l(p)$ for the closest-matching pixel p, and the pixel that matched best is recorded in $s_l(q)$.

In actual usage, image analogy involves two stages. In the design (or training) phase, a designer (possibly an expert) creates a filter by selecting the training images A and A' (for example, from scanned imagery), annotating the images if desired, and (directly or indirectly) selecting parameters that control how various types of image features will be weighted in the image analogy. The filter can then be stored away in a library. Later, in the application phase, a user (possibly someone with no expertise at all in creating image filters) applies the filter to some target image B. Fig. 4.41 gives some examples of converting source images into artistic effects with image analogy.

Fig. 4.41 Examples of image analogy [Hertzmann *et al.*, 2001]. Copyright of ACM, used with permission

The major advantage of image analogy is that they provide a very natural means of specifying image transformations. Rather than selecting from among a myriad of different filters and their settings, a user can simply supply an appropriate exemplar (along with a corresponding unfiltered source image) and say, in effect: "Make it look like this." Ideally, image analogies should make it possible to learn from a very broad variety of complex and non-linear image filters by analogy, with actual (real-life) renderings in these styles. By contrast, the previous artistic rendering works are that the methods have had to be specifically tailored to a specific rendering style (or space of styles).

4.4.2 Artistic Painting Generation by Stroke Templates from Examples

The aforementioned image analogy technique synthesizes a new "analogous" image B' that relates to an input image B in "the same way" as the example image A' relates to A. This technique, while good at mimicking the local relationships from image pair (A', A) to (B', B), lacks the power to capture the high-level structural information. Therefore, Chen *et al.* [2004] proposed a composite sketching approach for portraits by examples. Each example sketch is a highly abstract representation of the original source image, using realistic as well as exaggerated features to achieve an evocative likeness. The basic idea is to first decompose the data into components that are structurally related to each other, such as the eyes or mouth. After these have been independently processed, these components are carefully recomposed to obtain the final result. As shown in Fig. 4.42, a global model of face is defined, and 14 global features $(w_1/w, w_2/w, w_3/w, w_4/w, w_5/w, w_6/w, w_7/w, h_1/h, h_2/h, h_3/h, e_1, e_2, e_3, e_4)$ are carefully chosen from a pool of approximately 30 recommended facial features in a caricature drawing textbook. These relations describe the proportion of the face devoted to a particular facial feature. w_4/w, for instance, relates the width of the head to the width of the mouth. By not tying these relations to fixed values, the model can adjust the size of the features as the overall size of the head is changed.

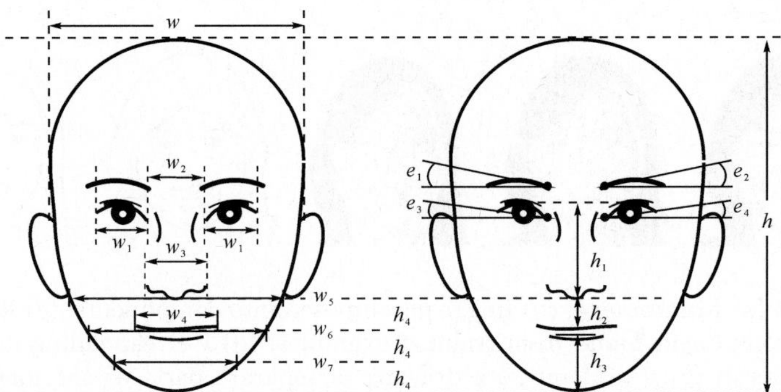

Fig. 4.42 Global features of face [Chen *et al.*, 2004]. Copyright of ACM, used with permission

A human face is decomposed semantically into 6 local components, one for each of the major facial elements, of 4 types. They are left and right eyebrows, left and right eyes, a nose, and a mouth. Each type of feature is further divided into several prototypes based on their appearance in the training data (see Fig. 4.43). The *eyebrow* component has two prototypes which are classified as thick and thin. The *eye* component has 11 prototypes which could be roughly clustered into 2 classes, those with or without a contour above the eye and below the eyebrow. The *nose* component has 3 and the *mouth* component has 4 prototypes.

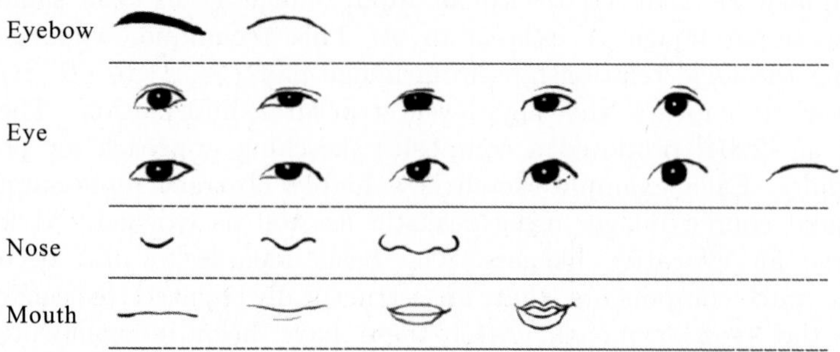

Fig. 4.43 The prototypes extracted from the training set [Chen *et al.*, 2004]. Copyright of ACM, used with permission

For an input image of a face, it is firstly decomposed into components. Secondly, the best match for each component is found from training examples. Thirdly, corresponding drawings of components are generated, and the drawings of separate parts are composited into the final drawings. Fig. 4.44 shows the pipeline of generating a portrait from an example.

Fig. 4.44 (a) Input image; (b) Image decomposed into components; (c) Best match for each component found from training examples; (d) Corresponding drawings of components in (c); (e) Composite drawing of separate parts as the final drawing [Chen *et al.*, 2004]. Copyright of ACM, used with permission

The principal advantage of this component-based approach is its capacity to capture large-scale correlation within the components and its ability to create an overall picture in the style intended by the artist. Fig. 4.45 shows the stylized portraits generated from images.

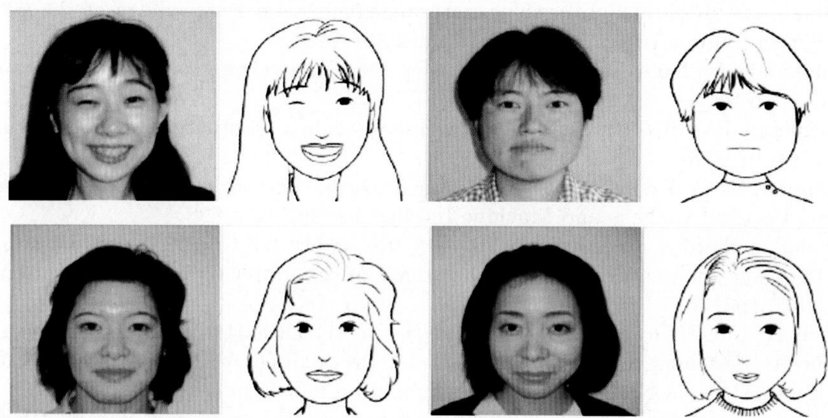

Fig. 4.45 Stylized portrait generation by stroke-based templates [Chen *et al.*, 2004]. Copyright of ACM, used with permission

4.5 Summary

Image-based painting offers several advantages over the rendering from 3D models [Salisbury *et al.*, 1997]. First, it greatly reduces the tasks of geometric modeling and of specifying surface reflectance properties, allowing much more complicated models (such as furry creatures and human faces) to be illustrated. Second, an image based system provides the flexibility of using any type of physical photograph, computer-generated image, or arbitrary scalar, vector, or tensor field as input, allowing visualization of data that is not necessarily even physical in nature. Finally, image-based systems offer more direct user control: the ability to more easily modify tone, texture, or stroke orientation with an interactive digital-paint style interface.

Although the image-based painting techniques have made great progress, there are several limitations in terms of artwork creation. First of all, the artistic effects are constrained by the content of source image. Second, the interaction pipeline is not flexible enough to create artistic drawings from images. The long-term goal of interaction is to make the interaction pipeline to be more consistent with the conventions of artists. And at the same time, the tedious technical aspects of drawing are shifted to the computer side, while providing the user with expressiveness and a new kind of freedom on the creative and aesthetic side.

References

Ashikhmin M(2001) Synthesizing natural textures. In: Proceedings of the 2001 Symposium on Interactive 3D Graphics 217–226

Ashikhmin M(2003) Fast texture transfer. Computer Graphics and Applications 3(4):38–43

Buchanan JW(1996) Special effects with half-toning. Computer Graphics Forum 15(3):97–108

Canny J(1986) A computational approach to edge detection. IEEE Transactions on Pattern Analysis and Machine Intelligence 8(6):679–698

Chang Y, Saito S, Nakajima M(2003) A framework for transfer colors based on the basic color categories. In: Proceedings of Computer Graphics International 2003, 158–163

Chen H, Liu Z, Rose C, Xu Y, Shum H, Salesin D(2004) Example-based composite sketching of human portraits. In: Proceedings of the 3rd International Symposium on Non-photorealistic Animation and Rendering 95–153

Collomosse JP, Hall PM(2003) Cubist style rendering from photographs. IEEE Transactions on Visualization and Computer Graphics 9(4):443–453

Curtis CJ, Anderson SE, Seims JE, Fleischer KW, Salesin DH(1997) Computer-generated watercolor. In: Proceedings of the 24th Annual Conference on Computer Graphics and Interactive Techniques 421–430

DeCarlo D, Santella A(2002) Stylization and abstraction of photographs. ACM Transactions on Graphics 21 (3):769–776

Deussen O, Hiller S, Overveld CV, Strothotte T(2000) Floating points:a method for computing stipple drawings. Computer Graphics Forum 19(3):40–51

Durand F, Ostromoukhov V, Miller M, Duranleau F, Dorsey J(2001) Decoupling strokes and high-level attributes for interactive traditional drawing. Rendering Techniques 2001. Springer-Verlag/Wion, NewYork

Elber G, Wolberg G(2003) Rendering traditional mosaics. The Visual Computer 19(1):67–78

Freudenberg B, Masuch M, Strothotte T(2002) Real-time half-toning:a primitive for non-photorealistic shading. ACM International Conference Proceeding Series 28:227–232

Fritzsche L P, Hellwig H, Hiller, S, Deussen O(2005) Interactive design of authentic looking mosaics using Voronoi structures. In: Proceedings of 2nd International Symposium on Voronoi Diagrams in Science and Engineering

Gooch B, Coombe G, Shirley P(2002)Artistic vision: painterly rendering using simple vision algorithms. In: Proceedings of the 2nd international symposium on Non-photorealistic animation and rendering 83–89

Guo Y, Yu J, Xu X, Wang J, Peng Q(2006) Example based painting generation. Journal of Zhejiang University, Science A 7(7):1152–1159

Haeberli P(1990) Paint by numbers:abstract image representations. In: Proceedings of the 17th Annual Conference on Computer Graphics and Interactive Techniques 207–214

Hausner A. Simulating decorative mosaics(2001) In: Proceedings of the 28th Annual Conference on Computer Graphics and Interactive Techniques 573–580

Hertzmann A(1998) Painterly rendering with curved brush strokes of multiple sizes. In: Proceedings of the 25th Annual Conference on Computer Graphics and Interactive Techniques 453–460

Hertzmann A, Jacobs CE, Oliver N, Curless B, Salesin DH(2001) Image analogies. In: Proceedings of the 28th Annual Conference on Computer Graphics and Interactive Techniques 327–3404

Hertzmann A(2002) Fast paint texture. In: Proceedings of the 2nd International Symposium on Non-photorealistic Animation and Rendering

Hertzmann A(2003). A survey of stroke-based rendering. Computer Graphics and Applications 23(4):70–81

Hiller S, Hellwig H, Deussen O(2003) Beyond stippling:a method for distributing objects on the plane. Computer Graphics Forum 22(3):515–522

Huang Z, Li N(2003) A method of feature-based pencil drawing. In: Proceedings of the 1st International Conference on Computer Graphics and Interactive Techniques in Australasia and South East Asia 135–140

Johan H, Hashimoto R, Nishita T(2004) Creating watercolor style images taking into account painting techniques. The Journal of the Society for Art and Science 3(4):207-215

Kim H, Jin H, Yu Y, Cho H(2001) Creating pen-and-ink illustration using stroke morphing methods. Computer Graphics International 2001 113–120

Lloyd S(1982) Least square quantization in PCM. IEEE Transaction on Information Theory 28(2):129–137

Luiz V, Jonas DMG(1991) Digital halftoning with space filling curves. Computer Graphics 25(4):81–90

Mao X, Nagasaka Y, Imamiya A(2001) Automatic generation of pencil drawing from 2D images using line integral convolution. In: Proceedings of the 7th International Conference on Computer-Aided Design and Computer Graphics 240–248

Mould D(2003) A stained glass image filter. In: Proceedings of the 14th Eurographics Workshop on Rendering 20–25

Ostromoukhov V, Hersch RD(1999) Multi-color and artistic dithering. In: Proceedings of the 26th Annual Conference on Computer Graphics and Interactive Techniques 425-432

Ostromoukhov V(1999) Digital facial engraving. In: Proceedings of the 26th Annual Conference on Computer Graphics and Interactive Techniques 417–424

Reinhard E, Ashikhmin M, Gooch B, Shirley P(2001) Color transfer between images. Computer Graphics and Applications 21(5):34–41

Salisbury MP, Anderson SE, Barzel R, Salesin DH(1994) Interactive pen-and-ink illustration. In: Proceedings of the 21st Annual Conference on Computer Graphics and Interactive Techniques 101–108

Salisbury MP, Wong MT, Hughes JF, Salesin DH(1997) Orientable textures for image-based pen-and-ink illustration. In: Proceedings of the 24th Annual Conference on Computer Graphics and Interactive Techniques 401–406

Santella A, DeCarlo D(2004) Visual interest and NPR:an evaluation and manifesto. In: Proceedings of the 3rd International Symposium on Non-photorealistic Animation and Rendering 71–150

Secord A(2002) Weighted Voronoi stippling. In: Proceedings of the 2nd Annual Symposium on Non-photorealistic Animation and Rendering 37–43

Shiraishi M, Yamaguchi Y(2000) An algorithm for automatic painterly rendering based on local source image approximation. In: Proceedings of the 1st International Symposium on Non-photorealistic Animation and Rendering, 53–58

Sousa MC, Buchanan JW(1999) Observational model of blenders and erasers in computer-generated pencil rendering. In: Proceedings of the 1999 Conference on Graphics Interface '99 157–166

Wang B, Wang W, Yang H, Sun J(2004a) Efficient example-based painting and synthesis of 2D directional texture. IEEE Transactions on Visualization and Computer Graphics 10(3):266–277

Wang H, Zhang JJ, Li ST, Wang Y(2004b) Shape and texture preserved non-photorealistic rendering. Computer Animation and Virtual Worlds 15(3–4):453–461

Way DL, Shih, ZC(2001) The synthesis of rock textures in Chinese landscape painting. Computer Graphics Forum 20(3):C123–C131

Way DL, Hsu, CW, Chiu HY, Shih ZC(2001) Computer-generated Chinese painting for landscapes and portraits. Journal of WSCG 2001

Yamamoto S, Mao X, Imamiya A(2004) Colored pencil filter with custom colors. In: Proceedings of 12th Pacific Conference on Computer Graphics and Applications 329–338

5

Artistic Rendering for 3D Object

The problem statement of artistic rendering for a 3D object can be described as: Given a 3D model, the user specifies the viewing parameters, the rendering styles and features, the system automatically or semi-automatically creates the corresponding picture with the desired visual effect. The research methodology of 3D artistic rendering can be classified as follows:

(1) *Artistic simulation based on traditional 3D rendering pipeline.* The overall rendering pipeline is the same as the traditional one. However, its photorealistic lighting model, projection transformation, texture mapping are replaced with non-photorealistic ones. The artistic images are accordingly generated based on the traditional 3D rendering pipeline.
(2) *Artistic rendering based on interim image generated from 3D object.* The interim image, generated by traditional photorealistic rendering, is used as a reference image. The system then employs image-based artistic rendering techniques to create the corresponding artwork guided by the interim image and the salient 3D information of the 3D object to be depicted.
(3) *Artistic rendering based on shape features of 3D object.* The 3D shape features are firstly extracted from the 3D object to be depicted in terms of the specified viewpoint. The artistic rendering result is then created by the 3D shape features and the drawing style. This method is often utilized in the silhouette drawing of 3D objects.

However, detailed artistic rendering techniques are also heavily dependent on the representation model of 3D objects. We will further discuss the following three artistic rendering techniques:

(1) *Line-drawing for 3D surface.* Line-drawing is a popular rendition style that is closely related to the presentation of shape features. The line-drawing on the parametric surface and implicit surface is much more difficult to achieve than that for polygonal objects.

(2) *Artistic rendering for 3D natural scenes.* In the computer graphics community, there are no general representation forms for a 3D landscape such as trees and mountains. Therefore, the artistic rendering for a 3D landscape is unique in that we should take into account more information about the description of a 3D landscape, such as the overall shapes, the local shapes and the skeleton, and the 3D structures, etc.
(3) *Artistic rendering for 3D volume model.* The volume model is an approximate representation of a 3D object. The artistic rendering for a 3D volume focuses on the rendition of the features of the surface, boundary and its internal structure.

5.1 Artistic Rendering Based on Traditional 3D Rendering Pipeline

Traditional photorealistic rendering still plays the dominant role in the computer graphics community. When artistic rendering started being explored, it was natural for a researcher to manage to generate the artistic rendition by "borrowing" the 3D rendering techniques. For example, Masuch and Strothotte generated the artistic effects of line-drawing by post-processing the wireframe drawing in traditional 3D graphics [Masuch & Strothotte, 1998]. Markosian *et al.* proposed an improved hidden surface model algorithm for the artistic rendering of silhouettes [Markosian *et al.*, 1997]. This section will mainly discuss how to create the artistic rendering of 3D objects by embedding the non-photorealistic lighting models, the non-photorealistic projection transformation, or the non-photorealistic texture-mapping into the traditional 3D rendering pipeline, respectively.

5.1.1 Non-photorealistic Lighting Model

A non-photorealistic lighting model should go beyond the physical and optical laws in traditional photorealistic lighting models, and its illustrated visual effect should be consistent with intrinsic merit based on the evolutionary nature of art and visual perception conventions. For the time being, there are three typical approaches to building non-photorealistic lighting models:

(1) The non-photorealistic lighting model is created by improving and enhancing the traditional shading model in terms of the illustration conventions and general principles of visual perception.
(2) The non-photorealistic lighting model is built on the human-like approach by imitating the training process of the human artist in terms of the "divide and conquer" strategy. It is based on the fact that human artists usually start learning illustration skills from drawing primitives such as boxes, cylinders and spheres, etc., and finally they will be able to depict a 3D object with arbitrary geometric complexity by decomposing its 3D models into these well-known primitives.

(3) The non-photorealistic lighting model is generated by the quantitative distribution of artistic illumination and color that are interactively extracted from the painting artworks.

Gooch *et al.* are the pioneers in the exploration of non-photorealistic lighting models. They made the first approach and proposed a non-photorealistic lighting model for technical illustration based on cool-to-warm tones [Gooch *et al.*, 1998; Gooch, 1998]. Their lighting model uses both luminance and changes in hue to indicate surface orientation, reserving extreme light and dark for edge lines and highlights. The fundamental idea behind it is that when silhouettes and other edge lines are explicitly drawn, then very low dynamic range shading is needed for the interior. This is because adding a somewhat artificial hue shift to shading helps imply shape without requiring a large dynamic range. The lighting intensity of this modified shading model is calculated as follows:

$$
\begin{aligned}
I &= \left(\frac{1+\boldsymbol{I}\cdot\boldsymbol{n}}{2}\right)k_{\text{cool}} + \left(1-\frac{1+\boldsymbol{I}\cdot\boldsymbol{n}}{2}\right)k_{\text{warm}},\\
k_{\text{cool}} &= k_{\text{blue}} + \alpha k_d,\\
k_{\text{warm}} &= k_{\text{yellow}} + \beta k_d,\\
k_{\text{blue}} &= (0,0,b), b \in [0,1],\\
k_{\text{yellow}} &= (y,y,0), y \in [0,1].
\end{aligned}
$$

Where $\boldsymbol{I}$ is the RGB color to be displayed for a given point on the surface; $\boldsymbol{I}$ is the unit vector in the direction of the light source, and $\boldsymbol{n}$ is the unit surface normal vector at the point; k_d is the RGB diffuse reflectance at the point; k_{blue} and k_{yellow} are fully saturated blue and yellow in RGB space respectively. The values for b and y will determine the strength of the overall temperature shift, and the values of α and β will determine the prominence of the object's color and the strength of the luminance shift. Fig. 5.1 shows how to create the tone for a pure red object by summing-up a blue-to-yellow and a dark-red-to-red tone. Fig. 5.2 shows the shading instances with Phong and new lighting models respectively. The new illustration method gives a clearer picture of the shape, structure and material composition than traditional computer graphics methods. Moreover, this non-photorealistic lighting model is further improved by Winnemöller and Bangay, who successfully simulated the reflective visuals effect by modifying the calculation of the reflective component accordingly [Winnemöller & Bangay, 2002].

Fig. 5.1 The final tone is created by summing-up a blue-to-yellow and a dark-red-to-red tone [Gooch *et al.*, 1998]. (a) Blue-to-yellow tone; (b) Dark-red-to-red tone; (c) The final tone. Copyright of ACM, used with permission

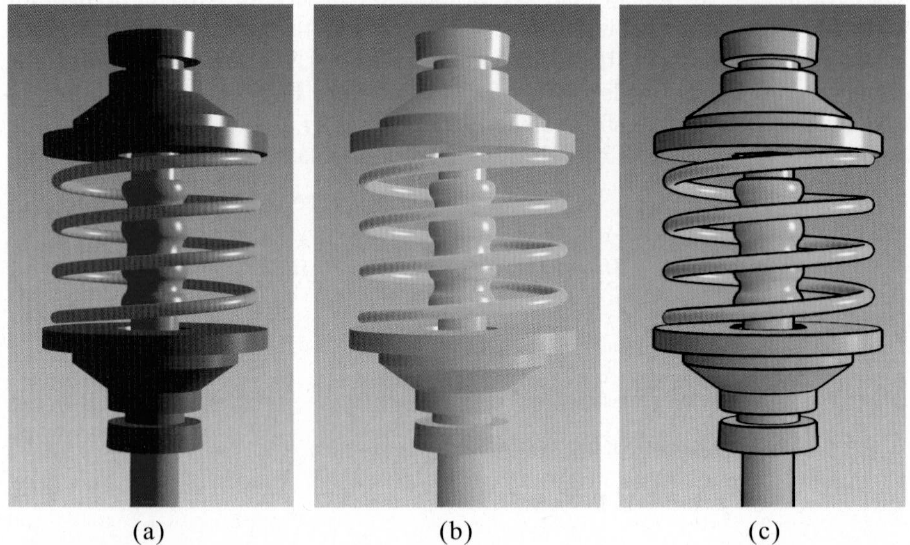

Fig. 5.2 Left to right: (a) Phong model for colored object; (b) New shading model with highlights, cool-to-warm hue shift and without edge lines; (c) New model using edge lines, highlights and cool-to-warm hue shift [Gooch *et al.*, 1998]. Copyright of ACM, used with permission

Geng *et al.* took the second approach to building the non-photorealistic lighting model by imitating the human depiction methods [Geng *et al.*, 2001; Geng *et al.*, 2005]. Regarding human depiction, Durand proposed a four-stage processing pipeline to render a mechanical product [Durand, 2002]:

(1) *Spatial mapping.* It handles the spatial properties, and generates the corresponding spatial layout in a 2D picture according to the viewpoint and projection type.
(2) *Pictorial units conversion.* It converts 3D primitives (points, lines, surfaces, volumes) into 2D pictorial units (points, lines, regions).
(3) *Attributes assignment.* It assigns visual properties such as color, texture, thickness, transparency, wiggliness, or orientation to the pictorial units.

(4) *Mark implementation.* It is responsible for medium simulation (e.g., oil painting, pencil brush, watercolor, engraving), mimics the physical strokes in traditional rendering, and realizes the visual effect of primitives placed at their spatial location.

By this pipeline, a technical illustration system for 3D constructive solid geometry (CSG) models is given in Fig. 5.3.

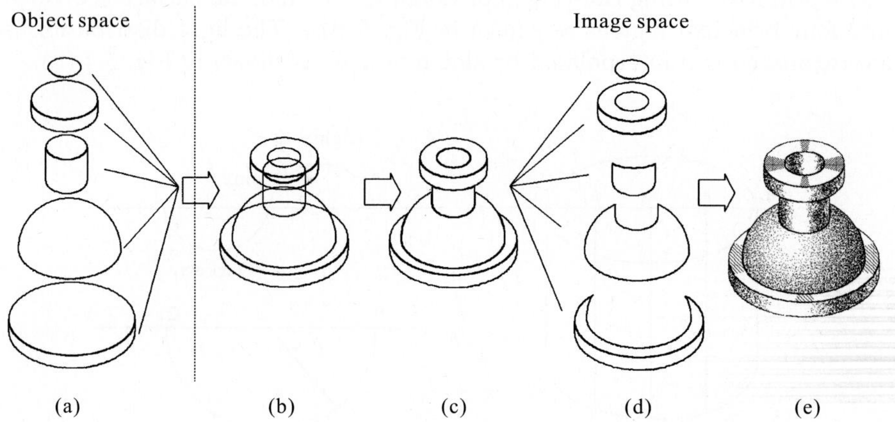

Fig. 5.3 The technical illustration pipeline based on CSG primitives. (a) Primitive types to be selected; (b) The object composed from primitives; (c) The object after hidden surface removal; (d) Spatial layout of the object to be rendered; (e) The resultant illustration

The remaining issue is how to define the non-photorealistic lighting model for technical illustration that is desired to preserve the correct geometric projection and lighting distribution. Geng *et al.* defined the following non-photorealistic lighting model for the technical illustration of CSG models [Geng *et al.*, 2005].

(1) The lighting intensity is represented as parameters of multiple discrete levels in terms of highlight, Mach bands, mid-tone, semi-dark and dark regions and so on. Their corresponding regions in image space are defined as "principal regions". For each level of lighting, the default value is calculated by the Phong illumination model.
(2) The spatial size, location and shape of these principal regions in image space are parameterized by projection conventions and type of CSG primitives.
(3) The lighting distribution over each CSG primitive is computed by interpolating the lighting intensities of its principal regions.

(4) Each CSG primitive has its own lighting model, and each level of the lighting is subject to the user's manual adjustment based on users' preferences or illustration styles.

Based on this definition, their NPR lighting models will have three major components: the multi-level lighting parameters, the parametric description of spatial occupations (principal regions) corresponding to each lighting level, and an interpolation method to calculate the lighting distribution over the entire primitive during run-time. For example, a cylindrical surface is divided into four principal regions as shown in Fig. 5.4(a). The light distribution is approximated and interpolated by sine function, as shown in Fig. 5.4 (b).

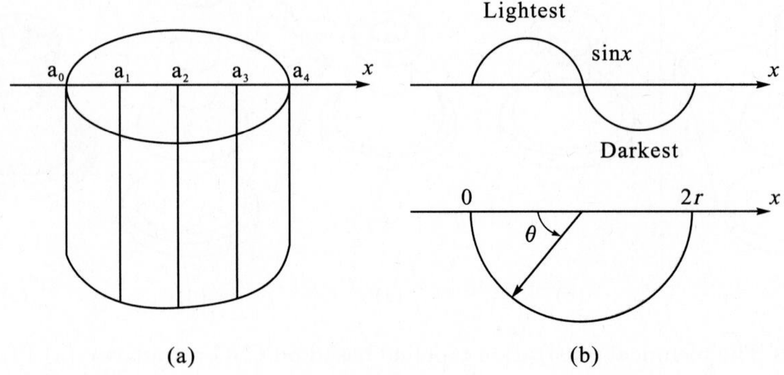

Fig. 5.4 (a) Segments on cylindrical surface; (b) Lighting model for cylinder

The default lighting for each primitive is the same as that of the Phong model, except that it employs a region-based discrete calculation of lighting intensity, rather than Phong's pixel-by-pixel calculation. This feature somewhat reflects the lighting calculation utilized by human artists, as it offers the user a flexible interface of local refinement of lighting [Geng *et al.*, 2005]. Fig. 5.5 shows a set of technical illustration samples generated by this non-photorealistic lighting model.

Sloan *et al.* took the third approach to create a non-photorealistic lighting model that can capture custom artistic shading models from sampled artwork [Sloan *et al.*, 2001]. When an artist draws or paints an object, he/she often starts with a shading study on the sphere that provides coverage of the complete set of unit normals, and then adapts this study to a complex object. In essence, the sphere serves as a surrogate for more complex objects in order to simplify the characterization of reflected light and assure sufficient coverage of normals. They refer to this "paint by normals" method of shading as the *lit sphere* model, which is built by mapping shading from works of art to geometric models . The *lit sphere* model is based on the assumption that source materials are homogeneous, while artists often encode local surface features in

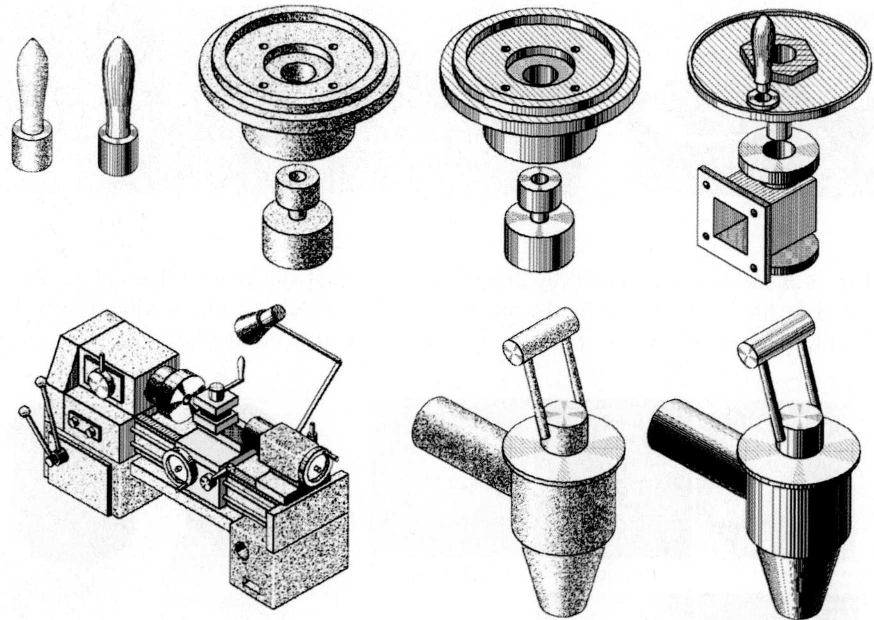

Fig. 5.5 Illustration samples by non-photorealistic lighting models

their artworks. Suppose that a piece of artwork contains surfaces with locally spherical patches. These patches possess an approximately correct distribution of normals. Thus, we can approximate the artistic lighting model by projecting the shaded patch onto a lit sphere. However, the patch may lack part of the hemispherical normal space or distort the distribution of normals. Therefore the system accordingly provides a method for modifying the mapping from the patch to the lit sphere environment map. Given an image of a shaded sphere, transferring a shading model from an image of a sphere to a complex 3D model is straightforward. It allows the user to interactively explore novel viewpoints of 3D models, and Fig. 5.6 shows the illustration samples applying the established lit sphere from different viewpoints. This lit sphere approach allows material properties found in 2D artwork retarget to 3D geometric models. It incorporates established principles from the art, computer vision, and rendering communities into a framework for non-photorealistic rendering. Fig. 5.7 gives an illustration sample of capturing shading from artwork via the lit sphere and re-projecting it onto geometry for human rendering.

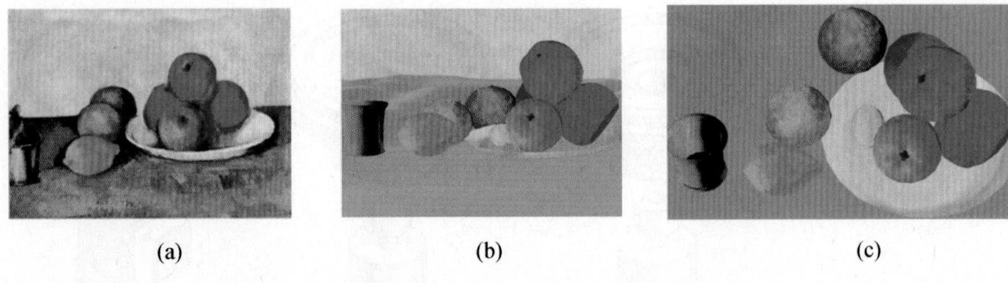

Fig. 5.6 Models illuminated by lit sphere from novel viewpoints[Sloan *et al.*, 2001]. (a) Still life by Cezanne for lit sphere; (b) The resultant illustration 1; (c) The resultant illustration 2. Copyright of ACM, used with permission

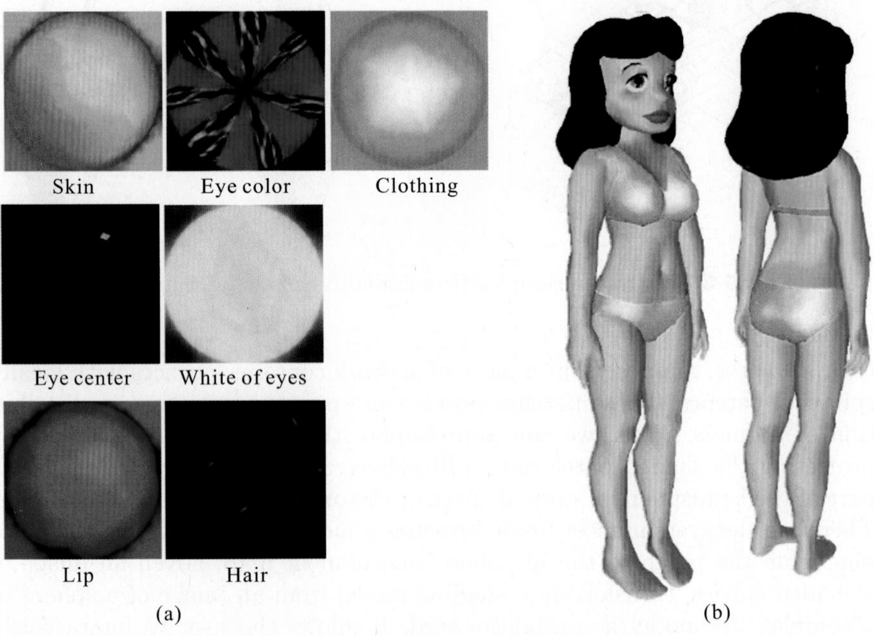

Fig. 5.7 The captured lit sphere and their application on the human illustration [Sloan *et al.*, 2001]. Copyright of ACM, used with permission

5.1.2 Non-realistic Projection

Perspective is the means by which cameras capture the 3D world in a 2D image. Projection techniques are particularly useful as means of controlling how information is presented to a viewer, expressing the various ways in which the shape of objects, and the spatial relations between them, can be represented in pictures. Levene informally characterizes a projection as being parameterized by [Levene, 1998]:

(1) The shape of the projection surface.
(2) The degree to which orthogonals converge to or diverge from a vanishing point in the image.
(3) The behavior of orthogonals as they converge or diverge.
(4) The subset of objects in the scene that are operated on.

The characteristics of each non-realistic projection are embedded in the transformation step. In formal terms, given point P in eye space, the transformation P' is given by

$$P' = (C_x + [f(P) \times V_x], C_y + [f(P) \times V_y], P_z),$$

where

- The point C, called the center of scaling, is a 2D point at the same eye space depth as P. The point C is used to control the location of the vanishing points in the image.
- The vector $\boldsymbol{V} = (P_x - C_x, P_y - C_y)$ is a 2D vector describing P relative to C.
- The function $f = R^3 \rightarrow R$, called the size-with-distance function, determines the factor to scale the x and y components of P, relative to C. f is used to control the degree to which orthogonals converge or diverge. f is defined as

$$f(P) = \left(\frac{d_P}{d_S}\right)^n.$$

As shown in Fig. 5.8, E is the eye point; S is the projection of P onto a viewing surface; $d_P = |P - E|$ is the radial distance of P from the eye; $d_S = |S - E|$ is the radial distance of S from the eye. n is a scalar that determines the degree to which orthogonals diverge or converge (see Fig. 5.8).

The shape of the projection surface determines d_s, influencing the degree to which a point is scaled in eye space. The surface is represented as a non-parametric cubic Bezier patch of the form

$$z = f(\alpha, \beta),$$

where $\alpha = \tan^{-1}(x)$ and $\beta = \tan^{-1}(y)$ are measures of a direction vector's angular displacement in x and y respectively. To convert a 3D vector to $\alpha - \beta$ space, it is first scaled until it intersects the plane z=1. Its $\alpha - \beta$ representation is then $(\tan^{-1}(x), \tan^{-1}(y))$. Converting back to Cartesian space would then yield

$$(x, y, z) = (\tan(\alpha), \tan(\beta), 1),$$

z is the depth of the surface point along the z direction in eye space. The surface point itself is calculated by finding where the direction vector (α, β) intersects the plane $z = f(\alpha, \beta)$.

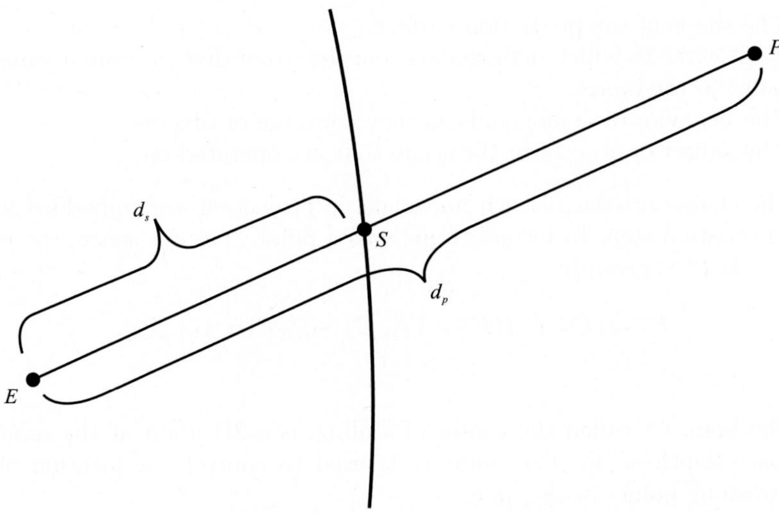

Fig. 5.8 Calculating $f(P)$, the size-with-distance function

The sixteen control points of the Bezier patch are evenly distributed in $\alpha - \beta$ space, and the user may interactively alter each point's corresponding depth.

In order to enable oblique projections, as is shown in Fig. 3.3, we allow the user to interactively skew the view volume in eye space by setting the x and y coordinates of a skew point, K. After a skew point is defined, each point P is skewed into point P_{skew}, before being transformed, according to:

$$P_{\text{skew}} = \left(P_x - \left[K_x \times \left(\frac{P_z}{K_z}\right)\right], P_y - \left[K_y \times \left(\frac{P_z}{K_z}\right)\right], P_z\right).$$

In order to combine the multiple projections, a 2D inertial fitting technique is proposed. If a scene is partitioned into m projections, one is arbitrarily assigned the "default" projection (which we call p_d). The image of each projection $p_i (1 \leqslant i \leqslant m-1)$ is then merged into that of p_d according to the following two steps:

(1) The objects assigned to p_i are duplicated. One copy is then transformed by p_i, the other by p_d. This yields two images of the original set of objects.
(2) The first image is fitted to the second, so that the position, orientation and size of the images are matched to each other.

The non-realistic projection framework provides a means of using curved projection surfaces. It controls both the degree to which orthogonals converge to or diverge from a vanishing point in the image, and the behavior of orthogonals as they converge or diverge. Different objects can be projected independently and their images can be composited together.

Agrawala *et al.* merely concentrated on how to create multi-projection images that can express a mood, feeling or idea, improve the representation or comprehensibility of the scene, and visualize information about the spatial relationships and structure of the scene [Agrawala *et al.*, 2000]. The input to the algorithm is a set of camera groups, each associating a collection of geometric objects with one local camera. The first stage of the algorithm renders each camera group into a separate image layer. All the image layers are then merged together to form the resultant multi-projection image. Their main difficulty in the compositing stage is the absence of natural visibility ordering. The solution is to let the user simply specify a master camera (often a local camera doubles as the master), and the master camera is employed to resolve visibility through a combination of two automation techniques: 3D depth-based compositing and standard 2D compositing based on object-level occlusion constraints. If necessary, the user can directly modify the visibility ordering by specifying additional pairwise occlusion relationships between image layers. They also set-up a series of constraints for the camera, including object-size constraint (keeping the object's size and position approximately constant while changing its perspective convergence), fixed-view constraint (maintaining a particular view of the object), and fixed-position constraint (maintaining the position of the object in the image plane), etc. The resultant multi-projection images are generated by the constraints-based solver. Fig. 5.9 shows the simulation of the multi-projection from an artwork.

(a)

(b)

Fig. 5.9 A multi-projection artwork and its simulated multi-projection image [Agrawala *et al.*, 2000]. (a) Giorgio de Chirico's the mystery and melancholy of a street; (b) The simulated multi-projection image. Copyright of ACM, used with permission

Singh further generalized Agrawala's multi-projection model and proposed an incremental approach, which allows non-linear perspective views of a scene to be built gradually by blending and compositing multiple linear perspectives [Singh, 2002]. Let C_i represent the camera parameters for exploratory view $i \in \{1, \ldots, n\}$, let M_i represent the perspective projection matrix built from the parameters C_i. Given a viewport specification represented by matrix V_i, the resulting point in two dimensional screen space $\langle x_s, y_s \rangle$ is

$$\langle x_s, y_s, z_s \rangle = PM_iV_i.$$

Usually, $z_s = z$ is the depth value of the point P, unchanged by V_i. Singh extended the viewport transformations V_i so that the canonical depth of a point $z \in [0,1]$ is mapped to z in an arbitrary user specified range. While the relative depth values are preserved with respect to a single perspective view, this allows the powerful visual capability of intuitively altering the relative depths of points in a scene as one transition between the multiple linear perspectives. Supposing that a normalized weight vector $\langle w_{1p}, w_{2p}, \ldots, w_{np} \rangle$ is specified for any point P in the scene, the projection of P is defined as PM_PV_P, where M_p is the perspective projection of a virtual linear perspective camera C_p, which is calculated by the following equation:

$$C_p = \begin{bmatrix} C_1 \; C_2 \; ... \; C_n \end{bmatrix} \begin{bmatrix} w_1 \\ w_2 \\ \cdots \\ w_n \end{bmatrix}.$$

Similarly, V_p is generated by weighted averaging the affine components of viewport transformations $V_1, \ldots, V_n$ with the weights $w_{1p}, w_{2p}, \ldots, w_{np}$, i.e., V_p is

$$V_p = \begin{bmatrix} V_1 \; V_2 \; ... \; V_n \end{bmatrix} \begin{bmatrix} w_1 \\ w_2 \\ \cdots \\ w_n \end{bmatrix}.$$

The rationale for generating an interpolated camera and an interpolated viewport independently, rather than simply weighted averaging the projected points resulting from applying each linear perspective camera projection to P, is twofold. First and foremost, a number of camera parameters are angular and are best interpolated individually using quaternion. Secondly, the camera parameters have intuitive physical manifestations and their interpolation can be better understood and controlled by a user. Fig. 5.10 shows a group of non-linear projection instances.

Martín *et al.* employed the *Hierarchical extended non-linear transformations* to produce modifications in the visualization of the elements included

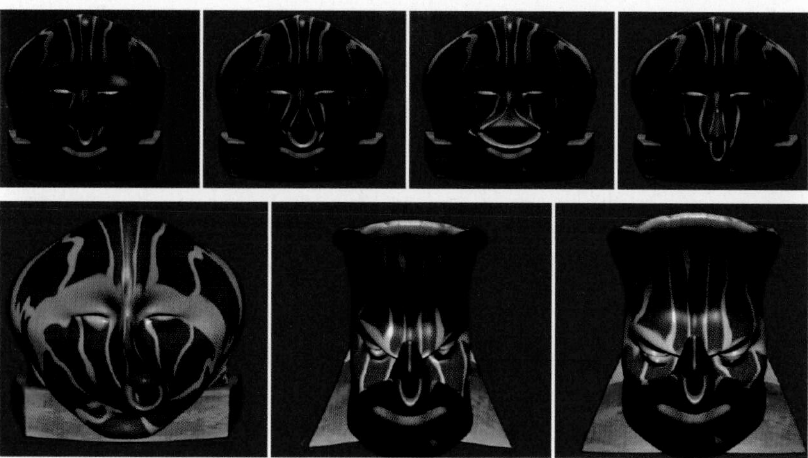

Fig. 5.10 Examples of non-linear projections [Singh, 2002]. Copyright of ACM, used with permission

in the scene [Martín *et al.*, 2000]. *Hierarchical extended non-linear transformations* are a variation of geometric transformations, translation, rotations, scale and so on. In non-linear transformations, the transformation itself is changed depending on the position. The function that relates position and transformation is called a control function. A geometric transformation can be seen as a non-linear transformation, for which the control function is constant (henceforth referred to as constant transformation). More formally, given a transformation, T, which is constant for all vertices, a point (x, y, z) is transformed into

$$(x', y', z') = T(x, y, z).$$

To which coordinate x, y, o, z, the selection axis points will be the independent variable in the control function, and a selection axis will be chosen for every transformation. A *control function* is a function that defines how the parameters control the deformation change. This function depends on the value of a coordinate, which itself depends in turn on the selection axis. Fig. 5.11 shows the control functions for orientation [Martín *et al.*, 2000]. Fig. 5.12 gives the examples of non-linear transformations.

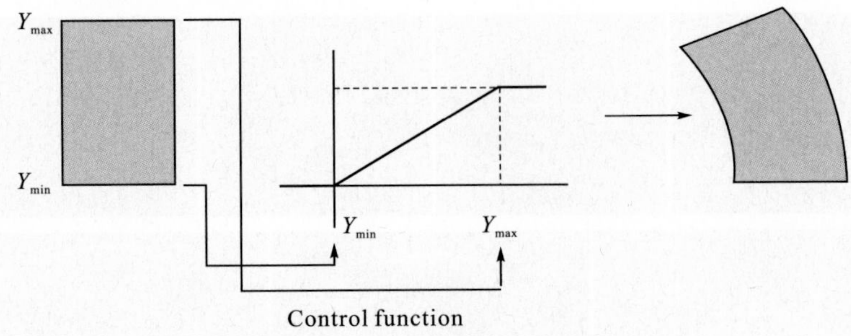

Fig. 5.11 General scheme of orientation and distance functions

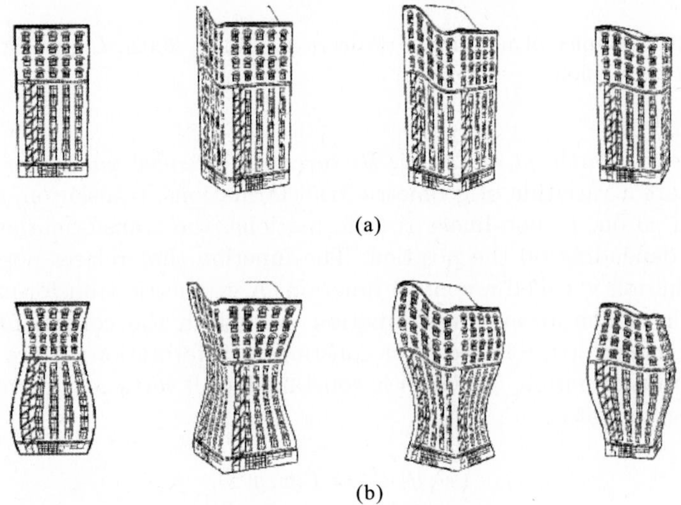

Fig. 5.12 Examples of non-linear transformations [Martín *et al.*, 2000]. (a) Orientation-dependent deformation; (b) Distance-dependent deformation. Copyright of ACM, used with permission

5.1.3 Non-photorealistic Texture Mapping and Synthesis

In photorealistic rendering, texture mapping is an important approach to enhancing the realism of the resultant image. This naturally motivates the NPR researchers to start exploring how to present the artistic effect of rendition by non-photorealistic texture mapping and synthesis.

Klein *et al.* presented how to synthesize imagery of architectural interiors using stroke-based textures [Klein *et al.*, 2000]. In a preprocessing stage, they captured photos of a real or synthetic environment, mapped the photos to a coarse model of the environment, and ran a series of NPR filters to generate textures. At runtime, the system re-renders the NPR textures over the geometry of the coarse model, and it adds dark lines that emphasize creases and silhouettes. Such a hybrid non-photorealistic rendering and image-based rendering approach makes it possible to reap the benefits of both technologies: an aesthetic rendering of the scene, and visual complexity from a simple model. Fig. 5.13 shows non-photorealistic texture mapping examples for a virtual environment.

Fig. 5.13 Image-based rendering using non-photorealistic textures [Klein *et al.*, 2000]. Copyright of ACM, used with permission

Praun *et al.* proposed a real-time system for non-photorealistic rendering of hatching strokes over arbitrary surfaces [Praun *et al.*, 2001]. It pre-renders hatch strokes into a sequence of mipmapped images corresponding to different tones, collectively called a *tonal art map* (TAM). Strokes within the hatch images are scaled to attain appropriate stroke size and density at all resolutions, and are organized to maintain coherence across scales and tones. In order to maintain both spatial and temporal coherence of the underlying strokes, TAM images are established with a nesting structure among the strokes, both between tones and between mipmap levels. Tone coherence is preserved by requiring that strokes in lighter images be subsets of those in darker ones. Resolution coherence is preserved by making strokes at coarser mipmap levels be subsets of those at finer levels (see Fig. 5.14). At runtime, hardware multi-texturing blends the hatch images over the rendered faces to locally vary tone by weighting each texture image according to lighting computed at the vertices. To render strokes over arbitrary surfaces, a lapped texture parametrization is built where the overlapping patches are aligned to a curvature-based direction field. Fig. 5.15 shows the resultant images rendered with different TAMs.

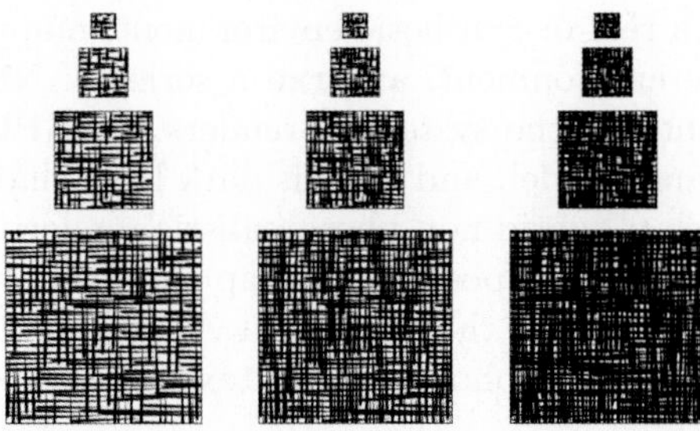

Fig. 5.14 A tonal art map. Strokes in one image appear in all the images to the right and down from it [Praun *et al.*, 2001]. Copyright of ACM, used with permission

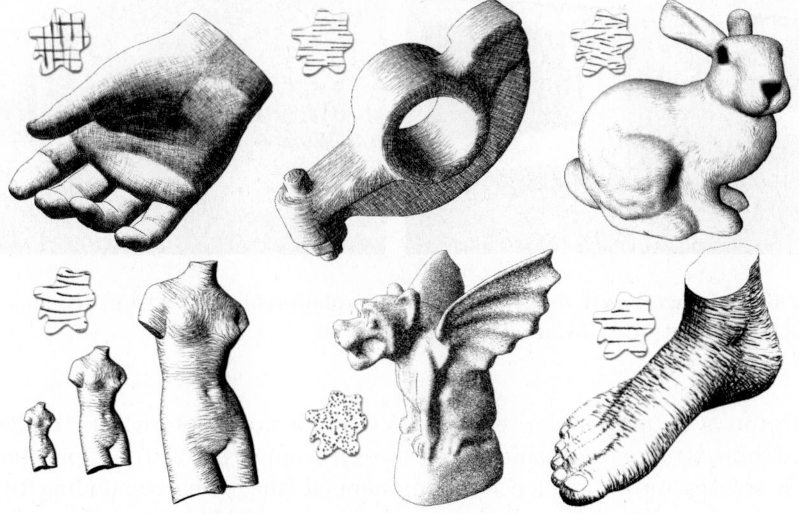

Fig. 5.15 Hatching examples rendered with different TAMs [Praun *et al.*, 2001]. Copyright of ACM, used with permission

Fung and Veryovka further extended the TAM approach that enables representation of arbitrary textures [Fung &Veryovka, 2003]. The TAM images are generated by distributing stroke primitives according to a probability density function. This function is derived from the input image and varies depending on the TAM's scale and tone levels. The distribution functions at multiple resolutions are computed according to some importance functions. Frame-to-frame coherence is preserved by copying drawing primitives from the light tonal textures into dark ones. The resulting depiction of textures approximates various styles of pen-and-ink illustrations such as outlining, stippling and hatching. Fig. 5.16 shows examples of stroke control using the probability density.

Fig. 5.16 The probability of a stroke becoming a hatching stroke increases as the tone darkens [Fung &Veryovka, 2003]. Copyright of ACM, used with permission

Kulla *et al.* presented a method to artistically control the brush stroke texture and color [Kulla *et al.*, 2003]. A scanned paint sample has two distinct properties: texture and color. The global color change across the sample is called the color trajectory, as it defines a path through color space. Texture change can be viewed as a local modulation of the color trajectory. It is created separately by subtracting the color trajectory from each pixel column of the original paint sample. An arbitrary color trajectory can then be added back into this texture difference image to obtain a sample with different colors but similar texture. Three methods, image-based texture synthesis, view aligned 3D texture projection and view-dependent interpolation, are explored to produce rendered, shaded images from the texture samples (see Fig. 5.17).

Hall presented a Q-mapping technique for rendering three-dimensional objects using non-photorealistic cues [Hall, 1999]. Q-maps are three-dimensional textures that make marks on objects, and thus providing visual cues for shape, shade and texture. Standard texture maps are applied before lighting calculations, Q-mappings are applied afterwards. Q-maps adapt to light intensity, typically by making more marks in darker areas. A Q-map can produce images with a very wide range of visual styles (e.g., half tone shading, and pen-and-ink color wash). A rendering system that includes Q-mapping has three parts:

(1) Compute the intensity of reflected light using any standard method, such as ray-tracing.
(2) Apply Q-maps to recolor the point. For each Q-map to be applied:
    - Adapt the Q-map using light intensity.
    - Transform the point from object into Q-map coordinates.
    - Decide if the point is in or out of the Q-map texture.
    - Decide a color for the point, and composite onto current color.
(3) Project the re-colored point onto the image using standard method.

Fig. 5.18 shows examples of the generation of non-photorealistic images by Q-mapping.

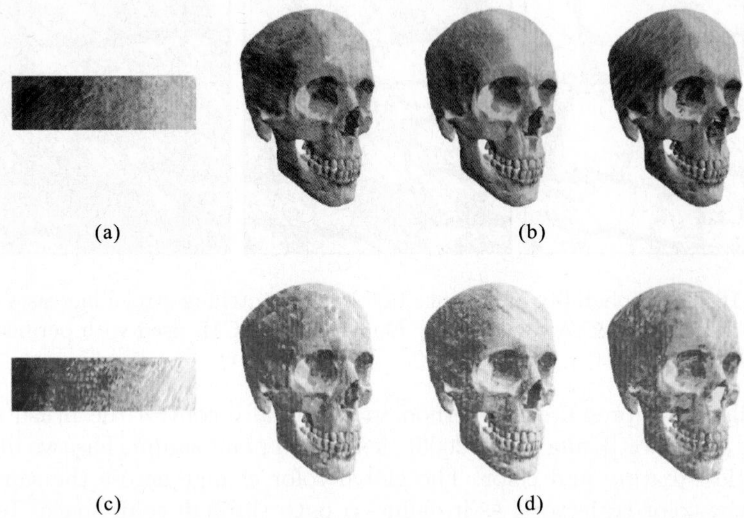

Fig. 5.17 Rendering a skull mesh with different paint samples [Kulla *et al.*, 2003]. (a) Paint samples; (b) Image based Texture Synthesis; (c) View aligned 3D texture projection; (d) View dependent interpolation. Copyright of IEEE, used with permission

Fig. 5.18 Examples of visual styles simulation by Q-mapping [Hall, 1999]. Copyright of Blackwell, used with permission

Veryovka extended threshold-function-based discrete color shading by specifying threshold values with an image or a procedural texture [Veryovka, 2002]. The threshold textures are constructed from texture images using the adaptive histogram equalization algorithm with clipping of values. The mip map filtering is modified to maintain uniform texture effects regardless of surface orientation and scale. Similarly, procedural line textures are constructed with the necessary distribution of values. In order to maintain constant spacing between the lines, it recomputes coordinates of procedural textures depending on surface position. The aliasing artifacts are addressed by filtering shading values produced with multiple threshold samples. The threshold textures are often employed to highlight important features and to suggest surface roughness, or the procedural textures are often used to convey surface curvature by approximating artistic hatching. Fig. 5.19 shows examples when applying the procedural textures.

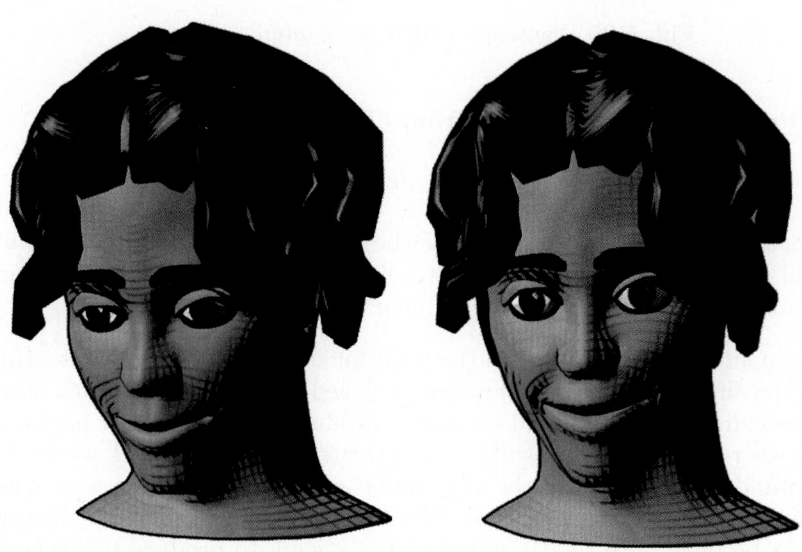

Fig. 5.19 Procedural line hatching is used to convey discontinuities of the hair surface. The spacing of hatching lines adapts to orientation, scale and deformation of the face model [Veryovka, 2002]. Copyright of ACM, used with permission

5.2 Non-photorealistic Rendering with Interim Images

It is easy to create the shading image from a 3D object by traditional computer graphics, and there also exists lots of work for converting the reference image into artistic effect (see Chapter 4). Therefore a hybrid approach for the NPR of a 3D object is proposed. It firstly generates the shading image of the 3D object and then, guided by the corresponding 3D geometry, the improved image-based artistic rendering is applied to generate the final rendition in terms of the visual styles specified by the users. Fig. 5.20 gives a non-photorealistic rendering diagram for it.

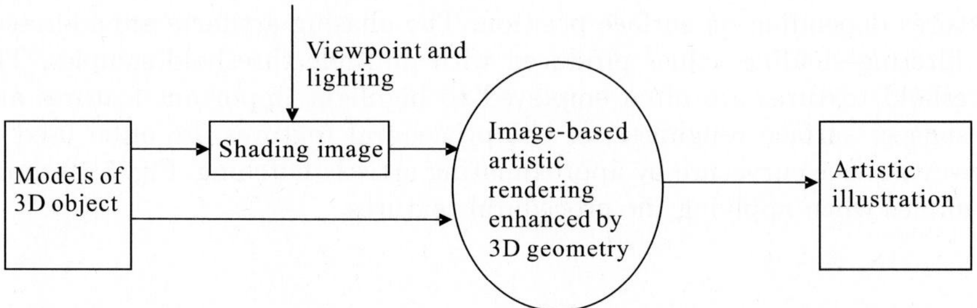

Fig. 5.20 Diagram for NPR using interim image

5.2.1 Pen-and-ink Illustration from 3D Object

Pen-and-ink illustration is a limiting medium. Its major components are strokes, tone, textures and outlines, etc. The pen itself gives off no color or tone, so both color and shading must be suggested by combinations of individual strokes. Compared with the traditional graphics pipeline, there are two fundamental differences between them:

(1) *The dual nature of strokes.* In the traditional graphics pipeline, a texture is typically defined as a set of images assigned to each surface, which affect the shading parameters and the tone is produced by dimming or brightening the rendered shades, while leaving the texture invariant. However, for pen-and-ink illustration, the very same strokes that produce tone must also be used to convey textures (see Fig. 5.21). Thus, tone and texture must become more tightly linked in the system to produce this type of imagery.

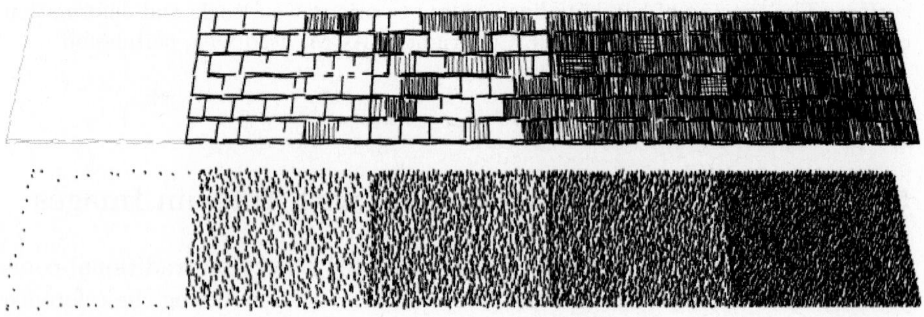

Fig. 5.21 The dual nature of strokes in pen-and-ink illustration [Winkenbach & Salesin, 1996]. Copyright of ACM, used with permission

(2) *The need to combine 2D and 3D information.* For pen-and-ink illustration, the 2D aspects of the particular projection used are every bit as essential as the 3D information for creating a proper rendering. The necessary 2D information takes a number of forms. For example, the size of the projected areas must be used to compute the proper stroke density, in order to accommodate the dual nature of strokes.

Winkenbach and Salesin introduced the "stroke texture", which can be used for achieving both texture and tone with line drawing [Winkenbach & Salesin, 1996]. To render a scene, their system begins by computing the visible surfaces and the shadow polygons. It then uses these polygons, projected to *normalized device coordinate space*, to build the 2D BSP tree and the planar map. Each visible surface is then rendered. The procedural texture attached to each surface is invoked to generate the strokes that convey the correct texture and tone for the surface. All the strokes are clipped to the visible portions of the surface using set operations on the 2D BSP tree. Finally, the outline strokes are drawn by extracting from the planar map all of the outline edges necessary for the illustration. The notable differences from the standard pipeline are given below:

(1) *Maintaining a 2D spatial subdivision.* The need to consider 2D adjacency information in rendering suggests the use of some form of spatial subdivision of the visible surface.
(2) *The rendering of texture and tone.* Polygons are no longer scan-converted, both texture and tone must be conveyed with some form of hatching.
(3) *Clipping.* The strokes must be clipped to the regions they are texturing. Since so many strokes are drawn, the clipping must be extremely fast. Moreover, the clipping should be stroke-based, allowing a wavy stroke to sometimes stray slightly outside of the clipped region.
(4) *Outlining.* Outlines play a significant role in pen-and-ink illustration. Outlines come in two varieties: boundary and interior outlines. The boundary outlines surround the visible polygons of the image, and must be drawn in a way that takes into account both the textures of the surrounded regions, and the adjacency information stored in the planar map. The interior outlines are used within polygons to suggest shadow directions or give view-dependent accents to the stroke texture.

In their system implementation, indication is also allowed. The pen-and-ink illustration required just enough detail in just the right places, and also the fading out of the detail into the unornamented parts of the surface in a subtle and unobtrusive way. The user interactively places "detail segments" on the image to indicate where detail should appear. Each segment is projected and attached to the texture of the 3D surface for which indication is being designed. Fig. 5.22 shows an example of a pen-and-ink illustration from a 3D model.

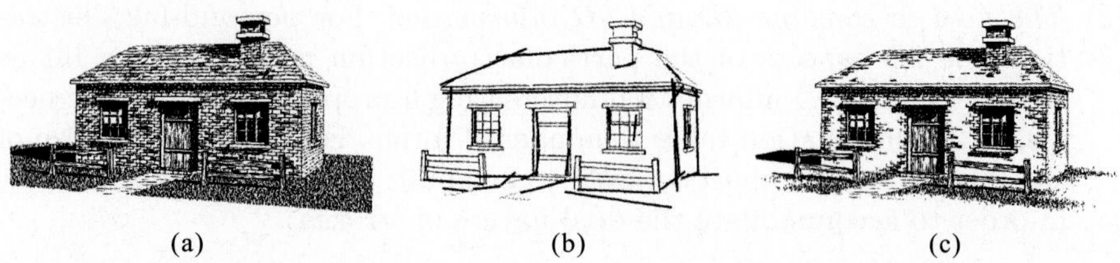

(a) (b) (c)

Fig. 5.22 Pen-and-ink illustration from 3D model [Winkenbach & Salesin,1996]. (a) Pen-and-ink illustration without indication; (b) Detail segments for indication; (c) Pen-and-ink illustration with indication. Copyright of ACM, used with permission

Sousa *et al.* presented a system for non-photorealistic rendering of precise pen-and-ink drawing strokes over dense 3D triangle meshes with arbitrary topology [Sousa *et al.*, 2003]. The precise drawing can effectively illustrate complex mesh models in a simple, informative manner that is valuable, especially for illustrating regions of interest while maintaining shape perception, where the short pen marks are used to depict the geometric forms that give 3D objects their characteristic shape. They utilize techniques from geomorphology to calculate shape measures across the surface of the models. Pen strokes are then modeled and rendered at each edge on the model with automatic thickness adjustment and interactive control over pen marking styles. The main strategies for their precise ink drawing are given below:

(1) *One stroke per mesh edge.* Each stroke has the same length and location of its corresponding edge, and is modeled and rendered individually (i.e., no chaining). This strategy provides rendering at reasonable rates with temporal coherence, as the strokes are fixed to their edges on the model, and are not redistributed for each frame.
(2) *Edge-based shape measures.* It calculates shape measures at every mesh edge, using only information from its two adjacent faces. This is achieved by extending the edge-buffer data structure and by adapting shape measure calculation schemes from geomorphology.
(3) *Pen stroke thickness and styles.* It automatically adjusts the thickness of each stroke as a function of surface curvature estimated at the edge; the user controls the parameters of stroke style for placing different types of pen marks and for achieving ink distribution visual effects.

In their system implementation, two styles are provided: filled and serrated (see Fig. 5.23). *Filled marks* are implemented by simply rendering the stroke defined by the ribbon in black. *Serrated marks* are modeled by distributing marks with different directions and lengths within the ribbon. During its pre-processing stage, a single 3D triangle mesh is read, with no need for either illumination or surface reflectance information. An edge buffer data structure is then constructed with automatic calculation of shape measures directly at each edge, by adapting numerical techniques used in digital terrain analysis (geomorphology). At runtime, the edge-buffer is traversed, carrying user information on (a) which shape measures to display, (b) threshold values for the shape measures and (c) parameters to adjust stroke style attributes. Each edge is then modeled and rendered as a single stroke, with a specific thickness and style. Stroke thickness is automatically adjusted by the pre-computed surface curvature measure associated with the edge. Stroke styles are provided by an interactive stroke model, which reproduces traditional pen marks and visual effects of ink distribution. Fig. 5.24 shows examples of precise drawing.

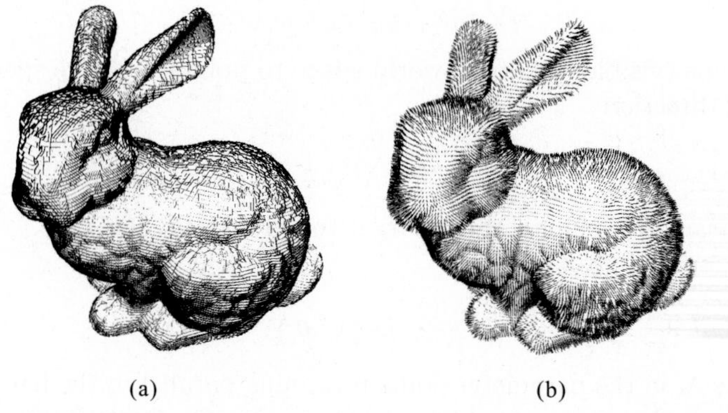

(a) (b)

Fig. 5.23 Filled style (a) and Serrated style (b) of precise ink drawing [Sousa *et al.*, 2003]. Copyright of Blackwell, used with permission

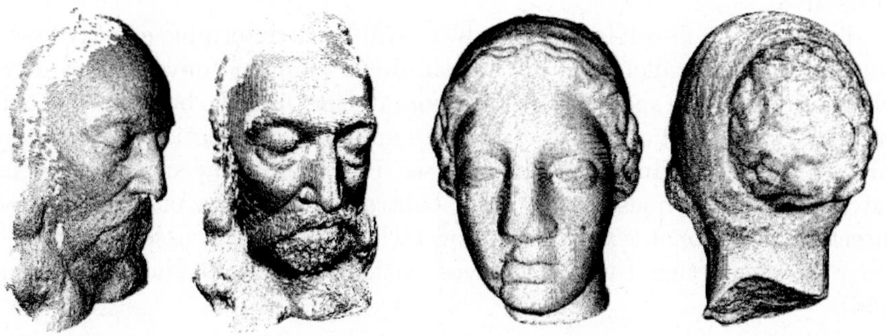

Fig. 5.24 Illustration examples of precise ink drawing [Sousa *et al.*, 2003]. Copyright of Blackwell, used with permission

Winkenbach and Salesin presented algorithms and techniques for rendering parametric free-form surfaces in pen and ink, and introduced the idea of "controlled-density hatching" for conveying tone, texture and shape [Winkenbach & Salesin, 1996]. The controlled density hatching problem is formally stated below:

Given a parametric surface

$$(u, v) \to (x_w, y_w, z_w),$$

which maps points in the parameter domain (u, v) to points in world space (x_w, y_w, z_w). A perspective viewing transformation

$$V : (x_w, y_w, z_w) \to (x, y),$$

which maps (visible) points in world space to points in image space (x, y). A hatching direction

$$h = (h_u, h_v).$$

in the parameter domain and a target tone function $T(x, y)$.

Find a set of strokes

$$\gamma_i = (\lambda_i, \theta_i),$$

with lines λ_i in the parameter domain running parallel to the hatching direction h, such that the apparent tone of mapping the strokes is $T(x, y)$.

Where a stroke γ is defined as a pair of functions (λ_t, θ_t), where λ_t is a line in the parameter domain (u, v), and θ_t is a thickness function, which describes the thickness used in rendering the stroke at every parameter value t. The apparent tone of an image in the neighborhood of a given point in image space (x, y) to the ratio of the amount of ink deposited in the neighborhood to its area .

The key step in solving this problem will be to determine exactly how the images of two parallel lines in the parameter domain converge and diverge when seen in image space. They approximate the distance between two curves in image space, and adjust the thickness and spacing function to compensate for any spreading and compression (see Fig. 5.25). The controlled-density hatching also provides "fine grain" control of the tone of an illustration, therefore traditional texture mapping techniques can be used to extend the range of effects that can be achieved with pen-and-ink rendering (see Fig. 5.26).

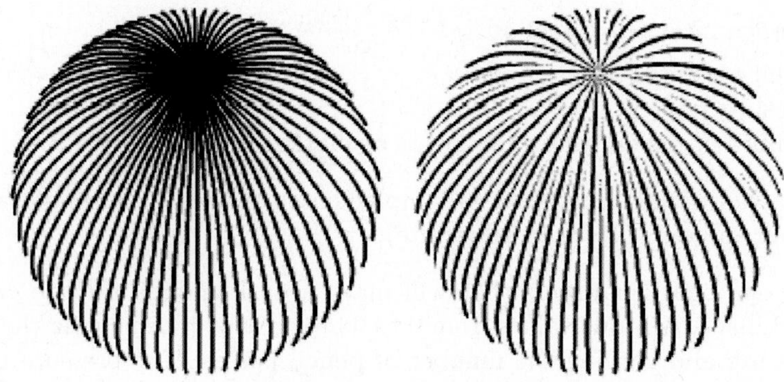

Fig. 5.25 Controlled-density hatching for the perspective of a sphere [Winkenbach & Salesin, 1996]. Copyright of ACM, used with permission

Fig. 5.26 Pen-and-ink illustration for parametric surface [Winkenbach & Salesin, 1996]. Copyright of ACM used with permission

5.2.2 Pencil Drawing from 3D Polygonal Object

A key work on pencil drawing from a 3D polygonal object comes from Sousa and Buchanan [1999a]. They described a 3D rendering, and broke the problem of simulating pencil drawing down into four fundamental parts:

(1) *Drawing materials.* Low-level simulation models for wood-encased graphite pencil and drawing paper, and for blenders and kneaded eraser.
(2) *Drawing primitives.* Pencil stroke and mark-making (for tones and textures) built on top of the drawing materials.
(3) *Rendering methods built on top of the drawing primitives.* Algorithms for outlining, shading, shadowing and texturing of reference images and 3D objects with a look that emulates real pencil renderings.
(4) *High-level tools.* Partial control of the drawing composition through ordering and repeating of drawing steps.

The matching between the tone of the interim image and pencil strokes is carried out by a tone value chart, which is defined as an array tvc_i ($3 \leqslant i \leqslant 11$). Each entry in tvc_i has the following information:

(1) Lightness intensity range $v_{\min}$, $v_{\max}$.
(2) Average intensity value: $av = \dfrac{v_{\max} + v_{\min}}{2}$.
(3) Pencil hardness ph.
(4) Pressure value p.
(5) Number of pencil passes (or layers of marks) np.

Two traditional approaches are implemented to create charts of a graded tone from value 0 (black) to 10 (white):

(1) Use one pencil hardness that will make a dark enough tone to create a solid black. All tone values from 0 to 9 are created by changing the pencil pressure and varying the number of pencil passes. The pressure applied to the pencil is adjusted according to the average tone intensity values and is given by: $p = 1.0 - av$. (see Fig. 5.27 top chart).
(2) Use seven pencils of grades 6B, 4B, 2B, HB, 2H, 4H, and 6H. Pencils are changed to create a gradual blending of the tones. There are slight or no variations on the pencil pressure and variations on the number of pencil passes from one value to the next (see Fig. 5.27 bottom chart).

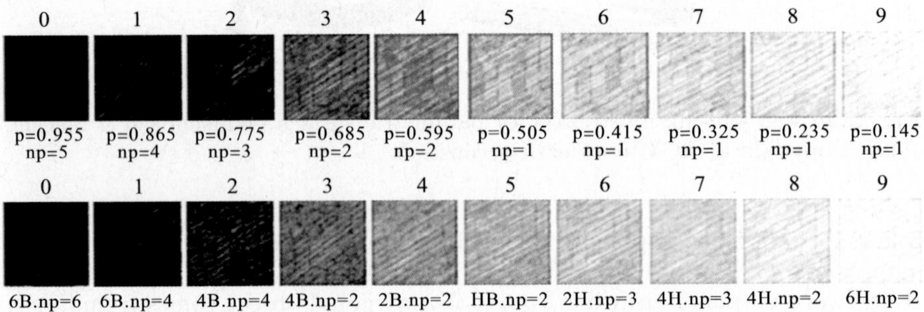

Fig. 5.27 Examples of tone value charts [Sousa & Buchanan, 1999b]. Copyright of Blackwell, used with permission

Its algorithmic pipeline to generate pencil drawing from 3D polygonal model is given in Fig. 5.28. They also provide the control of drawing steps from preparatory sketches to finished rendering results. The pencil drawing examples from a 3D object are given in Fig. 5.29.

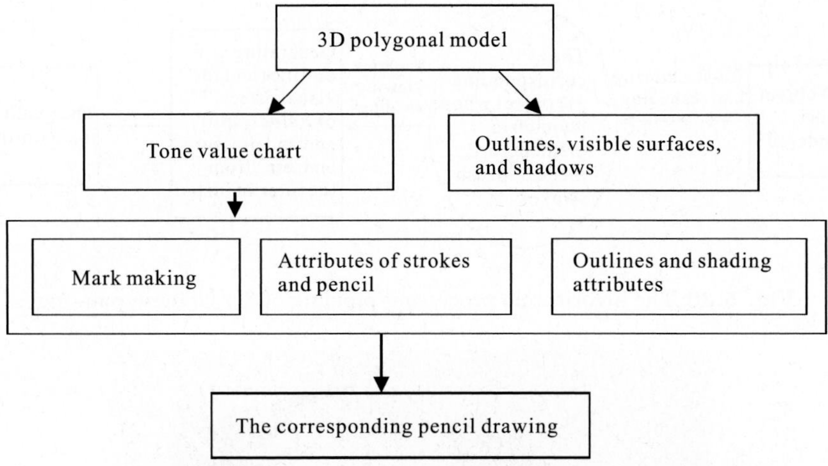

Fig. 5.28 The diagram of pencil drawing from 3D polygonal model

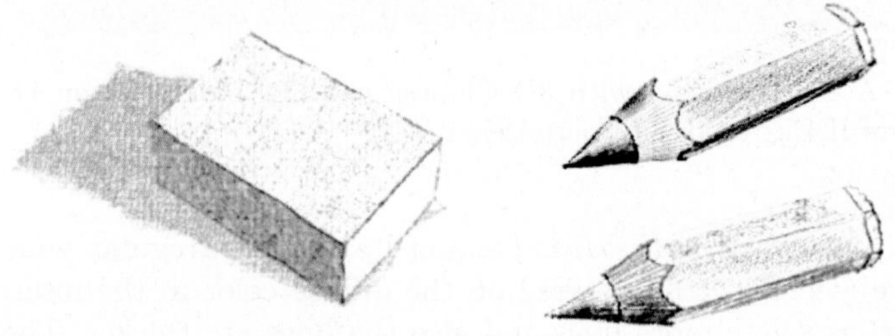

Fig. 5.29 Examples of pencil drawing from 3D polygonal model [Sousa & Buchanan, 1999b]. Copyright of Blackwell, used with permission

5.2.3 Chinese Painting from 3D Model

There are two typical approaches to creating Chinese painting from a 3D model. The first one is to manually re-structure and re-shape the 3D object to be rendered in terms of the characteristics of Chinese painting strokes. That is to say, the brush strokes are modeled as 3D geometric objects that form a 3D scene, and then the photorealistic rendering pipeline is employed to simulate the visual effect of *Feibai* (the white space showing through the strokes), split end (the ends of the brush stroke shape are made transparent), pressure end (the ends of the shape are made darker), etc. Fig. 5.30 shows its algorithmic processing pipeline.

In this method, the Chinese painting is actually modeled in 3D brush strokes (see Fig. 5.31). However, modeling shapes of a 3D object by these 3D brush strokes is a challenge since these strokes (geometric objects) need to be modeled in such a way that they will look interesting from every angle.

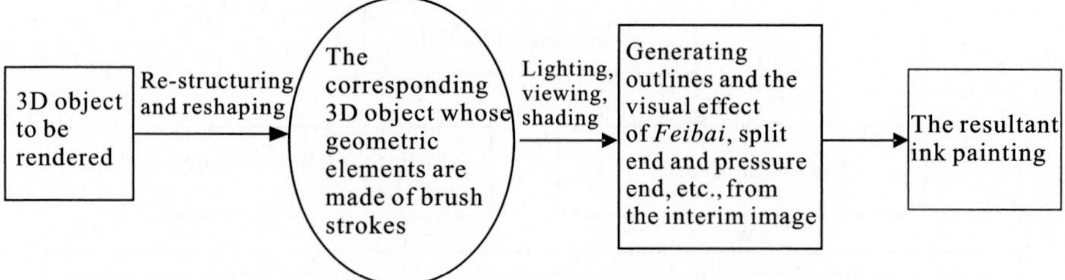

Fig. 5.30 The algorithmic processing pipeline of 3D Chinese painting

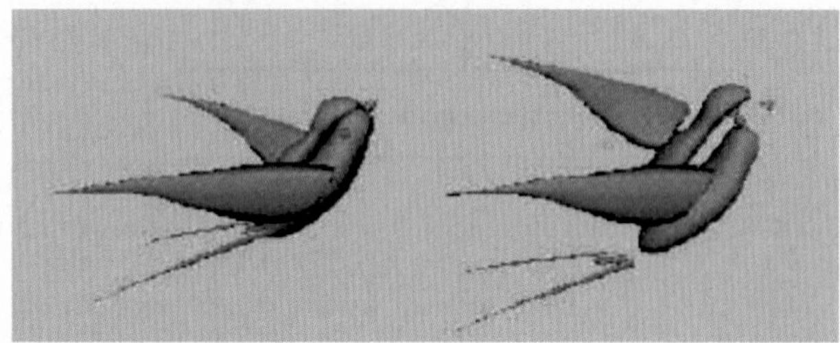

Fig. 5.31 A bird modeled with 3D Chinese painting stokes [Chan *et al.*, 2002]. Copyright of IEEE, used with permission

The visual effect of *Feibai* is created by adding irregular white lines to the surface (see Fig. 5.32). Based on the diffuse color in the interim image, the lighter area gets more lines and also the lines are thicker. The lines are created using a pulse function, whereas a noise function is used to make the lines irregular. The outline of the shape is created by determining the angle between the normal of the surface and the viewing vector. The bigger the angle, the thicker is the outline. The noise function is also used to make the outline irregular.

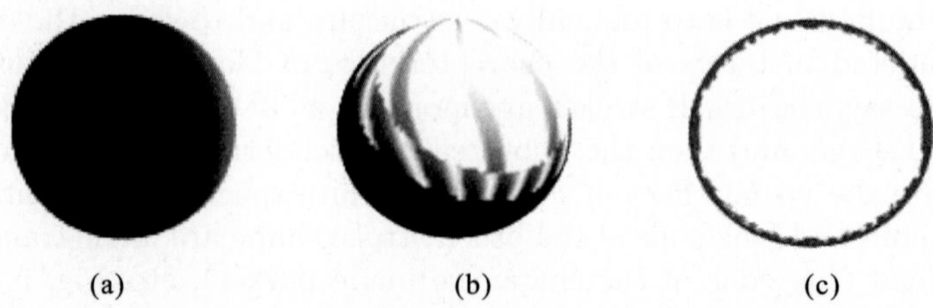

Fig. 5.32 *Feibai* effect and outlines for 3D Chinese painting [Chan *et al.*, 2002]. (a) Diffuse color shader; (b) *Feibai* effect; (c) Outlines. Copyright of IEEE, used with permission

Moreover, to achieve the atmospheric perspective or depth effect, their shaders detect the distance between the camera and the point being shaded. If the distance is large, meaning that the object is farther away, the point is shaded with less opacity, therefore it looks more transparent. Fig. 5.33 shows a 3D Chinese painting of bamboo.

Fig. 5.33 A 3D Chinese painting of bamboo [Chan *et al.*, 2002]. Copyright of IEEE, used with permission

The second approach to generating Chinese painting from a 3D object is shown in Fig. 5.34. It decomposes the rendering of Chinese painting into two parts: borderline drawing and shading of interior region [Yeh & Ouhyoung, 2002].

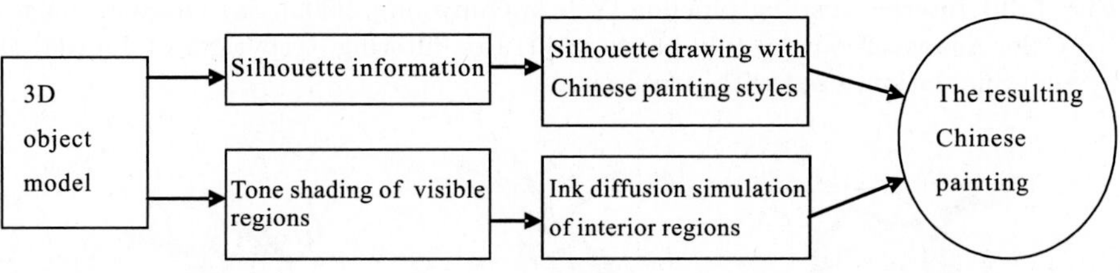

Fig. 5.34 The algorithmic pipeline for generating Chinese painting from 3D objects

In the borderline stroke making process, 3D model silhouettes are first calculated in real-time depending on the viewing direction of the user. After retrieving silhouette information from all model edges, a stroke linking mechanism is applied to link these independent edges into a long stroke. Finally, a plain thin silhouette line is stylized as a stylus stroke with various widths at each control point and a 2D brush model is combined with it to simulate a Chinese painting stroke (see Fig. 5.35). In the interior shading pipeline (see Fig. 5.36), three stages are used to convert a Gouraud-shading image to a Chinese painting style image: color quantization, ink diffusion and box filtering. The color quantization stage assigns all pixels in an image into four color levels and each level represents a color layer in a Chinese painting. The ink diffusion stage is used to transfer inks and water between different levels and to grow areas in an irregular way. The box filtering stage blurs sharp borders between different levels to embellish the appearance of the final interior shading image. In addition to automatic rendering, an interactive Chinese painting system which is equipped with friendly input devices can be also combined to generate more artistic Chinese painting images manually. Fig.5.37 shows examples of Chinese painting generated from 3D models.

Fig. 5.35 Examples of borderline drawing [Yeh & Ouhyoung, 2002]. Copyright of Journal of System Simulation, used with permission.

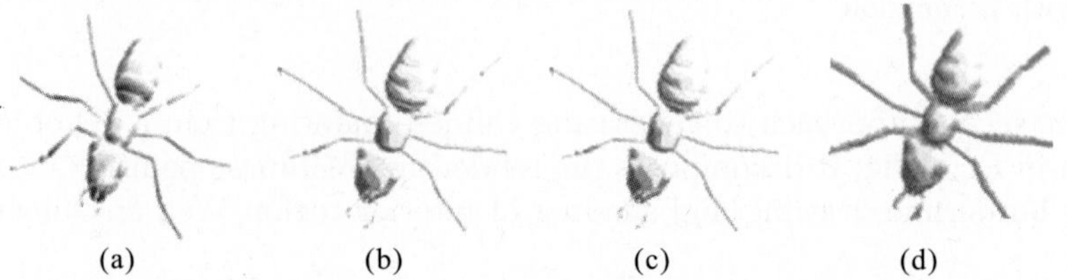

Fig. 5.36 Interior shading pipeline [Yeh & Ouhyoung, 2002]. (a) Original image; (b) Color quantization; (c) Ink diffusion; (d) Box filtering. Copyright of Journal of System Simulation, used with permission.

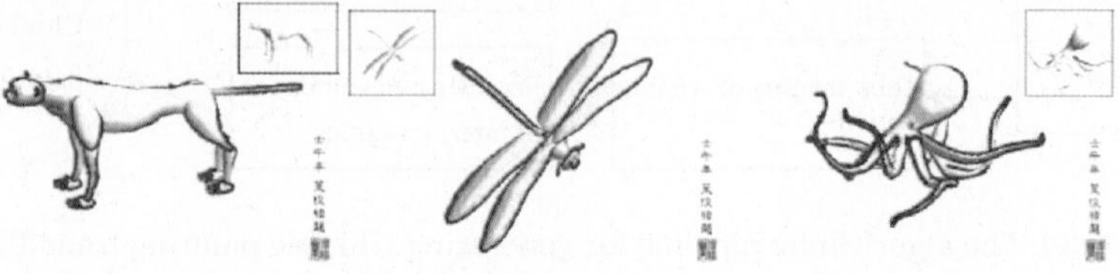

Fig. 5.37 The resulting Chinese painting automatically generated from 3D animal models [Yeh & Ouhyoung, 2002]. Copyright of Journal of System Simulation, used with permission.

5.2.4 Colorful Painting from 3D Model

The color information in the interim image plays a significant role in generating colorful images from 3D model. Some researchers explored forming colorful painting by adding artistic elements such as stylized outlines and shadows into the interim image generated by photorealistic rendering. For example, Decaudin added stylized silhouettes and shadows into the interim images to form a colorful cartoon style rendition [Decaudin, 1996]. Some researchers employed interactive colorful painting methods to generate the desired colorful illustrations, for example, Curtis *et al.* [1997] generated the watercolor painting by allowing the users to manually specify the parameters of strokes and pigments.

Later on, Lei and Chang proposed an approach to create the watercolor effects from a 3D model based on modern per-pixel shading hardware in real-time [Lei & Chang, 2004]. Their rendering pipeline is composed of two phases: color band specifying and watercolor shader. The color-band specifying phase lets the user create a color-band for each object in the scene, using an isotropic lit-sphere interface [Sloan *et al.*, 2001], which is set on top of a watercolor simulation engine, created using Curtis *et al.* [1997] water-flowing model. The watercolor shader takes the original 3D geometric models as the input, and applies the watercolor stylization to the 3D scene using vertex and fragment shaders. The 3D objects and the color-band are first taken to generate a color-map and a granulation-map using a vertex shader script. Then the color-map is further processed using a fragment shader, which takes the color-map and paper-texture as the inputs and combines them with a Sobel edge map to create various watercolor effects (see Fig. 5.38).

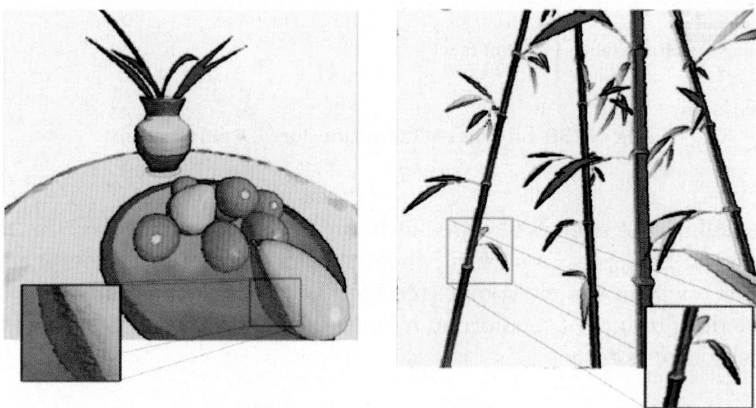

Fig. 5.38 Watercolor painting examples from 3D models [Lei & Chang, 2004]. Copyright of Springer Science and Business Media, used with permission

5.3 Artistic Silhouette and Line-drawing for 3D Model

Silhouettes and line-drawings provide one of the main cues for figure-to-ground distinction and play a significant role in shape conveying and recognition. In this section, we will mainly discuss how to generate silhouette rendition and line-drawing for 3D objects respectively.

5.3.1 Silhouette Rendering from 3D Polygonal Object

The silhouette of an object is the edge of a shape relative to a viewer, it is the boundary of the object's visible and invisible regions. The silhouette edges for 3D polyhedral objects are usually defined as those edges that mark the border between front-facing and back-facing polygons, and the visible parts thereof as visible silhouette segments (see Fig. 5.39). From the point of the drawing of strokes, a silhouette is the union of visible silhouette segments, which are connected to form silhouette strokes.

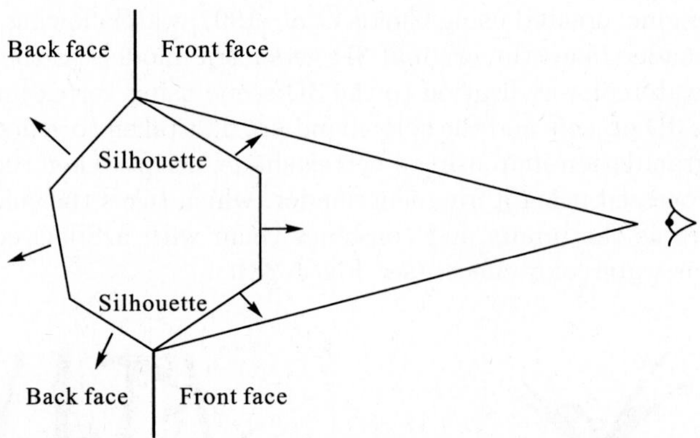

Fig. 5.39 Silhouette definition for 3D polyhedron

The silhouette edge S of a free-form object is typically defined as the set of points on the object's surface where the surface normal is perpendicular to the vector from the viewpoint (see Fig. 5.40). Mathematically, this means that the dot product of the normal n_i with the view vector at a surface vertex P's position p_i is zero:

$$S = \{P : 0 = n_i \cdot (p_i - C)\},$$

with C being the center of projection.

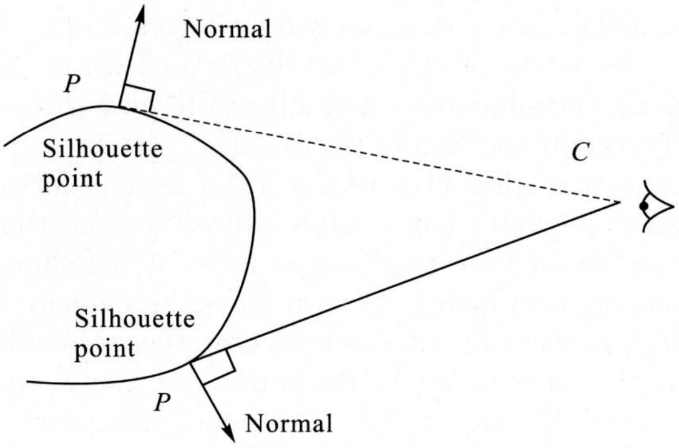

Fig. 5.40 Definition of silhouette for 3D surface model

Every silhouette rendering algorithm must solve two major problems: detecting the set of silhouette edges and determining the visible subset thereof (visibility culling). With respect to solving these two problems, the silhouette rendering algorithms can be categorized as image-based algorithms (the silhouette is represented in an image buffer), object-based algorithms (the resulting silhouette is represented by an analytic description of silhouette edges), and hybrid algorithms [Isenberg *et al.*, 2003].

The image-based silhouette rendering approach usually exploits discontinuities in the image buffer(S) that result from conventional rendering and extracts them using image-processing methods. It usually employs the depth buffer to detect the discontinuities which correspond to regions where there is a sudden change in the depth value of adjacent pixels. For example, Saito and Takahashi applied an edge detector such as the Sobel operator to detect the silhouettes [Saito & Takahashi, 1990]. This has the advantage of only finding object-relevant edges such as silhouette lines including contours, because at most of the places where silhouette lines are in the image there is a (C^0) discontinuity in the depth-buffer (see Fig. 5.41).

 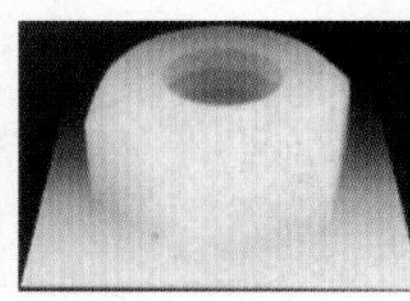 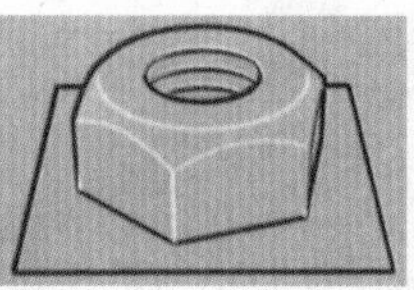 

Fig. 5.41 Image space silhouette detection based on edge detection operators on the Z-buffer [Saito & Takahashi, 1990]. Copyright of ACM, used with permission

Hagen extended this method by using a normal buffer, in which discontinuities correspond to regions where there is a sudden change in the surface normals [Hagen, 2004]. Discontinuities will be detected in both the depth and normal buffers. The union of these two discontinuities is stored in another buffer, representing the silhouette. The silhouette may then be refined using a thresholding function, and finally displayed.

In the object-space silhouette rendering, a straightforward way to determine a model's silhouette edges follows directly from the definition of a silhouette. It consists of two basic steps. First, it classifies all the mesh's polygons as front or back facing, as seen from the camera. Next, the algorithm examines all model edges and selects only those that share exactly one front and one back facing polygon. Buchanan and Sousa suggested using a data structure called an edge buffer to support this process [Buchanan & Sousa, 2000]. In this data structure they stored two additional bits per edge, F and B for front and back facing. When going through the polygons and determining whether they face front or back, they XOR the respective bits of the polygon's adjacent edges. If an edge is adjacent to one front and one back facing polygon, the F, B bits are 11 after going through all polygons. In order to speed up the silhouette detection for changing views, some algorithms use pre-computed data structures, while other algorithms achieve faster execution by employing stochastic methods.

Gooch *et al.* [1999] and Benichou and Elber [1999] presented a preprocessing procedure based on projecting face normals onto a Gaussian sphere. Here, every mesh edge responds to an arc on the Gaussian sphere, which connects the normal's projections of its two adjacent polygons. For orthographic projection, a view of the scene is equivalent to a plane through the origin of the Gaussian sphere. It is further observed that every arc intersected by this plane is a silhouette edge in the corresponding view. Applying this observation to silhouette edge extraction removes the need to check for each frame if every face is front or back facing. The arcs are computed in a preprocessing step and at runtime only the intersections with the view plane are tested. Fig. 5.42 shows an example rendering of the silhouette.

Fig. 5.42 Silhouette rendering based on projecting face normals onto a Gaussian sphere [Benichou & Elber, 1999]. Copyright of ACM, used with permission

Hertzmann and Zorin presented a method that uses a data structure also based on a dual representation [Hertzmann & Zorin, 2000]. This approach constructs a dual representation of the mesh in 4D space based on the position and tangent planes of every vertex. The viewpoint's dual (a plane in 4D) intersects the mesh triangles' dual. Beforehand, the approach normalizes the dual vertices using the norm so that the vertices end up on one of the unit hypercube's sides. (The normalization does not make a difference because the viewpoint's dual plane goes though the origin.) This means you need to intersect triangles in eight 3D unit cubes (the eight hypercube sides) with a plane. At runtime, the approach only computes the viewpoint's dual plane and then intersects it with each hypercube side, resulting in edges that intersect the silhouette. The major advantage of this approach over other methods is that it works for orthographic as well as perspective projections.

Kim and Choe presented a progressive silhouette edges rendering method using level-of-detail meshes, and the stylistic rendering was carried out with stylized brush functions [Kim & Choe, 2002]. The proposed progressive silhouette rendering framework consists of two major steps, one is mesh simplification for silhouette feature preservation and the other is the stylized silhouette edge rendering. The mesh simplification algorithm is based on local changes in volume over the surface and changes in area near surface boundaries. Silhouette information has been used to enhance artistic rendering of 3D objects, and the parameterized brush functions in various styles are employed to artistically render progressive silhouette rendering of triangle mesh of arbitrary topology.

In contrast to precomputation, Markosian *et al.* suggested a stochastic algorithm to gain faster runtime execution of silhouette detection [Markosian *et al.*, 1997]. They observed that only a few edges in a polygonal model were actually silhouette edges. In the hope of finding a good initial set of candidates for front and back face culling, they randomly selected a small fraction of the edges and exploited spatial coherence. Once they detected a silhouette edge, they recursively tested adjacent edges until they reached the end of the silhouette line. In addition, they also exploited spatial coherence, as the silhouette in one frame was typically not far from the (visually) similar silhouette in the next frame. The combination of these two parts of the algorithm yields most of the silhouette edges in one image. However this algorithm can't guarantee finding the entire set of silhouette edges for a certain view in the scene.

However, object space silhouette rendering is usually time-consuming, and a fast but less accurate way of determining silhouette edge visibility is an image space approach. But in many applications, such as the stylized silhouette rendering, only pixel accuracy is necessary. Thus, combining object space and image space approaches in a hybrid algorithm can achieve significant speedup for silhouette rendering. For example, Raskar and Cohen employed a depth buffer to find and display silhouettes based on a solver of partial visibility of a

3D model. The rendering process computes the intersection of adjacent front facing and back facing surfaces in image space at interactive rates [Raskar & Cohen, 1999]; Northrup and Markosian employed an ID buffer and a Z-buffer to determine silhouette edge visibility [Northrup & Markosian, 2000]. A unique color identifies each triangle and silhouette edge in this ID buffer. For each frame, the ID buffer is read from the graphics hardware and all reference image pixels are examined to extract all silhouette edges represented by at least one pixel. The approach then scan converts and checks for visibility the remaining silhouette edges according to whether a pixel with the edge's unique color exists in the ID buffer (see Fig. 5.43). Isenberg *et al.* used a similar approach in principle, and they directly exploited the analytic connectivity information of the mesh in combination with the available Z-buffer information during rendering [Isenberg *et al.*, 2003]. The silhouettes edges are the border between front facing and back facing polygons as silhouette edges and the visible parts thereof as visible silhouette segments. A silhouette stroke is a concatenation of visible silhouette segments that pairwise share a common vertex. The formed long smooth silhouette strokes can be the stylization algorithm.

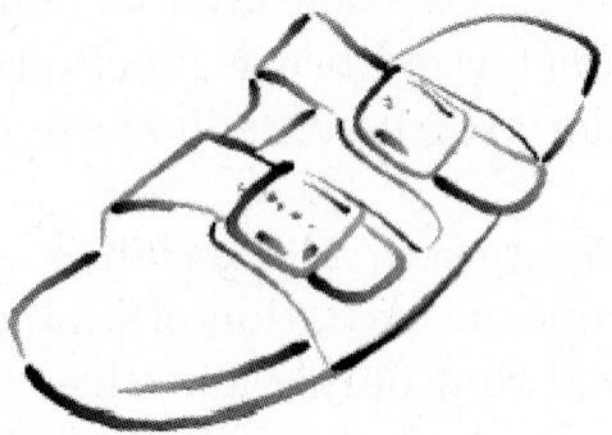

Fig. 5.43 Silhouette rendering in the hybrid approach [Northrup & Markosian, 2000]. Copyright of ACM, used with permission

This hybrid approach is also very popular in the artistic rendering of silhouettes. Martín and Torres developed the Virtual Lights model, which allows the user to define when, how and where the silhouettes will appear in an object [Martín &Torres, 2001]. The main advantage of the method is that it separates the location of the observer and the lighting process from the selection of silhouettes. This is done using external components, the *virtual lights*, which specify the silhouette's location in a more flexible way. The basic idea is to use virtual illumination, which produces virtual changes in shadows and color; these changes are then used to define the silhouettes. Two kinds of silhouettes, outlines and shape lines, are allowed in their system. Given an observer, the outlines are the lines that represent the limit between the visible and invisible parts of the object. Given one or more lights, shape lines are lines that represent the limit between different colors or shades. Fig. 5.44 shows the examples of silhouette rendering with the *virtual lights*.

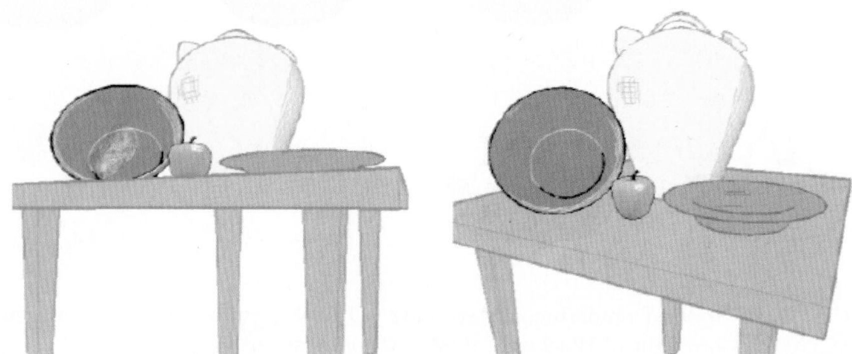

Fig. 5.44 Silhouette rendering with the *virtual lights* [Martín &Torres, 2001]. Copyright of Blackwell used with permission

Furthermore, Martín *et al.* employed the silhouettes to produce the plane elements, which are composed of an area part represented by a polygon, and one or more linear parts represented by silhouettes [Martín *et al.*, 2002]. The form of the object can be transformed artistically, not only by changing the attributes of the silhouettes, but also those of the polygons. The main idea is that, given a 3D scene, each component can be converted into plane elements that are parallel to the projection place, in such a way that the projected image of a 3D scene is equivalent to the composition of these 2D plane elements, like pushing the 3D objects until they are flat. The place representation is termed a layered plane element, LPE. Each LPE has two components: an area represented by a closed polygon, and a closed silhouette (which can be divided into two or more open silhouettes). An object can be divided into one or more LPEs. A convex object always produces an LPE with one polygon and one silhouette, which is closed. A concave object can produce one or more LPEs, each of which can have one closed silhouette or several open ones. The scheme to produce an LPE is as follows:

For each object **do**
  Define and extract the silhouettes
  Obtain LPEs using connectivity and visibility information
  Divide and clean the LPEs to eliminate useless information
End For

Once we have the LPEs of each object, they must be ordered. The correct image is obtained by drawing them from back to front. Fig. 5.45 shows the stylized rendering of flattening 3D objects into silhouettes.

Fig. 5.45 Stylized rendering of flattening 3D objects into silhouettes [Martín *et al.*, 2002]. Copyright of Blackwell, used with permission

5.3.2 Line-drawing for 3D Surface

Line drawing is one of the most common illustration styles, and can be found in many contexts, such as cartoons, technical illustration, architectural design and medical atlases. These drawings often communicate information more efficiently and precisely than photographs. From many points of view, a smooth object may have no visible silhouette lines, aside from the outer silhouette, and all the information inside the silhouette is lost. In these cases, the extra line-drawings should be added to indicate the shape of the 3D surface.

Elber preferred the strokes from isoparametric curves of a free-form surface for line art rendering [Elber,1995]. His strokes are defined as parallel lines in the parameter domain resulting in isoparametric curves. The density of the isoparametric curves are set to be a function of the illumination of the surface determined using a simple shading model, or of regions of special importance such as silhouettes. This works especially well with surfaces of revolution (see Fig. 5.46).

Afterwards, Elber extended these techniques to enable interactive rendering with isoparametric curves, isophotes or lines of curvature on free form surfaces [Elber, 1998]. For rendering, these stroke curves are approximated by piecewise linear polygons. They are then evaluated up to a certain length determined by the shader. For shading, the surface normals at the seed points of the polygons are used. In order to meet real-time demands, all possible strokes are precalculated. Furthermore, the number of polygons involved in the rendering process is effectively reduced by inserting the polygons into buckets. Geometrically, a bucket is a cone outgoing from the origin. The union of all buckets covers the unit sphere. Every bucket contains all normals falling into the corresponding cone. Fig. 5.47 shows an example line drawing of a free-form surface.

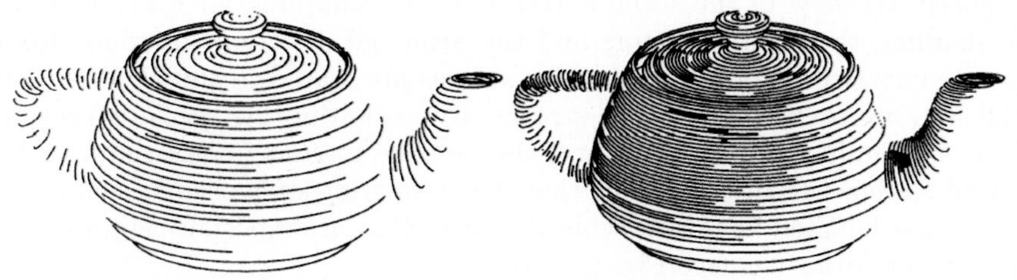

Fig. 5.46 Utah teapot line-art using isoparametric curves, with different densities [Elber,1995]. Copyright of IEEE, used with permission

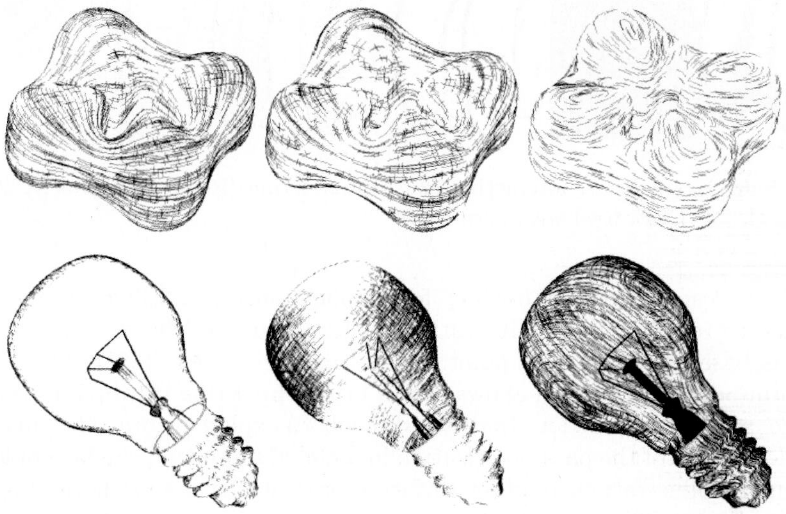

Fig. 5.47 Line-drawing of a wavy torus and a light bulb [Elber,1999]. Copyright of Blackwell, used with permission

Rössel *et al.* further expand Elber's method and utilize it on the triangle meshes, which are a universal representation of surfaces and they become more and more popular for geometric modeling[Rössel *et al.*, 2000]. Discrete curvature analysis on a triangulated surface allows the estimation of differential parameters. Lines of curvature are then constructed to be used as strokes. For the rendering of the scene, such lines are uniformly scattered over the surface. Depending on the point of view and the lighting, the strokes are drawn with different lengths.

Rössel and Kobbelt presented an interactive system for computer-aided generation of line art drawings to illustrate 3D models that are given as triangulated surfaces [Rössel & Kobbelt, 2000]. In a pre-processing step, an enhanced 2D view of the scene is computed by sampling for every pixel in the shading, the normal vectors and the principal directions obtained from discrete curvature analysis. Then streamlines are traced in the 2D direction fields and are used to define line strokes. By exploiting the special structure of the streamlines, an intuitive and simple tone mapping algorithm can be derived to generate the final rendering. The rendering style produces long single or cross hatched lines of varying thickness that are especially appropriate for technical drawings (see Fig. 5.48).

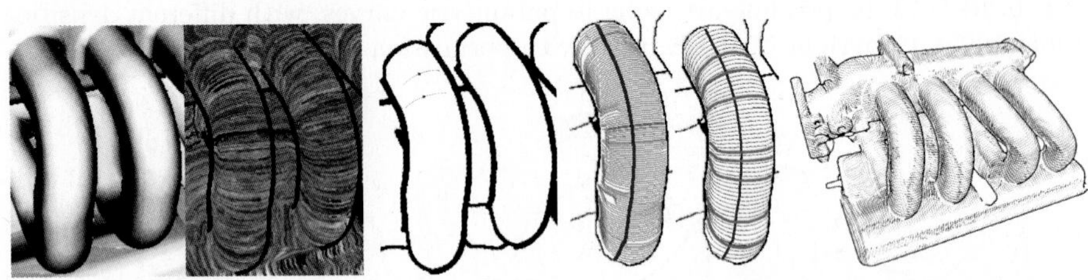

Fig. 5.48 Examples of interactive line art rendering [Rössel & Kobbelt, 2000]. Copyright of IEEE, used with permission

With respect to line-drawing for implicit surfaces, Elber presented a scheme to render line art illustrations of free-form models using a coverage that is based on a uniform point set distribution [Elber, 1998]. The use of uniform point distribution allows one to locally prescribe the direction of the stroke, a degree of freedom that was difficult to exploit before. The coverage is independent of the parameterization in a global sense, and can be employed for line art illustrations of other surface representations, most noticeably for implicit forms. The line art effect is parameterization-independent, and can be combined with traditional rendering techniques such as transparency and texture mapping (see Fig. 5.49).

Fig. 5.49 Examples of line art drawing by point-based coverage [Elber, 1998]. Copyright of IEEE, used with permission

Belyaev *et al.* employed ridges and ravines to depict the shape of the implicit surface [Belyaev *et al.*, 1998]. Ridges are the local positive maxima of the maximal principal curvature along its associated curvature line, and ravines are the local negative minima of the minimal principal curvature along its associated curvature line. They derived formulas to detect the ridges and ravines on a surface given in implicit form, and proposed an algorithm for obtaining the piecewise linear approximation of ridges and ravines as intersection curves of two implicit surfaces. The illustrated ridges and ravines are important for shape analysis and possess remarkable mathematical properties (see Fig. 5.50).

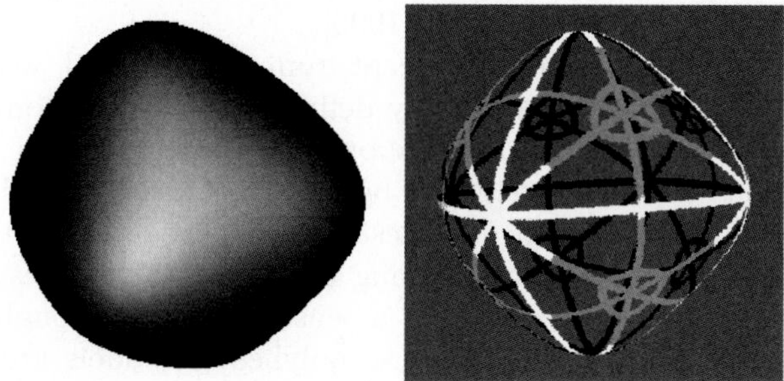

Fig. 5.50 Line drawing for implicit surface [Belyaev *et al.*, 1998]. Copyright of IEEE, used with permission

5.4 Artistic Rendering for 3D Landscape

The modeling of a 3D landscape is very complicated, and its representation forms also vary greatly. The approaches to the artistic rendering of a 3D landscape are classified in the following three ways, in terms of the representational models:

(1) The 3D polygonal or surface models are built as base models to approximate the 3D landscape, and the artistic particles and strokes are created to depict the details of the appearance of a 3D landscape. The resulting rendering is generated by placing these artistic particles or strokes on it directly.
(2) The 3D landscape is represented by special models such as the L-system or shape grammar. The artistic rendering algorithms are embedded into the modeling phases of 3D landscapes, and the resulting illustrations are then generated by the artistic simulation methods aforementioned.
(3) The 3D landscape is represented by point clouds from the 3D scanner, and the artistic illustration is generated by the point-based artistic simulation methods.

5.4.1 Artistic Simulation by Placing Artistic Particles and Strokes on the 3D Surface

In the modeling and rendering of a 3D landscape, artists are able to rapidly create an impression of free-form shape by drawing a few well-chosen strokes. However, it is difficult to do this with conventional 3D modeling systems in a computer graphics community. In order to ease the burden of modeling complex scenes such as 3D landscapes, Kowalski *et al.* treated the rendering strategy as an aspect of modeling, and used strokes to render 3D landscapes in a stylized manner, suggesting the complexity of the scene without representing it explicitly [Kowalski *et al.*, 1999].

They borrowed the "graftal" concept from Smith [1984], which is defined as particles, together with recursively defined L-systems. From the point of view of rendering, these "graftal"s are procedural stroke-based textures. The key requirements are that "graftal"s be placed with controlled screen-space density in a manner matching the aesthetic requirements of the particular textures, but at the same time seeming to "stick" to surfaces in the scene, providing inter-frame coherence and a sense of depth through parallax. In their system implementation, the base polyhedral models are divided into one or more surface regions (called *patches*), to each of which the user can assign one or more procedural textures (called *textures*), although just one is active at a time. The procedural texture elements are placed at specific areas of the surface via a modified version of the "difference image" stroke-placing algorithm, and the particular aesthetic effects are achieved by the customized "graftals" (see Fig. 5.51).

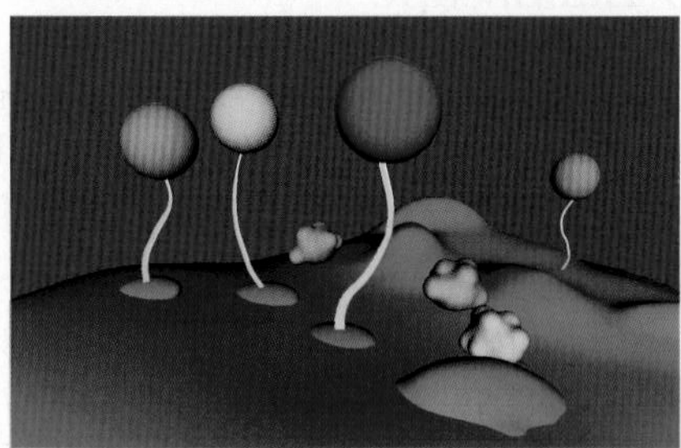

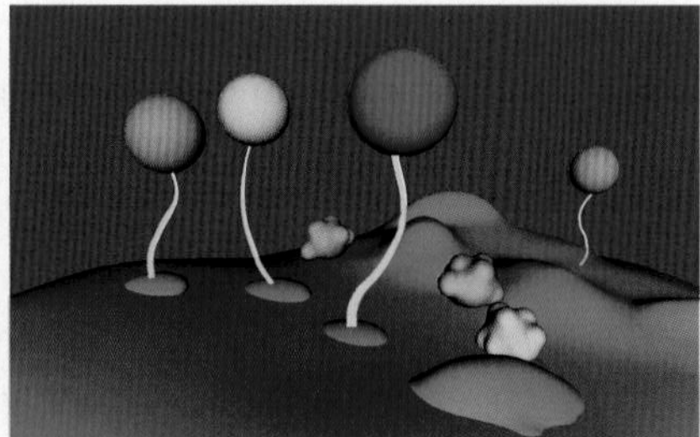

Fig. 5.51 The "graftal" rendering of a 3D landscape [Kowalski *et al.*, 1999]. (a) The 3D landscape represented with polyhedral models (b) The same scene drawn with "graftals". Copyright of ACM, used with permission

Kaplan *et al.* further extended the "graftal" to "geograftal", which are composed of common rendering-related attributes such as normals, positions, colors and highlights [Kaplan *et al.*, 2000]. Each geograftal is statically placed on a model's surface, the creator of a scene can edit the attributes of any geograftal to obtain full control over the look and feel of the hand drawn effects.

Each model within a scene is stored as a list of constituent quadrilateral surfaces which define the mesh. Individual geograftal objects are stored with each surface. Attributes such as location, width, height, type and color are stored with each geograftal object. It allows the user to completely control particle placement, size, shape and orientation on a per object basis, to generate a variety of artistic effects of significant complexity. The subdivision surface models of complex scenes are rendered in a variety of artistic styles, using this interactively editable particle system.

Cornish *et al.* proposed a framework that employs the hierarchical view-dependent clustering algorithm to regulate the number and placement of view-dependent particles, which are inspired by and built upon algorithms for view-dependent polygonal simplification [Cornish *et al.*, 2001]. The object-to-be-rendered is represented as a densely sampled polygonal model, the vertices of this model form the highest resolution of the view-dependent particle system. View-dependent particles provide an efficient multi-resolution structure for fine-grained control over the placement of strokes, and can be generated from any polygonal model. Each node in a view-dependent simplification hierarchy either represents a vertex from the original full-resolution model or a vertex created by a series of vertex merging operations. The nodes form a hierarchy called the particle tree. Each node represents a particle, leaf nodes are attached to a vertex of the original polygonal model, while internal nodes represent the result of particle merging operations. Internal nodes in polygonal simplification typically represent a sort of average of all vertices below them in the hierarchy (see Fig. 5.52).

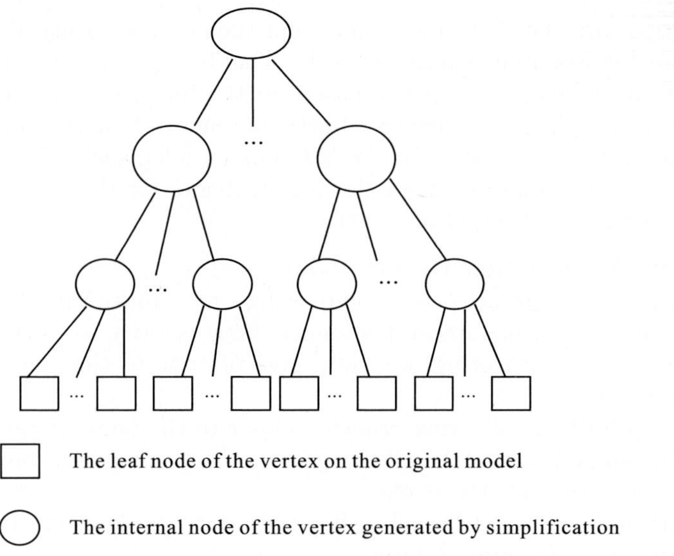

Fig. 5.52 A view-dependent simplification hierarchy

The multi-resolution nature of the structure provides efficient rendering on all scales, allowing densely populated scenes containing tens or hundreds of thousands of particles. Arbitrary scalar or vector fields may be defined over the particles to describe attributes, such as color or orientation, which affect stroke rendering. The view-dependent particles can be adjusted dynamically and continuously as viewing parameters shift, using the underlying multi-resolution structure to enhance interactivity. The resulting rendering can produce compelling artistic imagery of polygonal models in many varied artistic styles at interactive rates (see Fig. 5.53).

Fig. 5.53 Artistic rendering using view dependent particles [Cornish *et al.*, 2001]. Copyright of ACM, used with permission

5.4.2 Artistic Rendering of Plants Based on Their 3D Structure

Landscapes are one of the most important themes in painting. Plants such as trees are the essential painting objects. The 3D modeling method of plants such as the L-system is usually based on the integrated 3D structure and geometry. Therefore, the dedicated artistic rendering methods based on the 3D structure are developed for the 3D plants model, such as trees.

Zhang *et al.* employed the following strategies for their painting of trees by 3D structure [Zhang *et al.*, 1999]:

(1) Move the brush from the root to a branch.
(2) Draw a vital branch (internode) using one stroke. Vitality appears on a branch of strong apical dominance. Give priority to thick branches. If there are two offspring branches, give priority to the one closer to the parent branch.
(3) Give priority to offspring branches closer to the point of view.
(4) If the angle between the offspring branch and the parent branch exceeds a limit, terminate the stroke.
(5) Draw a background branch using a separate stroke if the branch is not hidden by a foreground branch.

Their geometrical models of trees are generated from a growth model, i.e., a tree is modeled on the simple dichotomy of its skeleton and thickness (diameter). A skeleton is a set of internodes of a tree. An internode of a tree is represented by a line segment $e = (p, q)$ and a diameter d_e, where p and q are position vectors of the terminal points. The entire rendering pipeline is composed of the following three major steps:

(1) Split the tree into strokes, i.e., sequences of line segments each of which represents an internode of the tree(see Fig. 5.54).
(2) Eliminate the hidden parts from each stroke under a certain criterion and define the substrokes for the remainder of the tree;
(3) Draw the strokes individually by applying the models for ink transfer, diffusion, paper and brush (see Fig. 5.55).

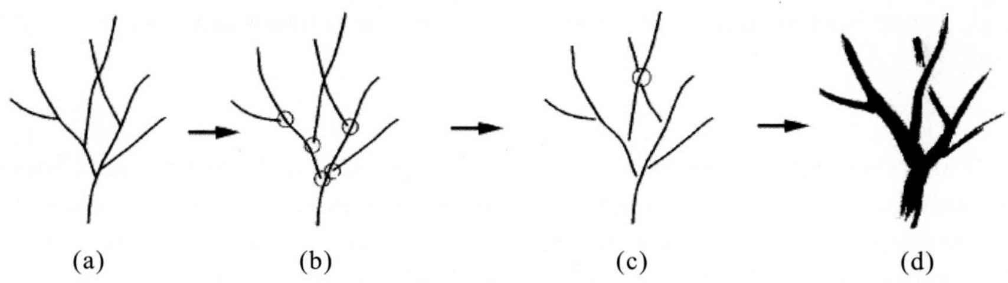

Fig. 5.54 The process of splitting a tree into strokes [Zhang *et al.*, 1999]. (a) The tree model; (b) The initial splitting of strokes; (c) The dividing of intersection strokes; (d) The final painting. Copyright of John Wiley & Sons, Ltd., used with permission

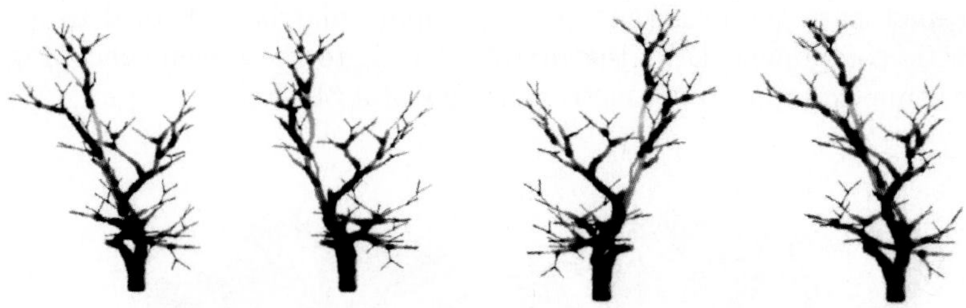

Fig. 5.55 The resulting painting of trees rendered from different view points [Zhang *et al.*, 1999]. Copyright of John Wiley & Sons, Ltd., used with permission

Way *et al.* presented a set of novel methods to automatically draw trees in Chinese ink painting from 3D polygonal models. Outline rendering and texture generation use the information of the silhouette, shade and orientation of the three-dimensional model's surface to draw a particular tree [Way *et al.*, 2002]. The depth map, normal map and curvature maps (see Fig. 5.56) are constructed as the reference maps to analyze the information for the bark texture.

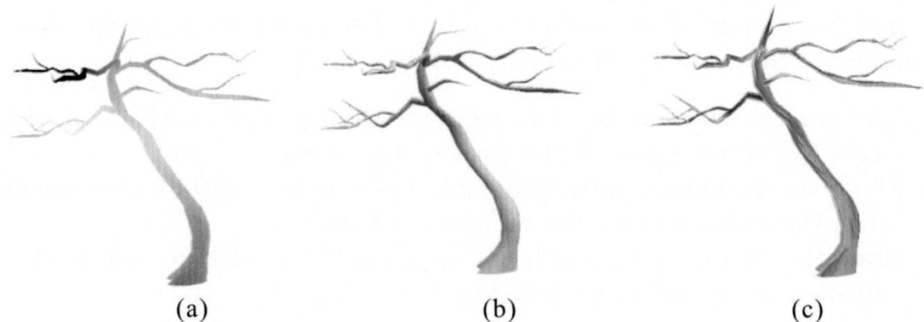

Fig. 5.56 Reference maps for the analysis of information for the bark texture [Way *et al.*, 2002]. (a) Depth map; (b) Normal map; (c) Curvature map. Courtesy of Way *et al.*

They employed a procedural textural approach to preserve the Chinese ink painting style from accurately rendering the surface. The texture shape is controlled by defining at least one brush stroke on the texture pattern. A 2D texture pattern is created to preserve both the stroke path and the brush profile. Let $\tau(G, B, s, t)$ be a unit texture pattern defined by the brush stroke set (G, B) at texture coordinate (s, t). Each brush stroke(g_i, b_i) of (G, B) is defined by two components—stroke geometry (path), g_i, and brush profile, b_i. In practice, g_i can be defined by a set of control points to specify the path of the stroke at a texture coordinate, and b_i can be defined by a set of parameters of the brush model. A mapping matrix is defined to map the geometric component, G, of texture pattern, τ, to the screen space. Fig. 5.57 shows some examples of Chinese paintings of a 3D tree.

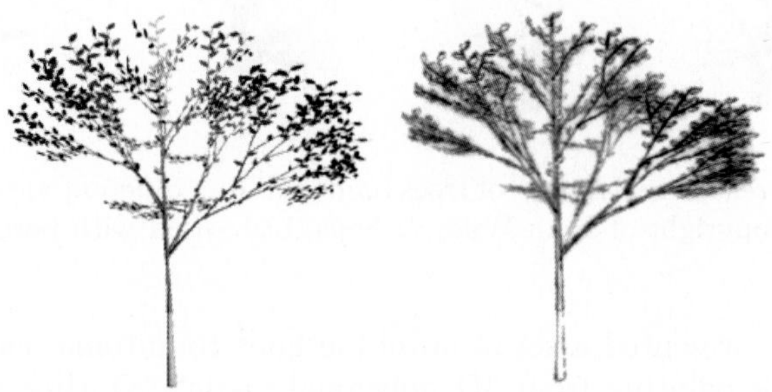

Fig. 5.57 Example painting of 3D trees [Way *et al.*, 2002]. Courtesy of Way *et al.*

Aiming to provide a transition from a tree illustration with a realistic plant-specific look to an abstract representation, Deussen and Strothotte presented a framework for a pen-and-ink illustration of a 3D tree model [Deussen & Strothotte, 2000]. They employed the "divide-and-conquer" strategy, and separately rendered the tree skeleton and the foliage. The tree skeleton is usually drawn up to the second branching level, and the trunk and branches are represented by silhouette lines augmented by crosshatching in dark areas (see Fig. 5.58). The foliage is drawn by using abstract drawing primitives that represent leaves. Such primitives can be circles, ellipses or other polygons. The visual appearance of the foliage can be divided into three areas. The top of the tree is usually in direct light and is therefore visualized by only some details and its outline. In the half shadow more details are drawn to achieve an appropriate grey level and the outline of the leaves is often drawn in detail. The third area is the shaded part. An interpolation scheme allows the users to adapt the form of the primitives to the normal vector of the particles that are used as input. Depth differences are used to determine which part of the primitives is drawn (see Fig. 5.59).

The depth differences can be computed from the depth values in eye coordinates to achieve linear differences or directly for the depth buffer values. The depth z in the eye coordinate system is calculated from a depth value d ($d \in [0, \ldots, 1]$) by the following equation:

$$z = \frac{\dfrac{z_1 z_0 (d_1 - d_0)}{z_1 - z_0}}{d - \dfrac{(z_1 + z_0)(d_1 - d_0)}{2(z_1 - z_0)} - \dfrac{(d_1 + d_0)}{2}},$$

where d_0 and d_1 are minimal and maximal values represented in the depth buffer, and, z_0 and z_1 are the corresponding depth values of the near and far clipping plane in the camera projection.

With this proposed method, the users are able to generate illustrations with different drawing styles and levels of abstraction. The illustrations generated are spatially coherent, enabling us to create animations of sketched environments (see Fig. 5.60).

Wilson and Ma attempted to deal with highly complex geometrical models, such as trees, in a way that gives clear, meaningful and artistically believable renderings [Wilson & Ma, 2004]. Unnecessary or incomprehensible details are removed while preserving important details and as much texture as possible. Their system supports two primary pen-and-ink styles for tree rendering: silhouette edge rendering, in which only edges are drawn and hatching, in which small groups of parallel lines are drawn. For silhouette edge renderings, complex areas are identified and important edges in those areas are drawn to match the greyscale value of a target rendering. For hatching, small blocks of the image with similar properties are extracted, allowing abstraction of low importance details but preservation of the more important

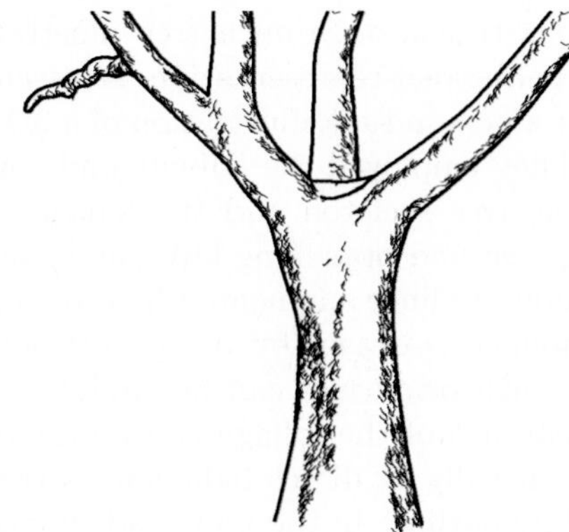

Fig. 5.58 The trunk and main branches of a tree are extracted and rendered by silhouette lines and cross hatching [Deussen & Strothotte, 2000]. Copyright of ACM, used with permission

Fig. 5.59 The pen-and-ink illustration with different threshold of depth discontinuities [Deussen & Strothotte, 2000]. Copyright of ACM, used with permission

Fig. 5.60 The pen-and-ink illustration examples of 3D trees [Deussen & Strothotte, 2000]. Copyright of ACM, used with permission

boundaries. These two methods can be combined in different amounts to achieve a range of rendering styles imparting different information and style. In the system implementation, they combined the two-dimensional image processing techniques and three-dimensional geometry-processing techniques in a hybrid pipeline to leverage the strengths of each. An intermediate rendering stage, combined with image processing techniques such as segmentation provides additional information to the final renderer about how the viewer will perceive the scene. These techniques, each with their own large range of stylistic control, can be combined to form a continuum of styles. This information is combined with the original geometry to generate the final stylized rendering. Fig. 5.61 shows the example rendering of trees.

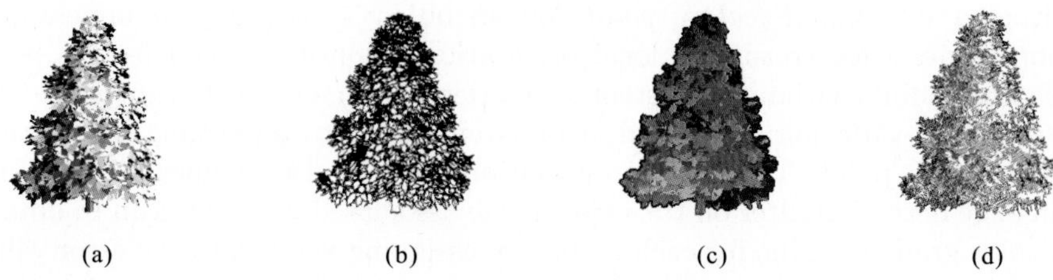

Fig. 5.61 The pen-and-ink illustration of trees with silhouettes and hatching [Wilson & Ma, 2004]. (a) Reference image; (b) Silhouette rendering; (c) Depth map; (d) Hatching illustration. Copyright of ACM, used with permission

5.4.3 Artistic Rendition for Point-based Models

Using points as alternative modeling primitives has been explored for over a decade and has recently received increasing attention. Points have been shown to be advantageous over polygons when representing highly detailed features. The output of the 3D scanner is usually represented as a point cloud. Recently, researchers have shown increasing interest in capturing and processing real-world 3D objects and scenes, as advances in 3D scanning technology are making this 3D acquisition method feasible for objects on ever larger scales. Outdoor scanning is becoming an efficient way to acquire real world environments.

Outdoor environment scans demonstrate the following properties [Xu & Chen, 2004]:

(1) Incompleteness. A complete scan of every object in the environment is impossible to obtain due to the usual obstructions caused by intervening objects, and the constrained accessibility of the scanner.
(2) Complexity. Natural objects, such as trees and plants are complex in terms of their geometric shapes.

(3) Inaccuracy. Distant objects are less accurate due to scanning hardware limitations, and plants and trees can be moved by wind during the scanning process.
(4) The data size is relative large, and holes and noise are also apparent in the dataset.

These properties raise unprecedented challenges for existing methods, as most of them have been focused on generating a complete polygon mesh from points. Certain heuristics or even manual controls have to be specified to smooth out noise and patch up holes, which can be a tedious and even prohibitive process.

In order to artistically render the point-based models, each point is first classified through a *feature degree* computation and a fuzzy classification as either a *directional feature point* (on an object's geometry or appearance boundaries with consistent local orientation), *non-directional feature point* (feature points without consistent local orientation), or *non-feature point* (the rest). The variation in normal error is employed to determine the feature degree of a point. The normal estimation error is also augmented by using an edge detection filter on the color image associated with the scan to obtain a color gradient value for each point. By assigning weights to the error value and the gradient value, a final feature degree is assigned to each point, with large feature degrees denoting points with high variation in normal estimation error and large color shifts. The points are sorted from low to high feature degree and divide the list evenly into bins. The bins are then used to produce iterations with decreasing brush size (see Fig. 5.62).

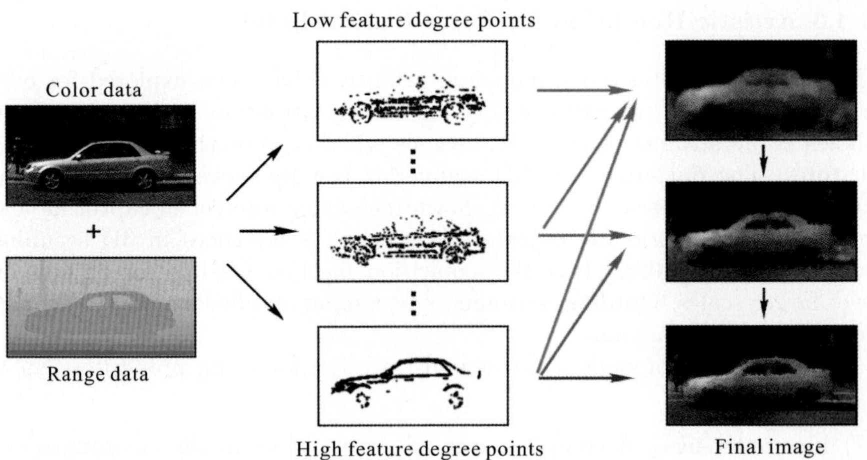

Fig. 5.62 The rendering pipeline for point-based models [Xu *et al.*, 2004]. Copyright of John Wiley & Sons, Ltd., used with permission

Once this classification is achieved, points of different classification are depicted using strokes of various styles. While the directional feature points are usually drawn using line segments or textured strokes with their orientation guided by the point's direction, the non-directional points are drawn using strokes of uniform direction (pre-determined) or isotropic strokes such as circular point sprites. To illustrate an object's shading tone, a subset of the non-feature points is also depicted, using strokes similar to those of non-directional feature points. These points are selected through a conventional dithering operation.

Adams *et al.* proposed a unified sample-based approach to represent the geometry and appearance of the 3D object as well as the brush surface [Adams *et al.*, 2004]. Their point-based model can be re-sampled dynamically and adaptively to store appearance detail across a wide range of scales. Each surface sample carries geometric attributes such as position, normal and radius, as well as a set of appearance attributes which represent the paint pigments: dry paint attributes, wet paint attributes and wet paint volume per unit area. The point samples are stored in a kd-tree which is used for efficient collision detection and neighbor collection during painting.

In their painting system, the user interface enables the artist to manipulate the brush, mix paint, move the object and apply paint in an intuitive manner. The virtual brushes are modeled by a geometric representation of the point-sampled surface, wrapped around a mass-spring skeleton, which is a physics-based skeleton to simulate the dynamic behavior of the brush (see Fig. 5.63). This flexible brush model enables us to define different brush types of various sizes and resolutions. Collision detection between the brush and complex 3D objects is possible at high rates. Since the paint transfer is handled locally between brush and surface samples, texture parameterization and patching become obsolete, it permits painting onto irregularly sampled object surfaces without distortions or visual artifacts, and supports a variety of paint effects, including paint diffusion, gold, chrome and mosaic paint, and renders the objects in high quality(see Fig. 5.64).

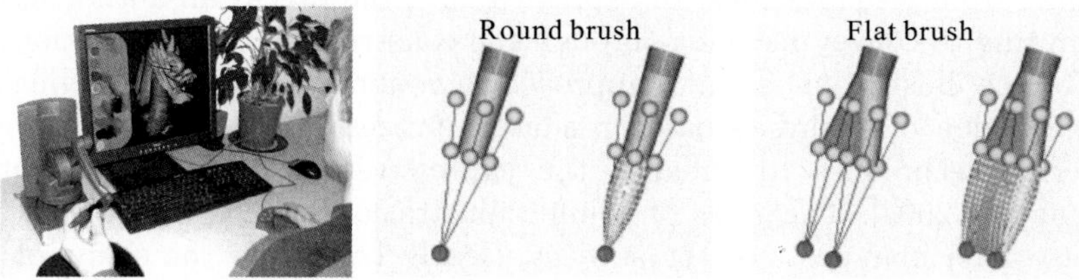

Fig. 5.63 The painting interface and the virtual brush model [Adams *et al.*, 2004]. Copyright of IEEE, used with permission

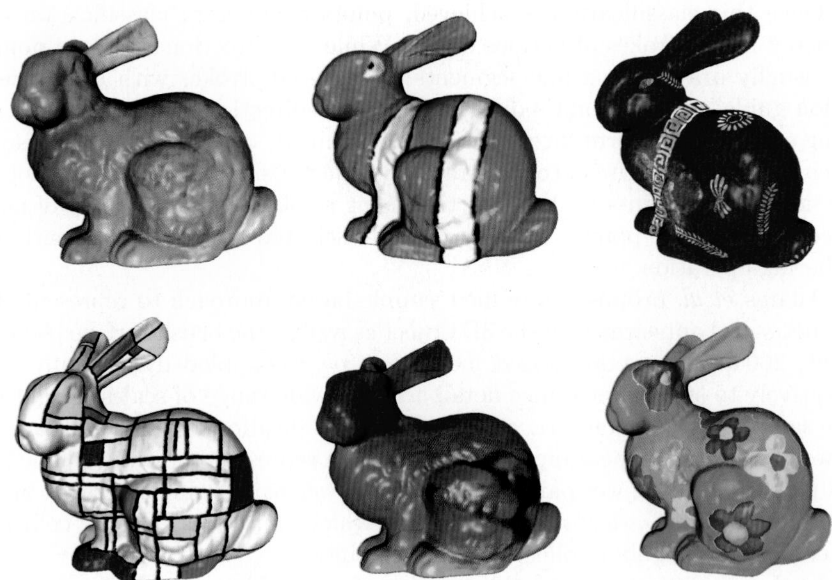

Fig. 5.64 Painting example of point-based Bunny models [Adams *et al.*, 2004]. Copyright of IEEE, used with permission

5.5 Artistic Illustration of Volume-based Models

A volume model is a visual representation of a large data set that can capture both interesting elements and interesting structure inside the data. It is often created for scientific visualization, whose main goal is to effectively convey information to the user using the wide input channel provided by the human visual system. The scientific visualization can be divided into two categories in terms of its expressive roles: interpretive and expressive [Gordin *et al.*, 1996]. In interpretive use, the user is primarily a viewer who is attempting to extract meaning from visualizations. In expressive use, the user is an author who is attempting to convey meaning through the construction of visualizations.

Volume illustration is a new approach to volume rendering, involving the augmentation of a physics-based rendering process with non-photorealistic rendering techniques to enhance the expressiveness of the visualization [Rheingans, 2004]. The goals of volume illustration include directing attention to particular parts of the subject, clearly conveying the shape of the subject, emphasizing depth relationships of items in the scene, and conveying the nature of the translucence of objects. The major differences between volume illustration and surface-based artistic rendering are summarized as below:

(1) In surface-based artistic rendering, the surfaces (features) are well defined, whereas, with volumes, the volumetric features vary continuously throughout three-dimensional space and are not as well defined as surface features.
(2) In a surface model, the essential feature is the surface itself. The surface is explicitly and discretely defined by a surface model, making "surfaceness" a Boolean quality. Many other features, such as silhouettes or regions of high curvature, are simply interesting parts of the surface. Such features can be identified by analysis of regions of the surface. In a volume model, there are no such discretely defined features. Additional processing is required to first identify interesting features in the volume.
(3) A few of the usual depth cues are present in traditional rendering of translucent volumes. Obscuration cues are largely missing since there are no opaque objects to show a clear depth ordering. Perspective cues from converging lines and texture compression are also lacking, since few volume models contain straight lines or uniform textures. The dearth of clear depth cues makes understanding spatial relationships of features in the volume difficult. Similarly, information about the orientation of features within the volume is also largely missing.

Algorithms for volume illustration can be categorized into two general approaches. Surface algorithms first map the volume data to representative geometry, such as an isosurface of constant value, and then render the geometric representation using artistic rendering techniques. The second type of approach, direct volume rendering, generates the image directly from the volume data, without first creating any geometry. We will discuss both of them in detail in this section.

5.5.1 Artistic Rendering of Surface Features of Volume Model

The features of surface and boundary in a volume model are composed of the overall shape of the representative geometry, silhouettes, border lines, tone, texture and shadow, etc. It is possible to generate a single scan-converted solid stroke texture that can be used to illustrate the essential shape information of any level surface in the data. For example, Interrante presented a method to place an evenly distributed set of tiny opaque particles on the surface via 3D line integral convolution through the vector field defined by the principal directions and principal curvatures of the level surfaces passing through each grid-point of a 3D volume [Interrante, 1997]. From the point of view of research methodology, the volume data is often converted into iso surfaces. In addition, there are also attributes associated with the whole volumetric object, such as texture identifier, normals, colors. Non-photorealistic rendering techniques are then employed to generate the resulting illustration. Fig. 5.65 shows an illustration example of a Microsoft mouse with various artistic rendering effects.

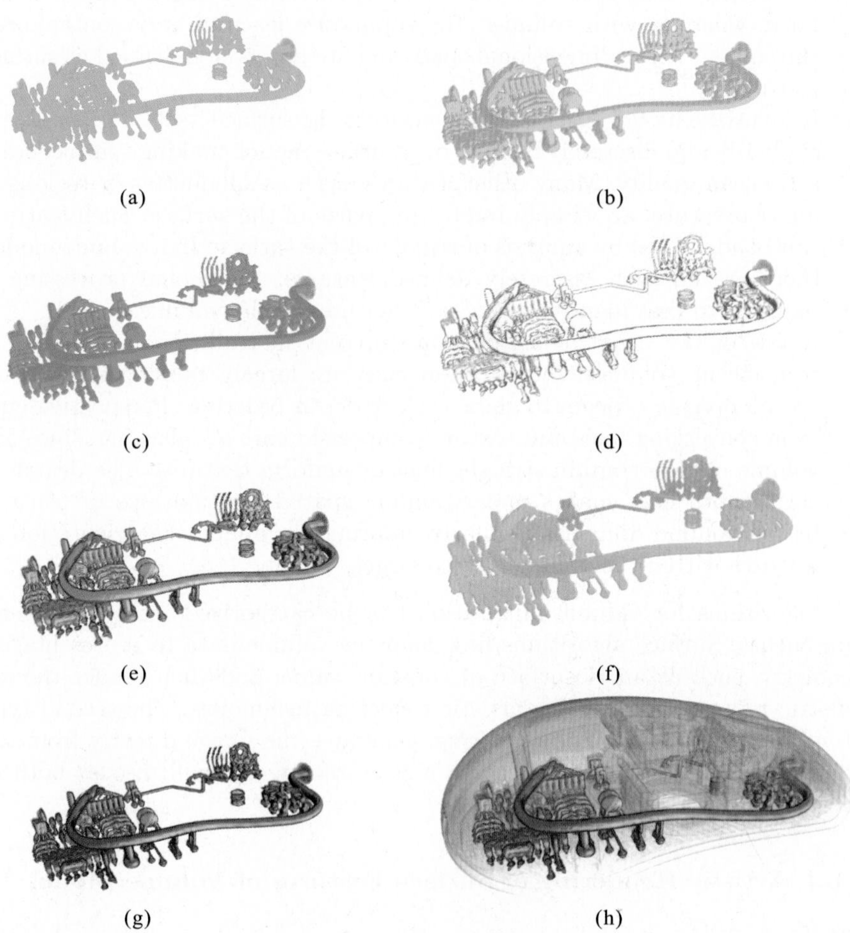

Fig. 5.65 An example of combined illustration techniques on the mouse data set [Lum & Ma, 2002]. (a) Volume without light; (b) Cool to warm shading contribution; (c) Volume with cool to warm shading; (d) Silhouette contribution; (e) Volume with silhouette; (f) Depth color cue contribution; (g) Volume with depth color cue; (h) Final volume illustration. Copyright of ACM, used with permission

Most artistic rendering techniques such as line-drawing, silhouette, pen-and-ink illustration, can be applied after the geometric representation of the volume model is built. For example, Nagy *et al.* employed the hatching technique to enhance the features of the volume model [Nagy *et al.*, 2002]. Their hatching fields coincide with the principal curvature directions along selected volume structures. To generate hatching strokes a number of seed points are scattered into the volume. The number of effectively placed seed points is determined by the normalized gradient magnitude and mean curvature information. The overall volume hatching is split into two passes. In the first pass hatching strokes are rendered as line strips starting at the currently selected seed points. In the second pass the volumetric dataset is rendered by means of three-dimensional texture maps. Later on, Nagy and Klein further presented an accurate, interactive silhouette extraction mechanism for texture-based volume rendering [Nagy & Klein, 2004]. It serves the purpose of visualizing silhouettes with an accurate width of one pixel. In a subsequent step, the silhouettes can be optionally broadened, either by a fixed pixel width or, depending on screen-space depth, using image processing. This illustration technique is in particular insensitive to coarse discretization in the dataset.

Treavett and Chen presented two pen-and-ink rendering methods based on the isosurface representation of the volume model [Treavett & Chen, 2000]. The pen-and-ink line-drawing are illustrated by the scalar fields, which are the underlying mathematical definition of a volume dataset coupled with an interpolation function. Their system implementation is built upon a traditional volume rendering pipeline integrated photorealistic rendering. It is demonstrated that such an integration facilitates an effective mechanism for enhancing visualization and its interpretation (see Fig. 5.66).

Dong *et al.* proposed a volumetric hatching approach for producing pen-and-ink drawings from medical volume data [Dong *et al.*, 2003]. Their hatching with line strokes accounts for data beneath the surface, and requires determining not just the position of the line strokes, but also their orientation. Thus, the strokes not only illustrate the subject's shape, but also describe its character in some way, for example, by displaying fiber orientations for muscles. This volumetric hatching approach is well-suited for medical illustrations. The results are pen-and-ink-style images (see Fig. 5.67).

Lu *et al.* employed the stippling technique to artistically illustrate the volume dataset [Lu *et al.*, 2003]. Stippling is effective for many applications and provides a quick and efficient method to investigate both volume and surface models. Lu *et al.* explored several feature enhancement techniques to create effective, interactive visualizations of scientific and medical datasets. These enhancements include a new method for silhouette curve generation, varying point sizes and stipple resolution adjustments based on distance, transparency and lighting effects. They provided an effective way to interactively preview large, complex volume and surface datasets in a concise, meaningful and illustrative manner.

Besides the geometric representation in isosurface form, the volume model of an object can also be directly converted into the polygonal mesh representation of its surface. Kobbelt *et al.* extended the well-known Marching Cubes algorithm for the surface extraction, and its sampling is feature-sensitive and thus reduces these alias effects, while keeping the simple algorithmic structure of the standard Marching Cubes algorithm [Kobbelt *et al.*, 2001].

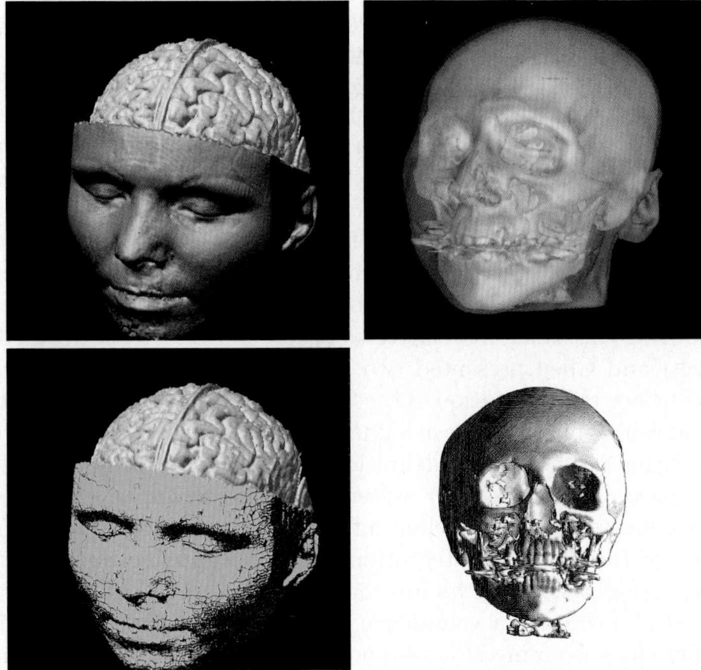

Fig. 5.66 Examples of traditional visualization and pen-and-ink based line-drawing of the volume dataset [Treavett & Chen, 2000]. (a) Traditional visualization of volume dataset; (b) Pen-and-ink based line-drawing of volume model. Copyright of IEEE, used with permission

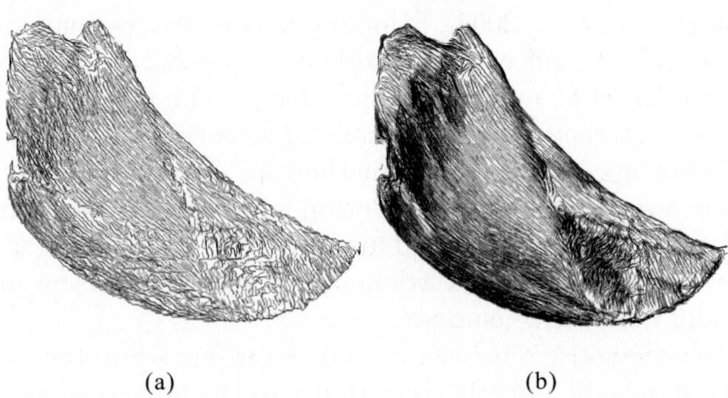

Fig. 5.67 Comparison of (a) Surface hatching with (b) Volumetric hatching. Volumetric strokes better describe the subject [Dong *et al.*, 2003]. Copyright of IEEE, used with permission

5.5.2 Artistic Illustration of Internal Structure of Volume Model

Surfaces are the most popular geometric representation for 3D models, as they are easy to construct, transmit, and render. However, the surface representation is limited because it lacks internal information. The key advantage of direct volume rendering over surface rendering approaches is the potential to show the structure of the value distribution throughout the volume, rather than just at selected boundary surfaces of variable value (by isosurface) or coordinate value (by cutting plane). There has been extensive research into illustrating surface shape using non-photorealistic rendering techniques. However, accurately and automatically conveying the structure of a volume model is a problem not fully solved by existing volume rendering approaches. Physics-based volume rendering approaches create images which may match the appearance of translucent materials in nature, but may not embody important structural details. Transfer function approaches allow flexible design of the volume appearance, but generally require substantial hand tuning for each new dataset in order to be effective.

One special challenge facing artistic illustration of internal structures of a volume model is the specification of features and parameters of visual effects such that the resultant images are in fact providing useful insights into the objects of interest. Rheingans and Ebert introduced a general method for creating halo effects during the illumination process using the local spatial properties of the volume [Ebert & Rheingans, 2000]. Halos are created primarily in planes orthogonal to the view vector by making regions just outside features darker and more opaque, obscuring background elements which would otherwise be visible. The strongest halos are created in empty regions just outside (in the plane perpendicular to the view direction) of a strong feature. The halo effect at a voxel is computed from the distance weighted sum of haloing influences in a specified neighborhood. In order to restrict halos to less interesting regions, summed influences are weighted by the complement of the voxel's gradient. The believable lighting and shadows can also enhance the spatial structure of internal objects inside the volume model. For example, a rim shadow, one particular form of stylized lighting effect, shows the periphery and distant areas of the subject to be in shadow, simulating a beam of light from the front. Tone shading adds warm/cool cues to shape, simulating the chromatic warming produced by a warm-spectrum light source. Outlines serve an important purpose in conveying shape by emphasizing important boundaries and providing detail in flat parts that would not be captured by lighting cues.

Overlaying the silhouettes on top of a volumetric image can help to better convey the geometric structure of inner objects that are exposed during a direct rendering process. Csébfalvi *et al.* utilized object contours to enhance the shape features of internal objects inside the volume model [Csébfalvi *et al.*, 2001]. Object contours are usually characterized by locally high gradient values. Based on the magnitude of local gradient information as well as on the angle between the viewing direction and gradient vector, data-values are mapped to visual properties (color, opacity), which then are combined to form the rendered image. This illustration approach varies the ways of visualizing the interior of a 3D dataset, and is very useful when the user aims to peer inside 3D objects (see Fig. 5.68).

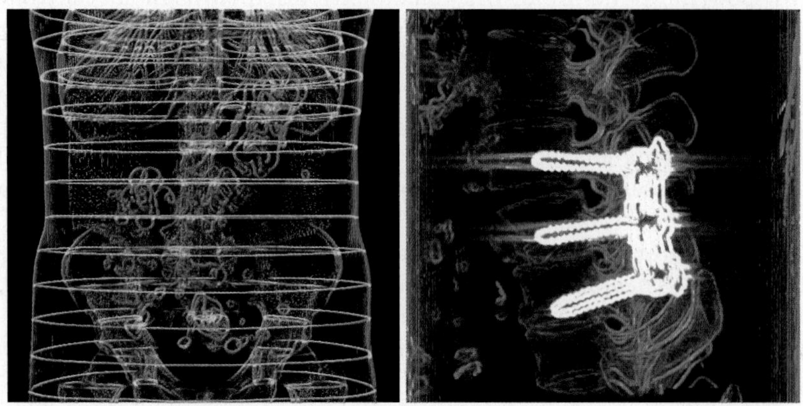

Fig. 5.68 Illustration examples based on contour enhancement [Csébfalvi *et al.*, 2001]. Copyright of Blackwell, used with permission

Schein and Elber presented an algorithm for silhouette extraction from volumetric data [Schein & Elber, 2004]. Trivariate tensor product B-spline functions are used to represent the data. An offline phase that arranges the data in a lookup table is employed to improve the computation time during an interactive session. A subdivision scheme is employed to extract the silhouette curves from an implicit trivariate B-spline function. It can generate high-quality smooth silhouettes that are of great value in the generation of technical illustrations. Fig. 5.69 shows a distance-based coloring scheme for the extracted silhouettes. Silhouettes that are close to the viewer are shaded in red, while silhouettes that are farther away are shaded in dark blue.

Burns *et al.* described a method for creating line drawings from volumetric datasets by extracting linear features such as contours and suggestive contours directly from the data [Burns *et al.*, 2005]. The resultant imagery is often more comprehensible than standard rendering styles, since it focuses attention on important features in the data. Both the efficiency and comprehensibility of these algorithms are demonstrated by creating a variety of figures based on a variety of datasets using a working system (see Fig. 5.70).

If there are no apparent objects inside the volume model, it will be difficult to express the internal structure merely by silhouettes or line-drawings. The texture mapping techniques are then employed to represent the internal information inside the volume data model. The user can visually obtain

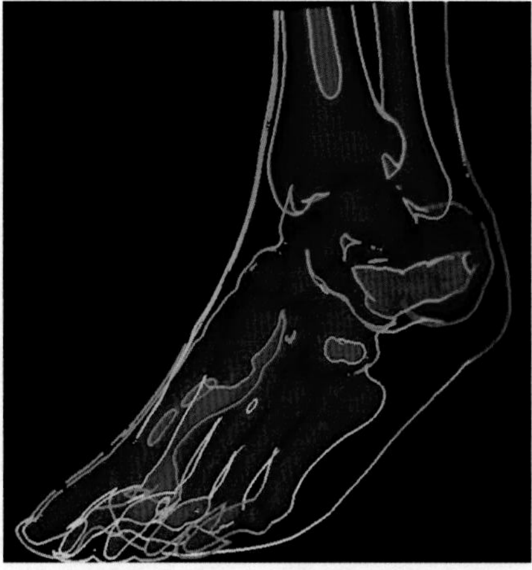

Fig. 5.69 The color-coded silhouette of the foot volume [Schein & Elber, 2004]. Copyright of Springer Science and Business Media, used with permission

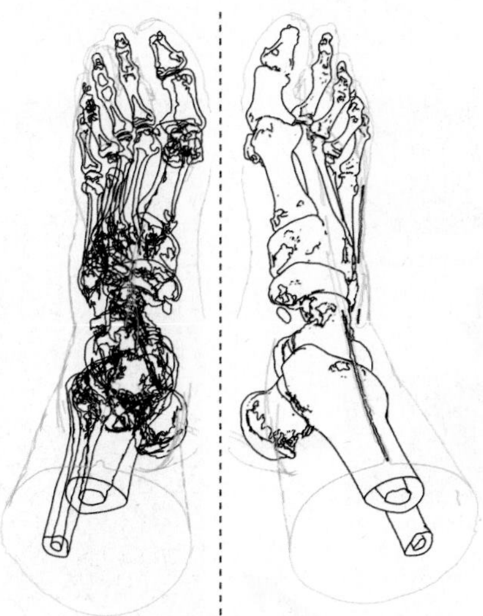

Fig. 5.70 Two volumetric line drawings. The left one is without hidden surface removal [Burns *et al.*, 2005]. Copyright of ACM, used with permission

the internal information of volume models by cutting the volume models at the desired locations, and browsing the cross-section with internal textures. Owada *et al.* developed an interactive designing and browsing system that allows the user to add interesting textures to surface meshes manually by using existing 2D reference images [Owada *et al.*, 2004]. To assign internal textures to a surface mesh, the designer cuts the mesh and provides simple guiding information to specify the correspondence between the cross-section and a reference 2D image. The guiding information, such as flow orientation, is stored with the geometry and used during the synthesis of cross-sectional textures. The texture synthesis technique is then employed to generate a plausible cross-sectional image using 2D reference images, instead of sampling directly from a complete 3D RGB volumetric representation. The overall pipeline to illustrate the internal information by textures is shown in Fig. 5.71. It supports three types of textures: isotropic, layered and oriented. Isotropic textures have a uniform distribution in 3D space with no dependency on position or orientation. All of the cross-sections of an isotropic texture look similar, regardless of their location or orientation. Layered textures have varying appearances according to their position in the axial or radial direction, and it requires depth information for the target 3D region. Oriented textures are defined by both a reference image and a flow direction, the appearance of an oriented texture depends on the orientation of the cut-plane relative to the flow-direction. Fig. 5.72 shows more illustration examples of a volume model with internal textures.

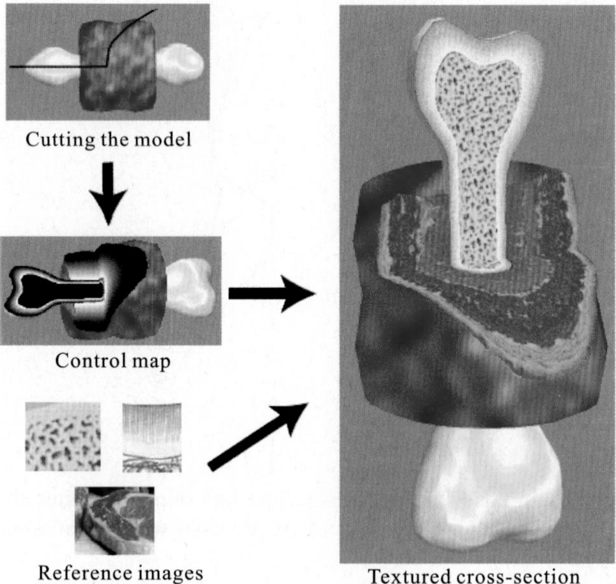

Fig. 5.71 The overall pipeline to illustrate the volume model with internal textures [Owada *et al.*, 2004]. Copyright of ACM, used with permission

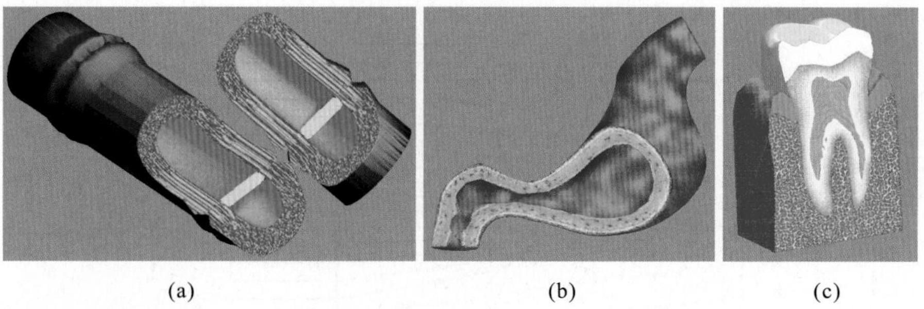

(a) (b) (c)

Fig. 5.72 Volume illustrations with internal textures [Owada *et al.*, 2004]. Copyright of ACM, used with permission

Wang *et al.* proposed a "focus+context" framework that uses various standard and advanced magnification lens rendering techniques to magnify the features of interest, while compressing the remaining volume regions without clipping them away completely [Wang *et al.*, 2005]. The magnification lens is based on the magnification model in optical physics. It provides users with a method for close inspection of regions of interest in volumetric objects. Fig. 5.73 illustrates the principle of a magnification lens. The blue line segment represents a magnification lens positioned on the image plane by the user. L_c is the center point of the lens and F is the virtual focal point. The transition region is represented by the red line segments on the image plane with a width L_b, L_r is the radius of the lens, and the magnification region of the lens is shown as the blue line segment. For a ray starting from a point P_l in the transition region, the direction is computed according to the distance from P_l to L_c as follows:

$$\frac{|P_F - F|}{L_r} = \frac{|P_l - L_c| - (L_r - L_b)}{L_b}.$$

Let P_F be the point at which this ray passes through the virtual lens focus plane, which is parallel to the image plane and includes the focal point F. P_F is calculated by the following equation:

$$P_F = F + \frac{P_l - L_c}{|P_l - L_c|} \times |P_F - F|,$$
$$\text{ray\_dir} = P_F - P_l.$$

Assuming that P_{RI} is the orthogonal projection of P_R on the image plane, the magnification factor mf for point P_R is calculated by

$$mf = \frac{|P_R - P_{RI}|}{|F - L_c|}\left(\frac{L_b}{L_r} - 1\right) + 1.$$

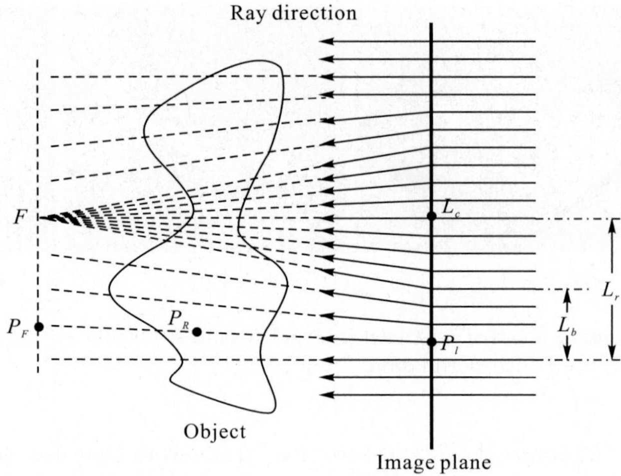

Fig. 5.73 The principle of a magnification lens [Wang *et al.*, 2005]. Copyright of IEEE, used with permission

When orthogonal incident rays hit the image plane, in the region of the magnification lens, then the ray directions are modified and go through the focal point F. Therefore, a ray cone is formed between the lens and F. The objects within this cone are rendered in a larger area on the image plane than their original size, while the other objects retain their original size. Consequently, the objects in the region of interest are magnified.

In feature-driven volume visualization, the free-form magnification lens can be employed to also achieve feature-sensitive and feature-centric object enlargement. The difference is that the shape of the magnification lens is defined dynamically by the shape of the features (represented by the segmentation information) in the dataset, within an arbitrary viewport (see Fig. 5.74). For each ray orthogonally incident upon the image plane, the new direction is computed as follows. Assuming all rays have changed directions to the focal point F,

(1) If a ray passes through the feature, then its new direction is pointing to F.
(2) If the ray does not pass through the feature but is inside the transition region on the image plane, the distance d (see Fig. 5.74) from its entry point to the boundary of the feature projected area is calculated. This distance is used to compute the new direction.
(3) Otherwise, the ray continues in its original direction.

Fig. 5.75 shows the illustration samples of feature magnification.

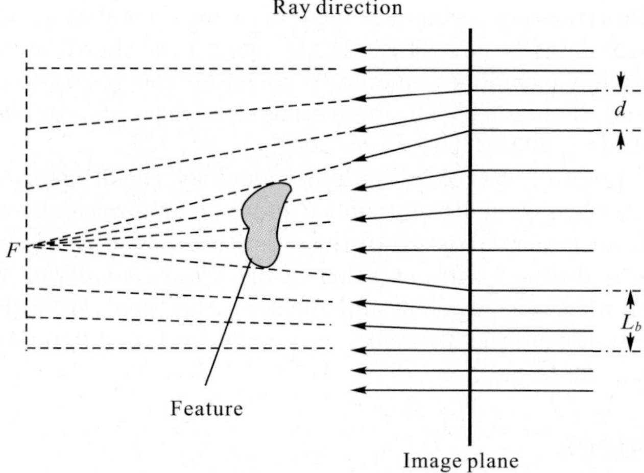

Fig. 5.74 Feature-based lens illustration [Wang *et al.*, 2005]. Copyright of IEEE, used with permission

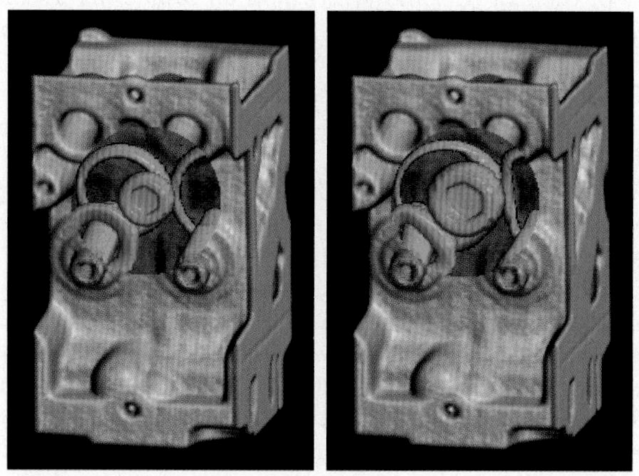

Fig. 5.75 Feature magnification illustration examples with different magnification factors [Wang *et al.*, 2005]. Copyright of IEEE, used with permission

5.6 Summary

In this chapter, the artistic rendering techniques for 3D objects are reviewed in terms of research methodology and drawing skills. In general, 3D artistic rendering techniques are becoming mature, and the modeling domain has been extended from 3D polygonal objects to 3D landscapes, 3D surfaces and 3D volume models, etc. For the time being, real-time artistic rendering techniques get more attention in the booming video game industry, and some of the artistic rendering techniques have been implemented in the 3D game engine [Freudenberg *et al.*, 2001]. At the same time, hardware-accelerated artistic rendering techniques emerge to speed-up the generation of artistic rendition, and it becomes an interesting tendency in non-photorealistic rendering [Raskar, 2001; Claes *et al.*, 2001].

From the point of view of research methodology, the 3D artistic rendering techniques should systematically embed more commonsense knowledge and experience from human artists into the algorithm. If a breakthrough can be made in the real-time implementation of 3D artistic rendering in the near future, it will be very convenient and effective when generating the resulting artistic rendition from the 3D model, especially for the illustration of a large scene or a huge dataset.

References

Adams B, Wicke M, Dutré P, Gross M, Pauly N, Teschner M(2004) Interactive 3D painting on point-sampled objects. In: Eurographics Symposium on Point-based Graphics 2004

Agrawala M, Zorin D, Munzner T(2000) Artistic multiprojection rendering. In: Proceedings of the Eurographics Workshop on Rendering Techniques 125–136

Belyaev AG, Pasko AA, Kunii TL(1998) Ridges and ravines on implicit surfaces. In: Proceedings of Computer Graphics International 1998 530–535

Benichou F, Elber G(1999) Output sensitive extraction of silhouettes from polygonal geometry. In: Seventh Pacific Conference on Computer Graphics and Applications 60–69

Buchanan JW, Sousa MC(2000) The edge buffer:a data structure for easy silhouette rendering. In: Proceedings of the 1st International Symposium on Non-photorealistic Animation and Rendering 39–42

Burns M, Klawe J, Rusinkiewicz S, Finkelstein A, DeCarlo D(2005) Line drawings from volume data. ACM Transactions on Graphics 24(3):512–518

Chan C, Akleman E, Chen J(2002) Two methods for creating Chinese painting. In: Proceedings of Pacific Graphics 2002 403–410

Claes J, DiFiore F, Vansichem G, Van Reeth F(2001) Fast 3d cartoon rendering with improved quality by exploiting graphics hardware. In: Proceedings of Image and Vision Computing 13–18

Cornish D, Rowan A, Luebke D(2001) View-dependent particles for interactive Non-Photorealistic rendering. No description on graphics interface 2001 151–158

Csébfalvi B, Mroz L, Hauser H, König A, Gröller E(2001) Fast visualization of object contours by Non-Photorealistic volume rendering. Computer Graphics Forum 20 (3) :452–460

Curtis CJ, Anderson SE, Seims JE, Fleischery KW, Salesin DH(1997) Computer-generated watercolor. In: Proceedings of the 24th Annual Conference on Computer Graphics and Interactive Techniques 421–430

Decaudin P(1996) Cartoon-looking rendering of 3D-scenes. Research Report INRIA #2919

Deussen O, Strothotte T(2000) Computer-generated pen-and-ink illustration of trees. In: Proceedings of the 27th Annual Conference on Computer Graphics and Interactive Techniques 13–18

Dong F, Clapworthy GJ, Lin H, Krokos MA(2003) Nonphotorealistic rendering of medical volume data. IEEE Computer Graphics and Applications 3(4):44–52

Durand F(2002) An invitation to discuss computer depiction. In: Proceeding of Non-photorealistic Animating and Rendering 2002 111–124

Ebert D, Rheingans P(2000)Volume illustration: Non-Photorealistic rendering of volume models. In: Proceedings of the Conference on Visualization 00, 2000: 195-200

Elber G(1995) Line art rendering via a coverage of iso parametric curves. IEEE Transactions on Visulization and Computer Graphics 1(3): 231-239

Elber G(1998) Interactive Line Art Rendering of Freeform Surfaces. Computer Graphics Forum 18(3):1–12

Elber G(1999) Line art illustrations of parametric and implicit forms. IEEE Transactions on Visualization and Computer Graphics 4(1):71–81

Freudenberg B, Masuch M, Strothotte T(2001) Walk-through illustrations:frame-coherent pen-and-ink style in a game engine. Computer Graphics Forum 20(3):184–192

Fung J, Veryovka O(2003) Pen-and-ink textures for real-time rendering. In: Proceedings of Graphics Interface 2003 131–137

Geng W, Ding L, Yu H, Pan Y(2005) Technical illustration based on 3D CSG models. Joural of Zhejiang University 6A(5):469–475

Geng W, Fleischmann W, Yu H, Pan Y(2001) Technical illustration based on human-like approach (short paper). In: Computer Graphics International 2001 343-346

Gooch A, Gooch B, Shirley P, Cohen E(1998) A non-photorealistic lighting model for automatic technical illustration. In: Proceedings of the 25th Annual Conference on Computer Graphics and Interactive Techniques 447–452

Gooch B, Sloan PJ, Gooch A, Shirley P, Riesenfeld R(1999) Interactive technical illustration. In: Proceedings of the 1999 Symposium on Interactive 3D Graphics 31–38

Gordin DN, Edelson DC, Gomez LM(1996) Scientific visualization as an interpretive and expressive medium. In: International Conference on the Learning Sciences 409–414

Hall P(1999)Non-photorealistic rendering by Q-mapping. Computer Graphics Forum 18(1):27-39

Hertzmann A, Zorin D(2000) Illustrating smooth surfaces. Proceedings of the 27th Annual Conference on Computer Graphics and Interactive Techniques 517–526

Interrante V(1997) Illustrating surface shape in volume data via principal direction-driven 3D line integral convolution. In: Proceedings of the 24th Annual Conference on Computer Graphics and Interactive Techniques, 109–116

Isenberg T, Freudenberg B, Halper N, Schlechtweg S, Strothotte T(2003) A developer's guide to silhouette algorithms for polygonal models. IEEE Computer Graphics and Applications 23(4):28–37

Kaplan M, Gooch B, Cohen E(2000) Interactive Artistic Rendering. In: Proceedings of the 1st international symposium on Non-photorealistic animation and rendering 67-74

Kowalski MA, Markosian L, Northrup JD, Bourdev L, Barzel R, Holden LS, Hughes JF(1999) Art-based rendering of fur, grass, and trees. In: Proceeding of 26th Annual Conference on Computer Graphics and Interactive Techniques 433–438

Kim SS, Choe SK(2002) Stylized silhouette rendering using progressive meshes (short paper). Journal of WSCG 2002

Klein AW, Li W, Kazhdan MM, Corrêa WT, Finkelstein A, Funkhouser TA(2000) Non-photorealistic virtual environments. In: Proceedings of the 27th Annual Conference on Computer Graphics and Interactive Techniques 527–534

Kobbelt LP, Botsch M, Schwanecke U, Seide H(2001) Feature sensitive surface extraction from volume data. In: Proceedings of the 28th Annual Conference on Computer Graphics and Interactive Techniques 57–66

Kulla CD, Tucek JD, Bailey RJ, Grimm CM(2003) Using texture synthesis for non-photorealistic shading from paint samples. In: Proceedings of the 11th Pacific Conference on Computer Graphics and Applications 2003 447–481

Lei E, Chang C(2004) Real-time rendering of watercolor effects for virtual environments. In: Pacific Rim Conference on Multimedia 474–481

Levene J(1998) A Framework for Non-Realistic Projections. Massachusetts Institute of Technology

Lu A Morris CJ, Taylor J, Ebert DS, Hansen C, Rheingans P, Hartner M(2003) Illustrative interactive stipple rendering. IEEE Transactions on Visualization and Computer Graphics 9(2):127–138

Lum EB, Ma K(2002) Interactive NPR. In: Proceedings of the 29th Annual Conference on Computer Graphics and Interactive Techniques

Markosian L, Kowalski MA, Goldstein D, Trychin SJ, Hughes JF, Bourdev LD(1997) Real-time non-photorealistic rendering. In: Proceedings of the 24th Annual Conference on Computer Graphics and Interactive Techniques 415–420

Matín D, Carcia S, Torres JC(2000) Observer dependent deformations in inllustration. In: Proceedings of the 1st international symposium on Non-photorealistic animation and rendering 75–82

Martín D, Torres JC(2001) Rendering silhouettes with virtual lights. Computer Graphics Forum 20(4):271–282

Martín D, Fekete JD, Torres JC(2002) Silhouettes and non-photorealistic rendering flattening 3D objects using silhouettes. Computer Graphics Forum 21(3):239–248

Masuch M, Strothotte T(1998) Visualising ancient architecture using animated line drawings. In: IEEE Conference on Information Visualization 1998 261–266

Nagy Z, Schneider J, Westermann R(2002) Interactive volume illustration. In: Proceedings of Vision, Modeling, and Visualization

Nagy Z, Klein R(2004) High-quality silhouette illustration for texture-based volume rendering. Journal of WSCG, 12(1-3):301-308

Northrup JD, Markosian L(2000) Artistic silhouettes:a hybrid approach. In: Proceedings of the 1st International Symposium on Non-Photorealistic Animation and Rendering 31–37

Owada S, Nielsen F, Okabe M, Igarashi T(2004) Volumetric illustration:designing 3D models with internal textures. ACM SIGGRAPH 322–328

Praun E, Hoppe H, Webb M, Finkelstein A(2001) Real-time hatching. Proceedings of the 28th Annual Conference on Computer Graphics and Interactive Techniques

Raskar R, Cohen M(1999) Image precision silhouette edges. In: Proceedings of the 1999 Symposium on Interactive 3D Graphics 135–140

Raskar R(2001) Hardware support for non-photorealistic rendering. The ACM SIGGRAPH/EUROGRAPHICS workshop on Graphics Hardware 41–47

Rheingans P(2004) Expressive volume rendering. Journal of WSCG 12(1–3)

Rössel C, Kobbelt L(2000) Line-art rendering of 3D-models. In: Proceedings of Pacific Graphics 2000 87–96

Rössel C, Kobbelt L, Seidel H(2000) Line art rendering of triangulated surfaces using discrete lines of curvatures. Journal of WSCG 2000 168–175

Saito T, Takahashi T(1990) Comprehensible rendering of 3D shapes. In: Proceedings of the 17th Annual Conference on Computer Graphics and Interactive Techniques 197–206

Schein S, Elber G(2004) Adaptive extraction and visualization of silhouette curves from volumetric datasets. The Visual Computer 20(4):243–252

Singh K(2002) A fresh perspective. In: Proceedings of Graphics Interface 2002

Sloan PJ, Martín W, Gooch A, Gooch B(2001) The lit sphere:a model for capturing NPR shading from art. In: Proceedings of Graphics Interface 2001 143–150

Smith AR(1984) Plants, fractals and formal languages. Computer Graphics 18(3):1–10

Sousa MC, Buchanan J W(1999b) Computer-generated graphite pencil rendering of 3D polygonal models. Computer Graphics Forum 18(3):195–207

Sousa MC, Buchanan, J W(1999a) Computer-generated pencil drawing. In: Western Computer Graphics Symposium

Sousa MC, Foster K, Wyvill B, Samavati F(2003) Precise ink drawing of 3D models. Computer Graphics Forum 22(3):369–379

Treavett SMF, Chen M(2000) Pen-and-ink rendering in volume visualization. In: Proceedings of the 11th IEEE Visualization 2000 Conference 203–210

Veryovka O(2002) Animation with threshold textures. In: Proceedings of Graphics Interface 2002 9–16

Wang L, Zhao Y, Mueller K, Kaufman A (2005) The magic volume lens: an interactive focus+context technique for volume rendering. In: Proceedings of the 16th IEEE Visualization 2005 367–374

Way D, Lin Y, Shih Z(2002) The synthesis of trees in Chinese landscape painting using silhouette and texture strokes. Journal of WSCG 2002 499–506

Wilson B, Ma KL(2004) Rendering complexity in computer-generated pen-and-ink illustrations. In: Proceedings of the 3rd International Symposium on Non-photorealistic Animation and Rendering 129–137

Winkenbach G, Salesin DH(1996) Rendering parametric surfaces in pen and ink. In: Proceedings of the 23rd Annual Conference on Computer Graphics and Interactive Techniques 469–476

Winnemöller H, Bangay S(2002) Geometric approximations towards free specular comic shading. Computer Graphics Forum 21(3):309–316

Xu H, Gossett N, Chen B(2004). Pointworks: abstraction and rendering of sparsely scanned outdoor environments. Eurographics Symposium on Rendering

Xu H, Chen B(2004) Stylized rendering of 3D scanned real world environments. In: Proceedings of the 3rd International Symposium on Non-photorealistic Animation and Rendering 25–34

Yeh J, Ouhyoung M(2002) Non-photorealistic rendering in Chinese painting of animals. Journal of System Simulation 14(9):1120–1224

Zhang Q, Sato Y, Takahashi J, Muraoka K, Chiba N(1999) Simple cellular automaton-based simulation of ink behaviour and its application to suibokuga-like 3D rendering of trees. The Journal of Visualization and Computer Animation 10(1):27–37

6

Expressive Rendering

The ultimate goal of computer graphics is to make the rendered image effectively convey the visual content that can be effectively recognized by human beings. Almost all physical surfaces contain some microstructure or texture visible to the human eye. It gives us information such as the type of material which composes the object and the relative smoothness or coarseness of the surface. Therefore, texture is an important surface characteristic which provides a great deal of information about the nature of a surface, and here are three characteristics of texture which provide this perceptual information: size, shape, and density [Schweitzer, 1983]. Perceptual psychologists have recognized the importance of surface texture as a cue to space perception, and lots of perceptual principles are newly developed for computer graphics [May, 2000].Changes in these components due to standard perspective and projective transformations provide knowledge about surface depth and changes in the orientation of the surface.

With the advent of expressive rendering [Landsdown & Schofield, 1995], the problem of computer graphics gradually changed from making displays recognizable, to ensuring that users notice what they are intended to see, without being distracted by irrelevant information. In expressive rendering, the resultant image will encourage the viewer to make the same imaginative, perceptual contributions they make to interpretive art. It is also desirable to be capable of interpreting all the data available in a 3D model in order to generate images that possess some internal meaning and structure. In this chapter we will mainly discuss how to make the resultant image comprehensible, how to convey the shape to the viewer, how to communicate meaningful information to the viewer, and how to depict the transparent surfaces or objects for the observer.

6.1 Comprehensible Rendering

Comprehensibility mainly depends on the object, purpose and sometimes the viewers' preferences, and cannot be expressed with theoretical definitions. The key point in synthesizing a comprehensible image is how to determine the most suitable combination of enhancement techniques. In general, there are three major approaches to improving the comprehensibility of the resulting rendition, there are:

(1) *The enhancement of visual cues for cognition.* The drawing primitives themselves or the attributes or features of the visual effect are augmented to attract the attention of the user, or to make the information-to-be-conveyed clear.
(2) *The composition of multiple views into one picture.* The points of view are carefully selected, controlled and the renditions from multiple views are seamlessly composed into the picture of the main view in which the user can simultaneously capture the necessary information from different views in the same illustration.
(3) *The exposure of hidden information by cutting-out.* The outer shape of the object is removed by cutting-out operations in terms of the user's interests, such that the user can easily see the hidden information or internal structure of the object.

6.1.1 Enhancement of Rendering by Emphasis of Visual Cues

In graphical rendering, the detailed visual cues, such as depth, light intensity, normals, contrast and hidden parts of the scene, often become unnoticeable in the flood of details in the resulting pictures, partly due to the limitation of the traditional rendering or modeling techniques. Therefore, it will be very useful for visual cognition tasks if these visual cues can be exposed or emphasized by alternative rendering or modeling approaches, which can effectively eliminate the vagueness of the resultant images.

The pioneer work on the emphasis of visual cues can be dated back to [Kamada & Kawai, 1987], in which Kamada and Kawai proposed a hidden-line indication scheme that can produce the explanatory nature of the resulting pictures. They developed a view-dependent picturing function to control how hidden parts of lines are displayed, such as removing all hidden lines or drawing all hidden lines in dashed style. Each part of a hidden line is characterized by the shielding set of surfaces that hide it (see Fig. 6.1). The display attribute of a part of a hidden line is determined by both its shielding set and the line to which the subpart belongs.

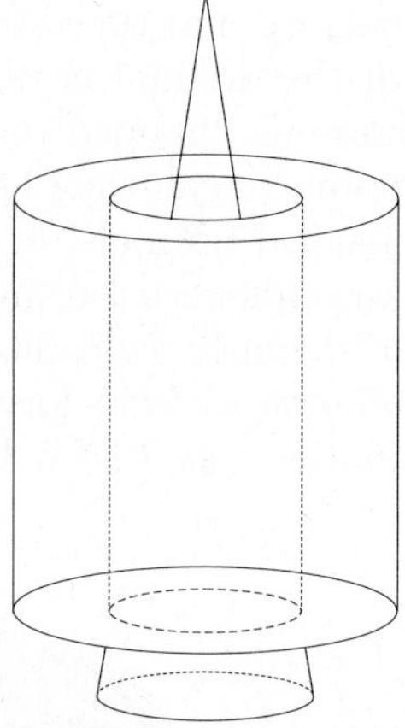

Fig. 6.1 Example of hidden line emphasis

6.1.1.1 Emphasis of the normal

Cignoni *et al.* proposed a normal emphasis technique that can enhance the shading and the perception of its features by modifying the normals of an object [Cignoni *et al.*, 2005]. The implicit idea behind this is that appropriate shading supplies the kind of information that is more qualitative than quantitative in the perception of an image (see Fig. 6.2). The enhanced normals are integrated into the model, either by assigning new normal values per vertex, or through re-sampled normal maps. The normal enhancement effect that can be obtained with the application of the formula $n_E{=}n{+}k{\times}(n-n_L)$ depends mainly on two parameters: the amount of low-pass filter that we use

Fig. 6.2 Comparison of traditional Phong shading and normal emphasis [Cignoni *et al.*, 2005]. (a)Phong shading; (b) Shading with normal variation. Copyright of Elsevier, used with permission

to generate the smooth normals n_L and the value of the weighting constant k used in the perturbation of the original normal vectors. During the rendering stage, the enhanced normals, mapped to the input geometry using a standard texture mapping approach, can then be used in any rendering subsystem that supports user-specified normals, or interactive bump mapping. In essence, the normal emphasis enhances the surface orientation, leaving the silhouette unchanged. It is particularly well suited to improve the rendering of mechanical parts where common straight-forward shading techniques can often generate shading ambiguities. (see Fig. 6.3).

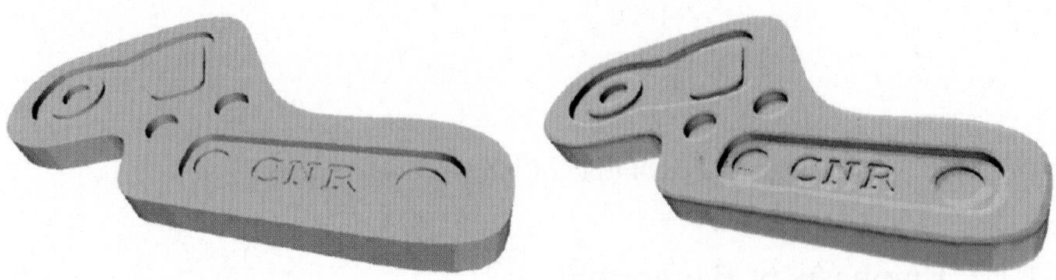

Fig. 6.3 Examples of synthesized images with normal emphasis [Cignoni *et al.*, 2005]. Copyright of Elsevier, used with permission

6.1.1.2 Emphasis on depth

Luft *et al.* introduced additional depth cues to improve the perception of complex scenes [Luft *et al.*, 2006]. The difference between the original and the low-pass filtered depth buffer is computed in order to find spatially important areas. This information is explicitly utilized to enhance the perceptual quality of the resultant images by locally altering the contrast, color and other parameters of the image. It allows us to emphasize objects in the foreground and to visually depict the spatial relation in complex scenes, especially the effect of depth darkening (the background objects are slightly darkened) and introduces a natural additional depth cue by usually increasing the local contrast. The method is useful for all scenes that contain spatially complex arrangements of objects. This approach can be applied to any image data with available depth information.

6.1.1.3 Emphasis on lighting

Tanaka and Ohnishi presented a regional emphasis of lighting intensity [Tanaka & Ohnishi, 1997]. Their intensity emphasis method is based on human vision. It simulates the adaptation of photoreceptor cells and the lateral inhibition of receptive fields. These attributes of a vision system are realized by the computation of relative intensity and differential intensity in small areas. The algorithm first converts a color image into a grey-scale image. The grey-scale image is normalized by its mean intensity, so that the average intensity of the image is equal to 1. The image is then emphasized by increasing local contrast while reducing global contrast, amplifying image intensity on shadowed surfaces, reducing intensity on illuminated surfaces and expanding contrast at intensity edges. The resultant image is amplified for display. This is the inverse process of intensity normalization. Finally, a color image is reconstructed with the original hue and chroma so the color of the original image is retained. This method can successfully generate painting-like artifacts, which greatly improves the perception of visual elements displayed in an image. As shown in Fig. 6.4, it exhibits contrast magnification along object boundaries. Darker backgrounds are drawn at the places where glossy objects are located. The same background is represented as a much brighter region around shadowed or shaded objects. This makes the silhouettes of the objects clear.

(a) (b)

Fig. 6.4 Example of intensity emphasis of computer generated images [Tanaka & Ohnishi, 1997]. (a) Original image; (b) Resultant image with intensity emphasis. Copyright of Blackwell, used with permission

Akers *et al.* further summarized that lighting can be used to convey the following features of the object [Akers *et al.*, 2003]:

(1) Orientation: On smooth portions of a curved surface, directional light is used to create diffuse shading, which helps viewers estimate the local orientation of the surface and differentiate between convex and concave parts of the shape.
(2) Curvature: Regions with high curvature or edge discontinuities are often emphasized with highlights. Photographers depict metallic objects using linear lights, aligning highlights with directions of zero curvature.

(3) Bumps and texture: Small-scale surface features are much easier to detect under side or raking lighting. Shadows cast by these features create regions of high contrast and reveal texture. The best landscape photographs are often taken at dawn or dusk; the best views of the moon's craters occur along its terminator.
(4) Silhouettes: The silhouette of an object is one of its most distinctive features. Rim lighting is often used along the edge of an object to distinguish it from a dark background. Rim shadowing serves the same purpose against a light background.

They accordingly presented a novel compositing process to allow the artist to quickly and easily create technical illustrations from a set of photographs of an object taken from the same point of view under variable lighting conditions (see Fig. 6.5). Each source photograph is associated with a matte image that modulates its contribution to the final image at each pixel. All the weighted source images are then added together to produce the final composite. It enables the final lighting in each area of the composite to be manipulated independently, as the source images are combined using spatially-varying light mattes. To ensure that the composite photograph has the same average brightness as the input images, it is required that the weights at each pixel add up to one. This image-based re-lighting technique makes it easy to create illustrations of complex objects that effectively communicate their shape and texture using common lighting design techniques (see Fig. 6.6).

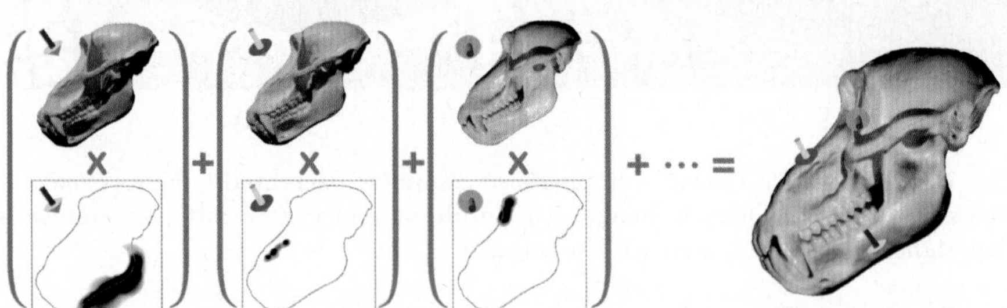

Fig. 6.5 Three sample photographs of a baboon skull cast taken under different lighting conditions, showing above their corresponding mattes. The composite image is shown on the right. Arrows indicate local variation in the lighting direction across the resultant composite [Akers *et al.*, 2003]. Copyright of IEEE, used with permission

Fig. 6.6 Above: three example images of a robotic assembly taken under three different lighting directions (indicated by arrows). Below: The resultant re-lighted image. The colored arrows indicate the predominant lighting direction used in selected regions of the composite. The first two are used to add highlights to the cylindrical base, while the third is used to reveal the brushed texture of a flat surface [Akers *et al.*, 2003]. Copyright of IEEE, used with permission.

6.1.1.4 Emphasis on discontinuity

Saito and Takahashi presented the rendering method to improve the comprehensibility of shape features by enhancing certain geometric properties [Saito & Takahashi, 1990]. Data about the geometric properties of the surfaces are preserved as Geometric Buffers (G-buffers). A G-buffer set is obtained by forming projection views and removing hidden surfaces. Each G-buffer contains one geometric property such as the depth or the normal vector of the visible object in each pixel. By using G-buffers as intermediate results, artificial enhancement processes are separated from geometric processes (projection and hidden surface removal) and physical processes (shading and texture mapping), and are performed as post-processes. If geometric factors (i.e., shapes and camera parameters) are fixed, any combination of enhancement can be examined without changing the contents of the G-buffers. This permits a user to rapidly examine various combinations of enhancement techniques without excessive re-computation, and easily obtain the most comprehensible image. The allowed basic enhancement operations are discontinuities, edges, contour lines and curved hatching. The most significant application of drawing discontinuity is edge drawing. Though all of them are line drawings, they are realized with 2D image processing operations instead of line tracking, so that they can be efficiently combined with conventional surface rendering algorithms.

Nienhaus and Döellner further extend the G-buffer technique to edge enhancing in real-time non-photorealistic rendering [Nienhaus & Döellner, 2003]. It is based on the edge map, a 2D texture that encodes visually important edges of 3D scene objects. The edge map is based on the following classification of edges: (a) A silhouette edge is an edge adjacent to a polygon facing towards the camera (front-facing); (b) one polygon facing in the opposite direction (back-facing); (c) a border edge is an edge to exactly one polygon. A crease edge is an edge between two front-facing (or back-facing, respectively) polygons whose dihedral angle is above some threshold. The dihedral angle defines the intensity of a crease edge. The implementation is based on multi-pass rendering: First, geometrical properties of 3D scene objects are extracted to generate image-space data similar to G-buffers. Next, discontinuities are extracted in the image-space data using common graphics hardware to emulate image-processing operations. In subsequent rendering passes, the algorithm applies texture mapping to combine the edge map with 3D scene objects.

6.1.2 Cutaway Illustration

Cutaway illustrations produce a visual appearance as if someone had cut out a piece of the object or sliced it into parts, and the entities lying inside or going through an opaque object are of more interest than the surrounding one itself. The purpose of cutaway illustration is to allow the user to view the interior of a solid opaque object. Illustrators often use cutaways to reduce occlusions and expose important internal parts, as most complex 3D objects contain many tightly connected and intertwined parts that occlude one another. Well designed illustrations reveal not only the shape and appearance of important parts, but also the position and orientation of these parts in the context of the surrounding structures. It avoids ambiguities with respect to spatial ordering, provides a sharp contrast between foreground and background objects, and facilitates a good understanding of spatial ordering.

From an algorithmic point of view, the most interesting question is where to cut the outside object, as naively cutting a hole through the occluding parts usually does not reveal the context of the surrounding structures. Cuts should respect the geometry of occluding parts. The most effective cuts should be carefully designed to partially remove occluding parts so that viewers can mentally reconstruct the missing geometry. Thus, the shape and location of cuts depend as much on the geometry of the occluding parts as they do on the position of the target internal parts that are to be exposed. Diepstraten *et al.* found some interesting common properties in many examples of traditional cutaway drawings [Diepstraten *et al.*, 2003], and summarized them in seven basic rules, including:

(1) Inside and outside objects have to be distinguished from each other.
(2) The cutout geometry is represented by the intersection of (a few) half spaces.
(3) The cutout is located at or around the main axis of the outside object.
(4) An optional jittering mechanism is useful to allow for rough cutouts.
(5) The possibility of making the wall visible is needed.
(6) The breakaway should be realized by a single hole in the outside object.
(7) All interior objects should be visible from any given viewing angle.

These rules allow the automatic generation of reasonable cutaways. Diepstraten *et al.* carried out two different subclasses of the general notion of a cutaway drawing: cutout and breakaway (see Fig. 6.7). These cutaway techniques can be readily combined with existing non-photorealistic rendering styles, such as silhouette rendering cool/warm tone shading, or pen-and-ink illustration. Several different NPR styles were implemented to demonstrate that our cutaway processes are independent of the rendering style (see Fig. 6.8).

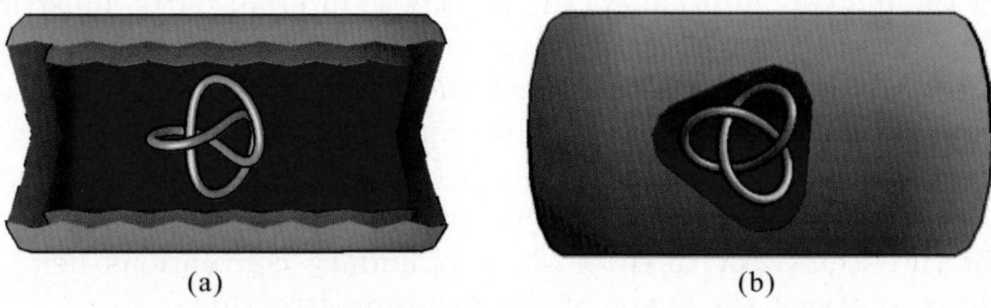

Fig. 6.7 Comparison of computer-generated cutout and breakaway illustrations [Diepstraten *et al.*, 2003]. (a) The image demonstrates the cutout technique with a jittering boundary; (b) The breakaway method is applied to the same scene. Copyright of Blackwell, used with permission

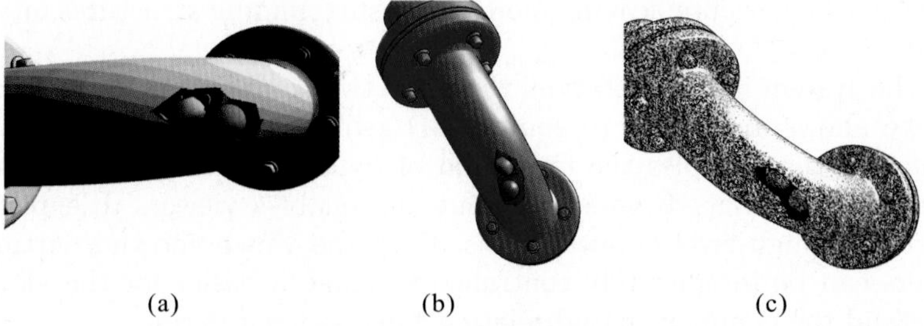

Fig. 6.8 Cutaway illustrations of a curved conduit [Diepstraten *et al.*, 2003]. (a) Toon shading and silhouette rendering; (b) Cool/warm tone shading with black silhouette lines; (c) Layered-stroke textures. Copyright of Blackwell, used with permission

Li *et al.* presented a system for authoring and viewing interactive cutaway illustrations of complex 3D models using the conventions of traditional scientific and technical illustration [Li *et al.*, 2007]. They simulated three classical cutaway illustrations: object-aligned box cuts, tube cuts, and window cuts. The object-aligned box cuts are aligned with the principal Cartesian coordinate frame of a part. This helps to accentuate its geometric structure. For man-made objects, the shape of the part usually implies the orientation of this frame. Such objects are typically designed with respect to three orthogonal principal axes and in many cases they resemble rectangular solids.

In the tube cuts, illustrators usually align the cut with the primary axis running along the length of the part. Often, illustrators will remove a section of the structure using a transverse cutting plane that is perpendicular to the primary axis. The tube cuts fit well with 3D models of both biological and man-made objects containing many structures that resemble tubes, either because they exhibit radial symmetry (e.g., pipes and gears), or because they are long and narrow (e.g., long muscles and bones, plumbing).

The window cuts fit well with complex 3D models that include thin extended enclosing structures (e.g., skin, the chassis of a car) that occlude much of the model's internal detail. To expose internal parts, illustrators often cut freeform or four-sided windows out of these structures. The window boundaries provide a useful cue about the shape of the enclosing structure. Boundary edges near silhouettes of the object help emphasize these contours. Another convention is to make the window jagged. This approach emphasizes that a cut was made and distinguishes the boundaries of the cut from other edges in the scene. All three of these boundary conventions help viewers mentally reconstruct the shape of the enclosing structure.

The view points should also be carefully chosen to help the viewer see the spatial relationship between the internal target parts they are interested in and the occluding parts. Typically, the viewpoint not only centers the target parts in the illustration, but also minimizes the number of occluding structures. This strategy makes it possible to expose the parts of interest with relatively few cuts, leaving more of the surrounding structures intact for context.

In the system implementation, there are two components. The authoring interface allows an author to equip a 3D geometric model with additional information that enables the formation of dynamic cutaways. The viewing interface takes a rigged model as input and enables viewers to explore the dataset with high-level cutaway tools. Both the viewpoint and cutting parameters can be interactively controlled to make it easier for the viewer to understand the complex spatial relationships between parts.

6.1.3 Comprehensive Rendering via Composite Viewpoints

There are two typical multi-viewpoint-based rendering methods to enhance the comprehension: the detail in context technique and surperspective projection technique.

The detail in context is defined as the ability to see simultaneously, for some chosen aspect of the information, sufficient local detail set in the overall global context. It strives to provide increased information comprehension, ease of navigation and effective use of screen space. There is a growing variety of types of distortion that can create detail in context viewing tools. Current techniques, which admit a greater variety of resulting views, are called distortion viewing, multi-scale viewing and detail in context views. Sheelagh *et al.* summed up the principles to create a multi-scale display as follows [Sheelagh *et al.*, 1997]:

(1) Avoid all occlusion if possible.
(2) Keep focal points in at least approximately the same location as in the initial layout.
(3) Smoothly integrate the focal point into its context.
(4) Use a familiar distortion curve (hemisphere).
(5) Preserve the mental map by maintaining orthogonality, proximity and topology.
(6) Animate transitions between views.

When the choice of focal sections changes in emphasis, location or number, a distortion viewing tool creates a new view of the same information representation. It is apparent that users cannot always recognize that they are actually looking at the same information (see Fig. 6.9).

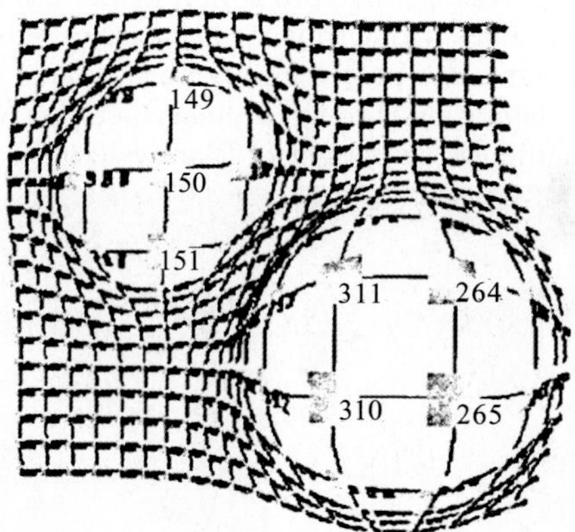

Fig. 6.9 Regular layout of a grid graph with two focal points [Sheelagh *et al.*, 1997]. Copyright of IEEE, used with permission

A surperspective projection is modeled as the target object is partitioned into several feature parts by analyzing its shape features, and each feature part has its own viewpoint. The 2D visual effects are calculated for the selected feature areas, and the final surperspective image is then created. Takahashi *et al.* presented a framework for generating surperspective images based on shape deformation techniques (see Fig. 6.10) [Takahashi *et al.*, 2002]. Using the ordinary perspective projection, the deformed shape is then transformed into a target guide-map image where each landmark enjoys its own vista points. Their framework consists of three algorithms. The first one is for partitioning terrain surfaces, and it extracts terrain features such as ridge and ravine lines, which partition the overall terrain surface into feature areas so that a designer can easily assign 2D visual effects to the portioned areas. The second one is for handling 2D visual effects, and it converts given 2D visual effects to 3D geometric constraints so that the designer can realize the surperspective effects in ordinary 2D perspective images after deforming the terrain surface under the converted constraints. The third one is for calculating such 2D visual effects, and it semi-automatically calculates the position and view direction of each partitioned feature area through the geographical shape analysis of the terrain surface. Fig. 6.11 shows the examples of surper-

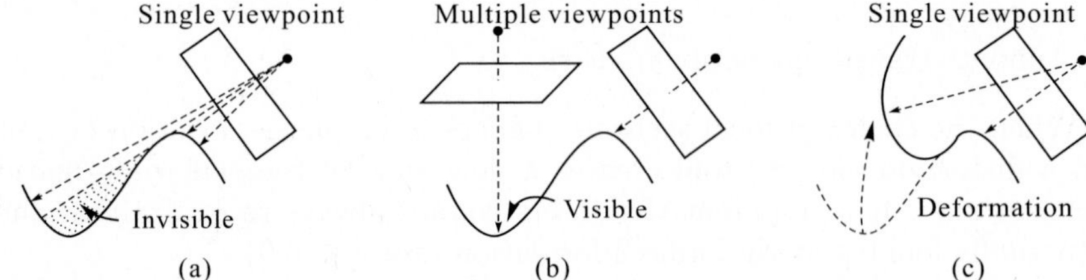

Fig. 6.10 Principle of surperspective projection model based on shapes deformation [Takahashi *et al.*, 2002]. (a) Ordinary perspective projection with a single viewpoint; (b) Multi-perspective projection where each area of interest has its own viewpoint;(c) Its implementation through ordinary perspective projection based on shape deformation techniques. Copyright of Blackwell, used with permission

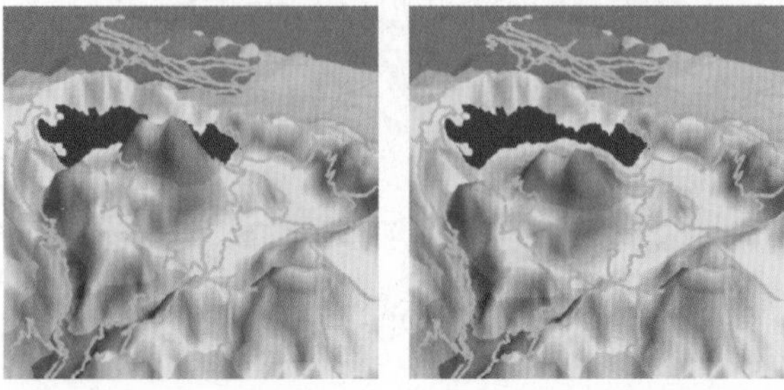

Fig. 6.11 Examples of surperspective guide-maps based on shape deformation [Takahashi *et al.*, 2002]. Copyright of Blackwell, used with permission

spective landscape images for guide-maps generated from 3D geographical elevation data.

6.2 Shape-conveying Illustrations

The effective expression and communication of 3D shapes is one of the major objectives in graphical rendering. Rodger and Browne designed and conducted a series of visual perceptual experiments to access the contribution of rendering parameters to the visual cognition of shapes of 3D objects, and they also provided a set of principles about how to choose the suitable displaying and viewing parameters to effectively convey the 3D shapes in realistic rendition [Rodger & Browne, 2000]. In non-photorealistic rendering, there are two typical approaches to conveying 3D shapes:

(1) *Expressing shape features via stroke texture.* The illustration technique, the position and modeling of lighting, stroke types and styles, etc., are carefully chosen to best express the desired shape features.
(2) *Shape expression via abstraction.* The abstraction rendering techniques such as line-drawing are employed to depict the significant shape features, ignoring the minor details of the 3D object. The user can quickly and clearly perceive the desired 3D shapes in the abstract illustration.

6.2.1 Expressing Shape Features via Stroke Texture

Although the mechanisms of the texture's effect on shape perception are not yet completely understood, numerous studies over the years have found evidence that the accuracy of observers' judgments of surface orientation and curvature can be significantly affected by the presence of a surface texture pattern. The existing theories of shape perception have not yet provided sufficient guidance to definitively answer the question of how to best define the surface material properties of an object in order to best facilitate the accurate understanding of its shape [Kim *et al.*, 2003]. But, much research work has been carried out to empirically find the solution to effectively express the shape features via stroke texture, e.g., Saito and Takahashi employed the stroke texture of hatching to convey the curved features of a 3D shape[Saito & Takahashi, 1990].

Veryovka and Buchanan presented a comprehensive half-toning technique in which the half-toning texture is explicitly employed to provide visual cues and to enhance the viewer's comprehension of 3D scenes [Veryovka & Buchanan, 1999]. The texture shape, scale, direction and contrast are adapted to the 3D information, and thus enhance the display with artistic elements providing visual cues of the form, position and illumination of the 3D scene. The algorithm is based on the property of the ordered dithering algorithm to define the appearance of the half-toning texture. The texture shape is controlled by constructing a dither matrix from an arbitrary image or a procedural texture. A mapping function is used to construct a dither screen from the resulting dither matrices and to adapt texture direction and scale to the control image. Texture contrast and the accuracy of the tone reproduction are varied across the image using the error diffusion process. The resultant half-toning image of 3D scene is generated in terms of the geometry, position and illumination information (see Fig. 6.12).

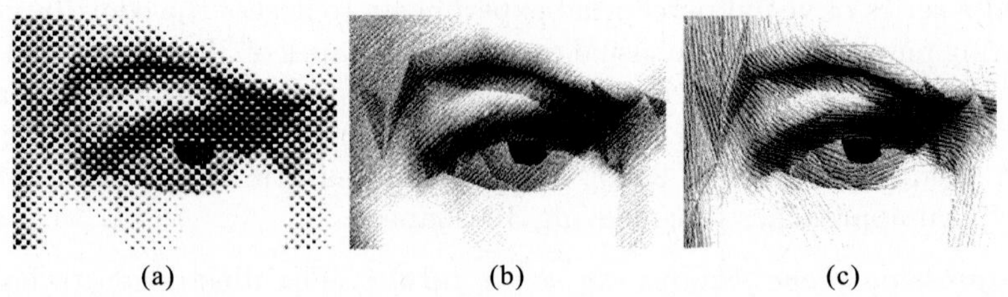

Fig. 6.12 An example of comprehensive half-toning [Veryovka & Buchanan, 1999]. (a)Ordered dithering with conventional clustered dither matrix; (b)Dither matrix generated from pencil stroke texture, cross-hatching is imitated; (c)Pencil stroke texture is adapted to object geometry. Copyright of Blackwell, used with permission

Deussen *et al.* presented a method for generating line drawings of complex geometries in the style of crosshatched illustrations [Deussen *et al.*, 1999]. The 3D models are first segmented into parts that will be handled by the desired line styles and intersection sets. For each part of the model, the set of intersecting planes is created. Computing a geometric skeleton allows us to determine automatically the orientation of the intersection planes for a wide variety of models. The hatching lines are generated by intersecting the geometry with a set of planes. The resultant curves are drawn in order to achieve half-toning which represent a given intensity distribution.

Aiming at evoking powerful expressive meaning, Sousa *et al.* simulate pen-and-ink style rendering of triangle-mesh surfaces by employing strokes that are short, straight and with very little width variation [Sousa *et al.*, 2004]. This illustration technique integrates two very important illustration strategies for depicting shape features: selection of drawing direction and the use of light. Drawing direction is given by four stroke directional fields. The lighting is based on the idea of "spotlight silhouettes", which consider only the regions on the mesh that are visible to the spotlight cone. The target tone is matched by adjusting the stroke length adaptively from parameters computed directly from the mesh, without the need for tone value charts or pre-generated stroke textures. At each edge of the mesh, a stroke is mapped directly to one of four possible directional fields. Finally, the stroke is stylized with path perturbation and ink weight distribution, imparting a less uniform look to strokes rendered on regular meshes. It also allows visual effects of reverse tone values and depth cueing. The resultant illustration provides good visualizations of shape features, creating convincing impressions of 3D forms (see Fig. 6.13).

Fig. 6.13 Examples of illustration in pen-and-ink edge-based strokes [Sousa *et al.*, 2004]. Copyright of IEEE, used with permission

In order to express meaningful information about a 3D terrain, manual sketching is usually employed to depict the relief features, such as watersheds, stream networks, breaks in the slope, ridges and edges of terraces. Lesage and Visvalingam provide an informal deductive analysis of the marks in sketches [Lesage & Visvalingam, 2002]. Fig. 6.14 shows an example of the sketching of a 3D terrain object.

Fig. 6.14 A sketching illustration of 3D terrain [Lesage & Visvalingam, 2002]. Copyright of Elsevier, used with permission

6.2.2 Expressing Shape Features by Selective Depiction

The interpretation of shape features is dependent upon a wealth of visual cues, including contours, surfaces, visibility of faces and edges, texture, shading, shadow, and many others. When artists design imagery to portray a 3D object, they do not just render visual cues veridically. Instead, they select which visual cues to portray and adapt the information each cue carries. These illustrations depart dramatically from natural scenes, but nevertheless convey visual information effectively, because viewers' perceptual inferences still work flexibly to arrive at a consistent interpretation of the 3D shape.

The line-drawing is one of the most popular forms for selectively depicting 3D shapes. This is mainly because, on the one hand, line-drawing can be interpreted remarkably well by humans, who are able to perceive and understand 3D object structures from very sparse collections of lines. The artists and scientific illustrators prefer to employ line-drawing to effectively represent the form of 3D objects. On the other hand, the line-drawing can well reduce the visual information, and the remaining information will not leave the impression that something about 3D shapes is wrong or missing. This will allow the viewer to focus on the information he or she wants, without being bothered by extra unnecessary and unwanted information. On the other hand, the line-drawing can effectively approximate the attributes of the surface of the 3D object by compressing the redundant information. Contours provide the simplest form of line-drawing, and many lines naturally come from contours. The visual system of humans is capable of relaxing the natural interpretation of contours, although contours are quite limited in the information they convey about shape on their own. Buchanan and Sousa proposed a dedicated data structure, edge buffer, for contour generation [Buchanan & Sousa, 2000]. This edge buffer is used a-priori to define which edges are to be rendered when visible, and is also updated each time the object is rendered so that silhouette edges can be drawn. It allows the users to portray the important features of a model by highlighting silhouette edges, boundary edges and artist defined edges.

Dooley and Cohen provided a line-drawing way of imparting meaning to visual representation of complex objects, and additional semantic attributes to be attached to objects [Dooley & Cohen, 1990]. They borrowed the experience and techniques of the art of technical illustration and employed four categories of lines: boundary lines, silhouette lines, discontinuity lines (folds), and contour or isoparametric lines, to indicate geometric meaning and help convey the curvature of the surface. A single line in their illustration is defined as being composed of line segments which define continuous portions of lines which do not cross in front of, or behind, other boundary or silhouette lines. A line segment has a thickness, a transparency and a style, i.e., solid, dashed, dotted, sketched, etc. Style and transparency and thickness attributes may convey different degrees of hiddenness or may indicate the importance of the object (or portion of the object) being drawn. A set of illustration rules takes the segment information and determines the drawing parameters for the specific segment. These rules are based on user specification and inferences drawn from artistic knowledge about illustration principles. This provides a balance between flexibility and automation of the production of final drawings (see Fig. 6.15).

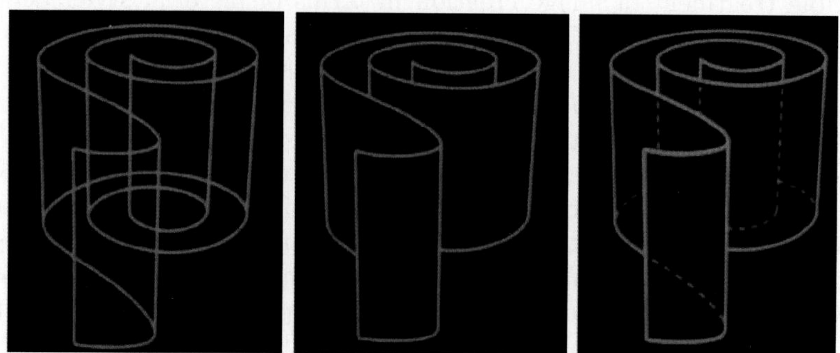

Fig. 6.15 Line-drawing examples with different illustration rules [Dooley & Cohen, 1990]. Copyright of IEEE, used with permission

Schlechtweg *et al.* developed tools for selectively mapping attributes of surfaces of an object onto lines based on the decomposition of the rendering process into a projection phase and an interpretation phase of an enriched 2D model [Schlechtweg *et al.*,1998]. Their enriched 2D model contains the following surface-oriented information:

(1) The projected geometry with all intermediate coordinates attached.
(2) Information about the visibility of parts of the geometry.
(3) Normal vectors or intensity values for model surfaces, edges and vertices, and connectivity information.

Within the second phase of the rendering pipeline, the enriched 2D model is interpreted in terms of mapping attributes contained in this model onto visual properties of a 2D image. For line-drawing, the following principles are employed to encode 3D information in line-drawing:

(1) Providing at least the silhouette of the objects to display helps to understand the structure of the observed scene. Different levels of detail can encode more information.
(2) Presenting the model with curved rather that with sharp polygonal borders.
(3) Encoding lighting by the use of lines of varying width and brightness.
(4) Suggesting surface properties by hatching or similar techniques.

Their line-drawing model also consists of two parts. The path determines the overall shape of the line as a parametric curve. Attributes may be attached describing, for example, the pressure and saturation of a drawing tool. These attribute values finally result in a certain appearance of the line. The style determines all deviations of the final line from this general path. This rich line drawing technique not only enables us to render images which encode only those properties which are needed for the application at hand, but also offers a flexible treatment of image creation in terms of pictorial style. Different interpretation leads to different pictorial styles and thus to different images from one given model.

DeCarlo *et al.* went beyond contours and explored how to depict and draw a new type of line: the suggestive contour [DeCarlo *et al.*, 2003]. The contours will appear where a surface turns away from the viewer and becomes invisible. The suggestive contours will be drawn on clearly visible parts of the surface, where a true contour would first appear with a minimal change in viewpoint. They can augment true contours to help convey shape. Consider a view of a smooth and closed surface S from a perspective camera centered at $\boldsymbol{c}$. The contour is mathematically defined as the set of points that lie on this surface and satisfy:

$$\boldsymbol{n}(\boldsymbol{p}) \cdot \boldsymbol{v}(\boldsymbol{p}) = 0.$$

where $\boldsymbol{p}$ is a point on the surface,$\boldsymbol{n}(\boldsymbol{p})$ is the unit surface normal at $\boldsymbol{p}$, and $\boldsymbol{v}$ is the view vector:

$$\boldsymbol{v}(\boldsymbol{p}) = \boldsymbol{c} - \boldsymbol{p}.$$

Informally, suggestive contours are curves along which the radial curvature is zero and where the surface bends away from the viewer (as opposed to bending towards them). DeCarlo *et al.* provided three mathematical definitions of suggestive contours [DeCarlo *et al.*, 2003]:

(1) The suggestive contour generator is the set of points on the surface at which its radial curvature k_r is 0, and the directional derivative of k_r in the direction of w is positive:

$$D_w k_r > 0.$$

The directional derivative $D_w k_r$ is defined as the differential of $k_r(\mathbf{p})$ applied to w, or $dk_r(w)$ (see Fig. 6.16).

(2) The suggestive contour generator is the set of minima of $\boldsymbol{n} \cdot \boldsymbol{v}$ in the direction of w.

(3) The suggestive contour generator is the set of points on the contour generator of a nearby viewpoint (of radial distance less than 90 degrees) that is not in radial correspondence with points on the contour of any (radially) closer viewpoint.

Based on the aforementioned definitions of suggestive contours, DeCarlo *et al.* presented two methods for calculating suggestive contours (one in object space and one in image space), including an algorithm that finds the zero crossings of the radial curvature. It is shown that suggestive contours

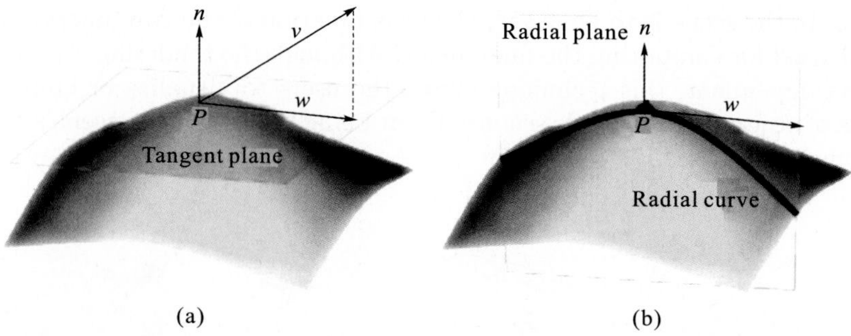

Fig. 6.16 (a) The view vector $\boldsymbol{v}$ is projected onto the tangent plane to obtain $\boldsymbol{w}$; (b) The radial plane is formed by $\boldsymbol{p}$, $\boldsymbol{n}$ and $\boldsymbol{w}$ and slices the surface along the radial curve, the curvature of which is $r(\boldsymbol{p})$ [Decarlo *et al.*, 2003]. Copyright of ACM, used with permission

can be drawn consistently with true contours, and the resultant images convey shape more effectively than contour alone, as the renderings of contour alone presented the limited shape information that seems to depict only an undifferentiated, smooth and round relief. However, suggestive contours enrich and differentiate the conveyed shape, e.g., they can convey small shape features as well as large ones, and can also convey folds in the surface when they are deep enough to contain an inflection point, as are the wrinkles on the hand.

However, the suggestive contours are heavily dependent on the viewing direction, and it is difficult to apply them in animation production, as the temporal coherence of suggestive drawing can't be guaranteed. In order to facilitate the problem of temporal coherence in suggestive contours rendition, DeCarlo *et al.* further embedded the temporal constraints into the rendering framework to generate the temporal-coherence suggestive contours [DeCarlo *et al.*, 2004].

In general, the line-drawing in non-photorealistic rendering computes the rendition effects as a function of the drawing style, the light intensity at an object and the distance from the viewer/camera to the point in space being visualized etc. However, these considerations are not rich enough to achieve the necessary repertoire of illustrative techniques as used in hand-drawn illustrations. In order to convey the 3D shape more effectively, there are two typical approaches for further enhancing the visual effect of line-drawing. One is to integrate the spatial effects into the line-drawing, e.g., Isenberg *et al.* employed the illustrative effects to describe the workings of illustrative techniques that rely on spatial location rather than just illumination or depth. This is based on specifying a general function $f_E(x, y, z)$ to describe the desired visualization effect to points (x, y, z) of the scene, combined with a function $f_S(\text{object})$ which determines the visualization style in which an object in the scene is to be drawn. The combination of the two functions, f_E, f_S, is used for computing the final image. Although the rendering style is still object-dependent, this technique allows the users to visualize or emphasize parts of objects or the whole scene without being limited by the scene's object decomposition (see Fig. 6.17).

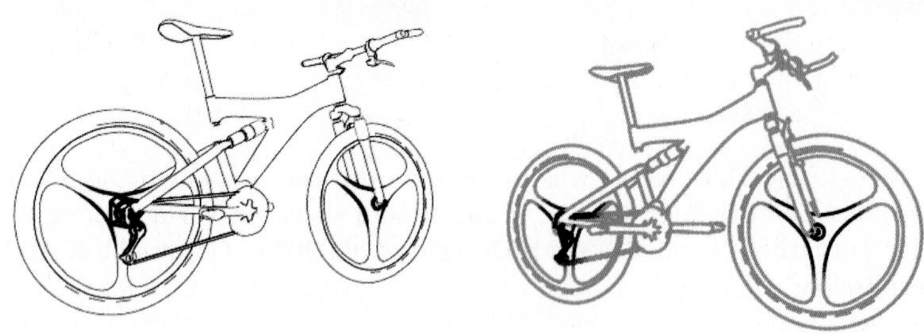

Fig. 6.17 Integration of spatial effect with line-drawing [Isenberg *et al.*, 2000]. Copyright of IEEE, used with permission

The other technique is to extract and emphasize a few good lines to enhance the line-drawing, i.e., a small number of lines with carefully chosen line qualities are drawn to suggest the 3D shape of the objects [Sousa & Prusinkiewicz, 2003]. Sousa and Prusinkiewicz extracted, segmented and smoothed feature edges related to the outline and interior of a given 3D mesh, yielding chains of lines with varying path, length, thickness, gaps and enclosures. The effects of ink fluidity, line weighting, connectives and enclosure are reproduced and this leads to results adding three-dimensional shape suggestion using selected feature lines [Sousa & Prusinkiewicz, 2003]. Their system takes as input a single 3D triangle mesh, and illumination and surface reflectance information are not taken into account. The main steps of the algorithm are performed in the object space and are as follows:

(1) Feature lines are extracted and classified.
(2) On this basis, several graphs are constructed as an input for chaining, which is the connection of lines of the same type into sequences.
(3) These chains are extruded into 3D (perpendicular to the object's surface), creating ribbons of width dependent on a selected measure of surface curvature.
(4) Spline curves are fitted to the edges of the ribbons, resulting in a smooth representation.

This suggestive drawing of a 3D model reproduces the artistic principle of suggestion or indication, in which lines are used with economy, and the expressive power of illustration results from engaging the imagination of the viewer rather than revealing all details of the subject (see Fig. 6.18).

Fig. 6.18 Examples of suggestive drawing of 3D models [Sousa & Prusinkiewicz, 2003]. Copyright of Blackwell, used with permission

6.3 Intent-based 3D Illustration

Intent consists of both the purpose and content of the communication. Intent-based illustration is to generate a picture that can fulfill a communicative intent, including the presentation of the position and orientation of an object, the moving state of an object and how to manipulate a product etc. However, intent communication is closely related to the interpretation. The same presentation, viewed by several people, may be interpreted to mean different things, while different presentations may be interpreted to mean the same thing. To further complicate matters, none of these interpretations may be the one intended by the presenter. Therefore, it is necessary to integrate the visual content with semantic meanings in terms of the cognitive models and principles [Geng *et al.*, 1999]. Although we are still lacking sophisticated theories to clearly explain the relationship between intent communication and visual cognition, lots of research has been done on how to effectively communicate the intent. For example, Csinger presented how to develop artificial intelligence techniques to acquire, represent and exploit such models, and probabilistic abduction is used to recognize user models and cost-based abduction to design tailored presentations [Csinger, 1995]; Giannini and Monti investigated the possible relationships between shape geometry and aesthetic character linked to the geometry and the design intent, and the formalization of these relations may allow the designers' aesthetic intent to be communicated through a product's shape and non-shape characteristics [Giannini & Monti, 2003]. Lu *et al.* employed context-dependent rendering to depict the internal flaws hidden in a design object [Lu *et al.*, 1996].

Intent-base illustration techniques can be summarized as follows:

(1) *Intent communication by multimedia presentation.* Aiming at the presentation of the desired intent, the visual content and semantic symbols

depicting the same object are composed together in terms of the aesthetic and cognitive principles.

(2) *Interpreting intent by graphical abstraction.* The 3D objects are hierarchically depicted and rendered from concrete geometry to abstract symbols, and the intent is effectively expressed by associating all these renditions with each other in terms of the conventions and empirical principles.
(3) *Visual explanation of iconic symbols.* It starts from the abstract symbols, which are semantically analyzed and interpreted, and then these iconic symbols are connected to the comprehensible visual content. Thus, the abstract symbols will be concretized as a visual icon and accordingly form an interpretation of the meanings embodied in the abstract symbols.

6.3.1 Intent Communication by Multimedia Presentation

The pioneer work on intent communication in 3D illustration is based on the multimedia presentation principle [Seligmann & Feiner, 1989]. They formalized the illustration process as a goal-driven process: the goal is to achieve a specified communicative intent within a complex of stylistic choices. The generate-and-test approach was employed to generate the intent-based 3D illustration, relying upon a rule base to make stylistic and design choices. Each rule in their system falls into one of two categories: method or evaluator. A method identifies what must be accomplished to satisfy a particular goal. An evaluator measures how well a particular goal is currently accomplished.

Later on, they implemented an intent-based illustration system (IBIS) that designs illustrations to fulfill a high-level description of the communicative goal. Communicative goals specify that particular properties of objects, such as their color, size, or location are to be conveyed in the illustration. An illustration's communicative goals are used to determine what is important to show in each illustration and to invoke rules that guide this decision process. The communicative goals that IBIS can satisfy are as follows:

(1) *Location.* Show the location of an object in a context (either explicitly specified or derived by the system).
(2) *Relative location.* Show the relative location of two or more objects in terms of a specified or derived context.
(3) *Property.* Show one of the following physical properties of an object: material, color, size, shape.
(4) *State.* Show an object's state.
(5) *Change.* Show the difference between a set of states.

Given an initial set of input goals, IBIS's rule-based control component builds and evaluates a representation of the illustration. Rules specify methods for accomplishing each kind of goal and methods for evaluation of goal achievement and interaction with other goals. IBIS first selects a set of achievement-methods to accomplish a goal and then uses evaluation-methods to rate how well the goal has been satisfied and to detect incompatibilities. When an incompatibility occurs, IBIS backtracks to select different achievement-methods. In addition to controlling the illustration process, evaluation methods can be queried directly, providing means for outside components to evaluate how well certain communicative goals are satisfied in an illustration. This in turn provides the necessary feedback for, as an example, a media coordinator to decide which medium is best suited to convey what information. The algorithmic pipeline of IBIS is shown in Fig. 6.19 [Seligmann & Feiner, 1991].

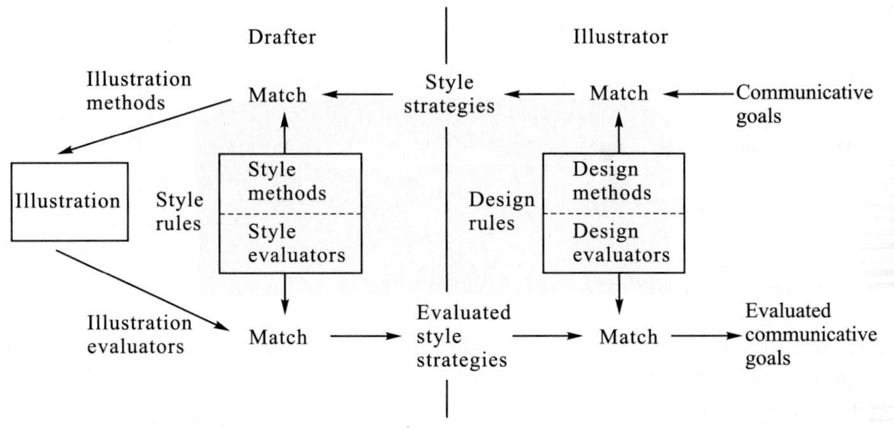

Fig. 6.19 The algorithmic pipeline in IBIS

IBIS is also provided with a knowledge base that specifies information about the objects in the world it depicts. This information includes the physical properties of the objects (shape, material, location and orientation), along with additional properties such as their type or purpose. Objects are organized in parts hierarchy in which leaf nodes constitute the indivisible physical objects and internal nodes represent composite objects. Each object refers to its shape by name, rather than storing its own geometry. The shape name indexes into a geometric object base, allowing multiple objects to share the same geometry. Facilities are provided to define new shapes in terms of the polyhedral geometry that IBIS supports. Any collection of objects that can be described in this form can be processed by IBIS.

The illustration contains all the information necessary to render it. Its members are a viewing specification, lighting specification, viewport specification and a display-list composed of illustrator-objects. The viewport specification denotes the placement of the illustration (inset in, overlapping, or non-overlapping its parent illustration's viewport), its range of acceptable viewport dimensions, and its location relative to its parent. Fig. 6.20 gives an illustration example showing the location of an object in a specific context, and the following strategies are employed for it.

(1) The object must be included in the illustration. The achievement threshold "highest" indicates that this style strategy must be fully satisfied.
(2) The object must be recognizable.
(3) The context object must be included.
(4) The object must be visible.
(5) The object must be highlighted.
(6) The context object must also be recognizable, but with a lower threshold.
(7) The context object must also be visible, but with a lower threshold.

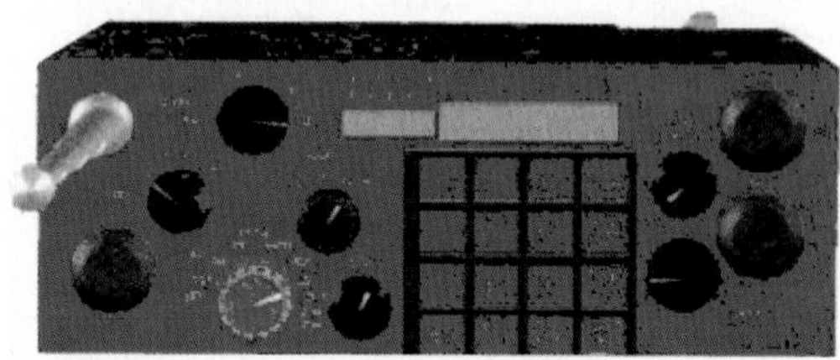

Fig. 6.20 Illustration example of the showing location [Seligmann & Feiner, 1991]. Copyright of ACM, used with permission

6.3.2 Interpreting Intent by Graphical Abstraction

Graphical abstraction is a simplification of an object's depiction. It could be abstract paintings, sketch drawings or pictures of technical documentations, etc. The model of graphical abstraction is to provide measures to evaluate and compare different graphical abstractions of the same object, assuming that graphics convey not only information, but also meaning, as part of a communicative act. From the point of view of intent communication, graphical abstraction not only reduces the probability of distracting the viewer's attention by unimportant details, but also enables the viewer's attention to be directed to relevant parts of the graphics, without using meta-objects or-colors (e.g., arrows, blinking objects, etc.).

In the context of intent-based 3D illustration, graphical abstraction is usually generated by simplification techniques. Different kinds of simplifications include: substitution of an object's colored parts by greyscales, unification of line styles (leading to a kind of sketch), smoothing the object's contour, suppression of some parts of the object. However, graphical abstraction is a special form of simplification, and a simplification becomes a graphical abstraction only if the viewer is still able to recognize the simplified depiction as a particular world object or as a member of a class of world objects. In order to distinguish simplification and graphical abstraction, Krüger introduced the concept of simplification degree to measure the syntactic and semantic simplicity which is dependent on the amount of information and the types of meaning conveyed by different depictions of the same object [Krüger, 1998]. Syntactic criteria of simplicity are the complexity of object composition, object shapes and object properties. For example: given two depictions G_1 and G_2 of the same object O, G_1 is simpler than G_2 if G_1 shows less object parts than G_2. Concerning O's shape depiction, G_1 is simpler if G_1's contour consists of less line segments or less noncontinuous parts or has less concave elements. If G_1 is a black and white picture and G_2 shows O colored, G_1 is simpler in respect of O's color property. The maintenance of object properties, like the object's main axis or texture is also a criterion to distinguish different syntactic simplification degrees. A semantic measure of simplicity can therefore be defined as follows: Given two graphical abstractions GA_1 and GA_2 of the same object O, if GA_1 is identifiable as O and GA_2 is only categorizable as a member of O's basic category, GA_2 can be considered as a semantically more simple depiction.

Krüger also presented an abstraction pipeline on each level of the image generation from a 3D model [Krüger, 1998]. Three major abstraction layers are distinguished: model space, generation space and image space. The model space describes all the initial 3D information (e.g., the location of objects and lights) needed to produce graphics. Different simplification techniques can be applied to the 3D models. Usually they aim at reducing the representational complexity of the 3D models, (e.g., in the case of a polygon-based representation to reduce the number of vertices that are needed to describe it). The modification in generation space includes changes in camera parameters and light conditions. Different shading techniques yield different results that may vary from photorealistic over shaded to wire frame depictions. The suppression of colors is another way to raise the degree of the depiction's simplicity. Rendering can also control the line thickness of depictions and a further method suitable for simplifying line drawings is known as hard edging. In the image space, a lot of different simplification techniques are available that manipulate the images directly. This includes a variety of filters, for example a Gaussian filter that blurs the image, color filters or erasers that completely remove image parts. Usually these methods do not need more information than the pixels of an image. However, in order to use them consciously to abstract certain parts, they must be restricted to some regions. Otherwise unwanted effects may occur and this will distort the attention of the user.

The key advantage of abstraction-based intent illustration is that both computational and cognitive resources are taken into consideration at the same time. By means of an evaluation component detecting artifacts, the results can be improved stepwise through a generate-and-test cycle.

6.3.3 Visual Explanation of Iconic Symbols

In essence, intent can be considered as a kind of semantic meaning, which is usually represented in textual symbols. However, the abstract symbol is not comprehensible, and therefore the semantic symbols are often interpreted in a specific context, expressing the user's intent together with the 3D scene. The major advantage of an iconic symbol is to better present the dynamic information in a single illustration. Preim *et al.* provided visual explanation of navigation intent by an integrated view of geometry, structure and rendering context [Preim *et al.*, 1997]. In the geometric view, it describes mathematical attributes for manipulating the 3D object, including graphical transformation, camera parameters and the picking-up of the object. In the structural view, it provides a visual tree of the entire 3D scene, where the nodes and edges represent the spatial order of each geometric primitive. In the rendering context view, it gives the textual description of non-geometric attributes such as the best-fit rendering parameters and the interaction strategies between user and the 3D scene. When the three views are presented to the user at the same time, all the information in one view will be reinforced in the other two views.

Nienhaus and Döllner employed dynamic glyphs to present dynamics in static media [Nienhaus & Döllner, 2003]. Dynamic glyphs are visual elements that symbolize dynamics in images of 3D scenes. For instance, arrows indicate the direction of movement, rays symbolize an extraordinary event, or clouds contain descriptions of the thoughts of an actor. Such depictions of dynamics in images enable observers to understand the dynamics of 3D scenery even in static images, to relate dynamics of the past and the future with the current state of a 3D scene, and to communicate all kinds of non-geometric information such as tension, danger and feelings. Dynamic glyphs are usually derived from a formal specification of dynamics based on a behavior graph. Different types of dynamics and corresponding mappings to dynamic glyphs can be identified, for instance, scene events at a discrete point in time, transformation processes of scene objects and activities of scene actors. Finally, an appropriate non-photorealistic rendering style is employed to produce the illustrations of 3D scenes and their dynamics.

In order to design step-by-step assembly instructions, Agrawala *et al.* examined how people mentally represent and communicate the process of assembling an object, and presented design principles drawn from cognitive psychology research [Agrawala *et al.*, 2003]. People's conceptual models of assembly and effective methods to visually communicate assembly intent are then investigated and the design knowledge is codified in computer programs, which can make it easier to produce clear drawings of 3D objects and more effective instructions. There are two primary tasks in designing assembly instructions: planning and presentation. The key-point in "planning" lies in that most objects can be assembled in a variety of ways, and the system should choose a sequence of assembly operations that is easy to understand

and follow. The challenge in "presentation" is how to convey the assembly operations in a series of operations. Their assembly instruction design systems are accordingly decomposed into two parts: a planner and a presenter. The planner searches the space of feasible assembly sequences to find one that best matches the cognitive design principles. To do this the planner must also consider many aspects of presentation. The presenter then renders a diagram for each step of the assembly sequence generated by the planner. The presenter also uses the design principles to determine where to place parts, guidelines and arrows. In particular, the presenter can generate action diagrams which use the conventions of exploded views to clearly depict the parts and operation required in each assembly step. Given object geometry, orientation and optional grouping and ordering constraints on the object's parts, the system can effectively produce good assembly instructions for it.

6.4 Expressive Rendering for Transparency

There are many potential advantages in using transparency to simultaneously depict multiple superimposed layers of information. The first advantage is simultaneity: displaying all relevant external and internal anatomical objects together in the context of each other allows better comprehension of the complex spatial relationships between two irregularly-shaped surfaces. The second advantage is completeness: a 3D display allows maximum comprehension of the 3D form, and the three-dimensional structure of a scene can be more accurately and efficiently appreciated when the layered elements are displayed in their entirety. However, the challenge is how to render the transparent surfaces in such a way that their three-dimensional shape can be readily understood and their depth distance from underlying structures clearly perceived, since in computer-generated images it can often be difficult to adequately perceive the full three-dimensional shape of an external transparent surface, or to correctly judge its depth distance from arbitrary points on an underlying opaque structure.

The representative work on transparency illustration comes from Interrante *et al.* [1995,1996,1997]. Inspired by artists' use of line to show shape, they explored methods for automatically defining a distributed set of opaque surface markings that intend to portray the three-dimensional shape and relative depth of a smoothly curving layered transparent surface in an intuitively meaningful (and minimally occluding) way. A transparent surface is "textured" with uniformly distributed opaque short strokes, locally oriented in the direction of greatest normal curvature and of length proportional to the magnitude of the surface curvature in the stroke direction. Adding such a sparse, opaque texture to a transparent surface can help make its location in space much more explicit, providing additional occlusion cues and possibly enabling a better estimation of relative depth from motion. (see Fig. 6.21).

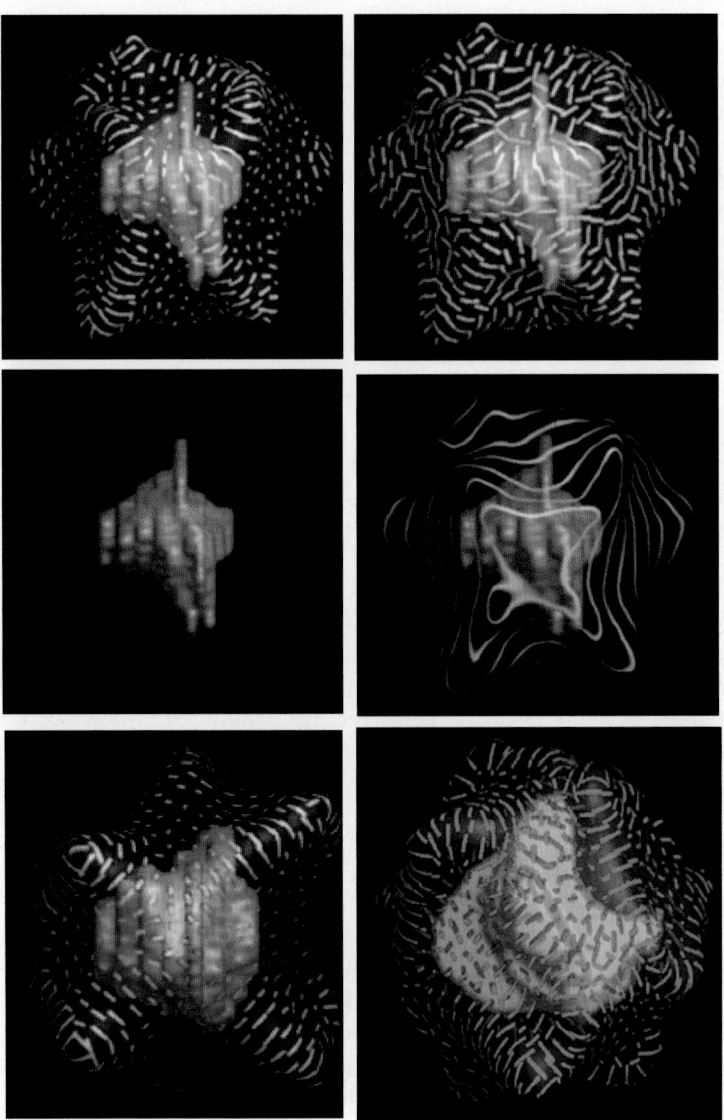

Fig. 6.21 Expressive rendering of transparency [Interrante *et al.*, 1997]. Copyright of IEEE, used with permission

Hamel *et al.* summarized principles of depicting transparency in hand-made line drawings, and developed a method to generate similar, but computer-generated line drawings [Hamel *et al.*, 1998]. Three different methods derived from traditional drawing techniques are simulated (see Fig. 6.22).

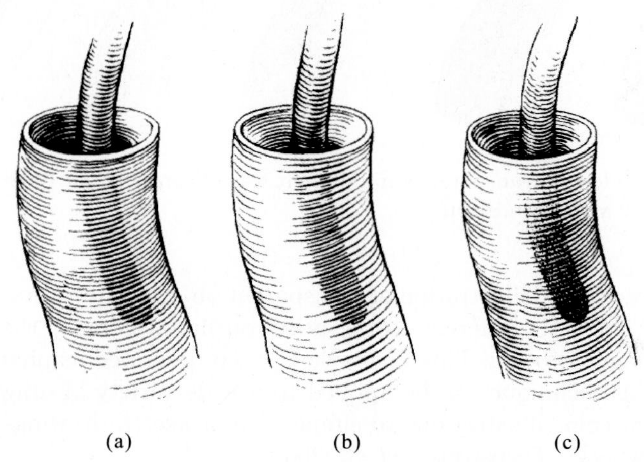

Fig. 6.22 Three different ways of expressing transparency in a line-drawing [Hamel *et al.*, 1998]. (a) Increasing the thickness of lines; (b) Inserting additional lines; (c) Using a different style (stippling). Copyright of IEEE, used with permission

In their system implementation, three different images are generated first: the "opaque" image, where all objects are rendered opaque and the outer parts brightness is faded to zero towards the edge between inner and outer parts; the "transparent" image rendered with a simple lighting model by a simplified transparency calculation; a mask, which masks out all pixels not concealed in the opaque image. Second, the three different ways of expressing transparency are simulated as follows (see Fig. 6.23):

(1) *Increasing the thickness of lines.* Lines are intersected with the edge of the mask and the part inside is drawn with a thickness based on the brightness of the transparent picture. The thickness of the line parts outside the masked area and all other lines are based on the opaque image.
(2) *Inserting additional lines.* Every second line is drawn on the tube, based on the opaque picture. The other lines are intersected with the mask edge and are drawn based on the transparent image.
(3) *Using a different style.* The lines are drawn on the basis of the opaque image, then the lines or dots are added, and, whatever the different style used, the primitives are drawn based on the transparent image and masked out.

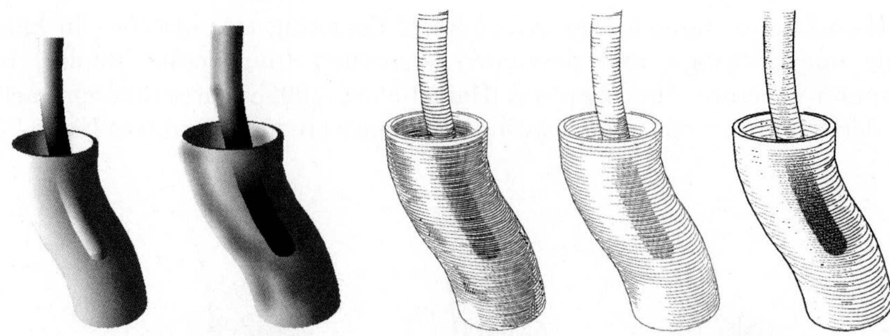

Fig. 6.23 Rendering transparency in different ways [Hamel *et al.*, 1998]. Copyright of IEEE, used with permission

In the traditional illustration of transparent objects, the outlines are often drawn in a line-style different to the other outlines, to make them distinct from the opaque objects. This line-style is often described as phantom lines. Although this technique can be applied to a wide variety of drawing styles, ranging from color illustrations to simple line or sketch drawings, there are certain drawbacks [Diepstraten *et al.*, 2002]:

(1) Details of the transparent objects are lost, as only their outlines are drawn.
(2) Material and surface information of transparent objects are ignored.
(3) There are only two transparency states: fully opaque or fully non-opaque, semi-transparency cannot be visualized.

In order to facilitate the aforementioned limitations, Diepstraten *et al.* [2002] introduced a novel view-dependent transparency model and carried it out based on the following empirical rules extracted from manual drawings:

(1) Faces of transparent objects never shine through.
(2) Opaque objects which are occluded by two transparent objects do not shine through.
(3) Transparency falls off close to the edges of transparent objects and increases with the distance to the edges.

Based on these rules, the basic algorithm is as follows. In the first step, all front-facing transparent surfaces are rendered to the depth buffer; afterwards, the depth buffer contains the depth values of the closest transparent surfaces. In the second step, the depth buffer is stored in a high-resolution texture and then the depth buffer is cleared. In the third step, the front-facing transparent surfaces are rendered to the depth buffer except the foremost ones, virtually peeling off the closest surfaces. In the fourth step, opaque objects are rendered. The depth test rejects all surfaces except for those lying in front of the second-closest transparent front faces. Finally, just the foremost transparent surfaces are blended into the frame buffer. Fig. 6.24 shows the comparative illustration of phantom lines showing transparent objects and view dependent transparency.

Fig. 6.24 The comparative illustration of transparency [Diepstraten *et al.*, 2002].(a)Phantom lines illustration of transparency of transparency; (b) View-dependent illustration. Copyright of Blackwell, used with permission

6.5 Summary

The traditional rendering process is mainly computed from the physical principles in an objective way. However, expressive rendering takes into consideration the subjective cognitive factors of human beings, such as the capability of visual perception and cognition. For the time being, research into expressive rendering is mainly driven by concrete applications, due to a lack of systematic cognitive theories and quantitative guidelines, although there are a few works that are starting to investigate the influence of subjective cognition and interaction between expressive goals and the objects-to-be-depicted[Seligmann & Feiner, 1993; Strothotte *et al.*, 1994], the cognitive model of sketch drawing of terrain [Visvalingam & Dowson, 2001], and the evaluation model of the resultant expressive illustration, etc. In order to deepen the research into expressive rendering, more work should be done on the systematic analysis and comparison of expressive rendering techniques and the quantitative construction of a series of computational models for expressive rendering, based on the relevant cognitive theories and principles.

References

Akers D, Losasso F, Klingner J, Agrawala M, Rick J, Hanrahan P(2003) Conveying shape and features with image-based relighting. In: Proceedings of the 14th IEEE Visualization 2003

Agrawala M, Phan D, Heiser J, Haymaker J, Klinger J, Hanrahan P, Tversky B(2003) Designing effective step-by-step. ACM Transactions on Graphics 22(3):828–837

Buchanan JW, Sousa MCThe edge buffer: a data structure for easy silhouette rendering. In: Proceedings of the 1st International Symposium on Non-photorealistic Animation and Rendering, 2000: 39–42

Sheelagh M, Carpendale ST, Cowperthwaite DJ, Fracchia FD(1997) Making distortions comprehensible. IEEE Symposium on Visual Languages 1997 36–45

Cignoni P, Scopigno R, Tarini M(2005) A simple normal enhancement technique for interactive non-photorealistic renderings. Computers and Graphics 29(1):125–133

Csinger A(1995) User models for intent-based authoring. The University of British Columbia

DeCarlo D, Finkelstein A, Rusinkiewicz S(2004) Interactive rendering of suggestive contours with temporal coherence. In: Proceedings of the 3rd international symposium on Non-photorealistic animation and rendering 15–145

DeCarlo D, Finkelstein A, Rusinkiewicz S, Santella A(2003) Suggestive contours for conveying shape. ACM Transactions on Graphics 22(3):848–855

Deussen O, Hamel J, Raab A, Schlechtweg S, Strothotte T(1999) An illustration technique using hardware-based intersections and skeletons. In: Proceedings of Graphics Interface 1999 175–182

Diepstraten J, Weiskopf D, Ertl T(2002) Transparency in interactive technical illustrations. Computer Graphics Forum 21(3):317–325

Diepstraten J, Weiskopf D, Ertl T(2003) Interactive cutaway illustrations. Computer Graphics Forum 22(3):523–532

Dooley D Cohen MF(1990) Automatic illustration of 3D geometric models: surfaces. In: Proceedings of the 1990 Symposium of Interactive 3D Graphics 307–314

Geng W, Pan Y(1999) A survey of computational models of integrating semantics and mental image. Pattern Recognition and Artificial Intelligence 12(1): 56–66

Giannini F, Monti M(2003) Design intent-oriented modelling tools for aesthetic design. Journal of WSCG 2003

Hamel J, Schlechtweg S, Strothotte T(1998) An approach to visualizing transparency in computer-generated line drawings. In: Proceedings of the 1998 IEEE Conference on Information Visualization 1998 151–156

Interrante V, Fuchs H, Pizer S(1995) Enhancing transparent skin surfaces with ridge and valley lines. In: Proceedings of the 1995 Symposium of Interactive 3D Graphics 52–59

Interrante V, Fuchs H, Pizer S(1996) Illustrating transparent surfaces with curvature-directed strokes. In: Proceedings of the 1996 Symposium of Interactive 3D Graphics 211–218

Interrante V, Fuchs H, Pizer S(1997) Conveying the 3D shape of smoothly curving transparent surfaces via texture. IEEE Transactions on Visualization and Computer Graphics 3(2):98–117

Isenberg T, Masuch M, Strothotte T(2000) 3D illustrative effcts for animating line-drawing. In: Proceedings of the IEEE Conference on Information Visualization 413–418

Kamada T, Kawai S(1987) An enhanced treatment of hidden lines. ACM Transactions on Graphics 6(4):308–323

Kim S, Hagh-Shenas H, Interrante V(2003) Showing shape with texture: two directions seem better than one. In: Proceedings of the 2003 IEEE Conference on Information Visualization

Krüger A(1998) Automatic graphical abstraction in intent-based 3D illustrations. Workshop on Advanced Visual Interfaces 98 47–56

Lansdown J, Schofield S(1995) Expressive rendering: a review of nonphotorealistic techniques. IEEE Computer Graphics and Applications 1995 29–37

Lesage PL, Visvalingam M(2002) Towards sketch-based exploration of terrain. Computers and Graphics 26(2):309–328

Li W, Ritter L, Agrawala M, Curless B, Salesin D(2007) Interactive cutaway illustrations of complex 3D models. ACM Transactions on Graphics 26(3)

Lu SC, Rebello AB, Cui DH, Yagel R, Miller RA, Kinzel GL(1996) A 3D contextual shading method for visualization of diecasting defects. In: Proceedings of the 1996 Symposium of Interactive 3D Graphics 405–407, 510

Luft T, Colditz C, Deussen O(2006) Image enhancement by unsharp masking the depth buffer. ACM Transactions on Graphics 25(3):1206–1213

May J(2000) Perceptual principles and computer graphics. Computer Graphics Forum 19(4):271–279

Nienhaus M, Döllner J(2003) Edge-Enhancement:an algorithm for real-time nonphotorealistic rendering. Journal of WSGG 2003

Preim B, Hoppe A, Strothotte T(1997) Enrichment and reuse of geometric models. Simulation and Animation 97 159–170

Rodger JC, Browne R A(2000) Choosing rendering parameters for effective communication of 3D shape. IEEE Computer Graphics and Applications 20(2): 20–28

Saito T, Takahashi T(1990) Comprehensible rendering of 3D shapes. SIGGRAPH Computer Graphics 24(4):197–206

Schlechtweg S, Schönwälder B, Schumann L, Strothotte T(1998) Surfaces To Lines:Rendering Rich Line Drawings. Journal of WSCG 1998 354–361

Schweitzer D(1983) Artificial texturing:an aid to surface visualization. Computer Graphics 17(3):23–29

Seligmann DD, Feiner S(1989) Specifying composite illustrations with communicative goals. In: Proceedings of the 2nd annual ACM SIGGRAPH Symposium on User Interface Software and Technology 1–9

Seligmann DD, Feiner S(1991) Automated generation of intent-based 3D illustrations. In: Proceedings of the 18th Annual Conference on Computer Graphics and Interactive Techniques 123–132

Seligmann DD, Feiner S(1993) Supporting interactivity in automated 3D illustrations. In: Proceedings of the 1st International Conference on Intelligent User Interfaces 37–44

Sousa MC, Prusinkiewicz P(2003) A few good lines: suggestive drawing of 3D models. Computer Graphics Forum 22(3): 381–390

Sousa MC, Samavati F, Brunn M(2004) Depicting shape features with directional strokes and spotlighting. In: Proceedings of the Computer Graphic International 214–221

Takahashi S, Ohta N, Nakamura H, Takeshima Y, Fujishiro(2002) Modeling surperspective projection of landscapes for geographical guide-map generation. Computer Graphics Forum 21(3) 259–268

Tanaka T, Ohnishi N(1997) Painting-like image emphasis based on human vision systems. Computer Graphics Forum 16(3) 253–260

Veryovka O, Buchanan J W(1999) Comprehensive half-toning of 3D scenes. Computer Graphics Forum 18(3):13–22

Visvalingam M, Dowson K(2001) Towards cognitive evaluation of computer-drawn sketches. The Visual Computer 17(4) 219–235

7

Computer-assisted Cartoon Animation by Traditional Production Pipeline

The production of 2D cartoon animation is in essence a process of drawing a series of pictures that are smooth and temporally-coherent, and the production pipeline is traditionally decomposed into three major phases:

(1) The extreme frames, in which the emotion, motion or color of the cartoon characters are changed rapidly, are first drawn by experienced animators in terms of the storyboard.
(2) The key frames are then further drawn by the assistant animators on the basis of commonsense and his personal understanding of the episodes in the story.
(3) At last all the in between frames are created in detail by the painters/inbetweeners in terms of the key frames.

Such a production pipeline is not only time-consuming, but also requires that the animators should have a rich experience of life and possess a sophisticated skill in drawing. In order to speed up the production of cartoon animation, lots of computer-assisted cartoon animation systems were implemented and commercialized in the animation industry [Fekete *et al.*, 1995]. The computer graphics community also proposed and designed many key techniques that could partially automate the production process of cartoon animation such as semi-automatic/automatic coloring and line-drawing generation of in-between frames. In this chapter we will first give a brief introduction of the traditional production pipeline of cartoon animation, and then discuss the techniques of computer-assisted coloring and generation of in-between frames in cartoon animation.

7.1 The Traditional Animation Process

The overall pipeline of the traditional animation process can be summarized as three linear phases: pre-production, production and post-production [Catmull, 1978; Fekete *et al.*, 1995; Patterson & Willis, 1995; Qiu *et al.*, 2005]. As shown in Fig. 7.1, the involved steps are:

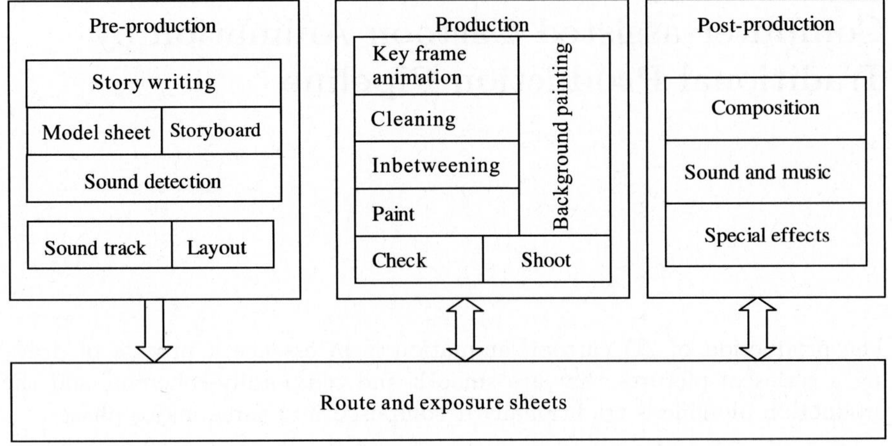

Fig. 7.1 The overall pipeline of the traditional animation process

(1) *Story writing.* Creates the drama script of the story of the animation narrated by text.
(2) *Story board.* Splits script into scenes with dialog and music.
(3) *Model sheet.* Designs and draws the characters in various poses.
(4) *Sound track.* Records dialog and music in prototype form.
(5) *Sound detection.* Fills the dialog column of an exposure sheet.
(6) *Layout.* Manages the drawing of backgrounds and main character positions, with specifications for camera movement and other animation characteristics.
(7) *Background painting.* Paints the background according to the layout.
(8) *Key frame animation.* Draws extreme positions of characters as specified by the layout. Provides instructions for the inbetweeners.
(9) *Cleaning.* Cleans up the drawings to achieve final quality of the strokes.
(10) *Inbetweening.* Draws the missing frames according to the key frame animator's instructions.
(11) *Paint.* Photocopies the clean drawings onto acetate celluloid (cel) and paints zones with water color.
(12) *Check.* Verifies animation and backgrounds according to the layout and approves for shooting.
(13) *Shoot.* Records frame-by-frame on film or video, using a rostrum.
(14) *Composition.* The recorded video clips are integrated into animation sequences by further editing and synthesizing.

(15) *Sound and music.* The sound effects and background music are synchronized with the video clips.
(16) *Special effects.* The special effects are created and inserted into the resultant animation sequence.
(17) *The route sheet.* Every scene is listed with its length, vital statistics and the name of the person in charge of the various stages. This allows the director to quickly determine the status and location of a scene.
(18) *The exposure sheet.* The exposure sheet has a line on it for every frame in the film. Each line indicates the dialogue for that frame, the order of all figures, the background and camera position. The exposure sheets are grouped according to scenes.

Whether it is generated by hand or by computer, the first goal of the animation is to entertain the audience. The animator must have two things: a clear concept of exactly what will entertain the audience, and the tools and skills to put those ideas across clearly and unambiguously [Lasseter, 1987].

Besides the well-defined pipeline, a set of drawing and production conventions are gradually formed in 2D hand-drawn animation, and finally become the fundamental principles of traditional animation [Lasseter, 1987].

(1) *Squash and stretch.* Defining the rigidity and mass of an object by distorting its shape during an action. The squashed position depicts the form either flattened out by an external pressure or constricted by its own power. The stretched position always shows the same form in a very extended condition. The most important rule of squashing and stretching is that, no matter how squashed or stretched out a particular object gets, its volume remains constant (see Fig. 7.2). If an object is squashed down without its sides stretching, it would appear to shrink; if it is stretched up without its sides being squeezed in, it would appear to grow [Lasseter, 1987].

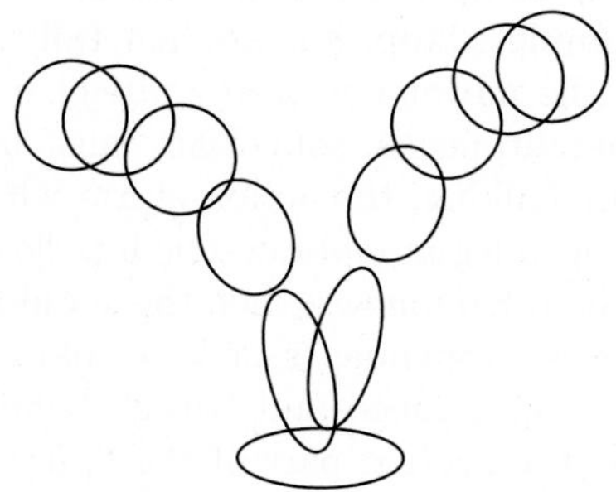

Fig. 7.2 Squash and stretch example in bouncing ball

(2) *Timing, or the speed of an action, is an important principle because it gives meaning to movement.* The speed of an action defines how well the idea behind the action will be read by an audience. It reflects the weight and size of an object, and can even carry emotional meaning. Proper timing is critical to making ideas readable. If too much time is spent on any of these, the audience's attention will wander. If too little time is spent, the movement may be finished before the audience notices it, thus wasting the idea.

(3) *Anticipation.* The preparation for an action. There are several facets to anticipation. In one sense, it is the anatomical provision for an action. Anticipation is also a device to catch the audience's eye, to prepare them for the next movement and lead them to expect it before it actually occurs. Anticipation is often used to explain what the following action is going to be. Anticipation is also used to direct the attention of the audience to the fight part of the screen at the fight moment. This is essential for preventing the audience from missing some vital actions. Without anticipation many actions are abrupt, stiff and unnatural.

(4) *Staging.* Presenting an idea so that it is unmistakably clear. This principle translates directly from 2D hand drawn animation. An action is staged so that it is understood; a personality is staged so that it is recognizable; an expression is staged so that it can be seen; a mood is staged so that it will affect the audience. It is important, when staging an action, that only one idea be seen by the audience at a time. If a lot of action is happening at once, the eye does not know where to look and the main idea of the action will be "upstaged" and overlooked. The object of interest should contrast from the rest of the scene. In a still scene, the eye will be attracted to movement. In a very busy scene, the eye will be attracted to something that is still. Each idea or action must be staged in the strongest and the simplest way before going on to the next idea or action.

(5) *Follow through and overlapping action.* The termination of an action and establishing its relationship to the next action. Actions very rarely come to a sudden and complete stop, but are generally carried past their termination point. In the movement of any object or figure, the actions of the parts are not simultaneous: some part must initiate the move. This is called the *lead.* In walking, the action starts with the hips. As the hip swings forward, it sets a leg in motion. The hip "leads", the leg "follows". As the hip twists, the torso follows, then the shoulder, the arm, the wrist, and finally the fingers. Appendages or loose parts of a character or object will move at a slower speed and "drag" behind the leading part of the figure. Then, as the leading part of the figure slows to a stop, these appendages will continue to move and will take longer to settle down. Slight variations are often added to the timing and speed of the loose parts of objects. This *overlapping action* makes the object seem natural, the action more interesting. Perhaps more important, overlapping is

critical to conveying the main ideas of the story. An action should never be brought to a complete stop before starting another action, and the second action should overlap the first. Overlapping maintains a continual flow and continuity between whole phrases of actions.

(6) *Straight ahead action and pose-to-pose action.* The two contrasting approaches to the creation of movement. Straight ahead action is used for wild, scrambling actions where spontaneity is important. In this approach, the animator literally works straight ahead from his first drawing in the scene. He knows where the scene fits in the story and the business it has to include. He does one drawing after another, getting new ideas as he goes along, until he reaches the end of the scene. In the pose-to-pose approach, the animator plans his actions, and figures out just what drawings will be needed to animate the business, makes the drawings concentrating on the poses, relates them to each other in size and action, and then draws the in-betweens. Pose-to-pose is used for animation that requires good acting, where the poses and timing are all important.

(7) *Slow in and out.* The spacing of the in-between frames to achieve subtlety of timing and movement. Mathematically, it refers to second-order and third-order continuity of motion. It is often achieved by interpolation along the trajectory of motion. It can also be achieved by breaking the motion trajectory using its continuity parameters.

(8) *Arcs.* The visual path of action for natural movement. Arcs in nature are the most economical routes by which a form can move from one position to another. In animation such arcs are used extensively, for they make animation much smoother and less stiff than a straight line for the path of action.

(9) *Exaggeration.* Accentuating the essence of an idea via the design and the action. A scene has many components to it: the design, the shape of the objects, the action, the emotion, the color, the sound. Exaggeration can work with any component, but not in isolation. If just one thing is exaggerated in an otherwise life-like scene, it will stick out and seem unrealistic. The principle of exaggeration in animation does not mean arbitrarily distorting shapes or objects or making an action more violent or unrealistic. The animator must go to the heart of anything or any idea and develop its essence, understanding the reason for it, so that the audience will also understand it. If a character is sad, make him sadder; if he is bright, make him shine; worried, make him fret; wild, make him frantic.

(10) *Secondary action.* The action of an object resulting from another action. Secondary actions are important in heightening interest and adding a realistic complexity to the animation. A secondary action is always kept subordinate to the primary action. If it conflicts, becomes more interesting, or dominates in any way, it is either the wrong choice or is staged improperly. The facial expression of a character will sometimes be a sec-

ondary action. When the main idea of an action is being told in the movement of the body, the facial expression becomes subordinate to the main idea.

(11) *Appeal.* Creating a design or an action that the audience enjoys watching. It means anything that a person likes to see: a quality of charm, pleasing design, simplicity, communication, or magnetism. Your eye is drawn to the figure or object that has appeal and, once there, it is held while you appreciate the object. A weak drawing or design lacks appeal. A design that is complicated or hard to read lacks appeal. Clumsy shapes and awkward moves all have low appeal.

7.2 The Role of the Computer in Traditional 2D Animation

With the advent of computer graphics, it enables the computer to aid the production process of traditional animation. Catmull made a systematic analysis of the problems in computer-assisted animation, and summarized that the computer can be used in the following steps in the traditional animation pipeline [Catmull, 1978]:

(1) *Inbetweening.* Given figures A and C, the computer is employed to find the correspondence between the figures, such that it can produce an interpolated figure B dependent on the correspondence.
(2) *Input of drawings.* Figures can either be drawn directly on the tablet, traced in, or scanned in with the aid of the computer.
(3) *Coloring.* An operator indicates what color each area is to receive. The figures are colored by some area filling program.
(4) *Composition and photographing or videotaping.* With the computer, this can be done in a frame buffer before sending the picture to the film or video recorder. The programs must include capabilities for zoom and pan of the components in the picture, etc.
(5) *Background painting.* The software system can be used for painting backgrounds by tablet, color monitor and frame buffer.
(6) *Sound track reading.* Digital sound equipment could also be used to synthesize sound or to fix errors, by expanding or contracting sound on a tape.
(7) *Check (pencil test).* Animators need to check the action in their scenes. With the computer, the artist can get real-time playback of a scene as soon as the figures are entered or synthesized.
(8) *Exposure sheets.* One can easily think of the exposure sheet as a data base management system. It is a natural implementation on a computer.

From the point of view of research methodology, the work of computer assisted 2D animation can be classified as two major approaches. One is to "digitize" the production process, such as digitization of the shoot [Stern, 1979], vectorization of cartoon drawing [Zou & Yan, 2001] and paperless 2D animation [Van Reeth *et al.*, 1994; Fekete *et al.*, 1995]. The other is to let the computer assist the animators in time-consuming or repetitive work such as coloring or inbetweening. For the time being, computer-assisted 2D animation has made significant progress, especially in "digitizing" the production process, and most steps in the production pipeline were supported in the commercialized 2D animation software systems such as TOONZ, RETAS PRO, ANIMO, AXA, etc. (see Fig. 7.3). It not only greatly reduces the workload of animators, but also has obvious advantages over the hand drawn work of dialog design, timing control and motion specification etc. [Kurlander *et al.*, 1996; Litwinowicz, 1991]. Moreover, with the aid of the computer, the temporal coherence between consecutive frames can be easily checked and preserved and the quality of the resulting animation is much better than before (see Fig. 7.4).

Fig. 7.3 Example of computer-assisted cartoon animation [Stern, 1979]. Copyright of ACM, used with permission

Although the computer can effectively aid many steps involved in the traditional animation pipeline, it is still facing challenges when used to assist the coloring and inbetweening in 2D animation production. The computer can only play a secondary role in these two steps. This is mainly because the traditional animation production is merely based on the 2D plane, and the 3D information about characters and scenes is mentally and implicitly represented in the mind of the animator. Moreover, the visual content of traditional cartoon animation is an aesthetic depiction of the world, requiring the artistic imagination to interpret it, and its motion content is embodied in the 2D line-drawing that is expected to behave the way the 3D models do. Therefore it will be very difficult for the computer to directly infer the 3D geometric information and motion of the 2D character and background scene. Consequently, it is not easy to make the computer effectively assist the coloring and inbetweening of cartoon animation when occlusion occurs among consecutive frames [Catmull, 1978; Patterson & Willis, 1995]. However, in the traditional animation production, most work and time is spent on two tedious tasks: drawing and inking/coloring of the individual animated characters for each frame, which takes up approximately 60% of total labor required in traditional animation [Durand, 1991], and it makes sense to continue the exploration and development of key techniques to speed up coloring and inbetweening steps. The remaining sections of this chapter will discuss computer-assisted coloring and inbetweening in detail.

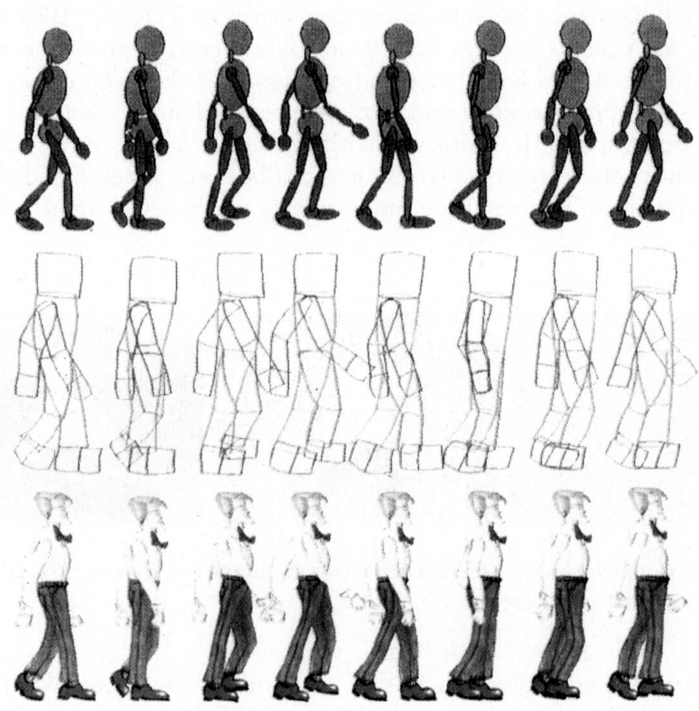

Fig. 7.4 Example of motion specification in traditional 2D animation [Litwinowicz, 1991]. Copyright of ACM, used with permission

7.3 Computer-assisted Coloring

The goal of computer-assisted coloring is to automatically fill each region of animation frames with the specified color. There are two major approaches to auto-coloring in cartoon animation production. One is based on the traditional animation pipeline, and the computer automatically fills the remaining frames with the specified colors in terms of the correspondence relationship of line-drawings and the reference frames, manually colored by the animator.

The other one aims at making the existing black-and-white animation clips colorful, and accordingly generates new colorful animation by transferring the desired colors into the entire animation sequence automatically.

7.3.1 Auto-coloring of Inbetweening Frames

The major task in auto-coloring of inbetweening frames is to find the correct correspondence relationship between regions to be colored in the current frames under consideration and the colored regions in the reference frames, and precisely propagate the colors in the reference frames into the regions in the remaining frames. The key technical point is how to build the correspondence relationship model between the regions to be colored and the regions manually colored by the animators. A typical solution for creating the correspondence relationship model is based on the visual similarities and motion principles of relevant regions, and the correspondence relationship among regions is usually determined by the means of quantitative computing of similarity between regions, qualitative reasoning of the neighboring relationship among regions, spatial reasoning of relative locations among regions, etc.

Madeira *et al.* estimated and evaluated the similarities among regions by shape-matching algorithms [Madeira *et al.*, 1996]. The user first chose an initial set of matched regions between the current and the reference frames. The matched regions in the reference and current frame under consideration are denoted as R and P respectively. R_i are the neighboring regions of R in the reference frame (i=1,. . .,n) and P_j are the neighboring regions of P in the current frame (j=1,. . .,m). For each candidate matched pair of (R_i, P_j), the Sobel operator is employed to compute the gradient of each pixel along the counters of the region, and then the shape of each region is then encoded as a sorted string in terms of the magnitude and sign of the calculated gradient. Given two encoded strings $A = A_1A_2 \ldots A_n$ and $B = B_1B_2 \ldots B_m$, a distance matrix of $(n + 1) \times (m + 1)$ is created and the cost of converting string A into B by inserting, deleting, replacing substrings is taken as the value of the difference in shapes in their corresponding regions. Let D_{ij} be the shape difference of (R_i, P_j), the impossibly matched regions are first removed by qualitative reasoning of the topological relationship among candidate regions, and the correspondence relationship model among the candidate regions is built by minimizing the overall cost of all the candidate matched regions as follows:

$$\min \sum_{i=1}^{m} \sum_{j=1}^{n} d_{ij} x_{ij},$$

where

$$\sum_{j=1}^{n} x_{ij} = 1, \quad i = 1, 2, \ldots, m,$$

$$\sum_{i=1}^{m} x_{ij} = 1, \quad i = 1, 2, \ldots, n,$$

where

$$x_{ij} \in \{0, 1\}.$$

Instead of minimizing the shape differences of all matched regions as in [Madeira *et al.*, 1996], Chang and Lee took the approach of creating a correspondence relationship model by maximizing the similarities between two matched regions. The similarity between two image regions, a target region and a reference region, is defined as the maximum number of similar features that are common between them, or is defined as the minimum changes that need to be performed on one object in order to produce the other region. They classified the region features into two categories: (a) Shape of regions, and attributes affecting their appearance such as area, bounding box, aspect ratio, density, and motion direction, etc.; (b) Spatial layout and connectivity of the components of each region. Moreover, a topological attribute graph is created to describe the planar spatial relationship of a drawing and is represented by the form

$$D_g = (V, E),$$

where $V = \{v_1, \ldots, v_n\}$ is a finite set of n region vertices with statistical region features and $E = \{e_1, \ldots, e_r\}$ is a set of r edges with adjacency relationship attributes, that is, relationships connected by border arc segments. This topological attribute graph is employed for the progressive matching of regions and the similarity between two graphs is evaluated by surrounding color, same surrounding edge with same color pair, extra neighbor color, and degree difference of edges, etc. The overall algorithmic pipeline of their automatic cel painting is summarized as: (a) Color the first drawing manually; (b) Obtain the next drawing and record all of the region feature information related to the drawings; (c) Perform image preprocessing for the new drawing to obtain a better drawing feature quality; (d) Establish region features and graph structures using an integrated labeling algorithm; (e) Make the matching and similarity measurement to find the color of the target region from the previous corresponding region, and fill colors into this target region; (f) Repeat steps (b)~(e), until all drawings in the current scene have been painted.

Seah and Tian presented how to automatically color line-drawings of cartoon animation by motion estimation [Seah & Tian, 2000]. The motion (displacement) vectors between two corresponding images are calculated by taking them as samples of a scene at a discrete time, and features such as intensities, edginess, cornerness (positive and negative), and regions (displacement orientation and magnitude smoothness) are selected as tokens that are to be matched. The employment of these multiple image features yields an over-determined system of matching constraints. This becomes an optimization problem, which can be solved with the least-square error technique. The following general principles are utilized to hierarchically match the line drawings:

(1) Preprocess the scanned line drawings to remove noises or broken lines.
(2) Establish the displacement vector field between the source and the target.
(3) Segment both images into regions and label them.
(4) Match all large regions in the source to those regions in the target one by one according to greatest similarity.
(5) Make small regions in the target correspond with respect to their neighboring relationships and information about the larger regions colored in the previous step.

The overall algorithm for the hierarchical feature based matching technique is as follows.

(1) Extract the attribute images (intensity, edginess, and cornerness) from the two input drawings at the original resolution (lowest level).
(2) Recursively smooth these images for higher levels to generate lower resolution images.
(3) Start with the highest level.
(4) Initialize displacement vectors (DVs) at all pixel locations to zero.
(5) Iterate for a preset number of times, at all pixel locations.
    a. Compute the average displacement vector and hence the orientation and displacement residuals.
    b. Compute and update the DVs.
(6) Project the DVs downwards to the next lower level.
(7) Set the level to the next lower level.
(8) Repeat step (5) until the lowest level is reached.

Their experimental results show that this technique is robust enough to color most regions of the frames when differences between the reference and target frames are small enough, even though there are some inaccuracies in the computation of displacement vectors due to the least-squares matching approach (see Fig. 7.5). Very minor intervention or correction by the user is required to complete the rest (for different cartoon sequences, this requirement varies in terms of the complexity of the characters and the changes among frames).

In order to further improve matching accuracy and make it more robust, Qiu *et al.* (2005a) presented a Hierarchical Region Matching (HRM) approach for computer-assisted auto coloring, expanding the matching process from the scope of single level regions to that of multi-level components.

Fig. 7.5 Coloring examples by matching line-drawing [Seah & Tian, 2000]. (a) Reference frame painted by the animator in advance; (b) Successful coloring of the target frame; (c) Failure to be colored by the reference frame. Copyright of Springer Science and Business Media, used with permission

The hierarchization representation of the frame is carried out by the grouping method that expands the region level into several component levels. The regions which are grouped to form a component are called the component's element regions. After grouping, the shared border of each component's element regions will be removed so that the component can be combined into a new region. For some components at the higher level, the corresponding combined regions may have some inner element regions which do not have shared borders with them. This grouping and decomposition process will iterate at the lower level until no components can be found (see Fig. 7.6). After all stable relations for each level are reorganized, the stable topology for each level is recomposed from them (see Fig. 7.7). The stable topology for each level can also be manually defined by users.

After the hierarchization and the stable topology for each level is recomposed, components and regions are matched from the first to the last component level. At each level, the order for selecting the target region goes from combined regions of components to ungrouped regions. With the expanded hierarchy, candidate regions selection is confined within a range based on the matching result of the target region's parent. For each target region, the matching criteria are given below:

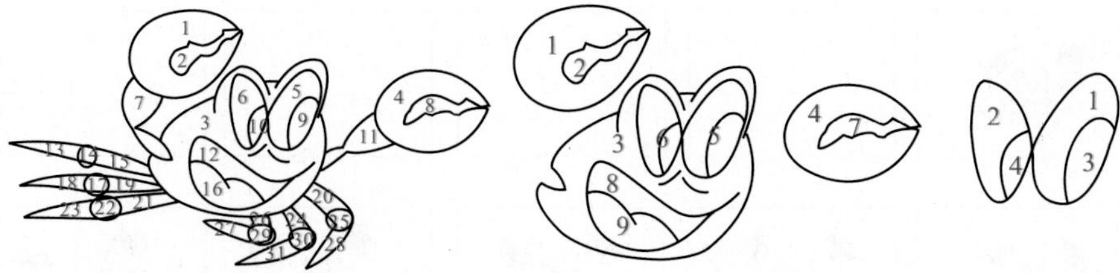

Fig. 7.6 Hierarchization result of a crab character [Qiu *et al.*, 2005a]. Courtesy of Zhongke Wu

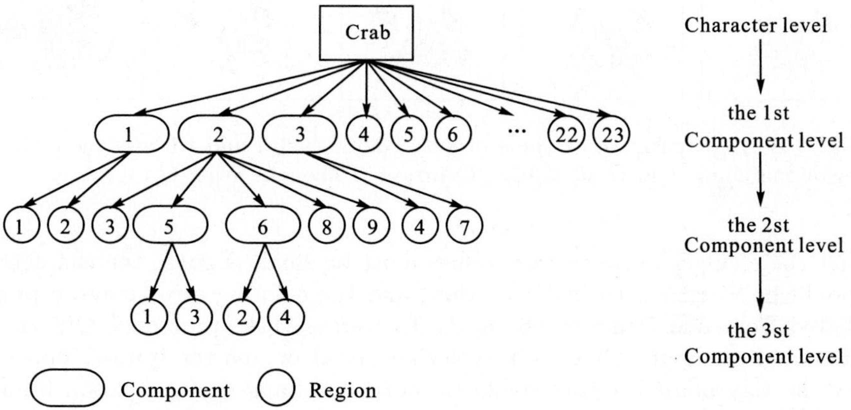

Fig. 7.7 Expanded hierarchy topology representation for the crab in Figure 7.3.2 [Qiu *et al.*, 2005a]. Courtesy of Zhongke Wu

(1) If its parent is matched to a component, candidate regions are selected from the component's children;
(2) If its parent is matched to a region, the region is its only candidate region;
(3) If its parent is not matched to any component or region, candidate regions are selected from all the components and regions at the same level and those regions which have not been matched at the higher level.

The matching process at each level is divided into two stages. (a) The matching is from the reference frame to the target frame, those components and ungrouped regions that constitute the stable topology are traced and bi-directionally matched. (b) Those unmatched components or regions in the target frame are matched with those in the reference frame. Examples have illustrated that HRM can improve matching accuracy, and could partly deal with matching errors caused by occlusion, making the matching more robust. A comparative example of auto coloring is given in Fig. 7.8.

The aforementioned algorithms can color successive frames according to the color information of their preceding frames. However, their limitation is

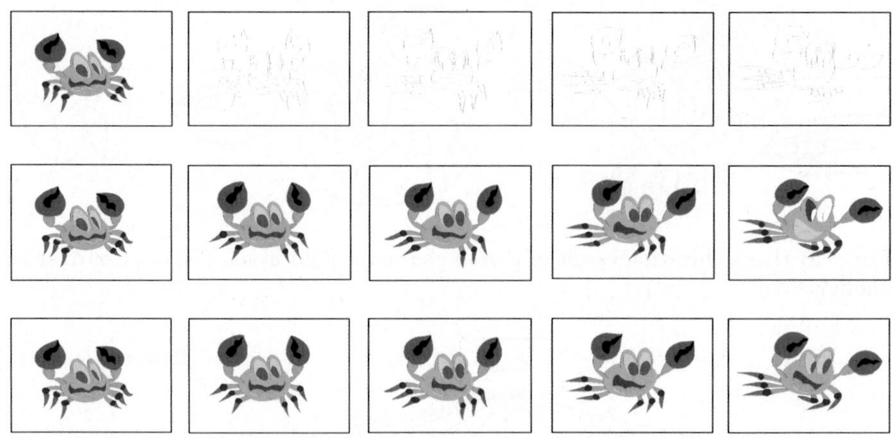

Fig. 7.8 A comparative example of auto coloring with and without hierarchical region matching [Qiu *et al.*, 2005a]. Courtesy of Zhongke Wu

that the changes between two frames must be small enough, the characters should be viewed with little rotations and the coloring error may be propagated from one frame to the next. To resolve these problems, Qiu *et al.* presented an approach to auto coloring based on master frames, mimicking the way humans apply colors to individual hand-drawn cartoon frames [Qiu *et al.*, 2003; Qiu *et al.*, 2005b]. Master frames are frames that define the appearance of the individual character to be animated, often containing the front, back and side views, or some specific postures of a character, as shown in Fig. 7.9. In traditional animation production, master frames are colored first. Animators can then color the character in any of the postures that appear in the animation, based on the color information of the master frames.

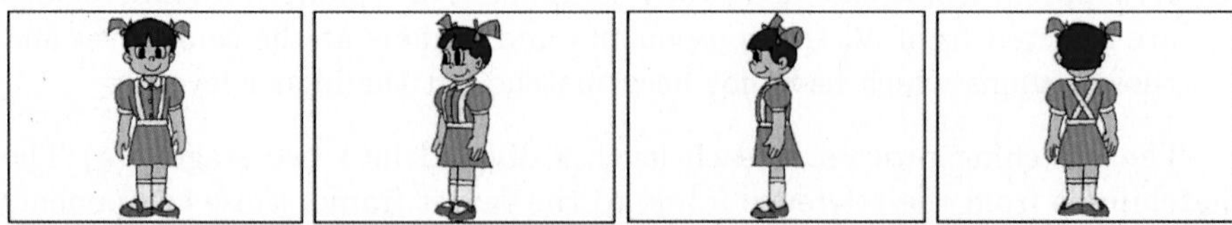

Fig. 7.9 Examples of master frames [Qiu *et al.*, 2005b]. Courtesy of Zhongke Wu

Assuming that objects that do not appear in master frames will not be drawn in the same layer as the character, the simulation of a human animator's auto-coloring by master frames is carried out in three algorithmic steps. It first matches a set of master frames to construct correspondences between regions in the master frames and extract a stable topology. The first frame of each scene is then colored, based on the set of master frames. With the painted first frame and an established stable topology, each region in subsequent frames is matched with regions in the previous frames and colored. Therefore, two types of matching are considered, one is the matching between painted master frames (master frames are both source frames and target frames), and the other is the matching from master frames (source frames) to an uncolored frame (target frame). To do matching from one or several source frames to one target frame, a region in the target frame is compared with all regions on the same scale in source frames, looking for the best-matched one. Compared with other algorithms, this approach is able to handle bigger changes between frames and automatically color the first frame of each sequence (see Fig. 7.10).

Fig. 7.10 Examples of auto coloring by the master frames in Fig. 7.12 [Qiu *et al.*, 2005b]. Courtesy of Zhongke Wu

7.3.2 Colorizing Black-and-white Cartoons

In the early history of cartoon-production, there was a lot of really valuable and artistically advanced work which stands up in front of world-wide, modern cartoon production. This provides an invaluable source of imagination for each new generation of children. However, these old cartoons were often shot in black-and-white film. It is desirable that color enhancement be applied to the black-and-white world, such that these old cartoons can be well perceived afresh, especially by an adolescent audience. Without the assistance of the computer, an artist who wants to color a black-and-white cartoon usually has to focus on featureless, repetitive work which prevents him from doing really creative artwork [Sýkora *et al.*, 2004].

For the point of view of technology, the colorization of black-and-white cartoon animation can be converted into a problem that transfers the color into a sequence of grey-scale images (see Fig. 7.11). Transferring color to a grey-scale image is a heavy under-constrained problem. The basic techniques for transferring color to grey-sale images can be found in a digital image processing textbook. A generic inking method is based on the user-defined look-up table, which converts each level of grey-scale intensity into the specified hue, saturation and brightness. Selected luminance values are converted, using a user-defined look-up table to the desired hue, saturation and brightness. Smooth selections of input luminance values are known as luminance keys. They could be used simultaneously on several regions with different luminance median and an almost disjointed deviation interval. The problem arises when one wants to apply different colors at the same intensity level. It is usually possible to overcome this limitation using simultaneously a few luminance keys for different manually segmented regions. This tedious process significantly increases the amount of hand-driven work.

Fig. 7.11 Color applied to the grey-scale image in the middle using left color image [Sýkora *et al.*, 2004]. Copyright of ACM, used with permission

Another color transfer approach is based on textural information [Welsh *et al.*, 2002]. Color transfer between an already inked source and a grey-scale target is based on local luminance distribution matching in LAB color space. Jitter sampling is used to select a subset of representative pixels in the color image. It is also possible to choose these samples manually as rectangular swatches in both images to reach better matching results. This technique is surprisingly successful in natural scenes (e.g., a tree in a meadow with sky on the horizon, a deep forest with brown tree trunks and green leaves, etc.). But cartoons have not enough textural information. Lots of frames only consist of almost plain regions and vary, above all, in global intensity and thus this simple process will fail.

Therefore Sýkora *et al.* started from scratch and developed an example-based inking framework that can effectively colorize the black-and-white cartoon [Sýkora *et al.*, 2004]. For this inking process, it is really important to determine which parts of the input image will be understood as background and foreground respectively. The dynamic foreground layer contains homogeneous regions surrounded by visible outlines and the background layer is usually a more complicated textural image which remains static during the animation. This important property enables one to divide the original greyscale image into the set of regions using robust outline detector and classify them roughly as foreground or background via region size thresholding (see Fig. 7.12). The overall algorithmic pipeline consists of contour detection, area segmentation, color indexation with prediction and final composition, with the restored or original background (see Fig. 7.13). On the segmented image the color transfer is applied only once using standard image manipulation software or some specialized colorization tool. In the dynamic foreground layer, color is applied frame-by-frame. It is based on the assumption that at least one animation frame is correctly colorized by a color expert. This means that each foreground region has associated with one index from the palette of available colors and it is possible to predict color-to-region assignment for the rest of the sequence using already colored frames as an example. Finally, color composition of each animation frame is made by pasting previously extracted and already colorized foregrounds into the correct position on the reconstructed and colorized background (see Fig. 7.14).

Bezerra *et al.* presented a colorization algorithm based on topological differences defined over a hierarchical graph of adjacent regions [Bezerra *et al.*, 2006]. It is based on propagating the structural information of the drawings from one frame to the next in an animation sequence. Each frame is described by a two-dimensional graph where nodes represent regions of the drawing and arcs their adjacency relationship (see Fig. 7.15). Nodes have several attributes that characterize the associated regions, such as centroid, area and shape. The topological difference between regions s and t is measured by the degree of topological difference DTD (s, t), which gives us the information about the proximity of the two regions based on a comparison of their adjacency functions. Multiple criteria are employed to establish the correspondence relationship between successive frames, and a match is only

Fig. 7.12 Segmentation of foreground layer [Sýkora *et al.*, 2004]. (a) The original image; (b) The edge detection; (c) The outline detection; (d) The outline extraction; (e) The final segmentation. Copyright of ACM, used with permission

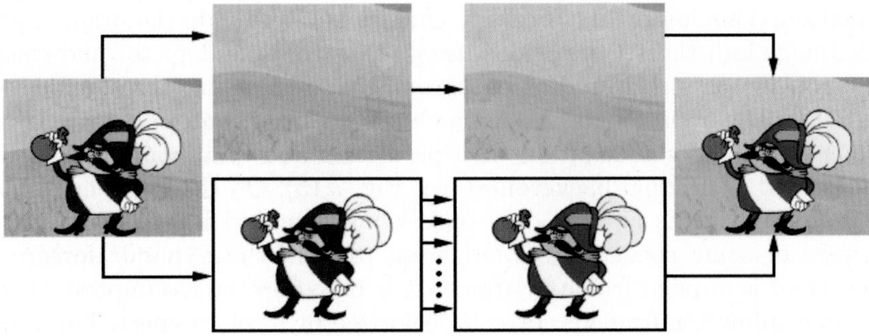

Fig. 7.13 The algorithmic diagram of coloring of black-and-white cartoon on the segmented image [Sýkora *et al.*, 2004]. Copyright of ACM, used with permission

Fig. 7.14 Coloring composition by patch pasting [Sýkora *et al.*, 2004]. Copyright of ACM, used with permission

accepted when all criteria agree. Although it was originally proposed for auto-coloring of in-between frames, it can also be applied to the colorization of black-and-white cartoons, as it propagates colors from the first frame of the sequence to all the other frames (see Fig. 7.16).

Qu *et al.* proposed a method that can colorize black-and-white "manga" (comic book in Japanese) which contains an intensive amount of strokes, hatching, half-toning and screening [Qu *et al.*, 2006]. The Japanese "manga" are distinctive from traditional western comic books in presenting fine details. The intensive use of strokes in "manga" causes discontinuities in intensity, imposing many difficulties for the aforementioned intensity-based colorization methods, which mainly rely on a "rough" continuity of grey levels to grow the affective regions and segment the image into color regions. However, the black-and-white patterns in "manga" preserve no grey-level continuity to facilitate the segmentation. Instead, "manga" exhibit a rough continuity of pattern. Therefore Qu *et al.* carried out the colorization of "manga" by propagating the colors over regions exhibiting pattern-continuity as well as intensity continuity in terms of the level-set principle.

The proposed technique starts by scribbling the desired color on the interested regions. The boundary is then propagated by the level set method that monitors the pattern /intensity continuity. The propagation stops accurately at the boundary where the pattern exhibits abrupt change, even if there is no apparent outline. There are two modes of color propagation for segmentation, pattern-continuous and intensity continuous propagations. The pattern-continuous and intensity-continuous propagations are designed for hatched/screened regions and intensity-continuous regions with/without unclosed outlines, respectively. The colorization over both pattern-continuous and intensity-continuous regions can be naturally formulated using the same mathematical framework. Besides the mathematical elegance, the level set provides several advantages. Its topological flexibility allows us to conveniently segment multiple disjointed regions with a single user scribble. Moreover, its capability in controlling local deformation allows us to conveniently

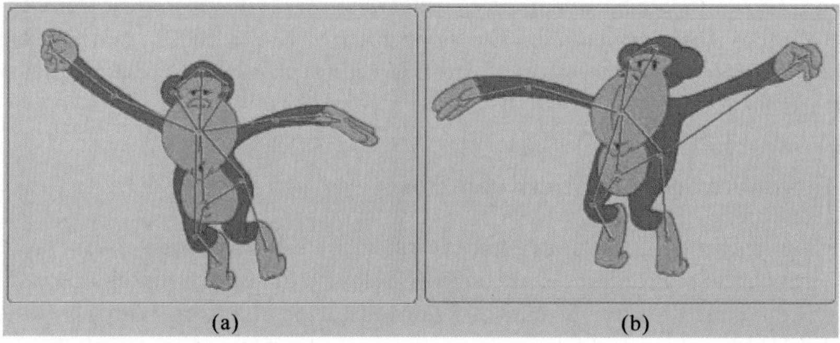

Fig. 7.15 Adjacency graph. Regions (circles) and their adjacencies (lines) represented on both source (a) and target images (b) [Bezerra *et al.*, 2006]. Copyright of ACM, used with permission

Fig. 7.16 Example of colorization for cartoon drawing [Bezerra *et al.*, 2006]. Copyright of ACM, used with permission

leak-proof during colorization. Once the regions are segmented, they can be colorized using stroke preserving colorization, pattern-to-shading and multi-color transition based on the user decision.

7.4 Computer-assisted Inbetweening

Inbetweening in traditional 2D animation is a process where animators draw a sequence of key frames first, and assistant animators then draw inbetween frames correspondingly. Drawing the inbetween frames is time-consuming and tedious. Given an animation, usually a huge number of inbetweens have to be drawn manually. Automation of these steps not only reduces a significant amount of time and labor, but also allows the artist to concentrate on more creative work such as drawing the key frames. But inbetweens are not just interpolations between key drawings. When drawing the inbetweens, the inbetweener utilizes: (a) His/her background knowledge of the physical rules of the world; (b) His/her expert knowledge as to when to bend or ignore these rules; (c) His/her idea of what emotions should be evoked by the animation.

For these reasons, automatic inbetweening will probably remain an unattainable goal, at least in the near future [Kort, 2002]. In this section we will discuss the generation of inbetweening poses and facial expressions respectively.

7.4.1 Generation of Inbetween Poses

The line-drawing of cartoon characters with different poses is in fact the contours of the characters, and the pose-to-pose in betweening is accordingly transformed into a kind of contour animation production [Kunii & Maeda, 1996]. Melikhov *et al.* [2004] summarized that the generation of inbetweening poses in traditional animation should meet the following requirements:

(1) Motion shall be smooth.
(2) Edges and curves shall remain as smooth as they are on given key frames.
(3) Lines and strokes shall not be thin and sometimes shall have a complicated texture. Therefore, inbetweening shall be performed by morphing the textures from one into another, in order to stylize the inbetweens.
(4) Curvature of strokes shall change from the first key frame into another, so dynamics of curvature and line length shall be considered.

The key frames are usually drawn on 2D canvas, and therefore the early work of computer-assisted in betweening was usually carried out in the 2D image plane, and the pixels are directly manipulated to create the inbetween frames. For instance, Bourdev designed and implemented an automatic inbetweening approach for the strokes with repetitive patterns by means of the image processing of silhouetted figure drawing and one-dimensional texture mapping [Bourdev, 1998]. A more sophisticated inbetweening approach is based on multi-layer representation of key frames by taking much of the animator's expertise into consideration [Melikhov *et al.*, 2004]. The preparatory work for layer-based matching and inbetweening consists of the vectorization of the key frames and construction of a polygonal core model linked with correspondent splines and textures. The vectorization of strokes in key frames is performed by finding their centers which form their skeletons. These centers are called skeletal points and computed by segmenting strokes with rectangles. A rectangle's centre is that of the stroke segment enclosed by the rectangle, and its direction follows the tangent of a stroke segment's edge. The size of the rectangle is determined by a threshold which represents the average difference of all points in the segment from one side of the rectangle. The vertices of the polygon core are feature points of the vectorized lines, including intersections of initial strokes and ends of strokes. If a curve's curvature changes significantly (according to the second derivatives of points of the curve), additional feature points are chosen on the curve in order to split it into several simpler parts.

Each key frame therefore is represented as a non-weighted graph which is used for matching. Graph representation builds a correspondence based on the structure (topology) of objects. After correspondence between each stroke of both key frames is built, the interpolation process is applied to each pair of strokes. This is divided into several levels with the following features:

(1) Stroke positions, defined by coordinates of their ends, are the feature points of images. The interpolation of the positions is an interpolation of two pairs of points in 2D space.
(2) Stroke curvature is defined by the stroke spline curve.
(3) Stroke texture is represented by needles of a hedgehog model computed for each skeleton stroke.

Interpolation of positions forms a motion of objects while that of curvatures and textures contributes to stroke styles.

Another layer-based auto-inbetweening approach was proposed by Kort (2002). The content of each key drawing is analyzed and classified into strokes, chains of strokes and relations of adjunction/occlusion with the following assumptions:

(1) Each drawing is made of stroke chains, structures consisting of one or more connected strokes.
(2) A stroke chain in one key drawing may have a corresponding stroke chain in another key drawing.
(3) The transition between stroke chains is modeled by animation paths. These animation paths indicate both the correspondence between stroke chains in key drawings and the spatial interpolations between them.

Stroke chains of connected visible and invisible strokes are the building blocks both for the matching algorithm and the generation of inbetweens. The best overall matching is found by building up an assignment tree between the stroke chains $\{a_1, \ldots, a_m\}$ and $\{b_1, \ldots, b_n\}$ of the stroke chain graphs G_1 and G_2. In this tree, every node corresponds to

- a matching between two stroke chains $a_i \rightarrow b_j$;
- an unassigned matching $a_i \rightarrow 0$;
- a surplus matching $0 \rightarrow b_j$.

The nodes are attributed with the cost of the matching. In each path from a leaf to the root node, each stroke can appear only once. No forbidden mappings are allowed in any path from leaf to root node. Non-assignment of stroke chains is punished with high costs, but it is explored whenever possible. Even when a match would be possible, the variant with the involved stroke being unassigned is tested as well. Finally, one or more complete paths in this tree remain, that involve all stroke chains in the two key drawings. The path with the least cost is chosen as the match. Animation path A_i:[0, 1]$\rightarrow R^2$ is defined as the correspondence model of stroke chains. A mapping function m: [0, 1]$\rightarrow$[0, 1] specifies the correspondence of points on these chains. A_i and m define the location of the morphed points on the inbetweens. Let $t \in [0 \ldots 1]$ be the time and $s \in [0, 1]$ be the scalar value of the point on the first stroke to be morphed. The path from $S_1(s)$ on the stroke chain S_1 ends at point $S_2(m(s))$ on stroke chain S_2. The corresponding interpolated point is given by

$$\begin{aligned} I(s,t) =&(1-t)S_1(s) + tS_2(m(s)) + (1-s)A_i(t) + sA_{i+1}(t) \\ &- (1-s)(1-t)A_i(0) - (1-s)tA_i(1) \\ &- (1-t)sA_{i+1}(0) - stA_{i+1}(1). \end{aligned}$$

It is applied to two stroke chains S_1 and S_2 with neighboring animation paths A_i and A_{i+1}. Generated animation paths between corresponding strokes determine the resultant inbetweens (see Fig. 7.17).

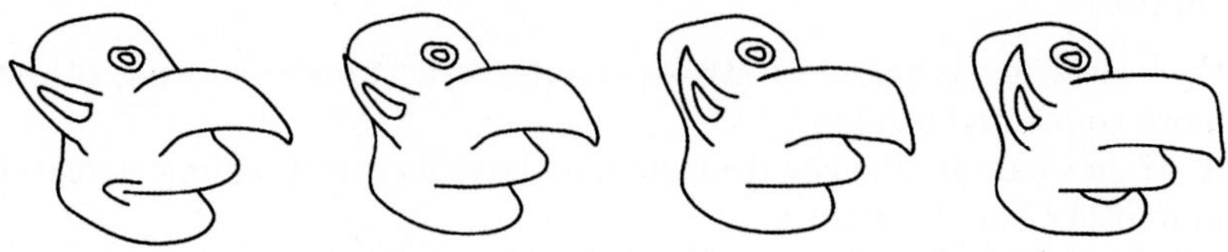

Fig. 7.17 A successful inbetweening with the key drawings [Kort, 2002]. Copyright of ACM, used with permission

The further improvement of the visual effect of auto-inbetweening is based on a more sophisticated stroke model in [Seah *et al.*, 2005]. They proposed the Disk B-Spline Curve (DBSC) that represents not only the 2D region of the stroke but also its centerline, so that various attributes like the scalar and vector field can be applied to the stroke (see Fig. 7.18). Given two or more animation drawings represented by DBSC, the intermediate frames can be automatically generated to form a smoother sequence, either linearly or non-linearly.

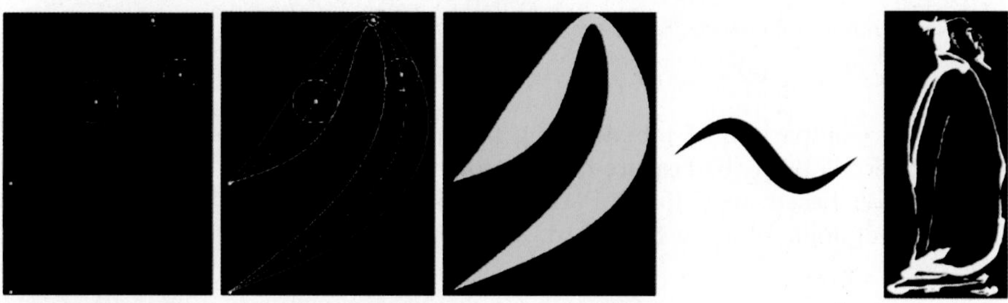

Fig. 7.18 Stroke example of DBSC[Seah *et al.*, 2005]. Copyright of ACM, used with permission

However, the linear interpolation of two DBSCs without incorporating characteristics of shape or motion will result in distortion and unrealistic motion in the inbetweening frames. In order to facilitate this problem, Chen *et al.* extracted and utilized more information in key frames in the generation of inbetweening frames [Chen *et al.*, 2006]. Points with high curvature are computed and corresponded between strokes in interpolation, which preserves features of strokes in animation (see Fig. 7.19).

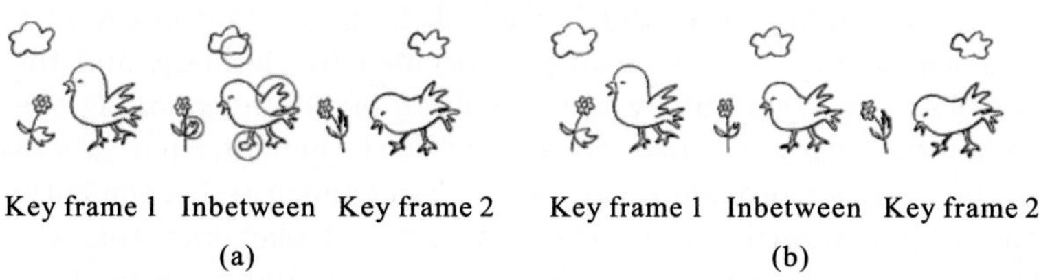

Fig. 7.19 Comparison of stroke interpolation techniques: a cartoon scene [Chen *et al.*, 2006]. (a) Previous method (main distortion in circles); (b) Feature-enhanced stroke interpolation. Copyright of John Wiley & Sons, Ltd., used with permission

In addition, the global motion of a character or its various components is estimated and interpolated as well, which retains the shapes during the

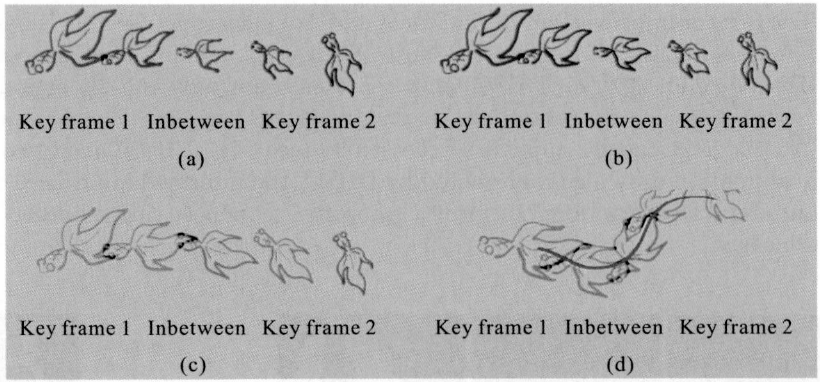

Fig. 7.20 Comparison of inbetweening techniques: Fish [Chen *et al.*, 2006]. (a) Linear interpolation; (b) Feature-based stroke interpolation; (c) Motion-enhanced interpolation based on (b); (d) Path-driven inbetween generation based on (c). Copyright of John Wiley & Sons, Ltd., used with permission

motion (see Fig. 7.20). Both the feature and motion enhanced methods incorporate properties of the drawing, which eliminate distortion and achieve a smoother sequence of animation (see Fig. 7.21).

The aforementioned auto-inbetweeing approach is mainly based on the pose-to-pose technique to generate the actions in hand-drawn animation. Another typical action generation technique in traditional animation is based on the straight-ahead mode, in which the animator literally works straight ahead from his first drawing in the scene (see Section 7.2). Assuming that the motion of the animation character is driven by a group of skeletons, and the line drawings of contours of characters will be changed according to the movement of skeletons, the animator's straight-ahead action mode could be simulated by the skeleton-based auto-inbetweening method.

For example, Hsu & Lee implemented an auto-inbetweening approach by skeleton strokes [Hsu & Lee, 1994]. Each skeleton stroke consists of a stroke path and width. Its "ink" is an image specified by the user, and the drawing of strokes is carried out by the morphing of the image along the stroke path. When the skeleton strokes are applied to the generation of inbetweening frames, they further provide an anchoring mechanism to conveniently transform the arbitrary image into a single skeleton stroke, such that the width and skew angle of the skeleton stroke can be fixed, and accordingly generate a pseudo 3D effect while drawing the character (see Fig. 7.22).

Key frames skeletons with feature points optimized skeletons

(a)

Key frame 1 Inbetweens Key frame 2

(b)

Key frame 1 Inbetweens Key frame 2

(c)

Fig. 7.21 Comparison of motion interpolation techniques [Chen *et al.* 2006] (a) Global motion estimation; (b) Previous method (main distortion in red circles); (c) Motion-enhanced in between generation; (d) Align all nodes. Copyright of John Wiley & Sons, Ltd., used with permission

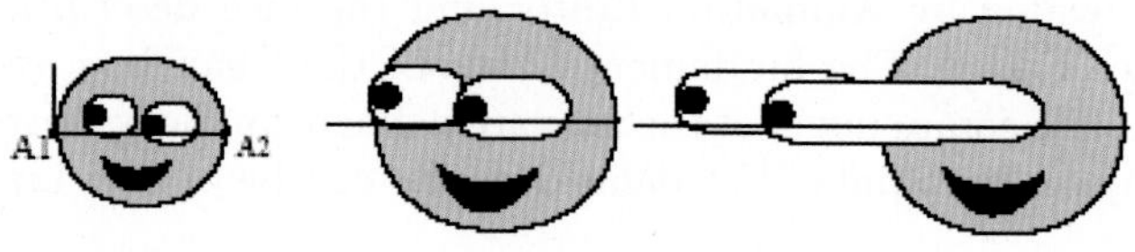

Fig. 7.22 The auto-inbetweening approach based on an anchoring mechanism [Hsu & Lee, 1994]. Copyright of ACM, used with permission

7.4.2 Generation of inbetweening Facial Expression

Computer facial animation has been a flourishing research topic over the past decades, aiming at models that can be animated and used to easily convey distinctive communicational (e.g., paying attention), cognitive (e.g., agreeing) and emotional (e.g., surprise) expressions. A synthetic human face can attract the user's attention, improve the effectiveness of using the computer and even have an influence on the cognition of users. However, making facial computer animation look convincing has proven to be a difficult task, as facial animations are usually complex, and drawing all emotions for all characters is without doubt a labour-intensive process. There is a clear need for a simple yet versatile method to speed up the generation of inbetweening facial animations, while not limiting the animation artists in their creativity.

Thorisson presented a ToonFace system that can create facial expressions in real time in response to a human interacting with it [Thórisson, 1996]. The scheme divides the face into seven parts: two eyebrows, eyes and pupils, and one mouth. Each part is associated with a specific number of control points. The eyebrows have three control points each, the eyes and mouth have four and pupils one each. As the control points are moved, either in one or two dimensions, the shape and position of animated polygons is modified to conform to the change, and thus change the facial expression. The resultant inbetweening facial expression frames are generated in terms of anatomical constraints and artistic conventions .

Inspired by the ToonFace system, Ruttkay and Noot extended the parametric keyframing technique and further implemented a CharToon system that supports the interactive design and animation of 2D cartoon faces [Ruttkay & Noot, 2000]. CharToon consists of 3 components: Face Editor, Animation Editor and Face Player. Face Editor is a 2.5D drawing program with which one can define the structure, the geometry, the colors and the potential motions of the face. Animation Editor is an interactive "animation composing" program, to define the time-behavior of a drawing's animation parameters, provided by Face Editor. Face Player actually generates the frames of an animation, on the basis of the animation parameter values in the movie script file provided by Animation Editor and the face description file provided by Face Editor. The fundamental part of the CharToon system is the Face Editor. The components of the face are defined similarly to vector-based graphical objects by points. The defined points can be of four kinds:

(1) Master control points which are used to animate the object, as the position of the control points is given by animation parameters;
(2) Slave control points which are assigned to a master control point and move as their master control point does;
(3) Frozen points which never move;
(4) Fixed points which may move, if driven by some control point, otherwise they remain in place.

While creating a component of a drawing, one also specifies its potential dynamical behavior to be used when animating it. The possibilities are:

(1) Change location;
(2) Change scale in the horizontal and/or vertical direction;
(3) Change visibility;
(4) Most of the components can change shape according to the changing position of the control points they contain.

CharToon also separates the appearance, the dynamism (possible deformations) and the behaviour of a face. The first two aspects are incorporated in the definition of the face, while the latter in the animation. Technically, CharToon supports the reuse of facial components and pieces of animations as building blocks. Based on careful analysis of specific facial features of the basic expressions—happiness, surprise, fear, sadness, anger and disgust— for each feature (eye, mouth, eyebrow...) different alternative designs are produced, forming together the feature repertoire. For each feature, the deformation for the basic expressions is given (in terms of animation parameters), forming the expression repertoire. The alternatives for a feature differ concerning the deformation control mechanism and/or structure. Variants of a face are built up from identical feature repertoire elements. The variants are gained by changing the rendering, the shape and color of the building blocks and the dynamism (ranges of control parameters).

From the point view of facial motion simulation, the aforementioned facial generation method mainly deals with the transformations in a plane parallel to the drawing canvas (the x-y plane), such as rotations around the z-axis and translations with a plane parallel to the x-y plane. However, there exists another kind of transformation that is outside the drawing plane, especially for all rotations around an axis different from the z-axis. The auto-inbetweening of this transformation needs the 3D structure underlying the objects and characters, and in traditional animation this 3D information is mainly presented in the animator's and viewer's mind, not in the 3D drawings. In order to explore the auto-inbetweening of 3D facial expression, Di Fiore and Van Reeth introduced the concept of facial emotion channels that represents a facial part expressing an emotion, and presented a novel approach through which an emotionally meaningful 2D facial expression, from one point of view, can be created from a reference expression, from another point of view [Di Fiore & Van Reeth, 2003]. The face modeling is implemented as a multi-layered 2.5D modeling system situated in their prior work [Di Fiore *et al.*, 2001]. The basic 2D drawing primitives (curves) are at level 0, and explicit 2.5D structure at level 1. The inclusion of 3D information by means of skeletons is at level 2 and high-level deformation tools (and possibly other tools for supporting specific purposes such as facial expression) at level 3. Multi-level 2D strokes, interpolation techniques and on-the-fly resorting are used to create convincing 3D-like animations starting from pure 2D information (see Fig. 7.23).

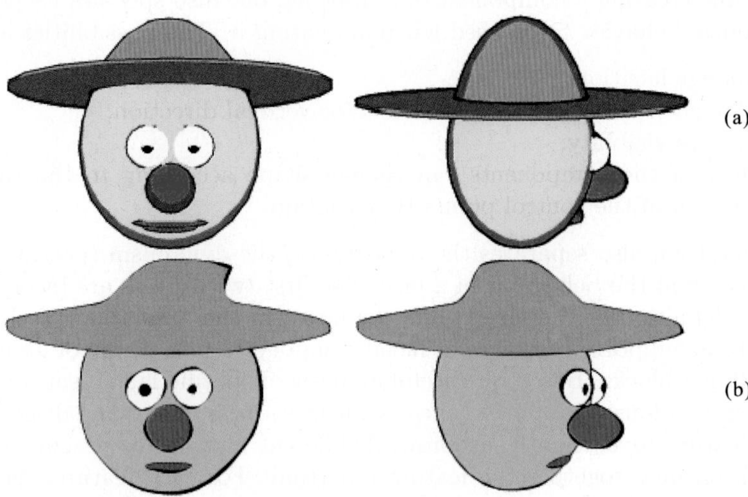

Fig. 7.23 Example of face modeling [Di Fiore *et al.*, 2001]. (a) shows a man's head face-on and a side-view obtained by NPR techniques; (b) shows the same views as an animator is likely to draw it. Copyright of IEEE, used with permission

Facial emotion channels can be seen as the building blocks of any facial expression. Instead of modelling a complete face at once, each individual facial part is modeled separately and independently. That is, for each individual part, the user models one neutral version (which depicts no emotion at all) and a set of emotional versions (one version for each emotion that has to be supported). Concerning the animation phase, the animator only has to specify key frames in time by entering parameters using the same methods as described in [Di Fiore *et al.*, 2001]. Afterwards, the automatic inbetweening method comes into play and generates the desired animation. This gives the animator the opportunity to create countless different facial expressions without having to model each expression manually, contrary to earlier systems.

7.5 Summary

In this chapter we mainly discuss computer-assisted techniques for auto- coloring and inbetweening based on the traditional animation pipeline. However, in traditional animation, modeling, motion and rendering are closely coupled to a single drawing process and the 3D information of objects and characters merely exists in the animator's mind, not in the 2D drawing. Therefore, it is difficult for the computer to acquire sufficient information to automate its inbetweening process, and the challenging technical problems in assisting traditional animation proposed by Catmull [1978] have not yet been solved.

For the time being, the researchers and artists in the animation industry are exploring novel techniques and the production pipeline for traditional animation, and we will discuss them in detail in the next chapter.

References

Bezerra H, Feijo B, Velho L(2006) A computer-assisted colorization algorithm based on topological difference. In: Brazilian Symposium on Computer Graphics and Image Processing 71–77

Bourdev L(1998) Rendering non-photorealistic strokes with temporal and arc-length coherence. Master's Thesis, Brown University

Catmull E(1978)The problems of computer-assisted animation. In: Proceedings of the 5th Annual Conference on Computer Graphics and Interactive Techniques 348–353

Chen Q, Tian F, Seah H, Wu Z, Qiu J, Konstantin M(2006) DBSC-based animation enhanced with feature and motion. Computer Animation and Virtual Worlds 17(3–4):189–198

Di Fiore F, Van Reeth F(2003) Mimicing 3D transformations of emotional stylised animation with minimal 2D input. In: Proceedings of the 1st International Conference on Computer Graphics and Interactive Techniques in Australia and South East Asia 21–28

Di Fiore F, Schaeken P, Elens K, Van Reeth F(2001) Automatic inbetweening in computer-assisted animation by exploiting 2.5D modelling techniques. Computer Animation 2001 192–200

Durand CX (1991) The "TOON" project: requirement for a computerized 2D animation systemComputers and Graphics 1991 15(2): 285–293

Fekete JD, Bizouarn É, Cournarie É, Galas T, Taillefer F(1995). TicTacToon: a paperless system for professional 2D animation. In: Proceedings of the 22nd Annual Conference on Computer Graphics and Interactive Techniques 79–90

Hsu SC, Lee IHH(1994) Drawing and animation using skeletal strokes. In: Proceedings of the 21st Annual Conference on Computer Graphics and Interactive Techniques 109–118

Kort A(2002) Computer aided inbetweening. In: Proceedings of the 2nd International Symposium on Non-photorealistic Animation and Rendering 125–132

Kunii TL, Maeda T(1996) On the silhouette cartoon animation. Computer Animation 1996 110–117

Kurlander D, Skelly T, Salesin D (1996) Comic chat. In: Proceedings of the 23rd Annual Conference on Computer Graphics and Interactive Techniques 225–236

Lasseter J(1987) Principles of traditional animation applied to 3D computer animation. ACM SIGGRAPH Computer Graphics 1987 21(4):35–44

Litwinowicz PC(1991) Inkwell:A 2D animation system. ACM SIGGRAPH Computer Graphics 1991 25(4):113–122

Madeira JS, Stork A, Groβ MH(1996) An approach to computer-supported cartooning. The Visual Computer 12(1):1–17

Melikhov K, Tian F, Seah HS, Chen Q, Qiu J(2004) Frame skeleton based auto-inbetweening in computer-assisted cel animation. In: Proceedings of the 2004 International Conference on Cyberworlds 216–223

Patterson J, Willis P(1995) Computer assisted animation: 2D or not 2D? The Computer Journal 1994 37(10):829–839

Qiu J, Seah HS, Tian F, Chen Q, Melikhov K(2003) Computer-assisted auto coloring by region matching. In: Proceedings of the 11th Pacific Conference on Computer Graphics and Applications 175–185

Qiu J, Seah HS, Tian F, Wu Z, Chen Q(2005a) Feature and region based auto painting for 2D animation. The Visual Computer 2005 21(11):928–944

Qiu J, Seah HS, Tian F, Chen Q, Wu Z(2005a) Enhanced auto coloring with hierarchical region matching. Computer Animation and Virtual World 16(3-4), 463–473

Qu Y, Wong T, Heng P(2006) Manga colorization.ACM Transactions on Graphics 25(3), 1214–1220

Ruttkay Z, Noot H(2000) Animated CharToon faces. In: Proceedings of the 1st International Symposium on Non-photorealistic Animation and Rendering 91–100

Seah HS, Tian F(2000) Computer assisted coloring by matching line drawings. The Visual Computer 16:289–304

Seah HS, Wu Z, Tian F, Xiao X, Xie B(2005) Artistic brushstroke representation and animation with Disk B-Spline curve. In: ACM SIGCHI International Conference on Advances in Computer Entertainment Technology (ACE 2005) 88–93

Stern G(1979) SoftCel an application of raster scan graphics to conventional cel animation. SIGGRAPH Computer Graphics 13(2): 284–288

Sýkora D, Buriánek J, Žára J(2004) Unsupervised colorization of black-and-white cartoons. In: Proceedings of 3rd International Symposium on Non-photorealistic Animation and Rendering 121–127

Thórisson KR(1996) ToonFace:a system for creating and animating interactive cartoon faces. Learning and Common Sense Section Technical Report 96–01

Van Reeth F, Lamotte W, E Fleracker(1994), ExTwAnPaSy: an extensible two-dimensional Animation/Paint System Computer Animation 1994

Welsh T, Ashikhmin M, Mueller K(2002) Transferring color to greyscale images. ACM Transactions on Graphics 21(3):277–280

Zou JJ, Yan H(2001) Cartoon image vectorization based on shape subdivision. Computer Graphics International 2001 225–231

8

Novel Approaches to Computer-assisted Cartoon Animation

In the production of traditional cartoon animation the computer does not play the key role as it does in generating 3D animations, although it has achieved much work in auto-coloring and inbetweening. With the advent of non-photorealistic graphics technology, researchers in the computer graphics community further explored how to improve the production efficiency by investigating many novel approaches to assisting 2D cartoon animation with artistic rendering, modeling and motion generation. From the point of view of research methodology, these novel approaches to cartoon animation production can be summarized as follows:

(1) *Video driven cartoon animation.* The performances of objects and actors are first extracted by image processing and computer vision techniques, etc., and then accordingly retargeted to the objects and characters in the cartoon animation sequence.
(2) *Carton animation production guided by approximate 3D geometry.* The objects or characters to be animated are modeled with 2.5D or 3D information, and the 3D computer animation techniques are borrowed to speed-up the production of 2D animation.
(3) *Cartoon generation by artistic rendering with temporal coherence.* The temporal coherence mechanisms are embedded into the artistic rendering techniques, and then the resulting cartoon sequences can be semi-automatically/automatically generated by them.
(4) *Cartoon production by "borrowing" 3D animation techniques.* 3D computer graphics techniques and animation methods are employed to explore and investigate the novel artistic modeling and rendering techniques that can improve the production efficiency of 2D cartoon animation.
(5) *Cartoon production by content reusing.* It acquires the relevant visual and motion content from the existing cartoon animation, and applies them to the production of new cartoon animation.

8.1 Video Driven Cartoon Animation

It is natural for researchers to take video into consideration while exploring novel approaches to assisting cartoon animation, as the video clips not only provide visual information (colors, textures and contours etc.) of objects of interest, but also indicate how this visual information changes with time. In essence, the algorithmic idea of video-driven cartoon animation is based on "rotoscoping", which traces and draws the contours of objects in the images and then generates the animation sequence frame by frame. Three major criteria for evaluating a successful video tooning system are summarized as follows [Wang *et al.*, 2004]:

(1) The result sequence should maintain spatio-temporal consistency to avoid significant jumps in frame transitions.
(2) The content of the video should be abstracted in such a way as to respect the higher level semantic representation.
(3) The artist should be able to express control over the style of the result.

The techniques regarding video-driven cartoon animation can be summarized as being of the following three types:

(1) The frames in the video sequence are directly processed in terms of cartoon animation conventions. The image-based artistic rendering techniques are intuitively applied to the overall image of each frame, converting the images in video clips into the corresponding frames in the resulting cartoon sequence. It is useful in creating the background in cartoon frames.
(2) The needed visual and motion content is extracted from the video clips for cartoon animation production, e.g., the contours can be traced and extracted from the video sequence, and the resulting animation clips can be generated by coloring the regions in terms of these contours. It is often used in foreground character drawings in cartoon production.
(3) Performance-driven facial animation. The facial expressions in the video are acquired by motion tracing and recovering, and the desired facial animations are created by retargeting them on the faces of the characters.

8.1.1 Directly Converting Video Segment into Painterly Animation

Painting each image in a video sequence is labor intensive, and even more work is necessary to produce a sequence that is temporally coherent. In order to automatically produce painterly animations from video clips, an example-based approach is usually employed to convert the video segment into cartoon sequence, i.e., a few frames from the source video are manually converted into the target cartoon frames with desired hand-drawn visual effect, and then the remaining frames of the source video are accordingly transformed into the resulting cartoon effect in terms of the artistic rendering parameters or templates applied to the reference frames. Its algorithmic diagram is shown in Fig. 8.1.

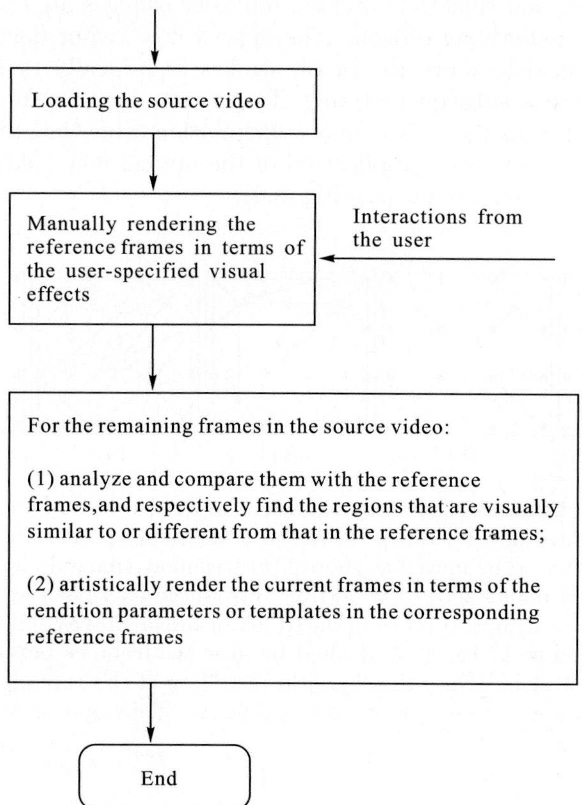

Fig. 8.1 The algorithmic diagram to convert video into cartoon sequence in terms of the reference frames

The simplest method for generating painterly video is to apply an image-based artistic rendering technique to each frame independently. As has been previously observed in the literature, subtle changes in the input can cause dramatic changes in the output, creating severe flickering in the output video. Therefore new approaches with a temporal-coherence mechanism should be explored for video-driven animation. Litwinowicz was the first to exploit temporal coherence in video clips to design an automatic filter with a hand-drawn animation quality [Litwinowicz, 1997]. It uses optical flow fields to push brush strokes from frame to frame in the direction of pixel movements. The pixel motions are tracked to produce a temporally coherent painterly style animation from an input video sequence. In order to move the brush strokes from one frame to the next, the optical flow between the two images is first calculated. Optical flow methods are a subclass of motion estimation techniques and are based on the assumption that illumination is constant, occlusion can be ignored, and that the observed intensity changes are only due to the motion of the underlying objects. The optical flow vector field is used as a displacement field to move the brush strokes (specifically their centers) to new locations in a subsequent frame. To generate new brush strokes in regions that are too sparse, a Delaunay triangulation using the previous frame's brush stroke centers (after application of the optical flow field) is employed to update the moved strokes (see Fig. 8.2).

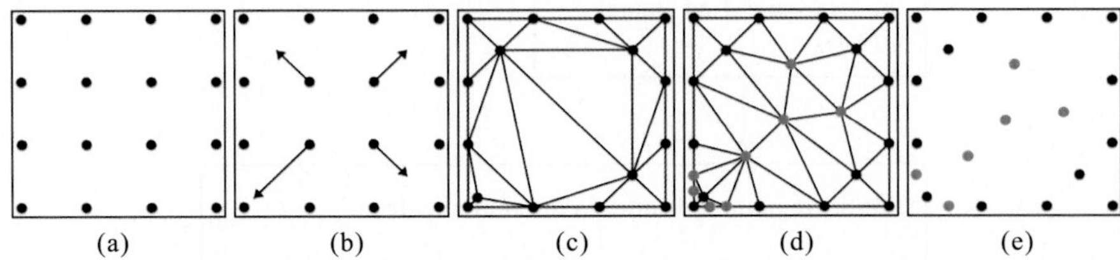

Fig. 8.2 Move brush strokes to new locations in a subsequent frame by Delaunay triangulation [Litwinowicz, 1997]. (a) Initial brush stroke positioning; (b) The four middle strokes are to be moved as shown; (c) Delaunay triangulation of the moved strokes; (d) Red points show new vertices introduced as a result of satisfying the maximal area constraint; (e) The updated list of brush strokes. The original lower left corner brush stoke has been deleted because the distance between it and another original stroke satisfies the closeness test. Two of the potentially added new brush strokes have also been removed from the list. Copyright of ACM, used with permission.

To render a brush stroke, an antialiased line is drawn through its center in the appropriate orientation. Brush strokes are oriented normal to the gradient direction of the original image; a scattered data interpolation technique is used to interpolate the gradient field in areas where the magnitude of the gradient is near zero. Randomness is used to perturb the brush stroke's length, color and orientation to enhance the hand-touched look. In order to preserve detail and silhouettes, strokes are clipped to edges that they encounter in the original image. Therefore, after a few initial decisions, such as what the brush stroke length, radius and texture should be, whether or not to use the gradient for brush stroke orientation, what filter kernels should be used, providing distances and areas for the closeness and sparseness tests, the source video can be automatically converted into the animation sequence with *Impressionist effect* (see Fig. 8.3).

Hertzmann and Perlin presented the approach of "painting-over" successive frames of animation based on their still image processing technique,

Fig. 8.3 Example of animation frame converted from video with *Impressionist effect* [Litwinowicz, 1997]. Copyright of ACM, used with permission.

which paints a rough sketch of the image with large brush strokes, and then refines it with smaller brush strokes [Hertzmann & Perlin, 2000]. The first frame of the video sequence is painted normally. For each successive frame, they "paint over" the previous frame only in regions where the source video is changing. This means that the painting of the first frame is used as the initial canvas for the second frame, which leads a natural mechanism of preserving temporal coherence in the resulting painterly video (see Fig. 8.4).

Fig. 8.4 Frames from a music video, illustrating various painting styles and resulting effects [Hertzmann & Perlin, 2000]. Copyright of ACM, used with permission

Mihai presented a system that can generate a stylized line-drawing based on the interesting features such as edges and large color areas [Mihai,1998]. Straight-line segments from the gradient of an image are extracted, and these are then combined into continuous strokes. Color areas are extracted using k-means clustering, working in HSV color space. The frame-to-frame coherence is established on the basis of optical flow.

Collomosse and Hall presented a novel framework for the automated synthesis of non-photorealistic animations from video sequences [Collomosse & Hall, 2005]. They interpreted the source video sequence as a spatio-temporal voxel volume, with time as the third dimension. Video frames are segmented into homogeneous regions, and heuristic associations between regions formed over time to produce a collection of conceptually high level spatio-temporal objects. These objects carve sub-volumes through the video volume delimited by continuous isosurface "*Stroke Surface*" patches. By manipulating objects in this representation it can synthesise a wide gamut of artistic effects, which allows the user to stylise and influence through a parameterized "*Video Paintbox*". The *Video Paintbox* consists of a single rendering framework which may be broken into a front and back end. The front end is responsible for the parsing of the source video to create an intermediate representation, and is largely automated through application of *Computer Vision* techniques. This abstracted video representation is then passed to the back end, where it is rendered in one of a range of artistic styles (see Fig. 8.5).

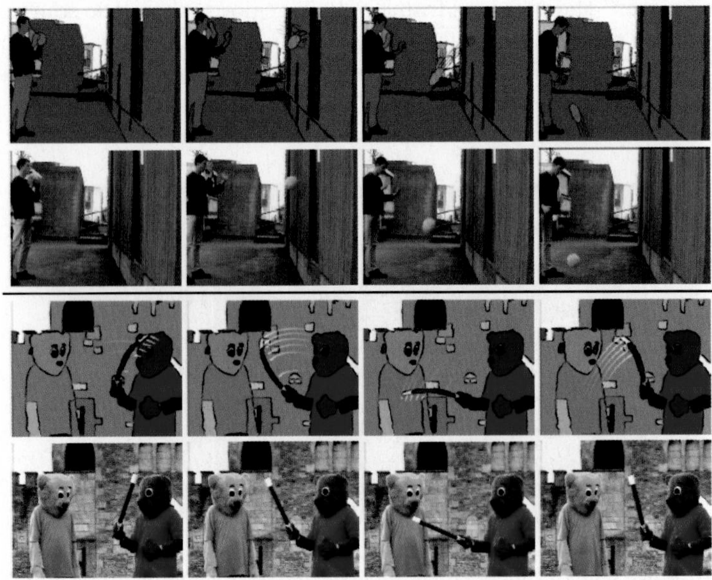

Fig. 8.5 Painterly animation generation based on "stroke surface" [Collomosse & Hall, 2005]. Copyright of IEEE, used with permission

Hays and Essa presented a new approach that builds on and refines several aforementioned techniques for generating painterly animations [Hays & Essa,

2004]. The central element in this approach is a brush stroke with dynamic properties. Each of these brush strokes has properties such as opacity, color, length, width, orientation and motion. The brush strokes are arranged in layers which are disjoint groups of brush strokes representing successive passes of refinement in a painting (see Fig. 8.6).

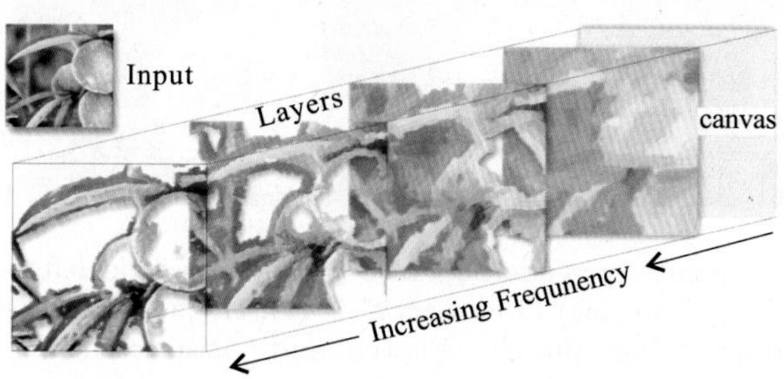

Fig. 8.6 Brush stroke layers and the canvas. The layers are independent meshes of brush strokes which successively refine the input frame [Hays & Essa, 2004]. Copyright of ACM, used with permission

Painterly animations are generated using a mesh of brush stroke objects with dynamic spatio-temporal properties. All brush stroke properties are temporally constrained to guarantee temporally coherent non-photorealistic animations. Their behaviors are governed by user-defined and selected styles as well information extracted from the input image, video, or motion information. A style is an encapsulation of parameters that control the analysis of input frames, the behavior of brush strokes, and the rendering of output. The images and videos can be transformed into painterly animations depicting different artistic styles (see Fig. 8.7). Its significant technical improvements in transforming video into painterly animations are as follows:

(1) Each brush stroke property is constrained over time to ensure that smooth, temporally constrained animations are produced. Brush stroke generation and deletion are performed smoothly through time by modifying brush stroke opacity.
(2) Radial basis functions (RBFs) are employed to globally orient brush strokes across time and space.
(3) Edge detection at varying frequencies is utilized to guide the creation of new brush strokes and the refinement of fine details.
(4) Rendering quality is improved by decoupling output resolution from input dimensions and by using real brush stroke textures along with a simple lighting model.
(5) The artistic versitility of motion is emphasized by synthesizing motion information for still images to produce animated stills as well as transplanting motion from video segments onto stills.

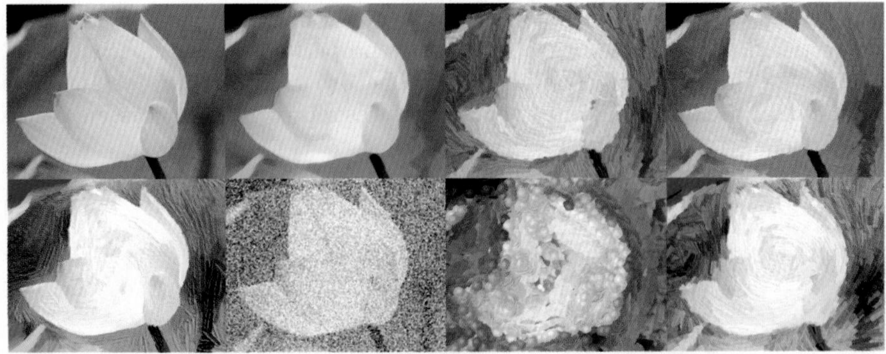

Fig. 8.7 Various painterly renderings of a pink flower (top left). Painterly renderings representing (top row) "watercolor", "Van Gogh", "Impressionism", (bottom row) "Abstract", "Pointillism", "Flower" and "Abstract" styles [Hays & Essa, 2004]. Copyright of ACM, used with permission

8.1.2 Contour-based Animation Generation from Video

The direct conversion of a video segment into painterly animation transformed the entire image into painterly effect, and this is useful in quickly creating the background in cartoon frames. However, in the foreground character drawing, users often identify and extract the foreground features in the image that they wish to include in the animation. Therefore, contour-based animation generation from video is proposed. From the point of view of technology, it is based on the common tracing techniques in rotoscoping, where cartoons are traced from film projected onto their desk, to handle especially complicated sequences. Children or untrained users often create better drawings than they could create alone by laying semi-transparent paper over an image and tracing it. However, cartoon rotoscoping is laborious, as it still requires the animator to hand-draw each frame of the animation.

In order to improve this situation, Agarwala combined this process of creating cartoons with video analysis, and implemented a SnakeToonz system which aims to give anyone with a video camera and a computer the ability to create compelling cel animation [Agarwala, 2002]. In SnakeToonz, the process of creating a cartoon is modeled as a dialogue between child and computer (see Fig. 8.8). The user first creates a cartoon of the first frame of the video by drawing curves directly on the image. The system responds by modifying the drawn curves to best fit the edges in the image as well as other aesthetic constraints. The system also snaps together small gaps between drawn curves. The user can advance to the next frames as the system attempts to automatically propagate the cartoon using video motion estimation. They can then edit the system's suggestion, if necessary, and is free to add or delete curves as occlusions occur or new perspectives of objects appear.

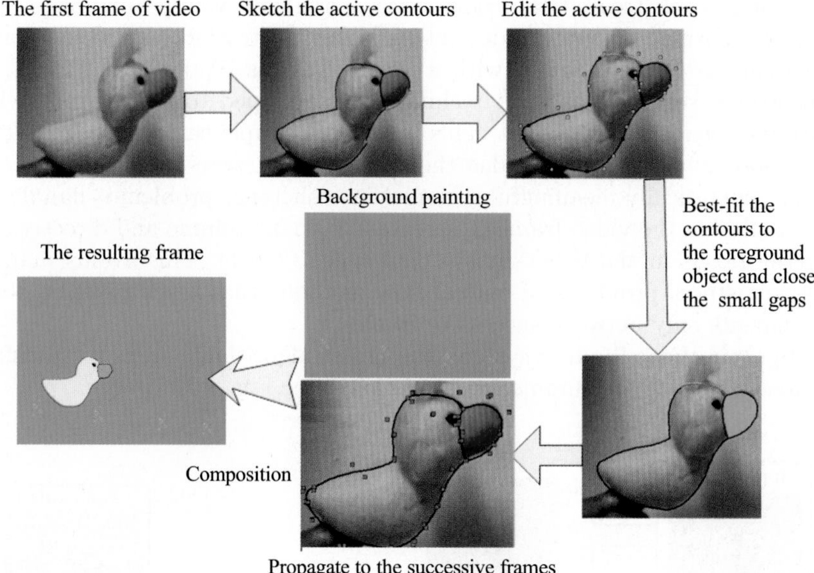

Fig. 8.8 The overall production pipeline in SnakeToonz

In SnakeToonz, its key technical point is contour tracking. It first copies the current frame's cartoon forward to the next frame along with the snapping information. A point tracking technique is employed to track the ends of the contours. Internal points are moved using a transformation space defined by the endpoints. The snakes are then relaxed to the edges in the new frame. It still requires significant and repetitive efforts in contour tracking. In order to facilitate this problem, Agarwala *et al.*, [2004] proposed a user-driven key-frame system for contour tracking. They combined the best features of user guidance and automated tracking: the user can specify constraints by manipulating any contour control point at any frame in the sequence; a space-time optimization, computed using a standard nonlinear optimization technique, then finds the best interpolation of the contours over time. The user can iterate by refining the results and restarting the optimization. Thus, the user can guide the automatic tracking in situations, and the optimization can significantly reduce the amount of human effort involved.

The goal of SnakeToonz is not to surpass professional animation, or to trivialize the medium. Instead, SnakeToonz allows those without experience in cel animation to express themselves in the medium at quality levels much better than they could have accomplished alone. It will help those of us who are brimming with creative vision but lack the skill and experience to map from this vision into results.

Wang *et al.* treated the video as a space-time volume of image data, and transformed an input video into a highly abstracted, spatio-temporally coherent cartoon animation with a range of styles [Wang *et al.*, 2004]. An anisotropic kernel mean shift technique is developed to segment the video data into contiguous volumes. This provides a simple cartoon style in itself, but more importantly provides the capability to semi-automatically rotoscope semantically meaningful regions. The coherence problem is handled by accumulating the video frames to create a 3D data volume and directly cluster the pixels in the three dimensional space (x, y, t). This avoids many of the robustness problems of optical flow methods that track pixel or object movements only between successive frames.

In their VideoTooning system, the major algorithmic steps to transform a video sequence are summarized as follows (see Fig. 8.9):

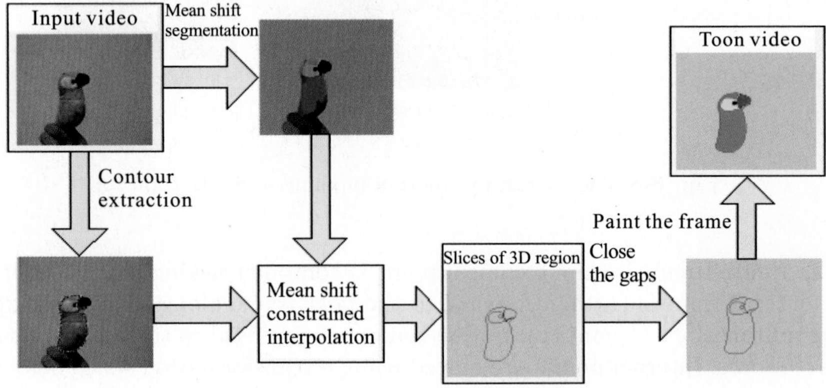

Fig. 8.9 The major algorithmic steps in VideoTooning

(1) A set of volumetric objects is determined by mean shift video segmentation.
(2) The user draws on a limited number of key frames to indicate how small segments should be merged into larger, semantic regions.
(3) The user's indications are interpolated between key frames by a mean shift guided interpolation technique propagating the user's input to all frames.
(4) The user can optionally draw paint strokes within regions at key frames. These are similarly interpolated.
(5) Semantic regions and surfaces are reconstructed and smoothed. Edge and stroke sheets are determined.
(6) At each frame, time regions and sheets are sliced to yield area and curve primitives.

(7) These primitives are rendered in desired style to create a final stylized video frame and output.

This VideoTooning approach provides a possible means to overcome the main challenge of providing temporal stability by leveraging a new mean shift method applied to video data. It is also shown that the mean shift results, together with the artist's input, can provide a variety of non-photorealistic styles (see Fig. 8.10).

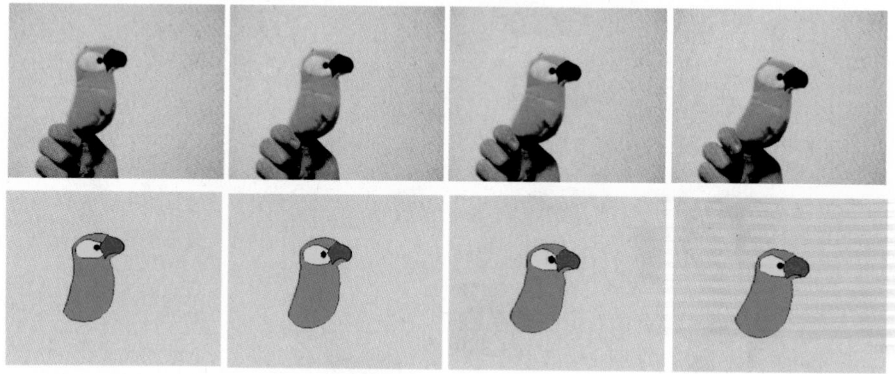

Fig. 8.10 Examples of animation generated based on VideoTooning approach

8.1.3 Video-driven Facial Animation with Style

The human face is one of the most complex and interesting objects that we come across on a regular basis. The face, the myriad expressions and gestures that are capable of making, are a key component of human communication. Human beings are extremely adept at recognizing faces. This attribute presents both an advantage and a challenge to any system that manipulates facial images. The viewer is likely to be able to instantly spot any defects or shortcomings in the image. If the image is not a perfect rendition of an actual face, both in appearance and in motion, the user will notice the discrepancies. Therefore, facial animation has become one of the most challenging tasks in producing character animation.

Video driven facial animation enables the user to create stylized facial animation by a small number of images and a few parameters for the inbetweening images. Buck *et al.* presented a system that can generate "hand-drawn" facial animation from video in real time [Buck *et al.*, 2000]. To construct a face, it requires an initial set of hand-drawn images to blend together. The artist draws this set, divided into mouth, eyes and background head images, all of which can be warped and blended independently (see Fig. 8.11).

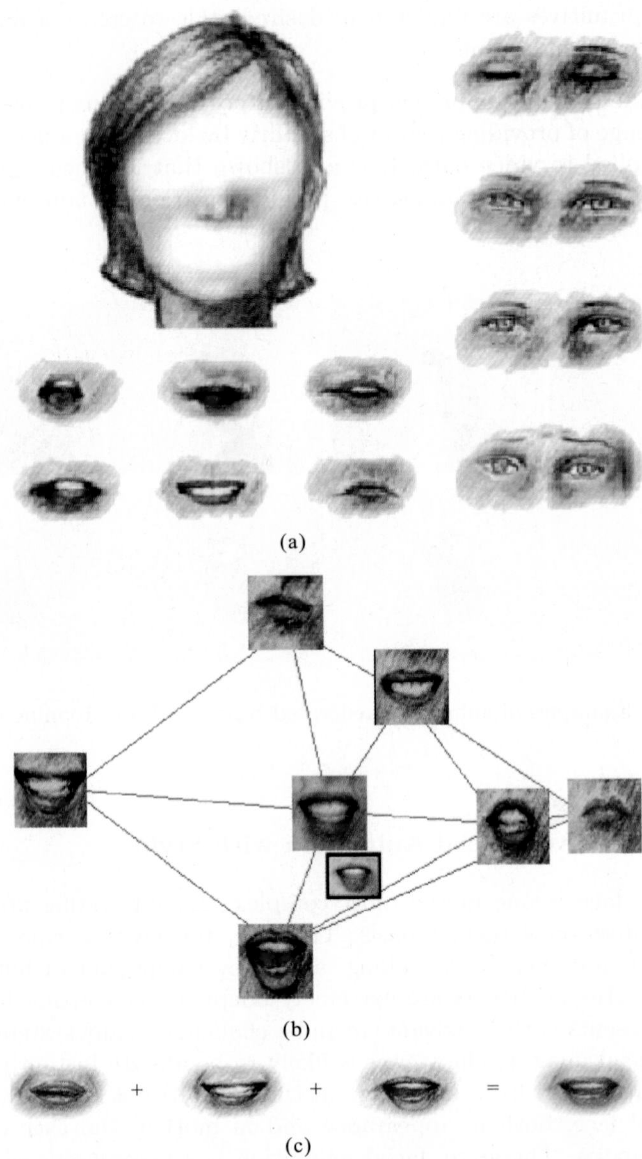

Fig. 8.11 A sample of facial expression, triangulation for mouth interpolation and multi-mouth morphing [Buck *et al.*, 2000]. Copyright of ACM, used with permission. (a) A full set of hand-drawn images; (b) A sample triangulation for mouth interpolation; (c) The three mouths on the left are warped and then blended to make the mouth on the right

A training step is also required to manually associate each eye and mouth expression from the set of artwork with an equivalent expression from a video frame. This correspondence allows the system to discern which tracked measurements of the real person's face best match each hand-drawn image. After this initialization, a person's facial features are tracked in real time. To draw the face, it first renders the warped versions of the eye and mouth regions of the face. Next, the head image, which contains "soft" alpha values in the eye and mouth areas to provide feathered masking, is placed on top of the rendered eyes and mouth. More than one such head image can be loaded, and the program will cycle through them at each frame. It demonstrates that a small set of hand-drawn artwork, in conjunction with a small amount of facial tracking data, can be used to create a real-time performance-driven animation system in which animations effectively mimic the expressions and facial actions of a human speaker (see Fig. 8.12).

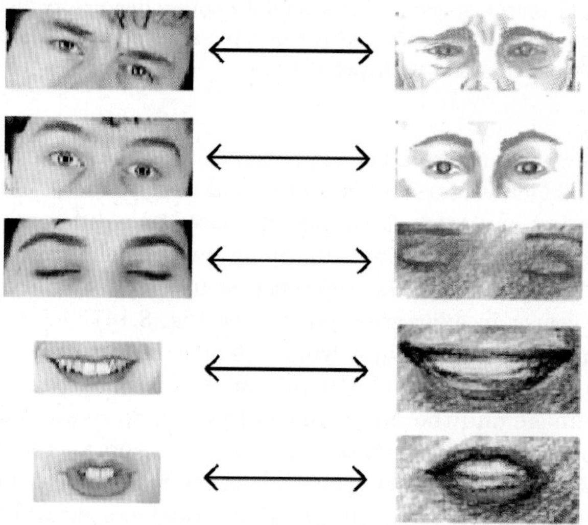

Fig. 8.12 Sample of hand-drawn eyes and mouths from videos [Buck *et al.*, 2000]. Copyright of ACM, used with permission

Blanz *et al.* presented a framework that can re-animate the faces in a single image or video based on a common representation of different faces and facial expressions in a vector space of 3D shapes and textures [Blanz *et al.*, 2003]. In this vector space, expressions can be changed continuously along any trajectory in face space, and transferred across individuals. Recorded from a single person, the expressions and mouth movements can be transferred to another person's neutral face by simple vector space operations (see Fig. 8.13). This procedure assumes that the 3D displacements of surface points are the same for all individuals, and they ignore the slight variations across individuals that depend on the size and shape of faces, characteristic patterns of muscle activation, and mechanical properties of skin and tissue.

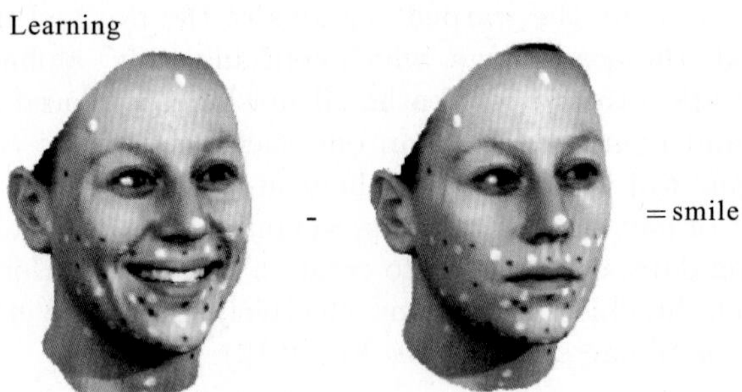

Fig. 8.13 In the vector space of faces, facial expressions are transferred by computing the difference between two scans of the same person [Blanz *et al.*, 2003]. Copyright of Blackwell, used with permission

To be able to transfer facial expressions, they combine the expression vectors with the face vectors of 200 individual neutral faces. The neutral face vectors have to be converted, since they are based on a different, closed-mouth reference surface. A point-to-point mapping between the two representations is established by matching the reference scan of personality space to the closed mouth vector in expression space (see Fig. 8.14).

The estimate of a 3D shape from a single image or a video frame is obtained by a fitting algorithm that minimizes the image difference between the synthetic image and the input image. In order to re-animate novel faces, the system automatically estimates the 3D shape and all relevant rendering parameters, and then adds the performed expression on them, and the desired facial expression is rendered from their neutral faces accordingly (see Fig. 8.15). More examples of re-animating facial paintings by video are given in Fig. 8.16.

However, the facial expression in cartoon animation is not just a reproduction of what is presented in the video sequence, the exaggeration of faces is always preferred by the animators. Aimed at facilitating the limitations of the aforementioned performance-driven facial animation, Liang *et al.* proposed an example-based approach to exaggerating the faces from input facial images [Liang *et al.*, 2002]. Their system learns how to identify facial features and exaggerate them using the artist's style, albeit implicitly. The exaggeration of faces is accomplished by a prototype-based method that captures the artist's understanding of what are distinctive features of a face and the exaggeration style. A prototype is defined on a subset of training data that

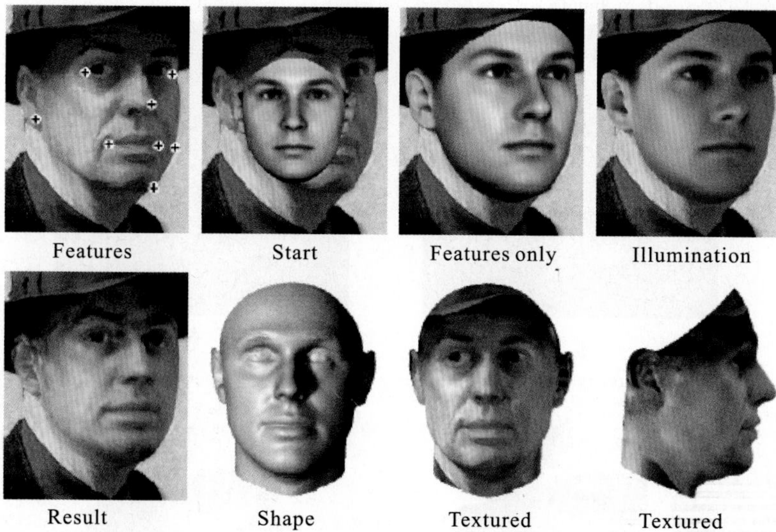

Fig. 8.14 Recovering a 3D face from E. Hopper's self-portrait: Initialized with manually labeled features (top, left) and starting from a front view of the average face, the algorithm automatically optimizes the shape and texture of the morphable model, and estimates pose, illumination and other parameters. The second row shows the result without (left) and with (right) texture extraction [Blanz *et al.*, 2003]. Copyright of Blackwell, used with permission

contains samples with a similar exaggeration direction. Each prototype corresponds to the exaggeration style of some facial features, such as elongating a face. Based on the training data, a set of such prototypes is picked out to represent different exaggeration directions of the artist. Then, given a new input face, the system decides which prototype this face most likely belongs to, then exaggerates it in the same direction as the samples that support this prototype. The overall process to generate the facial exaggeration consists of two parts (see Fig. 8.17): a training phase and a runtime phase. At the training phase, the training examples are analyzed to build the correlation between images and the exaggerated ones, and a set of exaggeration prototypes is constructed. At the runtime phase, the input shape is classified into one of the exaggeration prototypes, and the input shape is accordingly exaggerated by the selected prototype.

Their system can automatically identify facial features from input images, and exaggerate such features simulating the artist's style, and the significant facial features can be obviously exaggerated in a proper direction (see Fig. 8.18).

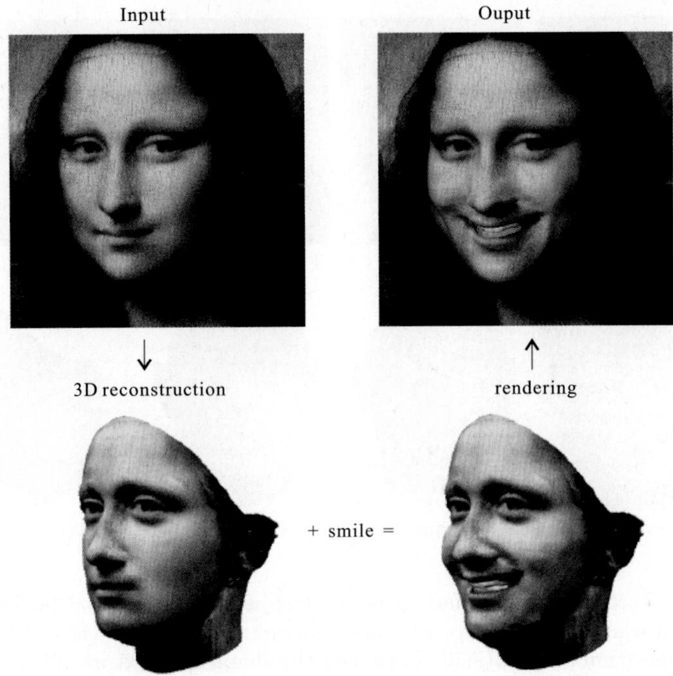

Fig. 8.15 The re-animation of the face of Leonardo's Mona Lisa. Her 3D face is reconstructed and the expression is added, and the new surface is rendered into the painting [Blanz *et al.*, 2003]. Copyright of Blackwell, used with permission

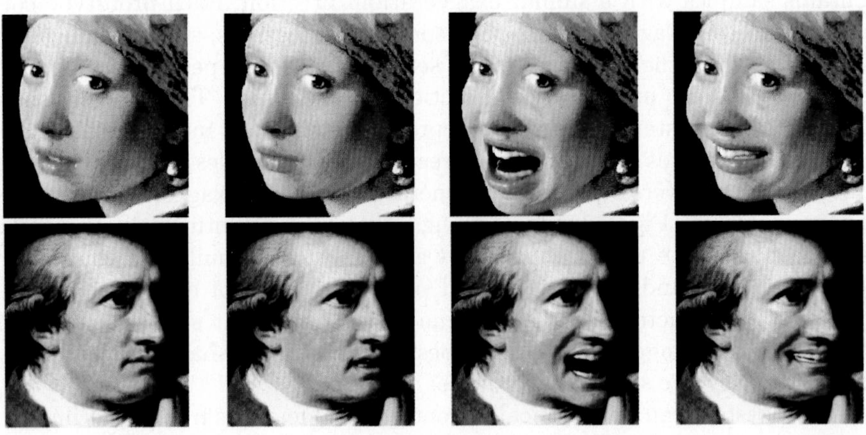

Fig. 8.16 Examples of facial animation driven by video sequence [Blanz *et al.*, 2003]. Copyright of Blackwell, used with permission

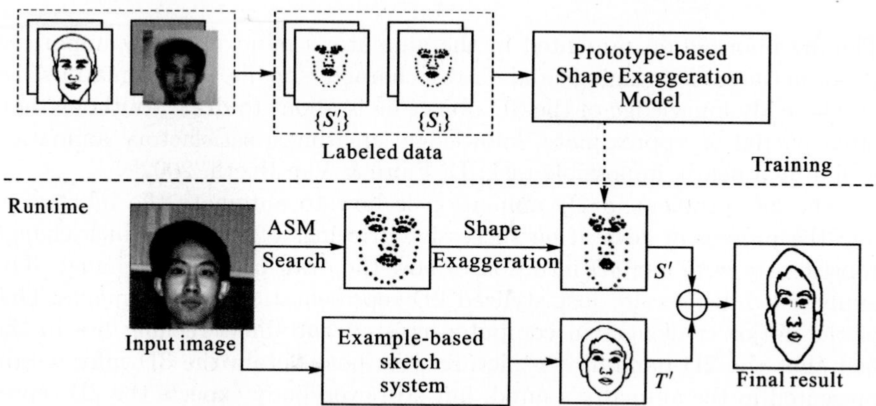

Fig. 8.17 The algorithmic pipeline of example-based exaggeration of faces [Liang *et al.*, 2002]. Copyright of IEEE, used with permission

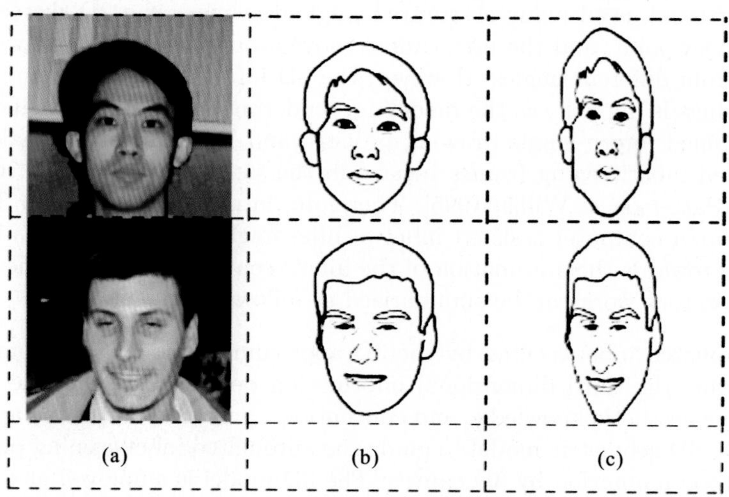

Fig. 8.18 Comparative examples of unexaggerated and exaggerated faces [Liang *et al.*, 2002]. (a) Original image; (b) Unexaggerated image; (c) Exaggerated image. Copyright of IEEE, used with permission

8.2 Cartoon Production Integrated with 3D Geometric Elements

The 3D information presented in the animator's mind is a very important factor in the art of bringing hand–drawn characters to life. The animator relies on his ready knowledge of the 3D object he is about to draw. Without that, often partial or approximate, knowledge, creating a satisfactory animation would be a nearly impossible task [Di Fiore & Van Reeth, 2002].

The key problem in 2D animation is how to automate the inbetweening: the process of generating successive drawings of a figure which change consistently with our 3D intuition of how the drawings should change. The animated drawings are just stylized 2D representations of 3D images. One of the major challenges in computer-assisted auto-inbetweening lies in the fact that the 2D hand-drawn picture does not contain the 3D information presented in the animator's mind, but still everybody expects the 2D representations to behave in similar ways as our 3D mental models do [Catmull, 1978]. Part of the current research focuses on employing full 3D input models, which are rendered and even animated in many different artistic rendering styles. Disadvantages are the need to create complicated 3D models and the many difficulties in achieving lively movements. Purely 2D approaches, on the other hand, need many elaborated single drawings, as a 2D sketch is to a single viewpoint, and the user cannot move around the object drawn, nor view it from different angles. However, the 3D information in the animated 2D drawings is implicit, as the modeling, rendering and motion specification are combined into a single drawing process, and it is difficult to make the automated inbetweening frames behave in the same way as our 3D mental models [Patterson & Willis, 1995]. Therefore, introducing minimum 3D information to computer-assisted inbetweening might be one of the valuable solutions towards the automation of the inbetweening process, and the existing exploratory work can be summarized as follows:

(1) Automated inbetweening by the 3D approximate model: The computer recovers the third dimensional information beyond the 2D plane based on the aesthetic knowledge and conventions, and then builds the approximate 3D geometric model to guide the automated inbetweening process.
(2) Cartoon animation by 3D canvas: The 3D model is employed as a "3D" painting canvas, and the animator directly paints on it on the principle of "what you see is what you get". The computer can then automatically generate the animated drawings with the desired artistic effect from a specified viewpoint.
(3) Cartoon animation based on view-dependent geometry: The view-dependent geometric model is constructed from a basic 3D model and a set of 2D drawings from various viewpoints. The 3D view morphing technique is employed to automatically generate the inbetweening drawings from a new viewpoint.

8.2.1 Automated inbetweening by the 3D Approximate Model

Di Fiore and Van Reeth introduced a novel approach in which approximate 3D models are used to guide the animator throughout various stages of the animation process [Di Fiore & Van Reeth, 2002]. They focused on its use as a tool for (i) depicting and retaining the volume and overall shape of the objects which make up the scene, (ii) rapidly inking the outlines by tracing silhouettes and marker lines of the objects, and (iii) providing frame-to-frame coherence. Drawing has long been an intuitive way to communicate complexity in a comprehensible and effective manner, due to visual abstraction. Drawing a sketch is much faster that creating a 3D model, and definitely more convenient to express ideas. Therefore, their basic shapes of approximate 3D models are input by the sketching (and possibly modifying) 2D circular and rounded forms as if drawing on paper, and then their system interprets these circular and rounded forms to automatically construct a 3D polygonal object of revolution. This modeling method enables the easy and rapid construction of the plain approximate shapes that traditional animators tend to use. The algorithmic pipeline to the 3D modeling is as follows:

```
While modelling:

Select underlying curve primitive
   adjust brush stroke parameters
For each stroke gestured by the animator
   collect 2D screen positions
   For each 2D screen position
      transform screen position to 3D object space
      create particle
      For all extreme frames
         calculate 3D position of particle
         transform 3D position to screen space
         store position
      End(for all extreme frames)
   End (for each 2D screen position)
End (for each stroke gestured by the animator)
```

Regarding the painting process, first of all the animator has to select one of the underlying curve primitives to which brush strokes are attributed. That way the underlying drawing order of the curve primitives specified in the extreme frames is utilized to determine the drawing order of brush strokes. As a result, this solves the problem of self-occlusions. At the same time (when gesturing the strokes), their system transforms the current position in 2D screen space to the object space of the underlying 3D surface at that moment. This is done at discrete moments in time and delivers a set of 3D points (which lie on the surface of the underlying 3D object). Then, with each of the points we associate a particle which stores the current selected brush, its position and orientation. Finally, for each extreme frame we calculate the 3D position of the particles by exploiting the underlying 3D surfaces. These 3D positions are then transformed to 2D screen space and rendering in a painterly style (see Fig 8.19). The animation process during run time is given as follows:

During animation(at runtime):

For each frame in time
  generate inbetween frame
  For each sorted primitive
    draw primitive
    For each associated particle
      orient particle orthogonal to view vector
      draw brush stroke into paint buffer
    End (for each associated particle)
  End (for each sorted primitive)
End (for each frame in time)

Fig. 8.19 Snapshots of an animation of the exotic bird guided by the approximate 3D model [Di Fiore & Van Reeth, 2002]. Copyright of IEEE, used with permission

Later on, Di Fiore *et al.* extended it to design artistic and believable trees in a cartoon-like style, which can be rendered by an animated camera to produce a convincing 3D-like experience [Di Fiore *et al.*, 2003]. However, the trees have a complex, recursive structure, and consist of numerous branches and leaves, and it is difficult for the animator to picture in his mind the trees he is about to draw. Therefore they employed realistic 3D geometries of trees as the underlying models to incorporate 3D information. Aimed at giving the animator the same freedom for expressing the artistic style he has in mind, as if drawing on paper, they presented a hybrid (2.5D) framework, combining the advantages of both 2D and 3D approaches. From an underlying 3D geometry they get the necessary information to obtain an acceptable level of 3D behavior and a good frame-to-frame coherence. In the same framework, 2D artistic input is employed to obtain any desired "look", both of the rendering and of the animation. In order to achieve convincing 3D-like animations, their system requires the object to be modeled as seen from different viewpoints. These different viewpoints can be seen as the extreme frames and will be used by our inbetweening method in the animation phase.

Cohen *et al.* focused on the automatic inbetweening of background painting, and presented an interactive system, Harold, for creating 3D worlds in terms of 2D drawings from a single point of view [Cohen *et al.*, 2000]. The interface paradigm in Harold is *drawing*: All objects are created simply by drawing them with a 2D input device. The primary geometric primitive in Harold is a *billboard*; these are commonly used in interactive systems to render complex yet unimportant objects with low overhead. A billboard is typically a plane with an image texture-mapped onto it that rotates about some point or axis to face the viewer as much as possible. Their billboards contain collections of planar strokes rather than textures. When the user draws a stroke over a billboard, Harold simply projects the stroke onto the billboard and stores it, then display the billboard and re-render each stroke, rotated appropriately. Most of the 3D objects in Harold are collections of planar strokes that are reoriented in a view-dependent way as the camera moves through the world. Virtual scenes created in Harold are rendered with a stroke-based system so that the resulting rendition will maintain a hand-drawn appearance as the user navigates through it (see Fig 8.20).

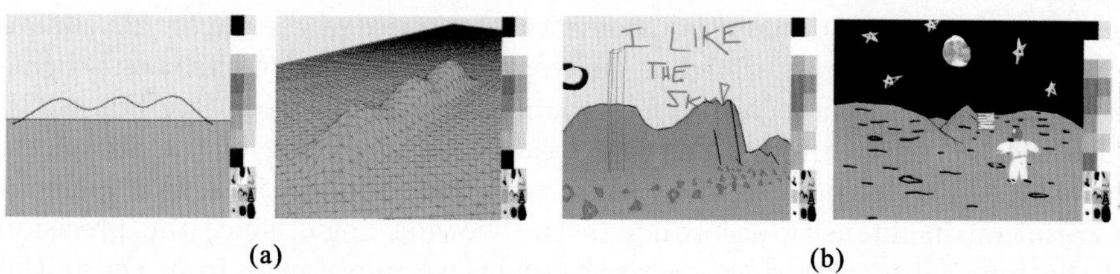

Fig. 8.20 The interface to create 3D terrain and examples of conceptual sketches of outdoor scene [Cohen *et al.*, 2000]. Copyright of ACM, used with permission

In order to better retain many of the characteristics of traditional 2D drawing, Bourguignon *et al.* built a sketching system that can employ the user-drawn strokes to infer the sketches representing the same scene from different viewpoints, rather than attempting to reconstruct a 3D model (see Fig. 8.21) [Bourguignon *et al.*, 2001]. Their work is a natural continuation of drawing or sketching tools which have been developed in computer graphics over the last few years. The central idea of their approach is to represent strokes in 3D space, thus promoting the idea of going from strokes to a fully-fledged 3D entity. Even in 3D, strokes are still an excellent way to indicate the presence of a surface silhouette: several neighboring strokes reinforce the presence of a surface in the viewer's mind, while attenuated strokes may indicate imprecise contours or even hidden parts. Two kinds of strokes are used in their system: line strokes that represent 1D detail and silhouette strokes that represent the contour of a surface.

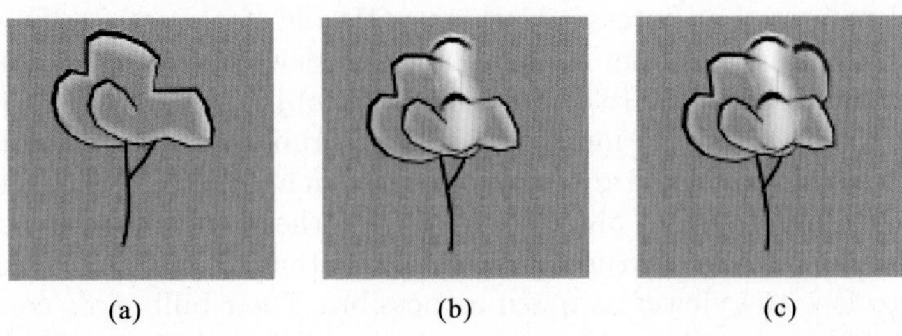

Fig. 8.21 An example of inferring the occluded strokes from a novel viewpoint [Bourguignon *et al.*, 2001]. Copyright of Blackwell, used with permission.

To enable the user to view stroke-based sketches from multiple viewpoints, their system interprets strokes as indications of a local surface silhouette or contour. Strokes thus deform and disappear progressively as the user moves away from the original viewpoint. Assuming that strokes are drawn in a plane, and by using differential geometry properties of the curve, 2D silhouette strokes can be interpreted as curves, and a curvature estimation scheme is employed to infer a local surface around the original stroke (see Fig. 8.22). This mechanism permits efficient stroke-based rendering of the silhouette from multiple viewpoints. In addition to stroke deformations, this includes a variation in intensity according to the viewing angle, since the precision of the inferred local surface decreases when we move away from the initial viewpoint. It also includes relative stroke occlusion, and additive blending of neighboring strokes in the image. It effectively enhances the traditional drawing process with 3D capabilities, notably by permitting multiple viewpoints for a single drawing based on the inferred local surface stroke, and well preserves the degree of expression, imagination and simplicity of use achieved by 2D drawing (see Fig. 8.23).

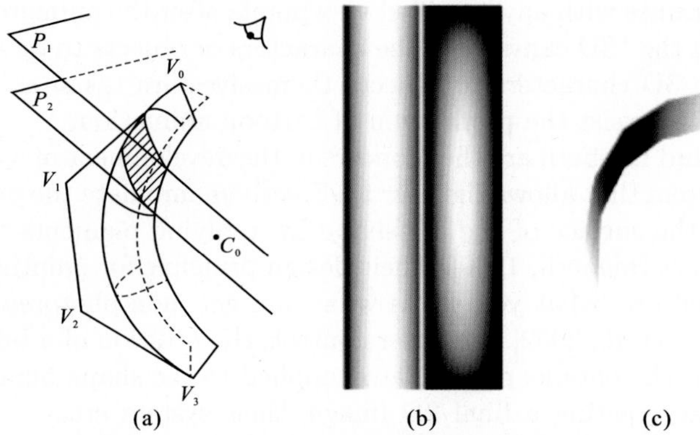

Fig. 8.22 Stroke representation and rendering [Bourguignon *et al.*, 2001]. In (a) the final stroke is a slice of Bezier surface obtained by using two clipping planes P_1 and P_2 facing the camera; C_B is the barycenter of C_i. In (b), two texture samples, one of "stroke texture" (left) and one of "occlude texture" (right). White corresponds to an alpha value of 1, black to an alpha value of 0. In (c), image obtained from rendering a black stroke against a white background, with the slice position corresponding roughly to (a). Copyright of Blackwell, used with permission

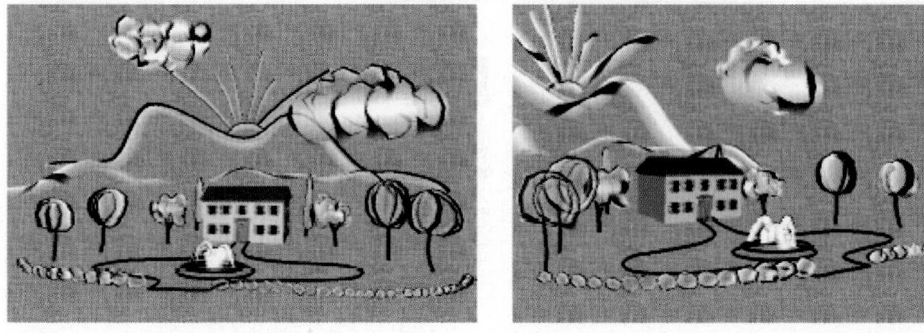

Fig. 8.23 Examples of generating a single landscape from two different views [Bourguignon *et al.*, 2001]. Copyright of Blackwell, used with permission.

8.2.2 Cartoon Animation by 3D Canvas

This approach is based on the assumption that the 3D characters or objects to be animated can be taken as a "3D canvas". The user can then interactively paint the pigments on the "3D canvas" to achieve the desired artistic effects, and with the help of the traditional 3D rendering techniques the system can automatically generate the resulting illustrations with the input artistic effects for the novel viewpoints. It not only imparts a personal aesthetic to the rendering of the object, but also helps automate the generation of inbetweening frames with any specified viewpoints after the animator finishes the painting on the "3D canvas" — the characters or objects to be animated. In essence, the 3D characters or objects themselves are taken as a kind of drawing media to assist the production of cartoon animation.

Hanrahan and Haeberli are the pioneers in the development of a 3D object space paint system that allows the user to directly manipulate the parameters used to shade the surface of the 3D shape by applying pigments to its surface [Hanrahan & Haeberli, 1990]. Their design principle for painting on "3D canvas" is based on "what you see is what you get, non-photorealistic rendering" [Kalnins *et al.*, 2002]. The user controls the position of a brush using a tablet; the brush contains paint that is applied to the shape being painted on. Rather than creating a final 2D image, their system creates an object description that describes the composite material properties everywhere on the surface of the object. The output of their painting system is a 3D model with associated texture maps. The resulting images of this object are then created by conventional rendering techniques as the user paints. The painting interface and an example of painting instance are shown in Fig. 8.24.

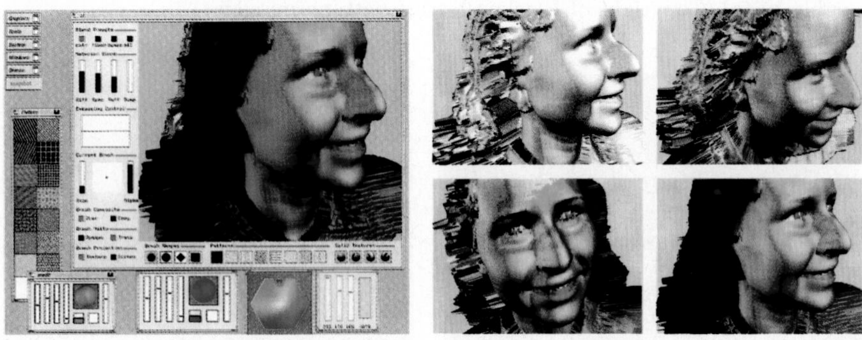

Fig. 8.24 The snapshots of the painting instance and a painting instance [Hanrahan & Haeberli, 1990]. Copyright of ACM, used with permission

Kalnins *et al.* further improved this approach by stoke-based rendering techniques [Kalnins *et al.*, 2002]. In their system, the artist can directly annotate a 3D model with three main categories of strokes: (a) Silhouette and crease lines that form the basis of simple line drawings; (b) Decal strokes that suggest surface features; (c) Hatching strokes to convey lighting and tone. The designer can apply strokes in each category with significant stylistic variation, and thus in combination achieve a broad range of effects (see Fig. 8.25).

The system offers direct user control over brush and paper styles, as well as the placement of individual marks and their view-dependent behavior by an interface with three editing modes. In the first, the artist can position each

Fig. 8.25 Examples of annotating 3D object with different rendering styles [Kalnins *et al.*, 2002]. Copyright of ACM, used with permission.

object and set its "base coat". In outline mode the artist can draw decals and stylize silhouettes and creases. In hatching mode, he can draw hatching strokes. In any mode, the artist can modify the current "brush style" that affects stroke properties. When the system renders the scene from any new viewpoint, it adapts the number and placement of the strokes appropriately to maintain the original look. Fig. 8.26 shows an example of the generation of an animation sequence.

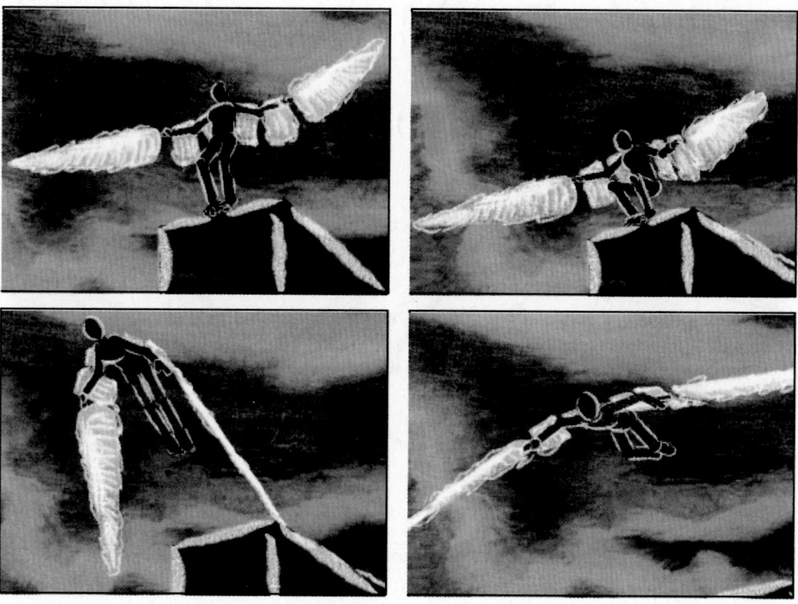

Fig. 8.26 Example of generation of an animation sequence [Kalnins *et al.*, 2002]. Copyright of ACM, used with permission

8.2.3 Cartoon Animation by View-dependent Geometry

When constructing 3D geometry for use in cel animation, the animators typically begin with a set of reference drawings of the object (the *model sheet*), showing it from different viewpoints. The artists who draw them try to achieve the best *aesthetic* effect, and are not bound to geometric precision. As a result, these drawings typically contain many subtle artistic distortions, such as changes in scale and perspective, or more noticeable effects such as changes in the shape or location of features. Because these distortions differ in each drawing and do not correspond to a 3D geometric space, conventional 3D models are unable to capture them all. Therefore, Rademacher proposed the view-dependent geometry technique, wherein a 3D model changes shape based on the direction it is viewed from [Rademacher, 1999]. A view-dependent model consists of a base model, a set of key deformations (deformed versions of the base model), and a set of corresponding key viewpoints (which relate each 2D reference drawing to the 3D base model) (see Fig. 8.27).

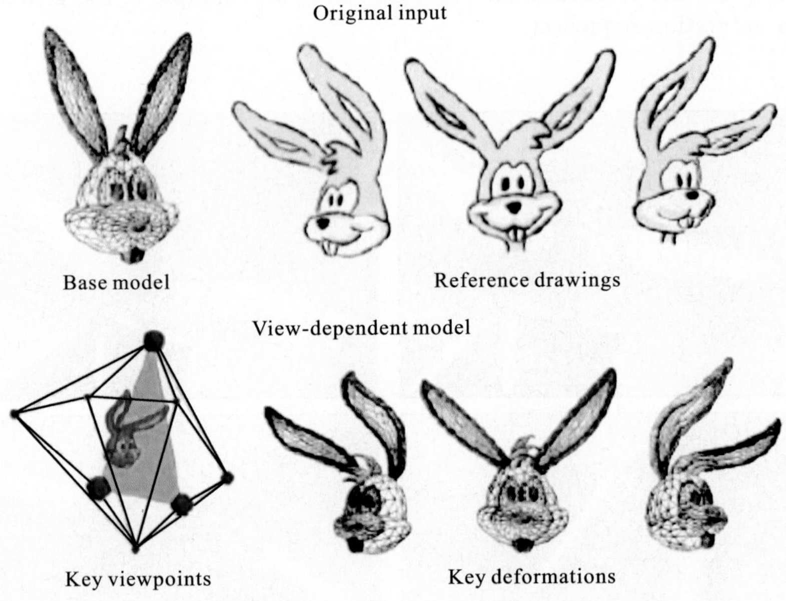

Fig. 8.27 Example components of a view-dependent model [Rademacher, 1999]. Copyright of ACM, used with permission

The first step in creating 3D view dependent geometry is determining a viewpoint for each drawing by calculating a projection that best matches the given drawings. The second step is to create key deformation by deforming the base model according to the reference drawings, and a set of key deformations are built to indicate what an object should look like from various viewpoints (see Fig. 8.28). Given an arbitrary viewpoint, the computer interpolates the key deformations to generate a 3D model that is specific to the new viewpoint– what the object's 3D shape should be. The rendering process proceeds as follows:

(1) Find the three nearest key viewpoints surrounding the current viewpoint.
(2) Calculate blending weights for the associated key deformations.
(3) Interpolate the key deformations to generate a new 3D model for the current viewpoint.
(4) Render the resulting interpolated 3D model.

Fig. 8.28 An example of creating key deformation by reference drawings [Rademacher, 1999]. Copyright of ACM, used with permission

From the point of view of animation production, these viewpoints in the view-dependent geometry model are known as the key viewpoints (which are independent of the camera path that will be used during rendering), and the corresponding object shapes are the key deformations. The key deformations are simply deformed versions of the base model, with the same vertex connectivity. Given an arbitrary viewpoint or camera path, the deformations are blended to generate a new, view-specific 3D model, and accordingly form the resulting animation sequence (see Fig. 8.29).

Aiming at enhancing the artistic impact of the characters and imparting them a personality of their own, Chaudhuri *et al.* presented a novel system for facilitating the creation of stylized view-dependent 3D animation by injecting view-dependent stylization into the animation [Chaudhuri *et al.*, 2004]. They embeded a multilayered deformation system into a view-dependent setting and integrated it with computer vision techniques for camera estimation. The technique of view-dependent geometry is enhanced by tying it up with the more conventional 3D character manipulation technique of inverse kinematics and direct free-form deformation. Their system allows the recovery of

Fig. 8.29 An example of generation of animation sequence by view-dependent model [Rademacher, 1999]. Copyright of ACM, used with permission.

a camera which best matches the intended view direction in the sketch. The skeletal pose of the 3D character is reconstructed in terms of the recovered camera (see Fig. 8.30). A base mesh model of the character can be modified to match closely to an input sketch, with minimal user interaction. After aligning the mesh model with the sketch, the system can then deform the mesh to match the deformation of the sketched character. This deformation model is coupled with the camera, and thus it gives a deformation consistent with the recovered view point. At every stage the system offers considerable

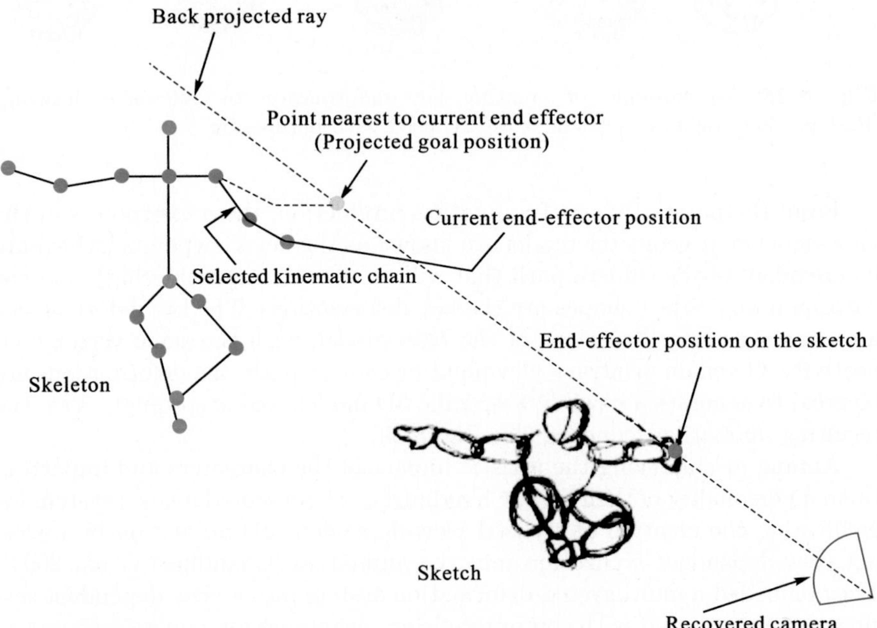

Fig. 8.30 Projecting the goal back using the recovered camera [Chaudhuri *et al.*, 2004]. Copyright of Blackwell, used with permission

flexibility to the user to correct the recovered view, reconstructed pose or the deformed mesh by manual intervention. Finally, their system is capable of creating view-specific distortions as a character moves from the traditional 2D world to the modern 3D world of computer animation (see Fig. 8.31).

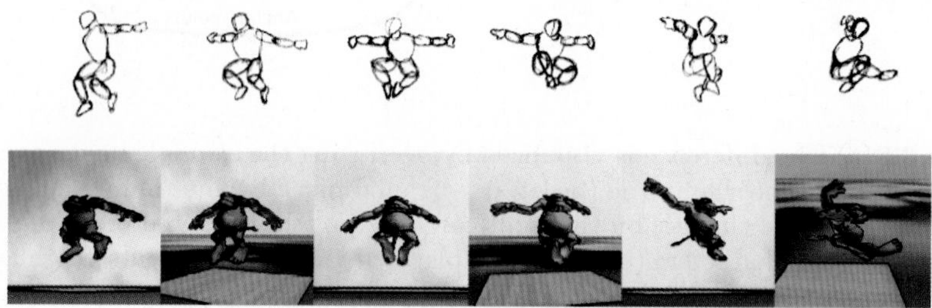

Fig. 8.31 Example of view-dependent animation by mannequin sketches [Chaudhuri *et al.*, 2004]. Copyright of Blackwell, used with permission

In order to further inject expression into the cartoon animation, Li *et al.* proposed a sketch-based stylization method allowing us to use an animator's talents to add exaggeration into the resulting animation [Li *et al.*, 2003]. The 2D sketches are seamlessly integrated into the original animation for emphasis, or purposefully shape the apparent silhouette to make the character easier to "read." The hand drawn images are called the *examples,* and the original computer drawing images are called the *rendering.* The differences between the example and the rendering represent the animator's intension of exaggerating or changing the appearance of the character, and these expressed changes are further divided into two parts: those that can be made by altering the skeletal animation, and those that must be made by altering the character's mesh geometry (see Fig. 8.32).

The algorithmic steps of this approach are given as follows:

(1) The user adjusts the skeletal pose that corresponds with the example image, and the system creates a new motion (and corresponding set of renderings) that interpolates this pose using motion warping.
(2) The user provides a small set of correspondences between the rendering and the example image and the system expands these points into curves.
(3) The system creates a dense image warp between the example and rendering using an interpolation technique based on the 3D structure of the model. This associates pixels in the example image with the 3D data.
(4) The system interprets the image-space field of the image warp as a vector field along the surface of the character.
(5) The character's appearance is computed at times other than in the example by driving the vector field along with the motion of the character.
(6) The system fades these changes in and out over time.

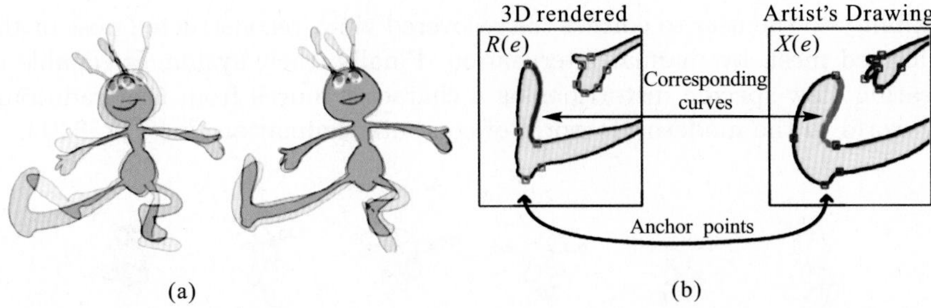

Fig. 8.32 (a) The difference is visualized by overlaying the example image over the rendered frame. The changes on the left can be minimized by fine-tuning the skeletal parameter, and the changes on the right can only be reduced by altering the mesh geometry of the character; (b) The user places a few anchor points (highlighted by squares), snapping them on corresponding positions in the example image. The corresponding curves inbetween these anchors are computed using a snake operator [Li *et al.*, 2003]. Copyright of ACM, used with permission

Fig. 8.33 gives a comparative example of the original animation and the stylized one.

Fig. 8.33 A comparative example of the original animation (top) and the stylized one (bottom) [Li *et al.*, 2003]. Copyright of ACM, used with permission

8.3 Cartoon Generation by Temporal Coherent Rendering

With the advent of artistic rendering techniques, it is possible to easily and automatically generate the artistic image from 3D objects in terms of the specified viewpoint and rendering style parameters. Therefore, it is natural for the animators to imagine directly generating the cartoon animation sequence merely based on the input 3D geometry. Aesthetically, a still frame in hand-drawn animation should have the following characteristics of painting [Meier, 1996]: details should be abstracted by shorthand brush strokes, the roundness of forms should be defined by brush stroke directions, color should break the boundaries of surfaces to create rhythm in the composition, brush stroke size and texture should be varied according to the kind of surface being depicted, and the effects of light should be exaggerated to help provide focus, all as if an artist had painted on a physical canvas. Technically, the rendered images in cartoon animation should maintain coherence in animated sequences and should not change in a random way every frame. Images should not have the gift-wrapped look of painted textures that are mapped onto the geometry using traditional methods. A human artist drawing each frame is better able to control frame-to-frame coherence, while maintaining a hand-crafted look. However, computer rendering usually creates static images that do not invite the viewer into the rendering process. Too much randomness often creeps in and makes the animation noisy while trying to mimic the wavering quality of hand-drawn animation. Therefore, the key point in using existing static image rendering techniques for animation is to get the paint to "stick" to surfaces rather than randomly change with each frame, while automating the drawing of brush strokes and retaining a hand-crafted look.

Meier was one of the pioneers who extended the artistic rendering methods for the static image to painterly animation by modeling surfaces as 3D particle sets which will be rendered as 2D paint brush strokes in screen space, much like an artist lays down brush strokes on a canvas [Meier, 1996]. The overall algorithmic pipeline is given in Fig. 8.34. It first generates a set of particles that describes a surface, depth-sorts the particles in camera space, and renders them as 2D brush strokes in screen space using a painter's algorithm. The look of the 2D brush strokes, including color, size and orientation, is derived from the geometry, surface attributes, and lighting characteristics of the surface. These attributes are designed by the user and either associated directly with the particles or encoded in rendered images of the geometry, called reference pictures. To maintain coherence, a seed is stored with each particle so that the same random perturbations will be used for a particular particle throughout an animation. The user specifies the amount of randomness by choosing a range about the given attribute.

This approach not only eliminates the "shower door" effect, in which an animation appears as if it were being viewed through textured glass, but also creates the desired painterly style of animation and forces the brush strokes to stick to animating surfaces (see Fig. 8.35). By varying lighting and choosing brush stroke parameters, the animator can create many varied painterly styles.

Based on similar principles of art-based graphics, Kowalski *et al.* employed "graftals" to model complex scenes (fur, grass and trees etc.) by treating the

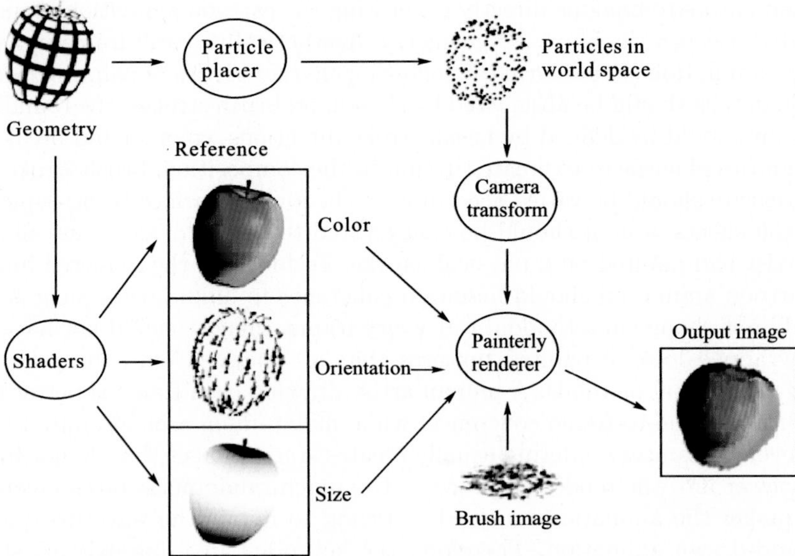

Fig. 8.34 The algorithmic pipeline of painterly rendering. The particle placer populates a surface with particles. The surface geometry is rendered using various shaders to create brush stroke attribute reference pictures. The orientations are encoded in the color channels of the image. The particles, which are transformed into screen space, the reference pictures, and the brush image are input to the painterly renderer. The renderer looks up brush stroke attributes in the reference pictures at the screen space location given by each particle's position and renders brush strokes that are composited into the final rendered image [Meier, 1996]. Copyright of ACM, used with permission

Fig. 8.35 Frames from a painterly rendered animation [Meier, 1996]. Copyright of ACM, used with permission

rendering strategy as an aspect of modeling [Kowalski *et al.*, 1999, Markosian *et al.* 2000]. In fact, the complexity of the scene is merely suggested by the stylized strokes, and these complex scenes are not explicitly represented. Basic graftals depict small detail elements such as individual leaves or blades of grass. Each graftal is composed of one or more drawing primitives, together with a set of 3D points or *vertices*. When a new graftal is copied from one of the example graftals, some of its parameters can be varied randomly, within a specified range of values. Graftals can scale their geometry and volume so that they tend to maintain a desired screen-space size and relative density. These graftals are constructed as procedural stroke-based textures that will be placed on polyhedral models. For the animation production, the key requirements of graftals placement are that graftals should be placed with controlled screen-space density in a manner matching the aesthetic requirements of the particular textures, but at the same time seem to "stick" to surfaces in the scene, providing interframe coherence and a sense of depth through parallax. In order to effectively maintain the coherence, a "static" placement scheme can be adopted to distribute graftals onto surfaces during the modeling phase, when the designer creates the scene [Markosian *et al.*, 2000]. Then, in each frame, graftals are drawn (or not) view-dependently. Fig. 8.36 gives some examples of the modeling and animation of a complex 3D scene with "graftals".

Fig. 8.36 Examples of modeling and animation of complex 3D scene with "graftals" [Kowalski *et al.*, 1999, Markosian *et al.* 2000]. Copyright of ACM, used with permission

In order to produce animations of polygonal 3D models rendered using the stippling style, Pastor and Strothotte explored frame-coherent stippling by taking the same idea of particle systems from painterly rendering, where particles, or graftals, are fixed on the surface of 3D models [Pastor & Strothotte, 2002]. Their algorithmic framework is based on the view-dependent particle system for real time non-photorealistic rendering [Cornish *et al.*, 2001]. Their hierarchical particles are constructed from a mesh simplification and subdivision scheme. Each input model's vertex is a particle that indicates a potential stipple location. Because each point attaches to a specific location on the surface of the model, points move along with the model as the model moves in an animated scene. In order to get even point distributions on the final rendition, they add and remove stipples from the surface of the models, using spatial criteria to meet this requirement as the animation occurs: new stipples, which are inserted lower in the particle hierarchy, are placed at locations roughly in the middle of existing stipples. Alternatively, when stipples are removed from the surface of a model, stipples at the bottom of the hierarchy are the ones that vanish first. The overall algorithmic steps to generate the animation with fame-coherent stippling rendition are given as follows:

(1) Compute a connectivity graph to operate on the input polygonal mesh.
(2) Apply a randomized phase on the vertices of the input mesh to reduce the presence of regular patterns that appear when the vertices of the input mesh are taken as locations for the stipples.
(3) Perform mesh simplification on the input mesh and simultaneously create a bottom-up hierarchy for the vertices in the input mesh.
(4) Render each frame of the animation using a series of key frames, interpolating values between each key frame to set the viewing parameters for each individual frame. These viewing parameters include the camera position and orientation, illumination and frame-rate among others, and determine whether more refinement is needed to fill in dark regions of the model.
(5) Assemble the rendered frames in an animation file.

Selection of particles during rendering also takes into account the screen space projection of the edges of a polygon fan that surround the particles and the desired tone at the position of the particles. This approach provides the frame-coherence effect at the stipple level, and can be applied to arbitrary polygonal meshes and can be extended to include grey scale textures, bump mapping and custom illumination models.

Kalnins *et al.* described a way to render stylized silhouettes of animated 3D models with temporal coherence [Kalnins *et al.*, 2003]. Stylized silhouettes can suggest surface texture, give an organic feeling to an overly-mechanical shape, or simply annotate features of a model such as the hidden silhouettes denoted by dashed lines. Temporal coherence is especially challenging for silhouettes because they may not have obvious inter-frame correspondence as they evolve over time. Strokes have two properties that affect coherence: the *path* in the image plane over which the stroke is applied, and the *parameterization* that defines how stylization (e.g., wiggles or texture) is mapped onto that path. Typically, silhouette paths in the image plane enjoy a natural coherence. Therefore, the key to achieving our goal is to provide coherence for the *parameterization* of silhouettes. Kalnins *et al.* addressed the coherence challenge by propagating the parameterization from strokes in one frame to strokes in the next. In their implementation, each mesh is assigned a stylization based on application-specific aesthetic concerns. The stylization is defined either as a set of brush marks or as a texture image. The mesh may be separated into patches, each of which receives a single stylization that is applied uniformly to all silhouettes. In order to maintain the coherence during rendering, stylization is mapped onto the brush path via a parameter that will be propagated from one frame to the next. This approach can effectively render coherent stylized silhouettes for animated 3D models (see Fig. 8.37).

Fig. 8.37 Temporal coherent stylized silhouettes on an animated figure [Kalnins *et al.*, 2003]. Copyright of ACM, used with permission

8.4 Cartoon Generation Together with 3D Graphical Processing Techniques

Many of the existing 3D graphics processing algorithms or principles can be borrowed, to enhance or speed up the 2D cartoon animation. In this section we will mainly discuss how to utilize the 3D artistic processing techniques such as affine transformation, texture mapping, shadows and highlight for cartoon animation production.

8.4.1 Cartoon Production Integrated with 3D Transformation

The 3D transformation can be applied on both background and foreground objects in cartoon animation production. Wood *et al.* employed the artistic transformation technique to simulate apparent camera motion through the background scene [Wood *et al.*, 1997]. In 2D cartoon animation, a background image (panoramas) is usually constructed to incorporate multiple views of a 3D environment as seen from along a given camera path. When viewed through a small moving window, the panorama produces the illusion of 3D motion. They explored how such panoramas can be designed by computer, and examined their application to cel animation in particular. Its major algorithmic steps are given as follows (see Fig. 8.38):

(1) A 3D modeling program is used to create a crude 3D scene and camera path.
(2) It takes the 3D scene and camera path as input, and outputs one or more panoramas, each with a 2D *moving window* for viewing the panorama during each frame of the animation. When viewed as a whole, the panoramas may appear strangely warped. However, when taken together, the panoramas and moving windows should produce the illusion of 3D motion along the camera path.
(3) An illustrator then uses each computer-generated panorama as a guide to produce a high-quality artistic rendering of the distorted scene, called an *illustrated panorama.* The illustrated panorama may be created with any traditional media and scanned back into the computer. Alternatively, the illustrated panorama may be created with a digital paint system directly on the computer.
(4) For each frame in the scene, images are extracted from the panoramas according to the moving windows. These images are composited (together with any additional foreground or computer-animated elements) to produce the final frames of the animation.

Fig. 8.38 An example of algorithmic pipeline based on Pan transformation of camera. (a) Views from a 3D camera path; (b) Computer-generated layout; (c) Illustrated panorama; (d) Frames from the illustrated panorama with a computer-animated bouncing ball [Wood *et al.*, 1997]. Copyright of ACM, used with permission

This automated process not only allows layout artists to work more efficiently and employ layouts more widely, but also leverages the strengths of both the computer and the artist. The computer permits the use of much more complex camera paths than can be created by hand; in addition, it allows easier experimentation in designing them. The artist, on the other hand, is free to create the panorama in any artistic style, and is not limited by the availability of any particular computer rendering technique (see Fig. 8.39).

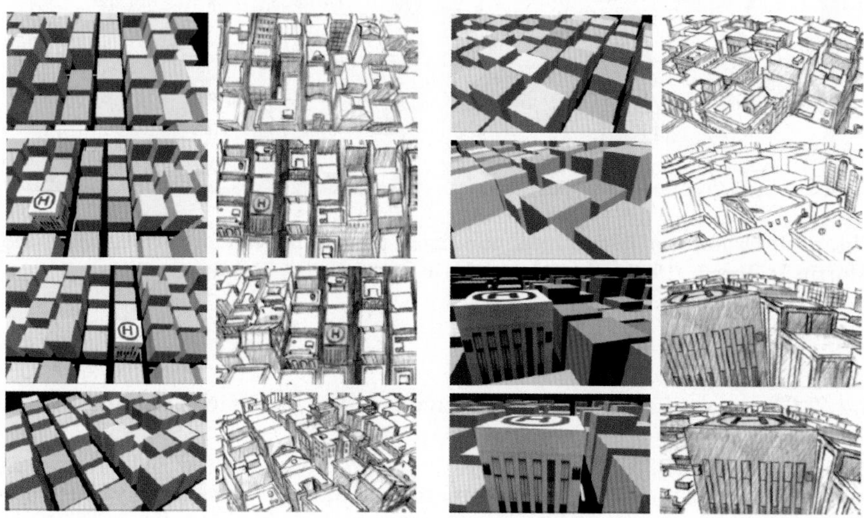

Fig. 8.39 Examples of 3D views of extracted frames in the resulting animation [Wood *et al.*, 1997]. Copyright of ACM, used with permission

Martín and Torres focused on the foreground characters and utilized the hierarchical non- linear transformations to produce computer animations that look like 2D classic cartoons [Martín & Torres, 1999]. They defined two axes for the non-linear transformation: one is the selection axis and the other is the application axis. The selection axis controls which coordinate is taken from the point to be transformed. This coordinate determines the value of the transformation that will be used with the point. The application axis controls which coordinate the transformation will be applied to. The transformations are made for each coordinate independent, which adds more computation but also provides more flexibility. However, for a given selection axis and value, the transformation is the same for all the points which have the same value in the selected coordinate. In order to facilitate this limitation, the hierarchical non-linear transformation is employed for cartoon animation production. That is, non-linear transformations can be passed down to other objects in the hierarchy. These transformations are inherited by the object, which can have its own local non-linear transformations. In some cases, the object is included in the application range of the object that is on a higher level in the hierarchy. In the other cases, the object is partially included or even totally excluded from the object at the higher level. An example of hierarchical non-linear transformation for cartoon animation can be seen in Fig. 8.40.

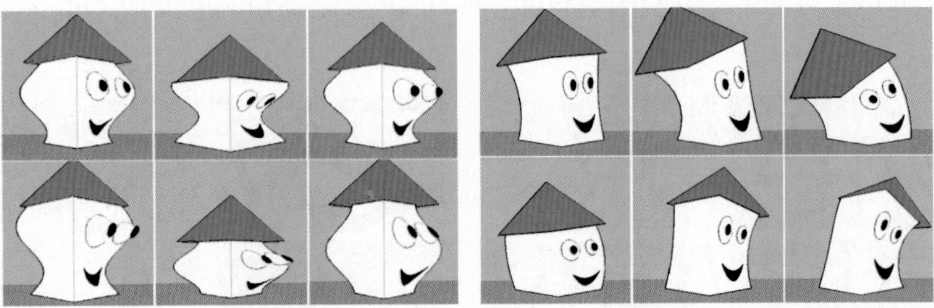

Fig. 8.40 Example of hierarchical non-linear transformation for cartoon animation [Martín & Torres, 1999]. Copyright of IEEE, used with permission

8.4.2 Cartoon Animation Enhanced with Artistic Texture Mapping

In traditional cartoon animation, foreground characters are usually illustrated with flat colors, whereas background scenery is often drawn in subtle detail. This disparity in rendition may be desirable to distinguish the animated characters from the background. But there are still many cartoon figures for which complex textures would be advantageous. Applying complex textures to hand-drawn characters in cartoon animation is extremely difficult. Corrêa *et al.* summarized that there are two major factors that prohibit animators from painting moving characters with detailed textures [Corrêa *et al.*, 1998]. First, foreground characters are drawn differently from frame to frame, requiring any complex shading to be replicated for every frame, adapting to the movements of the characters—an extremely daunting task. Second, even if an animator is to re-draw a detailed texture for every frame, temporal inconsistencies in the painted texture tend to lead to disturbing artifacts, wherein the texture appears to "boil" or "swim" on the surface of the animated figures.

Corrêa *et al.* presented a method that correlates features in a simple, textured, 3D model with features on a hand-drawn figure, and then distorts the model to conform to the hand-drawn artwork [Corrêa *et al.*, 1998]. Their system begins with hand-drawn characters created by a traditional animator. Next, a computer graphics animator creates a crude 3D model that mimics the basic poses and shapes of the hand-drawn art, but ignores the subtlety and expressiveness of the character. The 3D model includes both a texture and the approximate camera position shown in the artwork. The computer distorts the model within the viewing frustum of the camera, in such a way that the model conforms to the hand-drawn art, and then renders the model with its texture. Finally, the rendered model replaces the flat colors that would be used in the ink-and-paint stage of traditional cartoon animation.

For each shot in the animation, the detailed operational steps are given as follows:

(1) The user/animator scans in the cleaned-up hand-drawn artwork.
(2) The user/animator creates a simple 3D model that approximates roughly to the shape of the hand-drawn character.
(3) The computer finds border and silhouette edges in the model.
(4) The user/animator traces over edges of the line art that correspond to border and silhouette features of the 3D model.
(5) The computer performs depth-preserving warps for the 3D model to match the shape of the line art, and then renders the model.
(6) The computer composites the rendered model with the hand-drawn line art and background scenery.
(7) entire process requires relatively little effort per frame and allows animators to combine complex textures with hand-drawn artwork, leveraging the strengths of 3D computer graphics while retaining the expressiveness of traditional hand-drawn cartoon animation.

8.4.3 Cartoon Motions Augmented by 3D Physical Models

There are two typical expressive motions involved in cartoon animation production: apparent motion and squash-and-stretch motions. Apparent motion is a kind of global motion of foreground characters that comes from relative displacement between layers of characters and backgrounds, and there are no corresponding physical displacements for it. That is, the cartoon characters appear to move in the animated environment but they remain in the same position on a flat 2D screen. Squash-and -stretch motions address the interactions between foreground characters and the surrounding environment, in which the stretch anticipates the collision and the squash exaggerates its effects. That is, an object is stretched as it approaches a collision, and squashed through the collision, and then stretched again as it rebounds. Squash-and-stretch may also convey information about the physical properties of objects (their mass, hardness and so on).

In traditional cartoon animation, apparent motions are usually made from a series of drawings simulating motion by means of small progressive changes in the drawings. There are four well-known types of apparent motion: motion after effect (MAE) (e.g., upward motion of objects near a waterfall), phi phenomenon (e.g., filled in motion in a movie of flickering animation stills), induced motion (e.g., perceived movement due to a slowly moving train on the next track) and autokinetic movement (e.g., perturbation seen at low light in a dark room).

Raskar *et al.* exploited the induced motion effect generation by combining two-dimensional cartoon animation and static three dimensional dioramas of physical models into lively nonrealistic setups and non-realistic movement [Raskar *et al.*, 2002]. They illuminated the static physical models with projectors (see Fig. 8.41) and substituted the prerecorded sequence of images with real-time three dimensional computer graphics renderings to create an animated physical world with apparent motion effect. To induce motion, they segment a continuous static physical scene into sub-parts, so that the multiple movements appear compatible. They also force temporary and invalid 3D interpretation using shadows, lighting and texture movements.

Fig. 8.41 Setup with a projector and simple diorama of toy car [Raskar *et al.*, 2002]. Copyright of ACM, used with permission

In order to demonstrate the effectiveness of cartoon dioramas, they simulated a car driving along a road,on a rough surface, or in various other environments. To create apparent motion, they illuminated the wheels with images of rotating wheels. The images in the background (made up of the backdrop and ground) move in a direction opposite to the intended car movement. They implemented both a photo-realistic version and the cartoon-like version (see Fig. 8.42). The experimental results show that this technique can be used on similar setups while creating apparent motion for animation scenarios.

Chenney *et al.* presented a simulation system that uses a mixture of dynamic and kinematic techniques to squash-and-stretch objects with geometric deformations while preserving desirable qualities of the object's appearance and motion [Chenney *et al.*, 2002]. Their goal is to automatically add dynamic, cartoon style deformations to interactive models with the focus on the final appearance of the motion, rather than a physical model, and accordingly the following rules were summarized for generating squash-and-stretch motion:

Fig. 8.42 A comparative example of photo-realistic diorama (left column) vs. cartoon diorama (right column) [Raskar *et al.*, 2002]. Copyright of ACM, used with permission

(1) The object should squash during the collision by an amount that depends on how hard it hits the user-defined squash parameters.
(2) The deformation should vary smoothly through the collision, and should be continuous through the transition between ballistic and colliding motion.
(3) The object should appear to stick through the collision, rather than slide. The object must also rotate during the collision, to align its deformation axis with the outgoing direction of travel.

Their simulation process is initialized with the positions and velocities for each object. Assuming that no objects are inter-penetrating, and each simulation time step then performs the following steps:

(1) Update all the objects in free space according to ballistic point mass equations, and set their deformations and alignment according to rules described below. Objects are updated to either the next rendering frame time or the next collision time, whichever occurs first.
(2) Compute collision interpolation parameters for any new collisions found. Collision interpolations are based on velocities, contact conditions and our desired squash-and-stretch behavior. At each step, they serve as guidelines for the deformation and orientation of the colliding object.
(3) Update all objects involved in collisions, and set their deformations, orientations and positions.

The stylistic requirements for the squash-and-stretch deformations are:

(1) The deformations should be volume preserving.

(2) Each object has a natural set of deformation axes, including one principal axis, and scaling should always be done with respect to these axes. These axes define a deformation coordinate system with the x-axis aligned with the forward direction for the object.

It is demonstrated that the resultant motions generated by these requirements are pleasing for a range of objects (see Fig. 8.43). The major strength of this approach is its tight coupling between user controlled parameters and the appearance of the motion. The user can control that map directly onto properties of the motion, allowing the easy specification of particular styles.

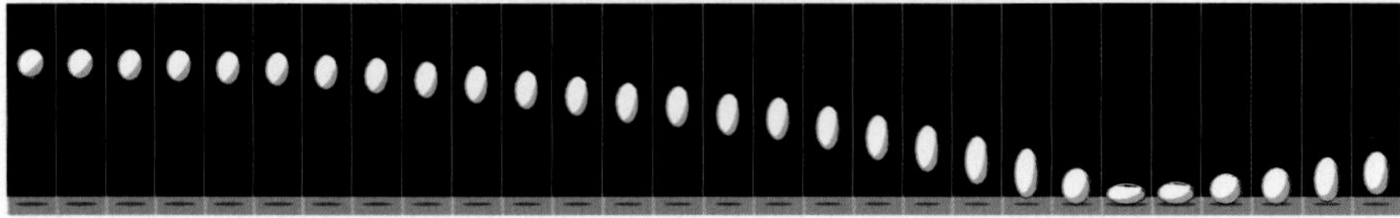

Fig. 8.43 Examples of simulated squash-and-stretch motions [Chenney *et al.*, 2002]. Copyright of ACM, used with permission

8.4.4 Stylized Highlight and Shadow Generation for Cartoon Animation

In traditional cartoon animation, highlights and shadows are semantic in that they imply an artistic and meaningful interpretation of the characters and scene. This highlight could be a kind of environment reflection or refraction, rather than the brightest area on the rear window. For example, a highlight on the swords, portraying that the swords are flat and shiny like plane glasses, and that they are so sharp that the heroine might be wounded in the next frame; the highlight on the monster's claws suggests that the claws are very hard, and that they can hurt someone easily (see Fig. 8.44). The practical requirements in making cartoon-style highlights for 3D objects are summarized as follows [Anjyo & Hiramitsu, 2003]:

(1) Shape: A simply shaped highlight should be created with a clear boundary. It won't always have a rounded shape, but can have rich variations such as crescents and squares.
(2) Animation: Highlight animation should be made smooth and dynamic, and therefore the temporal deformation of the stylistic highlight should be described.

Shadows provide important visual cues for depth, shape, contact, movement and lighting in cartoon animation. A moving figure and background scenery are illustrated in different layers with different styles, and therefore

Fig. 8.44 Various highlights suggest different artistic meanings of objects in the scene [Anjyo & Hiramitsu, 2003]. Copyright of IEEE, used with permission

shadows play an especially crucial role by integrating the character into the background. In most cases, shadows in cartoon animation serve to anchor the character to the ground, enhance the form of the figure, or suggest lighting or mood. Without some kind of contact with the background, the characters seem to float around, walk on air, no matter how much weight has been animated into their movements [Petrovic *et al.*, 2000].

By the aforementioned cartoon-like highlighting principles, Anjyo and Hiramitsu presented a novel highlight shader that can create cartoon-style highlights for 3D objects by a highlight vector field [Anjyo & Hiramitsu, 2003]. Without using a texture-mapping technique, their shader makes an initial highlight shape using the traditional Blinn's specular model. Then it interactively modifies the initial shape through geometric (local affine transformations such as translation, rotation and directional scaling), stylistic (a slight modification of the directional scaling operation or making a highlight area more square shaped, etc.) and Boolean transformations for the highlight vector field until the system gets our final desired shape. Moreover, once these operations specify highlight shapes for each key frame, their shader can automatically generate the highlight animation by linear interpolation (see Fig. 8.45).

Petrovic *et al.* proposed a semi-automatic method for creating shadow mattes in cartoon animation [Petrovic *et al.*, 2000]. Their system employs a scheme for "inflating" a 3D figure based on hand-drawn art. At a high level, the shadow creation process begins with hand-drawn line art created by a traditional animator, as well as hand-painted scenery created by a background artist. The user sketches over features in the painted background to establish the camera, ground plane and background objects. Using character mattes integral to the compositing stage of the normal cartoon animation pipeline, the system automatically "inflates" a 3D mesh for the character. The user specifies the depth for the character in the scene, as well as light positions. Next, based on the lights, the 3D character and the background objects, the

Fig. 8.45 Example of highlighting animation [Anjyo & Hiramitsu, 2003]. Copyright of IEEE, used with permission

computer renders three types of shadow mattes for the character: tone mattes indicate both self-shadowing and shadows of other objects on the character; contact shadow mattes emphasize contact between the character and the ground; and cast shadow mattes specify shadows cast by the character onto the background scenery. Finally, these mattes are composited into the scene as part of the conventional cartoon animation pipeline. This system requires a small amount of user input—less effort than would be required to draw the mattes by hand. Once the user has set up the scene, it is easy to alter the lighting conditions to produce very different kinds of shadows.

8.5 Cartoon Production via Reuse of Traditional Animation

The long history of cartoon animation provides a huge amount of artistically advanced art works, which give a valuable reference for the animators while creating new cartoon animation clips. The reuse of traditional animation will obviously speed up the production of new cartoon animations. Bregler *et al.* summarized that there are two dimensions in cartoon animation: the visual style (how the image looks, how it is rendered, the style of the drawing or model) and the motion style (how the characters move, the amount of exaggeration, use of cartoon physics and the way in which the animation principles are used) [Bregler *et al.*, 2002]. Therefore, we accordingly classify animation reuse into two types: reuse of visual style and motion style for cartoon animation.

8.5.1 Reusing Visual Style for Cartoon Animation

The key points in reusing visual styles for cartoon animation are how to effectively extract the desired visual content from traditional animation, and seamlessly apply them in the production of cartoon animation. Aiming at combining fragments of the original artwork to design new characters and poses, Sýkora *et al.* presented a novel example-based framework for reusing traditional cartoon animation [Sýkora *et al.*, 2005]. The input to their system is a set of classical cartoon images composed of two layers: background and foreground. In order to reuse shapes and regions stored in the foreground layer, the first step in their framework is an unsupervised image segmentation that allows us to partition the input image into a set of regions. Each region is then classified as to whether it belongs to the background or to the foreground layer. An interactive phase follows. In this step, the user simply selects a subset of interesting regions called a fragment. Afterwards, the system extracts the fragment together with corresponding outlines and performs vectorization. Finally, the user arranges it in a new position by sketching two composition scribbles that make it possible to define a combination of rigid transformation and free-form deformation. By this framework, the user can simply select an interesting part in the original image and then adjust it in a new composition using a few control scribbles. Practical results show that it can produce high-quality cartoon drawings within a much shorter time frame when compared with standard approaches [Sýkora *et al.*, 2005].

de Juan and Bodenheimer presented a semiautomatic segmentation and inbetweening method for reusing the cartoon characters [de Juan & Bodenheimer, 2006]. They employed support vector machines (SVM) to segment cartoon images from their backgrounds for incorporation into an image library. The first step in using SVMs to segment cartoon images is to classify the training data by selecting the appropriate attribute-label samples. Two feature sets are identified for classifying the data: color alone or color with optical flow vector magnitudes. Once the training data is classified, the SVM is trained to create a classifier model for each character. In order to generate the inbetween frames between the two newly reused key images, three steps are involved. In the first step, the character is partitioned into several layers such as head and torso. In the second step, inbetween shape contours are generated for each layer using an RBF-based technique, and in the final step the cartoon color or texture is fitted to the inbetween shape, using an elastic registration technique. The final inbetween typically requires only a small amount of touch up after generating the inbetween texture.

Besides the aforementioned character-reusing methods based on intuitive editing principles, some researchers explored the high-level reuse of visual effect or illustration styles in cartoon animation. For example, Sato *et al.* employed the data-mining concept to extract the accentuation effects in the hand-drawn images of the scene, and then the animation can be created interactively displaying the same accentuation effects [Sato *et al.*, 2004]. Hamel and Strothotte presented a solution to capture and re-use rendition styles for non-photorealistic rendering of 3D models, which is also applicable for the production of cartoon animation [Hamel & Strothotte,1999]. The rendition style is represented as a non-photorealistic template (NP-template for short) which describes the attributes of a rendition with respect to features of the underlying geometric model. In order to create an NP-template, the user initially works with the NP-renderer of his choice to construct a rendition R_1 from a geometric model M_1. This is a highly interactive process in which a considerable amount of fine-tuning is used to produce good-looking images. Next the final rendition R_1 and the Model M_1 are read by the non-photorealistic template extractor. The rendition is analyzed in order to map features of the geometric model onto the image. This mapping is recorded in the non-photorealistic template T_1, which now contains information about the objects in M_1 and the rendering styles in R_1 (see Fig. 8.46).

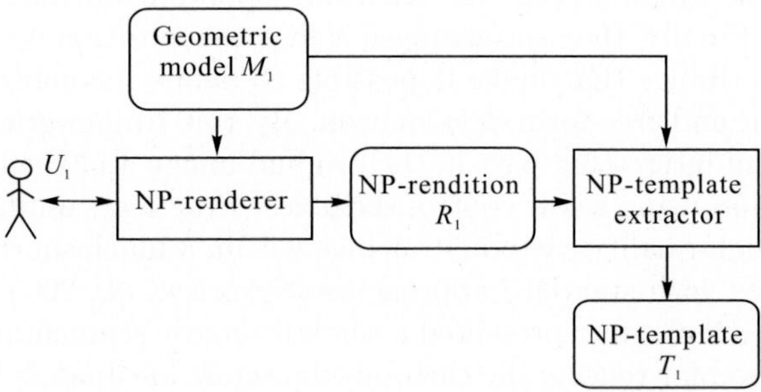

Fig. 8.46 Extraction of a template [Hamel & Strothotte, 1999]. Copyright of Blackwell, used with permission

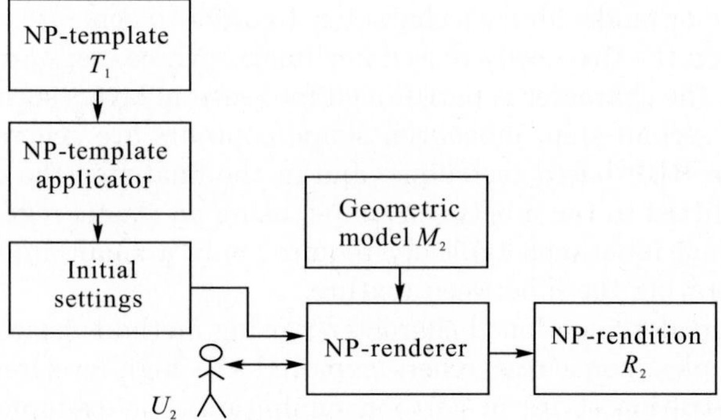

Fig. 8.47 Application of template [Hamel & Strothotte, 1999]. Copyright of Blackwell, used with permission

The application of the NP-template is shown in Fig. 8.47. The user has chosen a new model M_2 which is to be rendered in the style of R_1. The corresponding template T_1 as well as M_2 is analyzed by the NP-template applicator to produce initial settings for the renderer. The settings are passed on to the renderer and applied to M_2 and the user is given the opportunity to carry out some more fine-tuning. The result is a new non-photorealistic rendition R_2. This template-based rendition reusing approach can effectively transfer the style of rendition from one model to another (see Fig. 8.48).

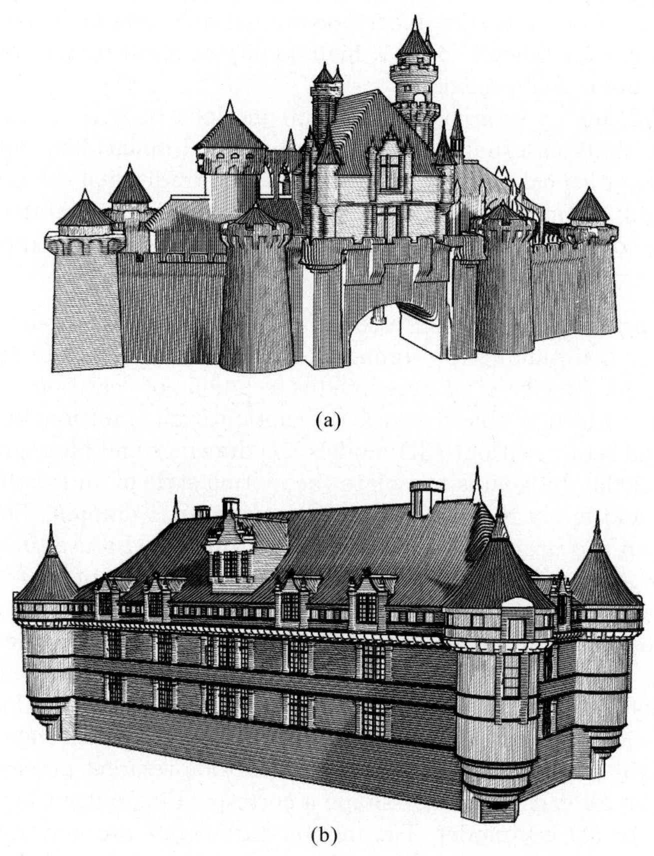

Fig. 8.48 Example of transferring rendition styles to new models [Hamel & Strothotte, 1999]. Copyright of Blackwell, used with permission. (a) The source rendition style; (b) The same rendition style transferred to a new model

8.5.2 Reusing Motions for Cartoon Animation

If the motion styles can be captured from existing cartoon animation and then applied to the production of new animation, the expressive characteristics, such as meaningful mood and exaggerations, will be naturally inherited in the new animation sequence. The main challenges in reusing cartoon motions are summarized as two aspects:

(1) It is difficult to effectively capture and extract motions from existing cartoon animations. There are no markers on the cartoon characters, and the typical vision-based tracking techniques can't be applied directly. Moreover, the frame rate in cartoon animation is relatively low, and consequently it is difficult to get a high quality of resulting motion from the source animation sequence.
(2) It is difficult to retarget the cartoon motions to new characters. The cartoon motions usually focused on the visual plausibility, ignoring the physical or logical plausibility. Moreover, the traditional cartoon motions are highly coupled with the exaggerated drawing of characters. It will often deform or degrade the cartoon motion greatly when applying it to new characters.

Assuming that most of the "essence" of the expressive movements will be preserved by maintaining the timing and motion parameters from the original animation, Bregler *et al.* presented a technique of "cartoon capture and retargeting", which is able to track the motion from traditionally animated cartoons and retarget it onto 3D models, 2D drawings and photographs [Bregler *et al.*, 2002]. Its goal is to isolate the motion style of an existing cartoon animation and apply the same style to a new output domain. The input to their cartoon capture process is the digitized video, and a user-defined set of key shapes (chosen from the source sequence). Cartoon capture transforms a digitized cartoon into a cartoon motion, which is represented as a composition of two types of deformations: (a) Affine deformations, that encode the global translation, rotation, scaling and sheer factors; (b) Key-shape deformations, that are defined relative to a set of key-shapes. This combination of affine transformation and key-weight vectors can describe a wide range of motion and non-rigid shape deformations. For the cartoon retarget process, the user has to define for each input key-shape a corresponding output key-shape, or key-image, or 3D key-model. The motion parameters are mapped from the source to the target. An overall algorithmic cartoon capture and retargeting pipeline is shown in Fig. 8.49.

By using animation as the source, the system can efficiently produce new animations that are expressive, exaggerated or non-realistic. Cartoon capture transforms a digitized cartoon into a cartoon motion representation. Using a combination of affine transformation and key-shape interpolation, cartoon capture tracks non-rigid shape changes in cartoon layers. Cartoon retargeting translates this information into different output media. The result is an

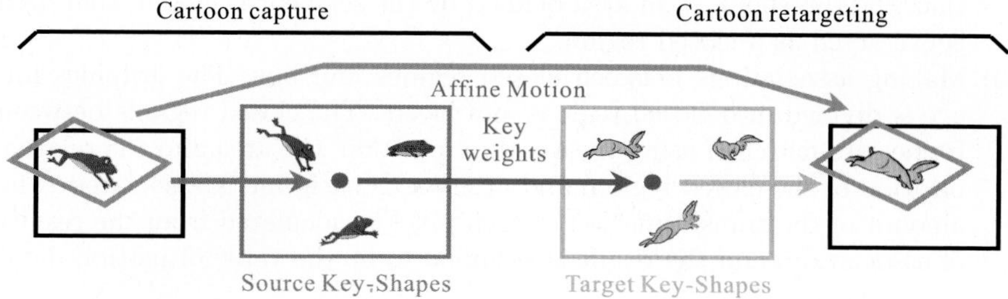

Fig. 8.49 The overall pipeline of cartoon capture and retargeting [Bregler *et al.*, 2002]. Copyright of ACM, used with permission

animation with a new look but with the movement of the original cartoon (see Fig. 8.50).

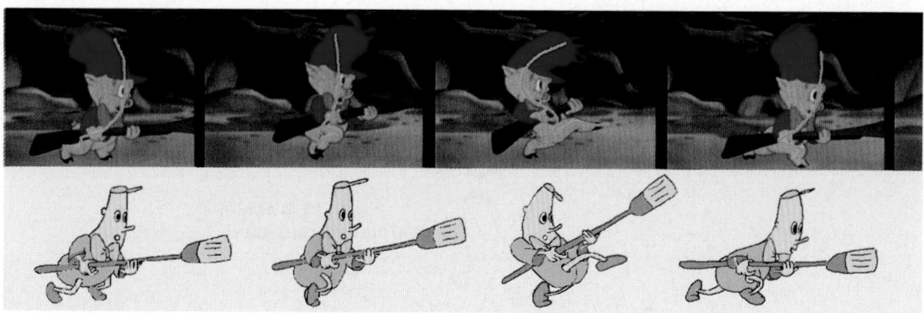

Fig. 8.50 Capturing line-of-action and retargeting onto a new 2D character [Bregler *et al.*, 2002]. Copyright of ACM, used with permission.

Sumi and Nakajima presented a motion reusing method by motion vector based on the model shapes [Sumi & Nakajima, 2003]. The overall algorithmic pipeline of motion reuse is shown in Fig. 8.51. It extracts motions at the same time as extracting the model shape from the existing animation sequence, and the major algorithmic steps are as follows:

(1) Binarization and making filamentation: The bitmap image from a frame of 2D animation sequences is binarized and the lines of the model shape are filamented.
(2) Extracting lines: The line of a segment is extracted by detecting the intersection points, and start and end points. A feature point is the pixel with the longest perpendicular line exceeding a user defined threshold length. The same process is repeated continuously for a line segment from the start point to the feature point until there is no length greater

than the threshold. If an area defined by the segment is closed, that area is extracted as a closed region.

(3) Making associations between closed regions and line: The graphics image is divided into closed regions and layers. The closed regions between frames are matched using the absolute position, the area and the relative position of the closed region, and afterwards each line is associated. The amount of the transformation of each pixel is calculated from the results of association, and the result is assumed to be the value of motion data.

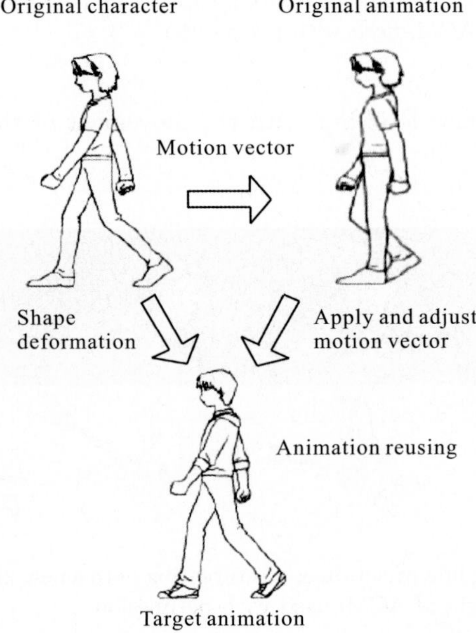

Fig. 8.51 The overall processing pipeline of motion reuse based on motion vector [Sumi & Nakajima, 2003]. Copyright of IEEE, used with permission

The resulting animation sequence of the target character model is generated by repeating the following two steps:

(1) The index to each pixel of the original image (original image index) is computed. At this time the target frame's correspondence point is to be the base value. Other original image indexes in between the correspondence points are calculated by a linear interpolation.

(2) The motion vector of the target image is calculated by using the original image indexes. At this time, use the weight of the decimal part of the original image indexes to create the motion vector of the target image

so that the amount of transformation of each pixel is proportional to its amount of position movement.

8.6 Summary

This chapter mainly describes and analyzes the novel approaches to speeding up cartoon animation production beyond the traditional computer-assisted coloring and inbetweening. The major algorithmic principles and key technical points are summarized in Table 8.1. These existing works clearly show that computer-assisted cartoon animation should go beyond 2D planes integrating with 3D information such as 3D geometry, video, emotions, etc. In the future, research into computer-assisted cartoon animation will still focus on the agile generation of high quality visual and motion content in cartoon animation, and the new generation pipeline of computer-assisted cartoon animation will achieve multi-discipline integration with techniques from computer vision, computer arts, artistic rendering, artificial intelligence and effective computing.

Table 8.1. A summary of novel approaches to assisting cartoon animation production

Novel approaches	Algorithmic principles	The key technical points involved
Video driven cartoon animation	It extracts the temporal features of visual and motion styles from the source video, and the new production of cartoon animation will be guided by them	The visual feature extraction and tracking, artistic rendering, performance driven deformation of 3D models or 2D images
Cartoon production integrated with 3D geometric elements	It usually reconstructs the 3D approximate geometry or transformations from 2D sketches or line-drawings, or pre-builds the base model of 3D object in advance. The resulting cartoon animation is generated by the 3D animation pipeline in terms of the newly-specified view points	Sketch-based 3D modeling, view-dependent geometry, image-based artistic rendering, view-independent artistic style simulation etc.

(to be continueed)

(Table 8.1)

Novel approaches	Algorithmic principles	The key technical points involved
Cartoon generation by temporal coherent rendering	The input is the 3D model of cartoon characters or scenes. The temporal coherence maintaining mechanism is embedded into the artistic rendering, and the resulting animation sequence is generated by the 3D computer animation pipeline	Artistic rendering, artistic styles rendition simulation with temporal coherence maintaining mechanism
Cartoon generation together with 3D graphical processing techniques	The input usually consists of both 2D hand-drawn images and 3D models. The 3D graphical processing techniques such as lighting model, digital geometrical processing, motion generation are modified to generate the desirable cartoon sequence in terms of the requirements of cartoon production	3D modeling integrated with cartoon rendering and motion generation respectively, the agile generation of cartoon scenes, cartoon stylized special effects simulation by 3D graphical processing
Cartoon production via reusing traditional animation	Its input is the traditional cartoon animation sequence. The visual style and motion styles are extracted from the input animation sequence. The desirable animation sequence is generated by applying the visual and motion style on the new foreground character or background scene	Segmentation of foreground characters and background scenes in cartoon image. The analysis and extraction of visual and animation styles from traditional animation sequence, simulation of artistic illustration styles, motion exaggeration and motion retargeting for 2D cartoon characters

References

Agarwala A(2002) SnakeToonz: A semi-automatic approach to creating cel animation from video. In: Proceedings of the Second International Symposium on Non-photorealistic Animation and Rendering 139–146

Agarwala A, Hertzmann A, Salesin DH, Seitz SM(2004) Keyframe-based tracking for rotoscoping and animation. ACM Transactions on Graphics 23(3): 584–591

Anjyo K, Hiramitsu K(2003) stylized highlights for cartoon rendering and animation. IEEE Computer Graphics and Applications 3(4):54–61

Blanz V, Basso C, Poggio T, Vetter T(2003) Reanimating faces in images and video. Computer Graphics Forum 22(3):641

Bourguignon D, Cani MP, Drettakis G(2001) Drawing for illustration and annotation in 3D. Computer Graphics Forum 20(3):114–123

Bregler C, Loeb L, Chuang E, Deshpande H(2002) Turning to the masters: motion capturing cartoons. ACM Transactions on Graphics 21(3) 399–407

Buck I, Finkelstain A, Jacobs C, Klein A, Salesin DH, Seims J, Szeliski R, Toyama K(2000) Performance-driven hand-drawn animation. In: Proceedings of the First International Symposium on Non-photorealistic Animation and Rendering 101–108

Catmull E (1978) The problems of computer-assisted animation. SIGGRAPH Computer Graphics 12(3): 348–353

Chaudhuri P, Kalra P, Banerjee S(2004) A system for view-dependent animation. Computer Graphics Forum 23(3), 411–420

Chenney S, Pingel M, Iverson R, Szymanski M (2002) Simulating cartoon style animation. In: Proceedings of the 2nd international symposium on Non-photorealistic animation and rendering 133–138

Cohen JM, Hughes JF, Zeleznik RC (2000) Harold: a world made of drawings. In: Proceedings of the 1st international symposium on Non-photorealistic animation and rendering 83–90

Collomosse JP, Hall P M(2005) Stroke surfaces: a spatiotemporal framework for temporally coherent non-photorealistic animations. In: IEEE Transactions on Visualization and Computer Graphics 11(5):540–549

Cornish D, Rowan A, Luebke D(2001) View-dependent particles for interactive non-photorealistic rendering. No description on Graphics Interface 01 151–158

Corrêa WT, Jensen RJ, Thayer CE, Finkelstein A (1998) Texture mapping for cel animation. In: Proceedings of the 25th Annual Conference on Computer Graphics and Interactive Techniques 435–446

de Juan CN, Bodenheimer B(2006) Reusing traditional animation: methods for semi-automatic segmentation and inbetweening. In: Eurographics/ ACM SIGGRAPH Symposium on Computer Animation 223–232

Di Fiore F, Van Haevre W, Van Reeth F(2003) Rendering artistic and believable trees for cartoon animation. In: Proceedings of Computer Graphics International 2003 144–151

Di Foire F, Van Reeth F(2002) Employing approximate 3D models to enrich traditional computer-assisted animation. In: Proceedings of Computer Animation 2002 183–190

Hamel J, Strothotte T(1999) Capturing and reusing rendition styles for non-photorealistic rendering. Computer Graphics Forum 18(3):173–182

Hanrahan P, Haeberli P(1990) Direct WYSIWYG painting and texturing on 3D shapes. SIGGRAPH Computer Graphics 24(4):215–223

Hays J, Essa I(2004) Image and video based painterly animation. In: Proceedings of the 3rd Internatioal Symposium on Non-photorealistic Animation and Rendering 113–120

Hertzmann A, Perlin K(2000) Painterly rendering for video and interaction. In: Proceedings of the First International Symposium on Non-photorealistic Animation and Rendering 7–12

Kalnins RD, Markosian L, Meier BJ, Kowalski MA, Lee JC, Davidson PL, Webb M, Hughes JF, Finkelstein A(2002) WYSIWYG NPR:drawing strokes directly on 3D models. ACM Transactions on Graphics 21 (3):755–762

Kalnins RD, Davidson PL, Markosian L, Finkelstein A(2003) Coherent stylized silhouettes. ACM Transactions on Graphics 22 (3):856–861

Kowalski MA, Markosian L, Northrup JD, Bourdev L, Barzel R, Holden LS, Hughes JF(1999) Art-based rendering of fur, grass and trees. In: Proceedings of the 26th Annual Conferences on Computer Graphics and Interactive Techniques 433–438

Lake A, Marshall C, Harris M, Blackstein M(2000) Stylized rendering techniques for scalable real-time 3D animation. In: Proceedings of the 1st International Symposium on Non-photorealistic Animation and Rendering 13–20

Li Y, Gleicher M, Xu Y, Shum H(2003) Stylizing motion with drawings. In: Proceedings of the 2003 ACM SIGGRAPH/Eurographics Symposium on Computer Animation 309–319

Liang L, Chen H, Xu Y, Shum H(2002) Example-based caricature generation with exaggeration. In: Proceedings of the 10th Pacific Conferences on Computer Graphics and Applications 386–393

Litwinowicz P(1997) Processing images and video for an impressionist effect. In: Proceedings of the 24th Annual Conference on Computer Graphics and Interactive Techniques 407–414

Markosian L, Meier BJ, Kowalski MA, Holden LS, Northrup JD, Hughes JF(2000) Art-based rendering with continuous levels of detail. In: Proceedings of the 1st International Symposium on Non-photorealistic Animation and Rendering 59–66

Martín D, Torres JC(1999) Alhambra:a system for producing 2D animation. In: Proceedings of Computer Animation 1999 38–47

Meier BJ(1996) Painterly rendering for animation. In: Proceedings of the 23rd Annual Conference on Computer Graphics and Interactive Techniques 477–484

Mihai P(1998) Image seqence stylization:a frame-to-frame coherent approach. Simulation and Animation 1998 101–112

Pastor QEM, Strothotte T(2002) Frame-coherent stippling. Eurographics 2002

Patterson JW, Willis PJ(1995) Computer assisted animation: 2D or not 2D? The Computer Journal 37(10):829–839

Petroic L, Fujito B, Williams L, Finkelstein A(2000) Shadows for cel animation. In: Proceedings of the 27th Annual Conferences on Computer Graphics and Interactive Techniques 511–516

Rademacher P(1999) View-dependent geometry. In: Proceedings of the 26th Annual Conferences on Computer Graphics and Interactive Techniques 439–446

Raskar R, Ziegler R, Willwatcher T(2002) Cartoon dioramas in motion. In: Proceedings of the Second International Symposium on Non-photorealistic Animation and Rendering 7–12

Sato T, Dobashi Y, Yamamoto T, Takao K, Anjyo K(2004) Extracting 3D stylized accentuation effects from a painted image. In: Proceedings of Computer and Graphics International 2004 222–228

Sumi F, Nakajima M(2003) A production method of reusing existing 2D animation sequences (short paper). In: Proceedings of Computer Graphics International 2003 258–263

Sýkora D, Buriánek J, Žára J(2005) Sketching cartoons by example. In: Eurographics Workshop on Sketch-based Interfaces and Modeling

Wang J, Xu Y, Shum HY, Cohen MF(2004) Video tooning. ACM Transactions on Graphics 2004 23(3):574–583

Wood DN, Finkelstein A, Hughes JF, Thayer CE, Salesin DH(1997) Multiperspective panoramas for cel animation. Computer Graphics 243–250

9

Perspectives of Non-photorealistic Computer Graphics

Non-photorealistic computer graphics has created an intriguing new field espousing expression, abstraction and stylization in preference to traditional computer graphics concerns about photorealism. It has two complimentary goals: the communication of information using images and rendering images in interesting and novel visual styles which are free from the traditional computer graphics constraint of producing images which are life-like. Many artistic and visual styles have been realized in non-photorealistic computer graphics, including interactive and automated systems for drawing and painting [Sayeed & Howard, 2006]. There is an international symposium NPAR (non-photorealistic animation and rendering) dedicated to non-photorealistic computer graphics, sponsored by the ACM SIGGRAPH and in co-operation with Eurographics. In 2009 it is the second time for NPAR to be collocated with SIGGRAPH, and this allows us to raise attention to this important field, and to open it to new people from academia, arts and industry.

From the point of view of research methodology, non-photorealistic computer graphics involves three major components: techniques, arts and human factors. The "techniques" related to non-photorealistic computer graphics are composed of artificial intelligence, virtual reality, human computer interaction, computer vision, multimedia computing, visualization, image/video processing, computer-aided design, computer graphics, computer animation, etc. The "arts" refer to calligraphy, painting, sculpture, literature, film, animation, dancing, drama, etc. Human factors are playing a more and more important role in future research, including visual cognition, thinking based on a mental image, affective computing, aesthetical assessment, subjective perception, psychology, etc. Fig. 9.1 shows a diagram of their relationship.

In essence, the scientific problems involved in non-photorealistic computer graphics can be summarized as (see Chapter One): (a) How to create art crafts from a blank canvas? (b) How to convert the source images into pictures with the desirable visual effects? (c) How to generate artistic rendition from 3D models? (d) How to synthesize expressive pictures from textual, graphical

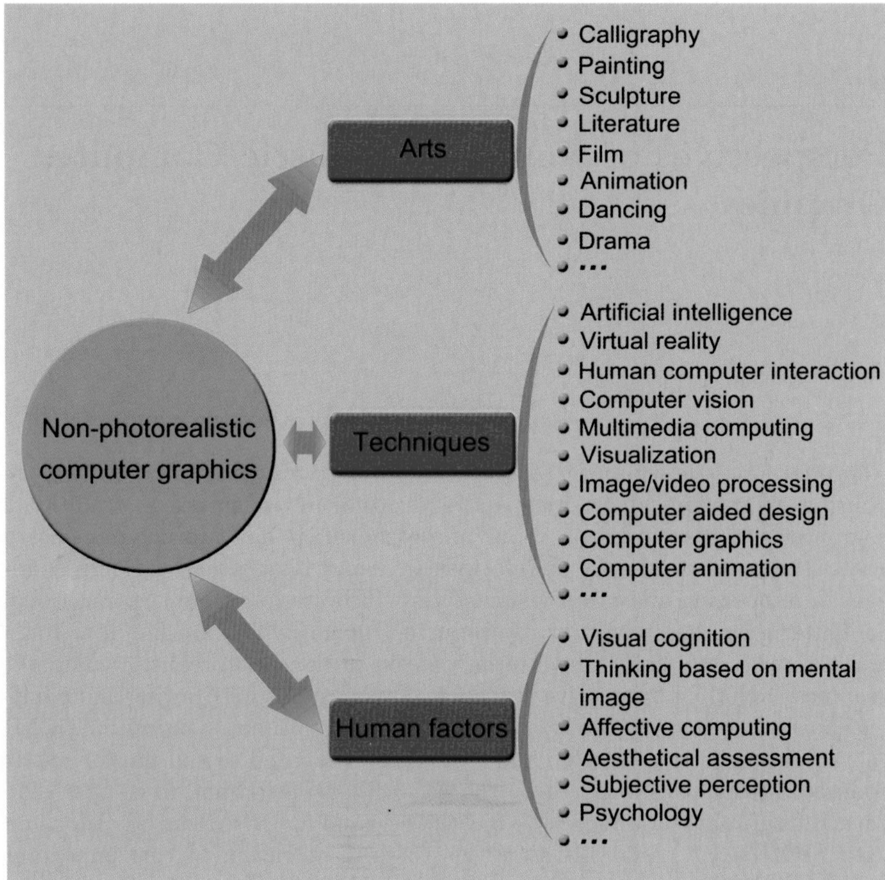

Fig. 9.1 A diagram of the relationship between techniques, arts and human factors in non-photorealistic computer graphics.

or pictorial data? (e) How to speed up the production of cartoon animation sequences with temporal coherence. There are more than 20 topics listed in the symposium of non-photorealistic animation and rendering in recent years, including:

- Simulation of traditional and new graphical styles;
- Simulation of natural media;
- Hardware-accelerated non-photorealistic algorithms;
- Level-of-detail in image space;
- Abstraction and composition in rendered images;
- Synthesis of stroke-based patterns;
- Style transfer;
- Automatic painting from photographs and video;

- Temporal and spatial coherence in non-photorealistic rendering;
- Motion blur and depth of field in non-photorealistic images;
- Lighting models for NPAR;
- Non-traditional perspective;
- Non-photorealistic modeling;
- Animation systems;
- Computer-aided cartoon animation;
- 2D/3D integration;
- Live-action integration;
- Computer-aided inbetweening;
- Computer-aided layout;
- Matting and compositing;
- Image-based rendering;
- Rendering languages and systems;
- Practical NPAR applications;
- Evaluation methods for artistic graphics;
- Computer-generated abstract art.

To the best of our knowledge, we correlate these specific themes with the five fundamental problems in non-photorealistic computer graphics (see Fig. 9.2). For the time being, the research into non-photorealistic computer graphics has made a significant advance in artistic rendering and cartoon animation. However, the perfect solution or computational models to solve the five problems have not yet emerged, and we still lack a technical breakthrough with great milestones. We believe that the future work on non-photorealistic computer graphics will remain centered on the aforementioned five problems.

From the point of view of evaluation criteria (the Turing test for non-realistic images), one of the biggest challenges faced by non-photorealistic computer graphics is the dependence on the human factors involved, because how humans perceive, think about and interact with images will affect their understanding of information presented visually, and most of the criteria used to assess the progress made, or the objective achieved in non-photorealistic computer graphics, is still subject-dependent. The graphics community has come to realize the importance of taking human factors into account and several research initiatives have begun to study them. Hapler *et al.* proposed the necessity of developing a theory of psychology within non-photorealistic computer graphics, and briefly discussed the functional and theoretical relationship of non-photorealistic rendering with general, social, biological and environmental psychology paradigms [Halper *et al.*, 2003]. Tory and Möller reviewed known methodology for doing human factors research and existing work on human factors, with specific emphasis on visualization, and identified promising areas for future research [Tory & Möller, 2004]. Sullivan *et al.* made a survey of the computational models of various perceptual functions in the graphics community, and the new insights into both graphics and perception [Sullivan *et al.*, 2004]. Lee explored how to improve the comprehensibility

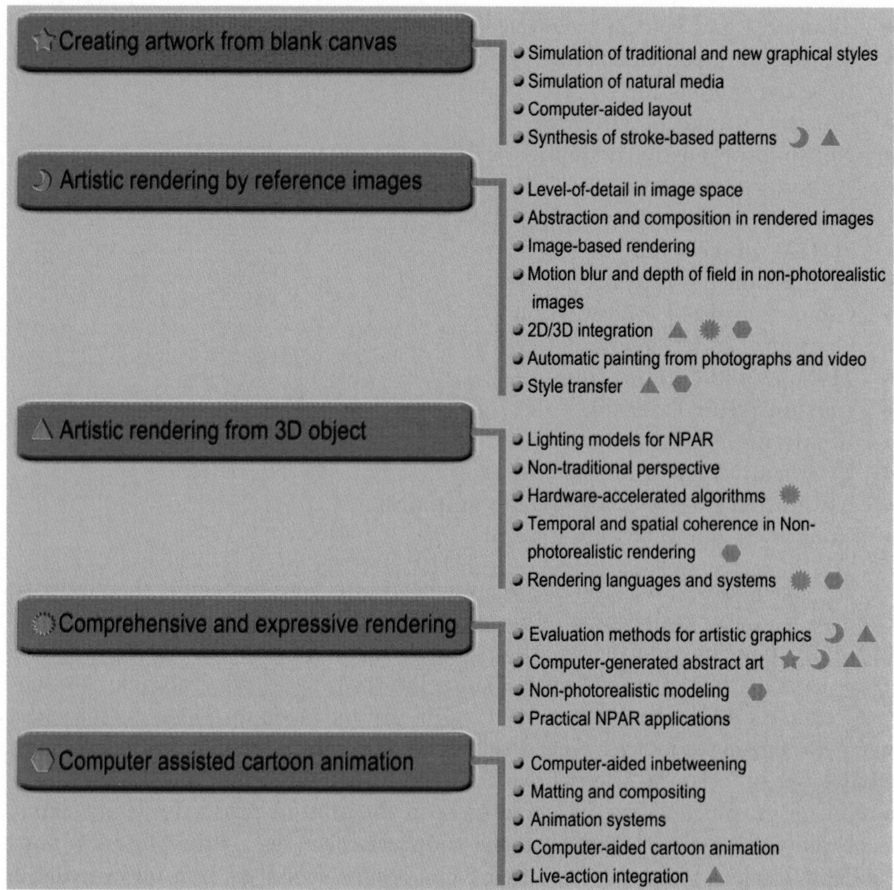

Fig. 9.2 The correlation of specific themes with the five fundamental problems in non-photorealistic computer graphics: The symbols that suffix a specific theme state that the current theme is also related to the corresponding problem annotated by this symbol.

of 3D graphics rendering using insights from human perception of geometry and illumination, and developed algorithms and systems to seamlessly integrate the low-level human visual system cues with object modeling and lighting for 3D graphics [Lee, 2005]. Santella presented several approaches for simplifying photographs to create concise, artistically abstracted images by the perceptual model based on eye movements, i.e., features in the image will be preserved where the viewer looked, and removed elsewhere. Some interesting insights into artistic abstraction and human visual perception are also provided, based on a series of experiments [Santella, 2005]. Winnemöller *et al.* studied the connections between non-realistic depiction and human perception, and proposed two non-realistic rendering frameworks for image abstraction and the generation of isolated visual shape cues, respectively [Winnemöller 2006, Winnemöller *et al.*, 2007]. Isenberg *et al.* presented an observational study of how people understand and assess both traditionally created hand-drawn and computer-generated non-photorealistic pen-and-ink illustrations, and revealed that hand-drawn images clearly still seem different from computer-generated images [Isenberg *et al.*, 2006]. Therefore, it is obvious that the non-photorealistic rendering work involving human factors is in its infancy, and many potentially promising areas have yet to be explored.

In the future, the research work in non-photorealistic computer graphics will still focus on the five aforementioned scientific problems, but more computational models of visual perception and cognition will be embedded into it. A breakthrough in formal evaluation and validation of non-realistic images will significantly help establish a major milestone in the non-photorealistic computer graphics community.

References

Halper N, Mellin M, Herrmann CS, Linneweber V, Strothotte T(2003) Psychology and non-photorealistic rendering: the beginning of a beautiful relationship. Mensch and Computer 2003 277–286

Isenberg T, Neumann P, Carpendale S, Sousa MC, Jorge JA (2006). Non-photorealistic rendering in context: an observational study. In: Proceedings of the 4th International Symposium on Non-photorealistic Animation and Rendering 115–126

Lee CH(2005) Perceptual graphics for effective visualization. PhD Dissertation, University of Maryland

Santella A(2005) The art of seeing: visual perception in design and evaluation of Non-Photorealistic Rendering. PhD Dissertation, The State University of New Jersey

Sayeed R, Howard T(2006) State of the art non-photorealistic rendering (NPR) techniques. EG UK Theory and Practice of Computer Graphics 1–10

Sullivan C, Howlett S, McDonnell R, Morvan Y, O'Conor K(2004) Perceptually adaptive graphics. Eurographics State of the Art Report

Tory M, Möller T(2004) Human factors in visualization research. IEEE Transactions on Visualization and Computer Graphics 2004 10(1):72–84

Winnemöller H(2006) Perceptually-motivated non-photorealistic graphics. PhD Dissertation, Northwestern University

Winnemöller H, Feng D, Gooch B, Suzuki S(2007) Using NPR to evaluate perceptual shape cues in dynamic environments. In: Proceedings of the 5th International Symposium on Non-photorealistic Animation and Rendering 85–92

Index

N

O

P

Q

R

S